# STORMING THE WORLD STAGE

STEPHEN TANKEL

# Storming the World Stage

## The Story of Lashkar-e-Taiba

OXFORD
UNIVERSITY PRESS

# OXFORD
UNIVERSITY PRESS

Oxford University Press, Inc., publishes works that further
Oxford University's objective of excellence
in research, scholarship, and education.

Oxford New York
Auckland   Cape Town   Dar es Salaam   Hong Kong   Karachi
Kuala Lumpur   Madrid   Melbourne   Mexico City   Nairobi
New Delhi   Shanghai   Taipei   Toronto

With offices in
Argentina   Austria   Brazil   Chile   Czech Republic   France   Greece
Guatemala   Hungary   Italy   Japan   Poland   Portugal   Singapore
South Korea   Switzerland   Thailand   Turkey   Ukraine   Vietnam

Copyright © 2013 Stephen Tankel

Published by Oxford University Press, Inc
198 Madison Avenue, New York, New York 10016

Published in the United Kingdom in 2013 by C. Hurst & Co. (Publishers) Ltd.

www.oup.com

Library of Congress Cataloging-in-Publication Data
Tankel, Stephen.
Storming the world stage : the story of Lashkar-e-Taiba / Stephen Tankel.
p. cm.
Includes bibliographical references and index.
ISBN 978-0-19-933344-8 (alk. paper)
1. Jamat al-Dawa Pakistan. 2. Terrorists—Pakistan—History. 3. Terrorism—
Religious aspects—Islam. 4. Islam and politics—Pakistan. 5. Jihad. I. Title.
HV6433.P18T36 2013
363.325095491—dc23
2013017006

1 3 5 7 9 8 6 4 2

Printed in India
on Acid-Free Paper

*For my parents Berta and Shelly and my wife Stephanie*

# CONTENTS

# ACKNOWLEDGMENTS

This book would never have happened were it not for my PhD supervisor Peter Neumann, who pushed me to put my thesis on hold in order to write it. He guided me through the book proposal process and has remained supportive throughout, providing the type of mentoring all PhD students hope to receive. I was doubly blessed in this department, as my secondary supervisor, Anatol Lieven, is an acknowledged expert on Pakistan. He not only provided critical feedback, but also an entrée to a number of sources in Pakistan. Peter Bergen offered early encouragement to pursue my interest in Lashkar at a time, well before the 2008 Mumbai attacks, when many did not view it as a major player in the jihadi movement. When I was ready to make my first field research trip, he also opened up his rolodex to me.

I conducted scores of interviews in India and Pakistan as well as various Western countries, speaking with many people who have become all-too-familiar with the costs of political violence. I am deeply grateful to all those who graciously offered me their knowledge and spoke of their experiences. I took more from them than I could hope to give back, and offer my thanks here once again. I was welcomed warmly everywhere I went and particularly so in Pakistan, where I conducted the majority of my field research. Although this book is sometimes critical of Pakistan's policies this is not reflective of its people, who have been held captive to forces beyond their control for much of the country's short history. Of the many people recommended to me in Pakistan, no one was more helpful than Mohammad Amir Rana. As a former journalist and now the director of the Pak Institute for Peace Studies, Amir has a comprehensive grasp of the history of jihadi militancy in Pakistan. He was both a willing tutor and a warm host, opening the Institute to me as a base of operations as well as allowing me access to the archived material that staff members collected over the years. Mubashir Bukhari acted as my compass in Lahore, and was of great help with the research I conducted there. I also benefited from my numerous interactions in India, in particular with Praveen Swami who continued to provide valuable insights regarding Lashkar's contributions to Indian jihadism throughout the drafting of this manuscript.

Two colleagues in London provided help with secondary sources. Jerry Moss, a veteran officer with the Metropolitan Police Service, is a trove of information regarding various activities associated with Pakistan-based militant groups in the United Kingdom. He gave freely of his time, helping to point me in the right direction for open source information on Lashkar's Europe-based activities. Dina Esfandiary at the International Institute of Strategic Studies kindly translated French materials regarding some of the group's France-based operatives.

This book benefited from a number of reviewers who offered comments at various stages of the drafting process. Rudy Chaudhuri, Polly Nayak, Peter Neumann and Saleem Vaillancourt offered helpful advice on sections of the manuscript. Sumit Ganguly and Frédéric Grare both provided useful guidance after reading an early draft. Alexander Evans, Arif Jamal, Myra MacDonald and Praveen Swami reviewed later drafts. By positing alternative analyses or proffering new facts all of them helped me to navigate the story of Lashkar's evolution. I could not have asked for a better publisher or editor than Michael Dwyer at Hurst who took great care in editing my manuscript. Thanks to Columbia University Press as well for agreeing to co-publish the book and to the Carnegie Endowment for International Peace, which hosted me for the final stages of writing.

To friends and family who patiently accepted my absence from events big and small, thank you for your support and understanding. I owe a particular debt to three people. First, to my mother and father. Throughout my life they encouraged me to expand my world, even if it meant missed time with them. Wherever I have gone in life, they were always there to support me. Second, to my wife Stephanie whose time I stole to write this book. Wherever I am in the world, she is home to me.

attacks raised questions about the direction of the organization. Was this evidence that Lashkar was moving deeper into al-Qaeda's orbit, and perhaps on a trajectory to displace Osama bin Laden's network as the next major global jihadi threat? Or were the attacks simply the group's latest attempt to harm Pakistan's rival, India? To understand the calculus that informed Mumbai and why Lashkar suffered little fallout in Pakistan as a result of the attacks, it is necessary to situate them and the group within a wider context over the last twenty years.

In this book I argue that Lashkar's evolution is informed by two defining dualities: the first is its identity as a militant outfit *and* as a missionary organization committed to promoting its interpretation of Ahl-e-Hadith Islam; the second concerns its military activities, namely that it is both a proxy used to further Pakistan's national interests against India *and* a pan-Islamist group dedicated to waging jihad against all enemies of Islam. As *Storming the World Stage* will demonstrate, Lashkar managed to evolve into a powerful and protected organization in Pakistan as a result of its ability to reconcile these dualities. A jihad against India to liberate Muslim land deemed to be under Hindu occupation aligned with Lashkar's ideological priorities and also with state interests. This enabled the group to become Pakistan's most reliable proxy, which brought with it substantial benefits including the support needed to construct a robust social welfare apparatus used for missionary and reformist purposes. Reconciling these dualities also necessitated deals and compromises, since preserving its position vis-à-vis the state sometimes forced the group to sublimate its pan-Islamist impulses. The need for such trade-offs became more acute after 9/11, and as the decade wore on pressure to expand its participation in the global jihad against America and its allies increased. Mumbai had multiple objectives, one of which was to generate momentum for the group at a time when it was in danger of being eclipsed by other outfits deemed more committed to that cause.

To appreciate Lashkar's dual identity as a missionary and militant organization, we must go back to 1982, when Zaki-ur Rehman Lakhvi, then a student from Punjab in Pakistan and now accused of masterminding the 2008 Mumbai attacks, went to Paktia in Afghanistan to wage jihad against the Soviets.[3] A member of the Ahl-e-Hadith sect of Islam, he initially fought alongside members of the Deobandi school of thought whom he believed were not waging jihad according to sharia [Islamic law]. The Ahl-e-Hadith are Salafist in orientation, meaning they believe Muslims must return to a pure form of Islam and advocate emulating the Prophet and his Companions in all areas of life.[4] In 1984, Lakhvi broke away and formed a small Ahl-e-Hadith group of his own. A year later, Hafiz Mohammad Saeed and Zafar Iqbal, two teachers at the University of Engineering and Technology (Lahore) Pakistan, formed Jamaat-ul-Dawa [Organization for Preaching, or JuD]. This was a small missionary order primarily dedicated to preaching the tenets of Ahl-e-Hadith Islam as interpreted by its founders. Soon after, the two joined forces.[5]

In 1986 Lashkar's parent organization Markaz al-Dawa wal-Irshad [Centre for Preaching and Guidance, or MDI] was formed to 'organize [Ahl-e-Hadith] Pakistanis participating in [the] Afghan Jihad on one Platform.'[6] But MDI was never intended to be simply another militant outfit. It had seventeen original founders who shared the aspiration of uniting the small Ahl-e-Hadith movement in Pakistan and promoting the purification of society, which it would rebuild based on their interpretation of Islam. Waging violent jihad was an essential part of this, but not the group's sole purpose. It was for this reason that Saeed was chosen to lead the nascent organization. Although Lakhvi had founded the first Pakistani Ahl-e-Hadith group to wage jihad against the Soviets, he was not a respected scholar. Saeed, on the other hand, was among the most influential of the Pakistani Ahl-e-Hadith ulema [scholars of Islamic law] involved in the Afghan jihad and was thus regarded as the best person to unite the Ahl-e-Hadith movement around MDI's objectives.[7]

The group had three functions: 'Jihad in the way of Allah preaching the true religion and the training of [a] new generation on Islamic lines.'[8] It regards jihad as waging war and sees doing so as obligatory for all Muslims until Islam emerges victorious against the unbelievers. This interpretation is at odds with that held by most Muslims, but in line with that of so-called 'jihadis,' a term that gained currency to connote those Sunni Muslims who share this extreme interpretation of jihad. The group places an equally strong emphasis on dawa, which literally means 'a call to God' and may include activities ranging from proselytizing to providing social services and charity. In this regard it stands out among major jihadi organizations, many of which rely primarily on violence and propaganda to achieve their objectives. MDI officially launched Lashkar as its military wing around 1990, after which the former was technically responsible for dawa and the latter for jihad.[9] However, as one former member explained, 'If you know their philosophy then you cannot differentiate between MDI and Lashkar.'[10] To avoid confusion this book refers to the group as Lashkar (or LeT) except in those instances where specific MDI activities are discussed.

Although Lashkar was born during the anti-Soviet jihad and its militants fought on several open fronts thereafter, regional dynamics associated with the India-Pakistan rivalry exerted the heaviest influence on it; shaping its dual identity as a state proxy and as a pan-Islamist group. The animosity that besets India-Pakistan relations is not reducible to their historic dispute over the divided region of Kashmir, but that issue remains a major impasse to peace between the two. When an insurgency erupted in the portion controlled by India [hereafter Indian-administered Kashmir] in 1989 the army and its Inter-Services Intelligence Directorate [ISI], the best known and most powerful of the country's intelligence agencies, began supporting militant outfits committed to liberating Kashmir. This was not the first time Pakistan had supported proxies there, nor was this the only territory in which the state promoted pan-Islamic jihad to serve national interests. This policy stretches back to the earliest days of Pakistan's history, as does the practice of building up the notion of Hindu India as an existential enemy of Islamic Pakistan. One result of these policies was to promote the idea that liberating Kashmir was the most legitimate of jihads. Another was to reinforce the idea among the country's Islamists that Pakistan was an Islamic vanguard responsible for protecting Muslims everywhere and so jihad would not end with Kashmir. Meanwhile, the state was supporting jihadi proxies for nationalist, rather than Islamist purposes. So long as this support remained extant, however, official policy aligned with jihadi objectives.

# INTRODUCTION

When the government of President Pervez Musharraf allied with America against al-Qaeda and the Taliban after 9/11, it fractured this alignment. The US did not give his government much choice, threatening military retribution if Pakistan did not get on board. Though he received no such guarantees from the US, Musharraf's decision to ally with America was predicated in large part on the hope that by doing so he could insulate some of Pakistan's proxies from the war against al-Qaeda. The Musharraf regime subsequently divided militant outfits into 'good jihadis' and 'bad jihadis' based on their perceived controllability and utility against India. This was an unsustainable model, since it proved impossible to enforce these divisions. By the end of the decade, Pakistan was facing its own jihadi-led insurgency. Yet the army and ISI remained committed to preserving Pakistan's proxy capabilities, creating a situation in which the state was both the supporter and victim of jihadi violence.

Lashkar's leaders also tried to have it both ways after 9/11. The jihad to liberate Indian-administered Kashmir brought with it significant state support for Lashkar, enabling it to grow militarily as well as to establish a robust social services apparatus, which the group used to pursue its missionary objectives in Pakistan. Lashkar had won its spurs in Kashmir, becoming the state's most reliable proxy there. Moreover, its leaders continued to view this as the most legitimate of jihads and also placed a premium on protecting the group's infrastructure in Pakistan. As a result, Lashkar remained more amenable to the Musharraf regime's agenda after 9/11 than any other outfit, focusing primarily on the fight against India and on expanding its social outreach. However, the global jihad was impossible to ignore and Lashkar also began contributing to the fight against America and its allies. Viewed through one lens, it remained a Pakistani proxy against India; through another it seemed to behave like an al-Qaeda associate. And to segments of the population in Pakistan, it appeared to be primarily a social welfare provider. The group's growth during this decade was due in large part to its ability to continue harmonizing operations in these different spheres; an approach which benefited from the fact that it remained more cohesive and methodical than most of its militant brethren in Pakistan. However, as with Pakistan's decision to divide its militants, attempting to balance these competing identities is a recipe for internal discord. Tensions emerged after 9/11 over the leadership's adherence to the Musharraf regime's agenda and were exacerbated during the middle of the decade when state support for the Kashmir jihad slowed while the insurgency against America and its allies in Afghanistan simultaneously gained strength. Lashkar subsequently opened up a second front there, though its leaders continued to place a premium on liberating Kashmir. Waging jihad in Afghanistan exposed its cadres to outfits that not only prioritized bringing the fight to the US, but also to waging war in Pakistan. This put pressure on the leadership to expand further the scope and scale of its jihad, which contributed to the audacity of the 2008 Mumbai attacks and the inclusion of foreign targets. The assault on Mumbai had minimal impact on Lashkar's ability to operate as a result of the group's continued utility as a proxy, its prominent role as a social welfare provider and the possible consequences that taking serious action against it could bring. Since November 2008 its militant activities in Afghanistan and throughout South Asian have expanded, while its operational integration with the jihadi nexus in Pakistan has grown.

*Storming the World Stage* traces Lashkar's evolution since its inception in order to assess its effects on the security of India, Pakistan and the West as well as on the stability of South Asia. The book consists of three parts: Part I contextualizes the group's evolution by discussing first the jihadi milieu in which it developed (Chapter 1) and then its ideological and strategic precepts as they developed during its formative years and which inform its behavior (Chapter 2). The remainder of the book proceeds chronologically. The second part focuses on the group's activities in the 1990s: Chapter 3 details Lashkar's activities in Indian-administered Kashmir, and Chapter 4 explains how the group built its infrastructure in Pakistan as well as its transnational networks abroad. Chapter 5 focuses on two inflection points for Lashkar, its jihadi brethren and the Pakistani state in late 2001: the 9/11 attacks and the decision by the Musharraf regime (taken under intense international pressure) to outlaw Lashkar and several other jihadi outfits following an assault by

Pakistani militants on the Indian Parliament in December. Fore-warned of the impending ban, MDI changed its name to Jamaat-ul-Dawa [JuD], that of Saeed's initial missionary organization. JuD leaders claimed the new organization was entirely discrete from the outlawed Lashkar; in reality, many jihadi groups orchestrated name changes of this sort in concert with the Pakistani security services to protect their leadership and assets. Lashkar and JuD remained two wings of the same organization. The third part is dedicated to Lashkar's evolution from 2002 onwards. Chapters 6 and 7 look at the group's development from roughly 2002–2005 and 2005–2008 respectively. Taken together these two chapters illustrate the evolving contours of its jihad against India and Lashkar's expanding focus on the fight against America and its allies. They also detail the repercussions of its increasing collaboration with other militants. Chapter 8 is dedicated to exploring the objectives, planning and execution of the Mumbai attacks in detail, while Chapter 9 revisits Lashkar's activities on multiple fronts to demonstrate how the group has expanded since Mumbai. The final chapter spotlights some of the possible implications this may have for Lashkar as well as for India, Pakistan and the West.

When gathering information I relied a great deal on field research conducted in Pakistan and India. Owing to the sensitivity of the material, some interview subjects requested anonymity. Because of the personal and professional risks involved for a number of those who spoke with me, I have approached identification of my sources with great caution. Anonymous sourcing is widely recognized as necessary when researching clandestine militant groups. It is also undeniably contentious because it removes accountability for both the source and, to a degree, the author. This is magnified by the fact that some interview subjects had a stake in skewing facts and analysis. To mitigate this I attempted to solicit enough information from different sources to redress the bias of any one party. In addition to field research, I also relied heavily on primary source material in the form of statements by the group and legal documents. This is supplemented with media accounts and the existing literature. I have tried to support anonymous assessments with those from on-the-record sources or written accounts, and in general endeavored to pursue a policy of dual sourcing wherever possible. All direct quotations appear as found in the original source material; [sic] is not used, though in some instances language has been inserted in brackets for clarification.

In gathering material for this book, it became clear that Lashkar is often misunderstood, owing partially to the fact that it wishes to be. Where myths exist, I try to debunk them using facts. However, ambiguity still surrounds many of the group's activities. When this is the case I make clear that uncertainty exists. I also attempt to outline competing claims, to identify clues or trends that might point the way forward and to suggest possible explanations as well as the alternative consequences different scenarios could create. Although this opens the door to possible errors of fact or analysis, this is a risk that accompanies any empirical work about clandestine phenomena. I am confident the material gathered is extensive enough to chart the significant trends in Lashkar's evolution, but caveat lector: the group's story continues to unfold and with it comes additional data about the current state of play. It is inevitable that by the time this book is in print more will be known about Lashkar. The best this book can hope to do is to serve as a foundation for future analysis and to provide a baseline for critical debate.

# PART I

1

# THE PAKISTANI JIHADI MILIEU

*Storming the World Stage* seeks to explain to the reader Lashkar-e-Taiba, not Pakistan, but exploring the former's evolution is impossible without addressing some of the centrifugal forces that shaped the latter's development. Pakistan has faced serious domestic and foreign challenges during its short history. These, in turn, influenced the country's engagement with Islamist parties and militants, and thus the jihadi milieu in which Lashkar developed. There are several ways to comprehend the dynamics of jihadism in Pakistan during Lashkar's early years. One is to distinguish militant groups based on their Islamic school of thought, with the major players representing the Deobandi and Ahl-e-Hadith sects of Islam. Another is to situate a jihadi group's focus of activity, to the extent possible, in one of three theaters: Afghanistan; Indian-administered Kashmir; and sectarianism in Pakistan.[1] These loci were never discrete and have shifted of late, while former divisions between Deobandi militants and the Ahl-e-Hadith Lashkar became less marked over time as well. Nevertheless, these categories remain useful analytic tools for situating Lashkar during its formative years, and are explored below. Before doing so, this chapter first provides a broad overview of Pakistan's history from the Partition of British India to its participation as a US ally in the Afghan jihad against the Soviets.[2]

Pakistan was created via partition from India in 1947 as a home for South Asia's Muslims. Like other countries that brought together

11

disparate ethnicities as the colonial era came to a close, Pakistan became a state before it was a nation. Unlike other post-colonial countries, which were created as the result of self-determination movements, Pakistan was not born in a struggle against colonial rule. Rather it was formed in opposition to an Indian nationalist movement that agitated for independence from the British Empire. From its inception, Pakistan's identity was molded partly in opposition to India.[3] The basis for partition from India was the two-nation theory, which argued Muslims and Hindus constituted two nations that could never live together. The man most responsible for the country's birth was Mohammad Ali Jinnah, who is officially known in Pakistan as Quaid-e-Azam [Great Leader] and Baba-e-Qaum [Father of the Nation]. As head of the Muslim League in British-controlled India, Jinnah called for the establishment of a new Muslim nation concomitant with Britain's granting of independence to Hindu-dominated India. Jinnah and the Muslim League appealed to religious sentiment and employed the mobilizing language of Islam to facilitate the transition from a Muslim community living in British India to a Pakistani nation.[4]

Islam was employed as a means to ensure Pakistan came into existence, but debates over what role it should play in governing the country continue to this day. The use of Muslim identity to mobilize support for Pakistan led some to interpret this to mean Pakistan was founded as an Islamic state. Others contended the intention was limited to creating a country in which Muslims could lead secure lives free from Hindu dominance. According to Farzana Shaikh, who explored this issue in *Making Sense of Pakistan*, the 'vexed relationship' between Islam and nationalism has proved to be the 'single greatest source of ideological uncertainty in Pakistan.'[5] However, as she notes, Islam and nationalism are not discrete concepts. There is significant interplay among the various ideas of Pakistan: as a cultural haven; a homeland; an Islamic state; or an Islamic vanguard.[6]

Although debates over the role of Islam in the nation continue, it is safe to say the majority of Pakistanis have no desire to live in a theocracy. No religious party has ever come close to winning power at the national level, though Islamist parties 'consistently punch above their electoral weight' in terms of influence on national politics.[7] This stems largely from effective mobilization of their political bases as well as their employment of Islamic identity and wedge issues to pressure successive national governments into adopting aspects of their platform.[8] The Islamist parties' success also has roots in the course charted by Pakistan's rulers from its inception, one that was intrinsically tied to the issue of how to build one nation out of the disparate ethno-linguistic groups inhabiting it.

At the time of Pakistan's founding there were already 70 million Muslims living within what became the borders of the new nation. Because Pakistan was contoured to include the Muslim majority regions of colonial India the new country consisted of two separate pieces of territory—West and East Pakistan—divided by 1000 miles of land belonging to India. Notably, the greatest support for the country's creation came from Muslims living outside of the regions that became modern day Pakistan.[9] The government was based in West Pakistan, which was at once less densely populated and more heterogeneous than its Eastern counterpart. Hindus and Muslims alike spoke Bengali in East Pakistan, which in 1971 seceded to form Bangladesh. In contrast, West Pakistan drew together the four provinces of Punjab, Sindh, Balochistan and the North-West Frontier Province [NWFP, now known as Khyber Pakhtunkhwa] along with the Federally Administered Tribal Areas [FATA or Tribal Areas].[10] Not only was West Pakistan home to people of different ethnicities, languages and cultures. It also had to absorb the approximately nine million Muslims, known as Mohajirs, who left India after Partition. Many of those who attempted the journey did not survive the furious communal violence that accompanied it. Hafiz Saeed, the man chosen to lead Lashkar at its founding, was born in post-Partition Pakistan. But thirty-six members of his family and clan were killed during their attempt to emigrate from India.[11]

Not long after independence Bengalis in East Pakistan were demanding Bengali as a national language. Meanwhile Sindhis, Pashtuns [the dominant ethnicity in the NWFP and FATA] and Balochs in West Pakistan were protesting over the fact that Punjabis and Mohajirs dominated the civil services and military officer corps. Among all of these ethnic entities, only Punjab never pressed for greater autonomy. This fact is explained by the province's predominant position within Pakistan: Punjabis are over-represented in the civil bureaucracy as well as in the army. Whether ruled by civilians or the military, the central government historically has been unrepresentative of the different ethno-linguistic groups brought together by Partition. Pakistan's central leadership feared disunity resulting from political opposition would weaken the country and leave it vulnerable to India. In response, it promoted Islamic unity to undercut competing ethno-nationalisms and bind the country together. The central government also instrumentalized hostility toward India as a means of enhancing national cohesion. Defending 'Islamic' Pakistan against 'Hindu' India became a national narrative.

Despite the sacrifices made in hopes of creating a home for South Asia's Muslims, Pakistan 'found in independence neither the peace, nor the security, nor the freedom of spirit that would enable it either to live in harmony with India, or ignore it.'[12] Instead, since its inception, the country has been forced to confront a more powerful external enemy. Partition left many Indians bitter and convinced the Pakistani experiment would fail. In turn, Pakistan's new rulers took a reflexively defensive posture, convinced of Indian intentions to re-conquer their new country. The two countries quickly found themselves at war over Kashmir, which compounded the enmity and distrust each had for the other.

In 1971, after twenty-four years of physical separation, East Pakistan cleaved itself politically from Pakistan and Bangladesh was formed. Making matters worse, India helped wield the knife by joining the battle on Bangladesh's side. Although India provided military support, the causes of this rupture were rooted in West Pakistan's refusal to allow East Pakistan a major role in governing the country despite the fact that it contained a majority of the citizenry.[13] Pakistani efforts to promote cohesion became more zealous and more militant after the loss of Bangladesh, which robbed the country of its justification as a homeland for South Asian Muslims. In response even greater emphasis was placed on Pakistan's Islamic heritage, and the concept of 'Islamic' Pakistan against 'Hindu' India was reinforced through constant propaganda and the educational system.[14] A nationally representative survey conducted in 2009 found that while better-educated Pakistanis were less likely to support the Taliban than their less-educated peers, the same did not hold true for those militant outfits fighting in Indian-administered Kashmir. The reason, according to those who conducted this research, is the presence of strong anti-Indian sentiment and support for the Kashmir struggle in the Pakistani school curriculum.[15]

Pakistan made use of non-state proxies during two wars with India over Kashmir in 1947 and 1965, a practice detailed in Chapter 3. The army did so again during the civil war in 1971, deploying them against Bangladeshi separatists. Following that conflict, a number of Pakistan's elected and martial governments continued to sponsor Islamist groups to serve internal and external political interests. Although these governments at times unleashed religious sentiments they could not control, for the first thirty years Islam was used primarily for instrumental purposes. This changed in July 1977 when General Zia ul-Haq seized power in a military coup d'état, after which he quickly declared martial law. During his reign, Zia promoted the expansion of Islamist influence in politics, the military and the civil bureaucracy.

General Zia's was not the first martial regime to govern Pakistan. More than half of the country's short history has been dominated by military rule, and even when not in power the army has exerted disproportionate influence on state policy from behind the scenes. There are several explanations commonly offered for the army's continued involvement—overtly and covertly—in Pakistan's governance. First, the nascent central government was unprepared for the refugee flows, communal violence and hostile geopolitical terrain that accompanied Partition. This led those in charge to cede much of the responsibility to the army, which set the tone for its future involvement in domestic affairs of state. Second, the new civilian leaders lacked legitimacy with the citizenry. The army, by virtue of its capabilities and its recognized position as the country's line of defense against India was viewed as the most legitimate actor in the country. Third, it has been argued that economic self-interest among members of the army contributes to its continued involvement in domestic affairs.[16] Ayesha Siddiqa, the Pakistani security analyst who posited this final explanation, asserts this involvement enabled the army to establish control over a vast economic empire, which it henceforth has sought to protect.[17]

The army historically has been a Punjabi-dominated institution, a development that can be traced back to a colonial pattern of military recruitment. During British suzerainty Punjabis were considered among the best soldierly material in the Indian colony. Soldiering opened up a major source of income since, on completion of military service, vast areas of arable land in Punjab were allocated to soldiers and veterans.[18] The result was a 'Punjabization' of the Indian army. Punjabis continued to dominate the army following Partition, though Zia helped to elevate the proportion of Pashtuns represented in its ranks.[19] Periods of military rule often witnessed a concomitant growth of Punjabi power, which in turn influenced Pakistani security priorities.[20] This is particularly true with regard to the Kashmir cause. Although it is generally less relevant to those living outside of Punjab, the army has projected the idea that a national consensus exists regarding the issue. Moreover, it has used the pretext of a consensus about Kashmir's importance as a means of retaining influence over national politics.[21]

Stephen Cohen, an American scholar who has written extensively on the subject, posits that three distinct generations joined the Pakistan army through 1982: a British generation; an American generation; and a Pakistani generation. The men comprising this third generation had less exposure to Western influences.[22] Many of those who constituted this third generation of Pakistani soldier also came from the lower middle class. Some of these men, who shared similar backgrounds with Lashkar recruits, were more susceptible to Zia's Islamization.[23]

This does not mean the Pakistan army is an Islamist one. To the degree that the army is associated with Islam it is in the communal form, i.e. in opposition to Hindu India as opposed to a universal or pan-Islamist conception.[24] However, the army has used pan-Islamic sentiment as pretext for projecting power beyond Pakistan's borders. Recourse to this latter path expanded as Pakistan sought to extend its influence into Afghanistan and Kashmir. Jihadi groups became ready allies of the Pakistan army's efforts to attain strategic depth in

Afghanistan and to bleed India via the Kashmir jihad. It is important to stress that these groups were used for nationalist purposes and that the army remains a nationalist—not an Islamist—organization. Nevertheless, the relationship between the military and its militant proxies was not a 'one-way street.'[25] Soldiers and civilian jihadis fought side-by-side in Afghanistan against the Soviets, and the two co-operated closely in Indian-administered Kashmir as well. Some soldiers were affected by this collaboration, and no doubt came to admire their civilian militant counterparts. Those espousing extreme views—of any variety—generally have not advanced to the upper military echelons.[26] The record is more mixed among mid-ranking officials, some of whom have embraced the ideological precepts for which their proxies fought.

This is also true among those seconded to the military's Inter-Services Intelligence Directorate [ISI]. Major General William Cawthorne, a British officer who served as the Pakistan army's deputy chief of staff following Partition, created the ISI to increase intelligence and military cooperation. It is one of two military intelligence services in Pakistan, the other being Military Intelligence [MI]. Some ISI departments focus on collecting and analyzing intelligence, while others conduct covert operations. It's directorate S, or S wing as it is sometimes known, is responsible for external operations and a specialized section within it has traditionally been responsible for working with non-state proxies. Because the ISI is both sprawling and compartmentalized, many units have little knowledge of the activities of those within it tasked to work with militant outfits like Lashkar. Pakistan also boasts two civilian intelligence agencies: the Intelligence Bureau [IB] and the police's Special Branch. The Federal Investigative Agency [FIA] is Pakistan's top criminal investigation agency and the country has established an anti-terrorism force as well. For the sake of simplicity, these various intelligence and investigative agencies are referred to collectively as the security services. Because the ISI is disproportionately powerful relative to these other agencies and plays a special role in coordinating militant groups like Lashkar, at times this book refers to it as a distinct entity.

The US initially shunned Zia, but the Soviet invasion of Afghanistan in December 1979 provided him with a route into America's

17

good graces. It also provided Pakistan a greater opportunity to influence events in Afghanistan, which was deemed necessary for its own security. Pakistan's geographic configuration meant the country lacked strategic depth within its borders should India invade from the east, and it sought to mitigate this by seeking strategic depth in Afghanistan. This necessitated a friendly and pliable government in Kabul, but historically Afghanistan had closer relations with India. Kabul also had designs on border territory inhabited by Pashtun tribes that became part of Pakistan, which feared India's support for these revanchist ambitions.[27] This heightened concerns in Pakistan about the threat of Pashtun separatism on its western border and fed the phobia that its enemies not only surrounded the country, but also sought to dismember it. Pakistan responded by using pan-Islamic sentiment to undercut separatist sentiment among the Pashtun tribes who lived on both sides of the Durand Line that serves as the Afghanistan-Pakistan border, as well as to thwart Indian influence in Afghanistan. This included providing financial and military support to Afghan Islamists beginning in the mid-1970s, a policy initiated before General Zia came to power.[28] The Soviet invasion presented a new threat, as Islamabad feared that if they occupied Afghanistan too easily then it would be a short step to Pakistan. Zia decided to covertly support the Afghan resistance fighters or mujahideen [the plural of mujahid or 'one who does jihad'].[29]

America began providing covert support to the Afghan mujahideen in 1980, but this remained at relatively low levels through 1984 when a US Congressman named Charlie Wilson and a small coterie of officers from the Central Intelligence Agency [CIA] precipitated a shift in US policy. In 1985 President Reagan signed National Security Directive 66, which established the objective of forcing the Soviets from Afghanistan. US support jumped to $250 million per year for weapons and other material, and grew significantly thereafter.[30] With Pakistan acting as a staging ground for the Afghan mujahideen, Zia demanded complete control over the dispersal of all of this hardware.[31] The Afghan mujahideen were organized into seven competing political parties and the ISI coordinated distribution to them, a role that helped it to grow into the powerful intelligence organization it is today.[32] Support was channeled primarily to hard-line Islamist parties in the hope of undercutting Pashtun nationalism and ultimately creating an Afghan government friendly to Pakistan.[33] In addition, the ISI also relied on Pakistani religious parties, most notably the Jamaat-e-Islami [Islamic Party, or JI] and the Jamiat Ulema-e-Islam [Assembly of Islamic Clergy, or JUI], to recruit Pakistani militants to participate in the jihad.

The government of Saudi Arabia, which had agreed to match US contributions, contributed a vast amount of support as well.[34] The Saudi ulema also steered millions of dollars via various establishment-controlled charities to support the Afghan jihad. In the late 1980s the Saudi government and ulema diverged in terms of their funding preferences, with the latter favoring Jamil al-Rahman in Kunar province because of his doctrinaire Salafism and the strong emphasis he placed on social and ritual issues compared with other Afghan factions.[35] Al-Rahman had previously been the provincial commander for Hizb-e-Islami, one of the seven Afghan parties and a favorite of the ISI's. He split with the party in 1986 or 1987 and, with the help of Saudi aid, established the Jamiat al-Dawa al-Quran wal-Sunna [Association for the Preaching of the Quran and the Sunna or JuDQS]. It emerged as the most powerful jihadi organization in the Salafi-stronghold of Afghanistan's Kunar province.[36] In addition to sending funds, the religious establishment also steered a high proportion of the Saudis who volunteered for the Afghan jihad to al-Rahman. Many of these men, as well as a number of Egyptian volunteers who also fought under him, came to consider Kunar province their home base.[37] Despite the Soviet retreat in 1989, Arabs continued traveling to Afghanistan. For the next several years, many Saudis, along with some Egyptians, continued to join Jamiat al-Dawa al-Quran wal-Sunna in Kunar and to train in camps there.[38] Then in 1991 Gulbuddin Hekmatyar's Hizb-e-Islami invaded Kunar, killing a number of al-Rahman's Arab allies and leading him to flee across the border to the Bajaur tribal agency in Pakistan. He was assassinated not long after.

Prior to launching MDI, Hafiz Saeed and several other founders had studied in Saudi Arabia. They had links to the Saudi ulema as well as to the Islamic University of Medina, where several of the teachers are believed to have contributed to the motivation for forming JuD by promising financial support. When MDI was founded a year later following the union with Zaki-ur Rehman Lakhvi's Ahl-e-Hadith outfit, al-Rahman's JuDQS also supported the nascent organization. Al-Rahman had a base in Bajaur as well, where another Salafi organization, the Jamaat-ul-Mujahideen, also provided early support.[39] MDI established its first training center in Paktia province in Afghanistan in 1987 and soon opened a second in Kunar province, where its cadres trained and fought alongside Jamil al-Rahman as well as the foreign fighters who had joined him there.[40] Like many of the outfits involved in the Afghan jihad, MDI was headquartered in the Pakistani frontier city of Peshawar.

With connections on both sides of the border and to Saudi Arabia, the group helped manage the flow of Arab volunteers, though its primary concern was mobilizing Ahl-e-Hadith Muslims in Pakistan. The Maktab al-Khidmat [Services Bureau], founded by Abdullah Azzam and sponsored by Osama bin Laden, was the major conduit for Arab volunteers traveling to fight in Afghanistan. Azzam was the man most responsible for encouraging Muslims from around the world to participate in the Afghan jihad, and he founded the Maktab al-Khidmat to accommodate the foreign fighters inspired by his call. It streamlined the mobilization process: raising money; recruiting and housing volunteers arriving in Pakistan; deploying them to Afghanistan; and providing them with weapons.[41] The Maktab al-Khidmat is typically considered a precursor to al-Qaeda, though by the time the latter was formed in 1988 bin Laden and Azzam had become estranged.[42] There were significant personnel overlaps between the two, as well as with MDI. Some of the Saudis based in Kunar, where the nascent Lashkar organization also trained, later joined al-Qaeda.[43] For example, a Saudi national named Abdul Rahman al-Surayhi [a.k.a. Abdul Rahman al-Sherahi] was Lakhvi's brother-in-law and reportedly played a role in organizing MDI's early training camps in Afghanistan, where Lakhvi is said to have been one of the main trainers.[44] He was also an associate of Osama bin Laden, on whose behalf he traveled back to Saudi Arabia to recruit others for the Afghan jihad.[45] The most obvious example was Azzam, who not only established and oversaw the Maktab al-Khidmat, but was also one of the original seventeen founding members of MDI.

After the Soviet withdrawal from Afghanistan, the call to jihad continued to resonate among the broader jihadi movement. Its leaders asserted that because Muslims remained oppressed by unbelievers in other locations around the world, defensive jihad must continue globally as part of an obligatory nomadic jihad.[46] The cessation of jihad in Afghanistan thus marked not an end, but rather the beginning of a transnational jihad waged on a number of fronts. Lashkar militants were part of this jihadi road show, and as the next chapter will detail its cadres fought in Tajikistan and Bosnia-Herzegovina as well as in Indian-administered Kashmir during the early 1990s. This reinforced its pan-Islamist tendencies and also enabled it to foster relationships with other jihadi outfits from beyond South Asia that were active on these fronts. However, Lashkar was arguably influenced more by local and regional dynamics.

*The Jihadi Milieu*

Approximately 95 per cent of the Pakistani population is Muslim, about 75–80 per cent of which are Sunni and 15–20 per cent Shia.[47] The Sunni Hanafi school of jurisprudence, to which both Barelvis and Deobandis subscribe, has predominated in South Asia since at least the turn of the thirteenth century CE.[48] Doctrinally, the Ahl-e-Hadith abjure association with any school of jurisprudence. Almost 80 per cent of Sunni Muslims in Pakistan, or close to 60 per cent of the overall population, subscribe to the Barelvi tradition of Islam, which is syncretic, blending Islam with ancient South Asian religious practices. This tradition has historically served as a check against Islamizing impulses taking root among the wider population. Deobandis represent a minority of Sunni Muslims in Pakistan, and the Ahl-e-Hadith an even smaller one. Despite their minority status, they are the two Islamic schools of thought to which Pakistan's major jihadi groups belong. Whereas multiple militant outfits adhere to the Deobandi school of thought and share a common ancestry as well as connections to the Taliban, Lashkar is the only major Ahl-e-Hadith jihadi group.

21

Deobandis are the second largest bloc within Pakistani Sunni Islam, but the most prolific in terms of political agitation and the promotion of militancy. However, at its inception the movement was apolitical. Deobandi Islam originated in 1867 in the Indian town of Deoband, approximately 100 miles north of Delhi. There a group of clerics founded the Darul Uloom Deoband, a school dedicated mainly to teaching the Hadith—the text that transmits the path or traditions of the Prophet Mohammad—and opposed to rational studies based on human reasoning.[49] It was one of a number of Islamic revivalist movements sweeping British India at a time when Muslims were the primary targets of a crackdown launched in response to the failed Rebellion of 1857 against the British Empire. While the early Deobandis opposed British rule, they were mainly 'inward-looking and primarily concerned with the Islamic quality of individual lives.'[50] Twelve years after the first Deobandi madrasa was founded, eleven more had opened across British India. Soon these seminaries were attracting a number of Afghan students as well.[51] Today, Deobandis have their strongest following among Pashtuns in Balochistan, the NWFP and FATA, all of which abut Afghanistan.[52] However, institutional links between Deobandi seminaries in Afghanistan and Pakistan and those in India were severed as a result of Partition.[53]

Prior to Partition, the Deobandi ulema were divided over whether to support the call for a separate state (Pakistan) by Mohammad Ali Jinnah and the Muslim League. The pro-Muslim league faction became the Jamiat Ulema-e-Islam. Many Deobandi clerics who opposed the creation of Pakistan moved there anyway following Partition, and joined the JUI. So too did many of the Deobandi ulema already living in what became Pakistan, but who initially had opposed the country's formation. Although the JUI had little political influence in Pakistan at Partition, as it was still intended to be a religious movement, it soon transformed into a political party. Over time it became a vigorously political actor, as well as a fractious one. A number of extremist factions emerged from the party, including the Sami ul-Haq faction [JUI-S] and the Fazl-ur Rehman faction [JUI-F], both of which sported ties to the Taliban movement that developed in Afghanistan during the 1990s.[54]

After Zia seized the levers of power in 1977 he set about enshrining Sunni Islam as the law of the land. Two years later, regime change came to Iran. The 1979 revolution that swept a Shia theocracy into power was a watershed event, which inspired and invigorated Shia Muslims worldwide. The ensuing mobilization of Shia identity 'galvanized the Shi'a into a distinct political group in Pakistan's politics.' This triggered an initial power struggle between the Pakistani state and its Shia community, followed by a broader and bloodier competition between Pakistan's Sunni and Shia Muslims.[55] The emboldened Shia community rejected Zia's Islamization program, which was based on Sunni interpretations of Islam. When Zia attempted to implement the Zakat Ordinance, Pakistan's Shia community objected and mobilized against it. Zakat is the practice of alms-giving and is obligatory for all Muslims able to do so, but Shias believe a ruler cannot impose it and so the ordinance violated their religious beliefs. The Shia community protested vigorously and Zia retreated, granting them an exemption. Pakistan's Sunni Islamists erupted in anger, with some arguing that the Shia, by refusing to submit to Sunni law, were 'outside the pale of Islam.'[56] Sunni and Shia organizations formed to protect their communities' interests and were soon engaged in sectarian attacks on one another. By 1988 the violence entered a new dimension with a series of sectarian assassinations and expanded during the 1990s, claiming almost 600 lives by 1997.[57]

The central government poured money into bolstering existing Sunni madaris [the plural of madrasa—religious school or seminary] and founding new ones. Much of this funding was diverted to the NWFP and Balochistan, provinces bordering Shia Iran. It also supported Sunni militant groups as part of its strategy to solve the 'Shia problem.'[58] External support further fueled the violence. Saudi Arabia, which considers itself the heart of the Sunni Muslim world, sought to check Iranian influence, leading the two countries to fund a sectarian proxy war in Pakistan. Iraq contributed as well and along with Saudi Arabia provided additional financing to Sunni madaris and militant organizations.[59] Deobandi madaris and militant outfits were major beneficiaries of this domestic and foreign largesse, which contributed to a growing Deobandi infrastructure. Because the central government was also channeling Saudi aid toward Deobandi militant groups to fight in Afghanistan, coupled with unofficial Saudi funding delivered to these groups directly, this helped to forge a nexus between sectarianism in Pakistan and attachment to the Afghan theater for many of the Deobandi jihadi outfits.[60] Some Pakistan-based scholars have also argued that Deobandi Islam in Pakistan and Afghanistan moved away from its Indian roots in part due to the influence of Saudi Wahhabism.[61]

The JUI took advantage of the situation to establish hundreds of madaris along the Pashtun belt that stretches across the NWFP and Balochistan. This contributed to a process of 'Pashtunization' in which Pashtunwali [the traditional Pashtun tribal code] fused with traditional Islamic interpretation.[62] With these madaris, the JUI was able to offer free education, food, shelter and military training to Afghan refugees and indigenous, but impoverished, Pakistanis. By the end of Zia's reign there were 8,000 official Deobandi madaris and an additional 25,000 unregulated ones.[63] As the quantity of madaris increased their quality declined and, in some cases, jihadi ideology built for mass consumption superseded traditional Islamic scholarship. One example of this phenomenon is the Darul Uloom Haqqania madrasa, headed by Sami ul-Haq. At least eight Taliban cabinet ministers and dozens more Taliban officials graduated from this madrasa. Another is the Jamiat-ul-Uloom-e-Islamiyah madrasa at Binori Town in Karachi, which also contributed a significant number of cadres to the ranks of the Taliban.[64]

In 1980, three students left the madrasa at Binori Town and headed for Afghanistan. There they founded a small group named Jamiat-ul-Ansar [Society of the Partisans] to take part in the jihad against the Soviets. The group was renamed Harkat-ul-Jihad-al-Islami [The Islamic Jihad Movement or HuJI] in 1988, after which it redirected its energies toward the Kashmir jihad. Following differences among the leadership, a splinter faction known as the Harkat-ul-Mujahideen [Movement of the Holy Warriors] emerged. This group also entered the Kashmir theater. The two later reunited briefly, before splitting once again in 1997. Two years later, HuM also splintered and another group called Jaish-e-Mohammad [Army of Mohammad or JeM] was formed. Many of the leaders and cadres from these groups could be traced back to the same Deobandi madaris, meaning they not only shared connections with one another but also with the Afghan Taliban.

These three groups—HuJI, HuM and JeM—also shared a connection to the Sipah-e-Sahaba Pakistan [Army of the Friends of the Prophet or SSP]. Haq Nawaz Jhangvi launched the SSP in 1985, a time when he was serving as the vice-chairman of the JUI in Punjab, to counter Shia influence in Pakistan. The party benefited from the majority of Zia's financing for those Sunni militant groups committed to beating back the Shia tide post-1979. The SSP also used the student body from its madaris in Punjab province to provide recruits for the Afghan jihad against the Soviets and later to the Taliban.[65] It split from the JUI and in 1994 birthed its own militant organization, Lashkar-e-Jhangvi [Army of Jhangvi or LeJ].[66] LeJ spent the late 1980s and all of the 1990s targeting Pakistani Shia, though it too forged ties with the Taliban alongside whom LeJ militants also fought. It became a close al-Qaeda ally after 9/11, and along with its splinter factions is responsible for many of the suicide bombing operations and assassinations that have racked Pakistan in the recent past.

Like the Deobandis, the Ahl-e-Hadith are a product of the colonial context in India where the movement was founded in the 1870s. Its leadership came from prominent families, which had become socially dislocated as a result of British colonization.[67] They too perceived the Muslim community to have strayed from its faith, believing that syncretism, Shiism and the British occupation were corrupting the purity of Sunni Islam. These Muslims condemned the accommodations their co-religionists had made to their Indian surroundings and urged a return to the Quran and Hadith as a way to restore Islam from the corruption of foreign influences.[68]

The Ahl-e-Hadith movement is essentially the South Asian variant of Salafism and the name literally translated means 'people of the Hadith,' which is the text that transmits the path or traditions of the Prophet Mohammad. The term Salafism derives from the name for the first three generations of Muslims, who were known as the al-salaf al-salih or pious forefathers. These men were participants in Islam's rise, and Salafis consider them examples of the correct way for Muslims to live.[69] They believe that these first three generations of Muslims had a pure knowledge of Islam, whereas subsequently this was 'sullied and distorted by the introduction of innovations and the development of schisms in the Muslim community.'[70] Salafis around the world, and the Ahl-e-Hadith in South Asia, preach a return to the study of the original sources of Islam. The Ahl-e-Hadith recognize only the Quran and the Hadith as legal sources in Islam, and reject all of the schools of Islamic jurisprudence that interpret those texts. Following any school of jurisprudence is considered to be tantamount to worshipping that school's founder, which violates the Islamic tenet to worship only God. Instead, they advocate engaging in what is known as ijtihad [individual interpretation] of the Quran and Hadith, though that interpretation is supposed to be confined to those who are sufficiently qualified.[71]

The Ahl-e-Hadith sect is often derogatorily referred to as the South Asian version of Wahhabism.[72] Beginning during the colonial era, the Ahl-e-Hadith interacted with Wahhabis while on the pilgrimage to Mecca as well as through their associations with the members of the Arab ulema who migrated to India at the time. However, the Salafis in India began drawing a distinction with Wahhabis soon after forming the Ahl-e-Hadith movement. This was done primarily to avoid the British suspicion that they followed the jihadi tradition of Syed Ahmed Barelvi and the so-called 'Wahhabi movement,' which had rebelled against the Empire.[73] The Ahl-e-Hadith openly professed loyalty to the British Raj and formally requested to be differentiated from the Wahhabis, even as they retained connections to some of those involved in the struggle against British colonialism.[74] This provided the required room for maneuver to propagate the Ahl-e-Hadith concept of Islam in colonial India and the movement continued to call for an 'intellectual jihad against fellow Muslims on moral and ethical grounds.'[75]

In return, the Ahl-e-Hadith were 'hated by the masses' and condemned in Muslim law books.[76] Their aversion to any of the schools of Sunni jurisprudence or form of syncretism put them at odds with the majority of South Asian Muslims, who follow the Hanafi school of Sunni jurisprudence and incorporate local practices into their approach to Islam.[77]Ahl-e-Hadith adherents reveled in this opposition, and courted an 'exclusionary identity.'[78] For example, the Ahl-e-Hadith introduced a new and highly visible style of prayer to distinguish themselves from those who follow the Hanafi school of jurisprudence.[79] Such visible demarcations of their faith further separated the Ahl-e-Hadith from other Muslims and marked them as an elitist group with a sense of 'moral superiority.'[80] This left them with a relatively small following in pre-Partition British India, which remained the case in Pakistan and India post-Partition.

The Ahl-e-Hadith movement has made gradual progress in Pakistan since Partition. By the end of the 1980s they were a small, but potent, force particularly in Punjab and the NWFP.[81] In part, this owed to state patronage. Like the Deobandis, the Ahl-e-Hadith benefited from funding for madaris during the 1980s. Saudi support played a prominent role in the movement's growth as well. In the 1920s, the Ahl-e-Hadith began developing international connections with Salafis and Wahhabis in what became Saudi Arabia.[82] Ahl-e-Hadith ties to the religious establishment there have grown stronger since the 1960s. In later years, alumni of Medina University in Saudi Arabia advanced the cause of Salafism as they returned to Pakistan.[83] The Ahl-e-Hadith also gained popularity as a result of the many Pakistanis working in the Gulf region who returned home with Salafi beliefs.[84] These connections to Saudi Arabia were reinforced when thousands of Arabs came to Pakistan to support the Afghan resistance against the Soviets. As described above, Saudi money had been pouring into Pakistan since the early 1980s. When the Jamaat-e Islami supported Iraq during the Gulf War in 1991 the Kingdom shifted the Saudi patronage it had been receiving to the Ahl-e-Hadith, channelling millions of dollars to the movement in Pakistan.[85]

While the number of Ahl-e-Hadith madaris remains miniscule relative to those affiliated with the Deobandi sect, they nonetheless increased from 134 in 1988 to 310 in 2000.[86] They have continued to grow since then. According to the Pakistani government, there were 34,000 students studying in Ahl-e-Hadith madrasas in 2006 compared with 18,800 in 1996.[87] This is almost a 100 per cent increase over ten years. The Ahl-e-Hadith's approach to education is partly responsible for the movement's growth in popularity. Ahl-e-Hadith madaris merge Islamic education with modern curricula, including Pakistan studies, English, mathematics and science. Adherents believe there is no harm in teaching these subjects provided students do not adopt Western culture. This is a markedly different approach from that taken in many Deobandi madaris, where the focus is mainly on religious learning. It makes Ahl-e-Hadith madaris an attractive option for lower middle class parents who cannot afford private schools, but want their children to receive the practical tools necessary for future economic success. The fact that students at these madaris generally achieve high exam results boosts their appeal.[88] It is important to note as well that madaris of all sectarian persuasions in Pakistan typically teach students to discount other sects. Thus, promoting one sect implies rejecting others.[89]

Despite these advances, Ahl-e-Hadith Muslims remain a small minority in Pakistan and the movement is also fragmented. Disagreements exist over ritual and strategy, participation in politics and the proper approach to jihad.[90] Similar differences among purists, politicos and jihadis are found in the wider Salafi movement as well.[91] The Markaz-e-Jamiat Ahl-e-Hadith [MJAH] is the main Ahl-e-Hadith organization. It participates in politics and is a member of the Muttahida Majlis-e-Amal [United Action Council or MMA], a coalition of religious parties.[92] The MJAH has several subsidiary organizations that have engaged in violence. One is the Ahl-e-Hadith Youth Force. It has been involved in sectarian disputes against Shia and Barelvi Muslims, including taking over Barelvi mosques to preach the Ahl-e-Hadith creed. Another is the Tehrik-e-Mujahideen [Movement of Holy Warriors], which emerged in 1989 in Indian-administered Kashmir to wage jihad.[93] It has also taken over a number of Barelvi mosques in Indian-Kashmir and converted them into Ahl-e-Hadith mosques. The Tehrik-e-Mujahideen was not connected to the MJAH until 2000, when the latter absorbed it in response to criticisms that it was only involved in politics and was not waging jihad.[94]

Lashkar avers participation in politics and considers the MJAH to be no longer a Salafi organization because it associates with non-Salafis.[95] The group is also at odds with the mainstream Ahl-e-

Hadith movement in general, and the MJAH in particular, over the issue of jihad. Although it is not the only Ahl-e-Hadith organization to wage military jihad, Lashkar is the only one to consider doing so to be an individual and compulsory obligation for all Muslims at the present time. The other Ahl-e-Hadith organizations that participate in jihad consider it to be a collective responsibility, meaning it is not obligatory for all Muslims. Because they do no promote jihad as an individual obligation, Lashkar leaders believe the other organizations within Pakistan's Ahl-e-Hadith movement have 'deviated from the pure Salafia school of Faith.'[96] This puts Lashkar at odds with the mainstream Ahl-e-Hadith organizations, which historically made it difficult for the group to recruit from Ahl-e-Hadith madaris, the great majority of which are controlled by the MJAH. Thus, it was forced to construct its own network and support structure. This is an entirely different situation from that which existed for the major Deobandi outfits.

Jihadi group decisions about where to operate, as well as the nature of objectives and activities in those loci of operation, are not as discrete as the division between the Deobandi and Ahl-e-Hadith schools of thought. Once again, the three loci are Afghanistan, Indian-administered Kashmir and sectarianism in Pakistan. The Afghan locus was connected to the Kashmir and sectarian loci during the 1990s because many of the major jihadi groups fighting in Indian-administered Kashmir or waging sectarian war in Pakistan trained in Afghanistan. Connections to Afghanistan for all of the major Deobandi militant groups were stronger than for Lashkar, and went beyond the use of the country for training purposes. Cadres from all of the major Deobandi outfits fought alongside the Taliban and some of their leaders held posts within the Taliban government as well. This inevitably brought them closer to Osama bin Laden's circle, a relationship explored in greater detail in Chapter 5. Specifically, Harkat-ul-Jihad-al-Islami [HuJI] and Harkat-ul-Mujahideen [HuM] fought in the Kashmir jihad, but as the 1990s progressed they became more motivated by events in Afghanistan. Sipah-e-Sahaba Pakistan [SSP] and Lashkar-e-Jhangvi [LeJ] were situated primarily within the locus of sectarian violence in Pakistan, but also shared similarly strong connections with the Taliban in

Afghanistan. When Jaish-e-Mohammad emerged it automatically had pre-existing connections with each of these three loci. Jaish was a splinter of HuM, from which it drew most of its cadres, and so it shared that group's connection to the Kashmir jihad and Afghanistan. It also shared members with SSP and LeJ, which meant it was situated in the sectarian locus as well. JeM's primary focus was on the Kashmir theater where it was a some-time ally and often a competitor with Lashkar, but had competing interests in the Afghan and sectarian loci as well as a weak ideological foundation owing to the nature of its emergence as a splinter group. The Deobandi groups were not only active in multiple loci, but, as already discussed, were all connected to one another as well. Thus a feedback loop existed in which their ties to one another reinforced the interconnectedness of the three loci in which they were active, while activity in each of these loci simultaneously compounded the relations among the groups.

Lashkar was part of the same jihadi galaxy as these other groups, but it moved in a separate orbit. Unlike the Deobandi groups whose cadres trained in Taliban-controlled territory from the mid-1990s onwards, Lashkar continued to use Kunar province as its primary Afghan training base after the Taliban came to power. The Afghan Salafis based there were antithetical to the Deobandi Taliban, which never invested too much effort in gaining control of the province.[97] Lashkar shared this sentiment and its cadres typically did not fight alongside the Taliban in Afghanistan, though contact between the two did occur. According to Noman Benotman, a former leader of the Libyan Islamic Fighting Group who worked with Lashkar during its early years, its members were only comfortable with other Salafis and viewed most Afghans as mushrikun[98]—the term used to denote those who commit shirk, which means polytheism, idolatry or the association of others with God. Salafis use the term against those Muslims who do not follow the Salafi creed.[99] Lashkar members felt similarly about many Muslims in Pakistan, especially Barelvi and Shia Muslims, and occasionally dabbled in sectarian violence against them as the next chapter will detail. These activities generally ceased after the group became the ISI's favored proxy for the Kashmir jihad in the early-to-mid 1990s. Thus, during the latter years of the decade when all of the Deobandi groups were increasing their ties to one another as well as to the Taliban and some of them were involved in sectarian violence in Pakistan, Lashkar was focused overwhelmingly on waging jihad in Indian-administered Kashmir. This meant it was a group apart within the jihadi milieu in terms of both its sectarian identity and its operations.

2

# LASHKAR'S IDEOLOGY

## DAWA AND JIHAD

The purpose of this chapter is to examine Lashkar's ideology, as it developed during the group's formative years in the 1990s. This provides a baseline for assessing its activities during the 1990s and its evolution after 9/11, as well as a means of situating the group within the wider jihadi movement. The term 'jihadi' is recognizably problematic and rightly controversial. It is a neologism that misconstrues the traditional and theosophical meaning of the concept of jihad. The term is used here to connote those Sunni Muslims who, in contradistinction to most Muslims, regard jihad primarily as waging war and believe doing so is an individual obligation. Jihadi ideology—in terms of objectives and approach—has theological as well as political dimensions. Strategic calculation also plays a role in a jihadi group's decision-making. The jihadi movement includes pragmatists and ideologues, making it no different from most social movements, political parties or even governments. In some instances, seemingly immutable principles are bent to fit strategic necessity. Theology is often employed selectively to reconcile what are essentially pragmatic calculations. Because jihadis are also human beings, ideological rigor and strategic calculus sometimes give way to more pedestrian influences such as greed, loyalty or simply the desire to survive.

Jihadis generally share the same long-term political aims. Most can agree on establishing a pan-Islamic Caliphate or achieving

Islam's complete dominance on Earth as end goals. Because these are utopian aims they offer limited utility for analysts who study jihadi groups, as well as for jihadis themselves. When considering where and how a jihadi group focuses its energy, it is better to focus on their short- and medium-term objectives. Despite the fact that jihadis constitute an incredibly small minority among Muslims, significant variegation exists within the jihadi movement over these objectives as well as a range of other issues, including which enemy to prioritize, where to fight, whether it is ever appropriate to make war against a Muslim regime, what to do about the Shia and whether it is permissible to kill other Sunni Muslims. There are also significant disagreements about the importance of dawa, with some jihadis advocating for a greater emphasis on non-violent outreach and others promoting a violence-only approach. How a jihadi group addresses these issues generally comes from a combination of its doctrinal precepts and strategic calculation.

Jihadis can be classified in a number of ways. This book employs a typology devised by Thomas Hegghammer, which focuses on the political content and strategic calculus of an actor's ideology. He posits five main rationales for Islamist activism: state-oriented, morality-oriented, sectarian, nation-oriented and umma-oriented. In each case, violent or non-violent approaches may be employed. Hegghammer argues that multiple rationales often motivate a jihadi group, but that traditionally a group had one dominant rationale guiding its violent behavior at a given time.[1] However, he also observes that there has been a trend toward ideological hybridization since the early- to mid-part of this decade, which has made it more difficult to determine what some jihadi outfits are fighting for.[2] Thus, when classifying jihadi rationales for activism, it is important to keep in mind that these are ideal types. The following summarizes descriptions drawn from Hegghammer's typology.[3]

State-oriented activism refers to a focus on changing the social and political order of the state. Its non-violent manifestation is reformism and its violent form is socio-revolutionary jihad. Socio-revolutionary jihadis prioritize defeating impious Muslim regimes, often termed the 'near enemy' and replacing them with men who will rule by sharia. This approach declares Muslim rulers to be kuffaar, or unbelievers, which most Muslims believe is not theologically justifiable unless the leader 'willingly implements non-Islamic law, understands that it does not represent Islam, and announces that it is superior to Islam.' This traditional reading of apostasy requires absolute proof of intentions, something that is nearly impossible unless the ruler publicly announces his disbelief.[4] For those waging a near enemy jihad, the bar is set much lower.

Morality-oriented activism describes a desire to reorient Muslims' social conduct in a more conservative direction and toward a more literalist interpretation of the Quran and Hadith. This is characterized by pietism in its non-violent form and vigilantism in its violent manifestation. Sectarian Islamism is defined by a desire to reduce the influence and power of a competing sect or sects. Violent sectarianism may aim to eliminate members of a competing sect altogether, or at least to cleanse a specific society of them. Like those motivated by state-oriented activism, sectarian and morality-oriented jihadis often look inward first, focusing on the population of the country in which they live.

Nation-oriented activism is characterized by a desire to establish sovereignty over specific territory perceived to be under non-Muslim occupation or domination. The designation of a specific piece of territory, as opposed to all territory under non-Muslim occupation or domination, suggests a nationalist as opposed to pan-Islamist orientation. This form of activism produces irredentist jihads. These are closest to the traditional Islamic rationale for war making, which encouraged Muslims to fight directly against infidels in order to liberate lands from foreign domination or protect Muslims under threat from an outside invader. Traditionally, this was an individual obligation only for Muslims living in the land in question, which is to say it was obligatory for all of them to participate. It was a collective obligation for all other Muslims, meaning the decision to participate was voluntary and that so long as some members of the umma answer the call, others need not fight. Thus, traditionally an irredentist jihad is inward looking and obligatory for Muslims living on the land in question and outward looking, but voluntary, for all other Muslims.

Umma-oriented activism is distinguished by a desire to protect the entire community of believers, known as the umma, from non-

Muslim threats. It may produce a soft or violent form of pan-Islamism. Those with a pan-Islamist rationale for jihad face a bevy of potential enemies, and can be further sub-divided into classical jihadis and global jihadis. Classical jihadi doctrine is close to the traditional conception of irredentist jihad outlined above, but with a modern twist: today's classical jihadis believe all Muslims, as opposed to the population directly effected by a non-Muslim occupation, are duty-bound to fight. Abdullah Azzam, bin Laden's mentor and a founder of Lashkar's parent organization, is the man most responsible for this modern twist. He declared in a highly influential fatwa that fighting to expel foreign occupiers from all Muslim lands was 'the most important of all compulsory duties.'[5] Classical jihadis also believe that any land ever controlled by Muslims is Muslim land. In this light, even a country such as Spain is in need of 'liberation.' Because pan-Islamist jihadis cannot fight everywhere at once it is necessary to make choices about where to focus their energies. Geography or the popularity of a particular front may play a role in the decision-making process, such that if a snapshot of an actor at war were taken it might be difficult to distinguish between a nation-oriented and umma-oriented jihad. The key distinction is that those motivated by nation-oriented Islamism theoretically would cease their violent activities once the specific territory for which they are fighting was liberated. Classical jihadis may focus on a specific piece of territory, but theoretically would not cease their activities once it was liberated so long as other Muslim lands were occupied.

While classical jihadis will fight against the US on open fronts, and may prioritize action on those fronts for any number of reasons, their main focus is not American-centric. This distinguishes them from global jihadis, who are characterized by a specifically anti-American agenda. Al-Qaeda pioneered the idea of prioritizing the fight against America, known as the 'far enemy' to distinguish it from local Muslim regimes or the 'near enemy'. In addition to an American-centric focus, this doctrine promoted a global view of warfare that entailed attacking US interests anywhere in the world. Global jihadism expanded after 9/11 to include military confrontation not only with America, but with its allies as well. Moreover, many militant outfits that continued to prioritize other enemies experienced a hybridization, whereby they began including America and its allies among their list of adversaries to be fought. Today, the term global jihad is used to describe the jihad against America and its allies as well as the nexus of actors who participate in that jihad.

The concept of jihad as religiously sanctioned war to protect the umma has a strong historical tradition in South Asia.[6] Successive governments in Pakistan have tapped into this tradition since Partition to support the use of militant proxies who were declared mujahideen and lauded for waging legitimate jihads abroad, at times fighting alongside active-duty soldiers. Although done to serve national interests, this practice reinforced the interpretation of Pakistan as an Islamic vanguard responsible for protecting Muslims beyond its borders. The state also promoted a vehemently anti-Hindu discourse, thus contributing to the conception that fighting against India was the most legitimate jihad.[7] One result was to blur the communal and universal interpretations of Islam in Pakistan, which helps to explain two important characteristics of Pakistani jihadism: first, most jihadi groups historically prioritized pan-Islamist campaigns abroad for which they enjoyed state sanction; and second, this pan-Islamism at times has been fused with a vicious anti-Hinduism. Finally, by promoting Islam as a means to bind the country together internally and project power externally, Pakistan's rulers also blurred the lines between Islamist activism at home and abroad. The major jihadi outfits that flourished during the past several decades were tied to religious parties that reaped domestic support for various reasons, enabling the construction of madaris as well as charitable institutions. This exacerbated sectarian competition among them as well as their militant offshoots for official support, but bolstered the collective belief that Pakistan's creation would not be fully complete until it was an Islamic state. It also contributed to their ability to penetrate pockets of Pakistani society through social outreach in order to advance their Islamist agenda.

Lashkar is a product of this environment. The group was always motivated by a pan-Islamist rationale for jihad, but has fixated overwhelmingly on India since the mid-1990s.[8] This preoccupation was compounded by the fact that its base of supporters was in Punjab province and Pakistan-administered Kashmir, where backing for the Kashmir cause is strongest. Lashkar was not immune to the increasing hybridization that has characterized many outfits in recent years, but the leadership's focus on India continues to rival al-Qaeda's historical preoccupation with America. It is also arguably more dedicated to dawa than any other Pakistani jihadi outfit. Indeed, the group pursues different rationales for activism—one violently and one non-violently—in different theaters with near equal vigor. The seeds of this dual focus were sown at the organization's founding, when Saeed's preaching organization merged with Lakhvi's military outfit. Although the group dedicated the majority of its resources to jihad during its earliest years, state support enabled it to actualize its commitment to non-violent reformism in Pakistan. Hafiz Saeed later explained the group's philosophy, saying:

Islam propounds both dawa and jihad. Both are equally important and inseparable. Since our life revolves around Islam, therefore both dawa and jihad are essential, we cannot prefer one over the other. This was also the practice of the Prophet (PBUH). If beliefs and morals are not reformed, dawa alone develops into mysticism and jihad alone may lead to anarchy. Therefore recognizing the salience of dawa and jihad, the need is to fuse the two together. This is the only way to bring about change among individuals, society and the world.[9]

The group outlines eight reasons for waging violent jihad, and asserts all Muslims are required to wage or support it until these objectives are met: to eliminate Muslim persecution; to achieve the dominance of Islam as a way of life throughout the entire world; to force disbelievers to pay jizya [a tax on non-Muslims]; to fight those who oppress the weak and feeble; to exact revenge for the killing of any Muslim; to punish enemies for violating their oaths or treaties; to defend Muslim states anywhere in the world; and to recapture occupied Muslim territory. Further, Lashkar considers any state that experienced Muslim rule to be Islamic territory that must be recovered.[10] After the Soviet withdrawal from Afghanistan in 1989, Lashkar militants joined the jihadi caravan and fought on multiple open fronts during the 1990s. Its militants were among the first foreign fighters to participate in the Tajik civil war [1992–1997], though they were not active for the entire conflict.[11] The group also sent cadres to

Bosnia-Herzegovina, where they fought under the command of Mahmoud Mohammad Ahmed Bahaziq, known by his kunya [nom de guerre] Sheikh Abu Abdul Aziz and sometimes referred to as Barbaros because of his red beard. A Saudi national of Indian descent (his mother was from Hyderabad), Bahaziq was one of the founders as well as a financier of MDI and headed its Department of External Affairs in the 1990s.[12] He was also one of the first veterans of the anti-Soviet jihad in Afghanistan to travel to Bosnia-Hezegovina and his efforts there helped to inaugurate a wave of fighters to that battlefield.[13] Some belonged to the nascent Lashkar, but most were veterans of the Afghan jihad (known as Arab Afghans), or new volunteers from various Arab countries.[14] An invitation in 1998 to MDI's annual conference lauded Bahaziq for his efforts stating 'Commander Abu Abdul Aziz of Markazul Dawa Wal Irshad laid the foundation of jehad in Bosnia.'[15] Once there, he stressed the need to convert Bosnian Muslims to Lashkar's interpretation of Islam. To this end he urged the same types of dawa-related activities Lashkar practiced in Pakistan:

We have to strengthen our Belief and the Belief of our Brethren the Bosnians by *all* means: through training, through education, through awareness programs and other means.[16]

He also believed that the Bosnian conflict presented the jihadi movement with an opportunity to 'make Islam enter Europe via jihad' according to an interview he gave to Lashkar's *Al-Dawa* magazine.[17] Jamal al-Fadl, a government informant and former member of al-Qaeda, reaffirmed this, testifying that Bahaziq stated a main objective of the Bosnian jihad was 'to establish a base for operations in Europe.'[18] The primary aim was to spread Bahaziq's (and Lashkar's) interpretation of the Salafi faith among Muslims in Europe and to develop a support base among them. To be sure, this included an emphasis on jihad, but the intent at the time was not to stake out terrain from which to begin launching terrorist attacks against the West.

While these peripatetic forays helped the group to begin weaving together the fabric of its transnational networks, it was the Kashmir jihad closer to home that enabled Lashkar to grow into the robust organization it is today. Some of Lashkar's militants began fighting in Indian-administered Kashmir as early as 1990. Before long other fronts were closing and Kashmir had become among the most active theaters for militants seeking to liberate occupied Muslim land. Many of the Pakistani jihadi groups that fought in Afghanistan against the Soviets began sending militants to Indian-administered Kashmir, where indigenous outfits were already active. The ISI was sponsoring a number of groups there, and Lashkar was not the first, second or even the third group the state threw its weight behind. General Javed Ashraf Qazi (Retd) was the Director-General of the ISI from 1993–1995, when the state began investing heavily in Lashkar. He described it as a 'very motivated group,' but also 'a very small one that was only just coming up.'[19] Ironically, it was the group's small size and weak position in Pakistan that contributed to its burgeoning relationship with the state. Because Lashkar was an Ahl-e-Hadith group and estranged from the wider Ahl-e-Hadith movement, it did not have a significant support base in Pakistan. With no natural allies or major funding flows of its own, the ISI presumed the group would be a more pliable proxy than other outfits. This proved an accurate assessment, even after Lashkar leveraged state support to develop its own infrastructure and economic interests in Pakistan. While doing so enabled the group to grow far more powerful domestically than the ISI might have anticipated, this infrastructure provided Lashkar's handlers with leverage over it. Were the group to act too independently of its handlers, they could threaten to shut down its domestic operations and seize its assets. Unlike the Deobandi groups, this infrastructure was specific to Lashkar and so the group did not have a wider support network to fall back on.

The 1993–95 period when the state began escalating its support for Lashkar marked a turning point for the group. Till then its militants had waged jihad on multiple fronts, but thereafter the focus was liberating Indian-administered Kashmir. However, it would be a mistake to view this as merely the result of practical calculation; Lashkar's leaders embraced an umma-oriented ideology, but viewed the Kashmir jihad as the most legitimate one for the group. They argued that because Indian-administered Kashmir was the closest occupied land, it was an Islamic obligation for the group's members to fight there and that this front took precedence over others. The Kashmir jihad was also among the most important because the ratio of occupying forces to the population was one of the highest in the world, and so it was among the largest and most heinous occupations in the Muslim world. Thus, Lashkar cadres were told they were doctrinally obligated to prioritize fighting in Indian-administered Kashmir, though they could volunteer to fight on other fronts and a small number are believed to have gone to Chechnya and the Philippines during the mid-to-late 1990s.[20] The core leadership of the group continued to hold these views after 9/11 according to Lashkar members who outlined these ideological arguments for the author.[21]

Lashkar's leaders also viewed the Kashmir jihad as only the latest chapter in a Hindu-Muslim struggle which has existed ever since the time of the Prophet Muhammad. They argue that Hindus are the worst of the polytheists and that the Prophet Muhammad singled out India as a special target for jihad. 'Whosoever will take part in jihad against India,' Lashkar's Muhammad Ibrahim Salaf has asserted the Prophet declared, 'Allah will set him free from the pyre of hell.'[22] Thus, Lashkar's jihad was not limited to liberating Kashmir, which helps to explain why the group began establishing networks to execute or support terrorist attacks against India as early as 1992. Once Kashmir was liberated, it could serve as a base of operations to reconquer India and restore Muslim rule to the Indian subcontinent. In other words, while the group's leaders spoke of waging jihad until the domination of Islam was achieved, for them the road to re-establishing the Caliphate ran through South Asia. Thus, while expanding its jihad after 9/11 to include America and its Western allies fit with Lashkar's pan-Islamist ideology, India would remain the primary enemy.

Lashkar's missionary ambitions are inherently sectarian. Its leaders state that the infidels invented sectarianism to divide Muslims and thwart them from waging jihad, and they have castigated other groups that engage in sectarian violence.[23] Yet Lashkar members were guilty of these offenses during the group's earliest years. As discussed in the previous chapter, the group was comfortable only with the Salafis in Kunar province and viewed most other Afghans as mushrikun. At the zenith of the Afghan jihad against the Soviets, some of its members were attacking non-Salafi Afghans instead. The practice of sectarian violence continued in Pakistan, where Lashkar members occasionally assaulted Shia and Barelvi Muslims, who they also denounced as mushrikun. These sectarian assaults in Pakistan stopped only when the group became more involved in the Kashmir jihad.[24] According to Noman Benotman, the leadership recognized the need to become more practical if it was going to increase its role in Indian-administered Kashmir, where most Muslims are Barelvi and Sufi. Lashkar's leaders asked him to spend time with its members and to serve as an example of a Salafi jihadi who had fought alongside non-Salafis in Afghanistan. He subsequently stayed at one of Lashkar's camps for several months in 1994, where he discussed with fighters the need to put sectarian differences aside and focus on fighting against the non-Muslim occupiers.[25] Efforts to take a more ecumenical approach were relatively, though not entirely, successful in Indian-administered Kashmir, where Lashkar militants still engaged in periodic sectarian assaults.[26]

Financial and organizational support from the state for Lashkar's participation in the Kashmir jihad enabled the group to build an infrastructure in Pakistan to pursue its missionary objectives via non-violent activism. The group's commitment to dawa had been extant since its inception, and once it began receiving state support Lashkar devoted significant resources to building additional mosques and madaris as well as to providing social welfare and educational services. Its growing reputation as a jihadi force fighting to liberate Indian-administered Kashmir also enhanced its standing among sections of the Pakistani populace, heightening its ability to raise money for missionary outreach and to recruit members from other sects, who were promptly converted upon joining.[27] Thus, while its sectarian orientation did not change, its approach did. In a sign of the group's maturity in this regard as well as of its growing stature in Pakistan, members of the federal and Punjabi governments reportedly solicited Lashkar's support against sectarian violence in 1998.[28]

Lashkar's leaders view missionary outreach as part of a larger reformist project to transform Pakistan. According to JuD spokesperson Abdullah Muntazir, 'Pakistan's foundation stone is La ilaha illa Allah [there is no God but The God] and so there is no difference between Pakistan and Islam.' However, the creation of Pakistan will be complete only when it becomes a truly Islamic country. Thus, the aim is to 'bring Muslims of Pakistan to the true meaning of Islam and to work not only for the purification of their beliefs, but also of their deeds.' This will enable the group to 'establish a society in Pakistan that is according to the true teachings of Islam.'[29] As Hafiz Saeed explained during an interview with Radio *Sada-e-Hurriyat*, 'We do not believe in revolutionary change in Pakistan rather we want a gradual reform through dawa.'[30]

The group's abstention from revolutionary jihad in favor of dawa is a function of doctrinal precepts and strategic priorities. In the Lashkar tract *Jihad in the Present Time*, Hafiz Abdul Salam bin Muhammad wrote that Pakistan's leaders 'do not at least outwardly and apparently disown Islam though they do follow a policy based on hypocrisy.' However, he argued there is a difference between a hypocrite and an avowed disbeliever, thus, the struggle in Pakistan 'is not a struggle between Islam and disbelief.'[31] Hafiz bin Muhammad elaborated on the importance of distinguishing between misguided Muslim rulers and non-Muslim aggressors in *Why We Do Jihad*, arguing that waging war against the former detracts from the ability to defeat the latter:

There are two kinds of infidels—one who has not professed the Faith, and one who has professed it. The former fights against us because we have professed the Islamic Faith. The latter will never fight against us because he has become our brother and entered our religion through professing the Faith. However, if he (the latter) is going astray, we will talk to him, persuade him to come to the way of religion. As long as he does not raise his hand against us, we will not raise ours against him. We will consider him wrong and misguided, and say that he is committing sins of un-belief (kufr) and associationism (shirk). But we will not declare war against him. Because if we declare war against those who have professed Faith, we cannot do war with those who haven't.[32]

He also made clear that Lashkar believes there is an 'essential difference between the utter brutalities and atrocities inflicted on the Kashmiri Muslims by the savage Hindus and the disregard for law and order which is a common scene in Pakistan and which is surely pitiable.' Thus, while appropriate to 'press the Pakistani rulers to enforce Islam' it is incorrect to directly fight against them since that would mean a cessation of jihad against the Hindu occupiers in order to 'set to killing our own brothers who declare their belief in the Islamic creed.'[33] In other words, Lashkar's prohibition against waging a jihad against Muslim rulers stems not only from the fact that it is considered doctrinally unacceptable as long as those rulers profess belief in Islam. It is also based on priorities and strategic calculation. Lashkar members were reportedly obligated during training to promise never to turn their guns on the state or use their martial skills within Pakistan.[34] Several militants confirmed this precept was drilled into them during training.[35] However, one of their number also admitted that debates often took place about whether to break with the prohibition against attacking the Pakistani state; a fact that was later confirmed by a high-ranking Jamaat-ul-Dawa official close to Hafiz Saeed.[36] These debates took place during the late 1990s and this decade, primarily coinciding with periods when Pakistan was restraining Lashkar's jihadi activities abroad. However support for these activities never ceased, and the leadership continued to direct the group's militant energies outward.

# PART II

3

# THE ISI'S BOYS

Jammu and Kashmir [hereafter Kashmir] was one of 565 'princely states' given the option of accession to India or Pakistan as Partition approached. The decision was to be based on the religious composition of their populations and contiguity to one of the two new countries. The Hindu Maharaja of Kashmir, Sir Hari Singh Indar Mahindar Bahadur ruled over a state whose population was approximately three-quarters Muslim and this created expectations that it would become part of Pakistan. However, the provisions made by the British for accession did not require the rulers of the princely states to consult their respective populations.[1] Further, the British demarcated the boundaries of the two new countries in such a way that Kashmir was contiguous to both India and Pakistan. Controversy surrounds the question of whether the British Viceroy at the time of Partition, Lord Mountbatten, influenced the head of the boundary commission to alter the final border in order to connect India to Kashmir via a land route. Many Pakistanis believe he did and that this was intended to queer the pitch in India's favor so that it might secure the accession of Kashmir. Nevertheless, it was still up to Hari Sing to determine which nation the princely state would join. Instead both Pakistan and India came into being on 14 August 1947 without the Maharaja making a decision. Soon Muslims in the Kashmir district of Poonch were calling for accession to Pakistan and a heavy-handed response by Hari Sing catalyzed a rebellion. Poonchis had strong geographical, economic and religious links to parts of Pakistan, which contributed to their initial demands for accession. Now they began crossing into the new country to prepare for armed rebellion back home. This practice continued in later years, as subsequent generations of Kashmiris made a similar trip. So too did the Pakistani policy of deploying proxies, which began not long after Partition when tribesmen from the NWFP were mobilized to join the fight in Kashmir. Although a small number of soldiers were with them, the Pakistan army was not deployed at this time.[2] Notably, the government invited religious scholars to issue fatwas [Islamic religious opinions] declaring this incursion a jihad and Pakistan described the tribesmen, as well as the soldiers assisting them, as mujahideen.[3]

Pakistan's aim at this stage was to internationalize the conflict and thus create a situation in which the Maharaja would be forced to accept a plebiscite.[4] One of the motives for using proxies, rather than deploying the army, was to avoid engendering an Indian military response. However, as reports of the gains made by the tribesmen reached India, its defense committee began discussing the provision of military assistance to the Maharaja. Lord Mountbatten insisted that the deployment of aid was dependent on Kashmir's accession to India.[5] While there is no question that Hari Sing signed a formal letter of accession to India, whether he did so before India mobilized its troops is another source of controversy. In either case, India deployed troops to Kashmir and Pakistan soon followed suit. The two countries were now at war. Fighting continued until a ceasefire was signed on 1 January 1949, by which time Pakistan controlled roughly one third of the former princely state and India the other two thirds with a ceasefire line separating their respective territories. Small pieces of land have changed hands since 1949, but this division remains the case today.[6] Pakistan controls Azad Jammu and Kashmir, or Pakistan-administered Kashmir, and Gilgit-Baltistan, formerly the Northern Areas. Indian-administered Kashmir consists of the Kashmir Valley, Jammu and Ladakh.

Pakistan did not incorporate the land it controlled, but rather treated it as administered territory. Thus if a referendum were ever held in the former princely state then Muslims living in the territory under Pakistani control would be able to participate. The government put measures in place to ensure the population remained on record as favoring accession. Pakistan-administered Kashmir has a separate government, but candidates must declare that they favor accession otherwise they are not allowed to contest elections.[7] It also has its own constitution, which stipulates that 'no person or political party in Azad Jammu and Kashmir shall be permitted to propagate against, or take part in activities prejudicial or detrimental to, the ideology of the State's [Kashmir] accession to Pakistan.'[8] A similar situation prevails in Indian-administered Kashmir, which is known in India as the state of Jammu and Kashmir. Technically this state has more autonomy than others in the Indian Union and its special status is enshrined in the Indian constitution. However, for most of its history, New Delhi has ruled Indian-administered Kashmir using a 'combination of direct control and intrusive intervention.' This included sponsoring local governments that were unrepresentative of and unaccountable to the populace.[9] The aim has been to marginalize independent leaders in favor of the pro-accession National Conference party, and as in Pakistan-administered Kashmir, those wishing to stand for election must swear allegiance to the Indian constitution, in effect acknowledging Indian sovereignty.[10] Pakistan has ingrained in its citizenry the importance of recovering the remaining two-thirds of Kashmir, just as India has promoted the idea among its populace that ceding any of this territory would threaten the entire nation's fabric. Many Kashmiris simply want independence, or at least greater autonomy.

War erupted again in 1965 when Pakistan launched Operations Gibraltar and Grand Slam. Pakistan had been attempting to sow the seeds of rebellion in Indian-administered Kashmir through covert various activities. Perhaps sensing Indian vulnerability following its defeat to China in the 1962 Sino-Indian War, it increased these activities while also planning a larger invasion. In August 1965 Pakistan launched Operation Gibraltar, so named for the invasion of Spain in 711 CE from the rugged Mediterranean promontory. Companies were formed consisting of irregulars, particularly from Pakistan-administered Kashmir, into which soldiers from paramilitary units were integrated. Army officers at the major rank commanded units consisting of four to six companies, which infiltrated across the LoC. Approximately 30,000 men were involved in the infiltration, which was intended to prepare the ground for a subsequent intervention by the Pakistan army. The plan was predicated on the belief that local forces would rise up and join a rebellion against Indian rule, but little local help was forthcoming. Rather than retreat, Pakistan launched Operation Grand Slam, which entailed deploying conventional troops. The army had early success, but an Indian counter-invasion soon threatened sovereign Pakistani territory, and by the end of September the two had signed a ceasefire. In early 1966 the two sides agreed to the positions they held prior to the August 1965 invasion.[11]

Five years later in 1971 the two countries fought another war, this time when India intervened in the Pakistani civil war that led to the creation of Bangladesh [formerly East Pakistan]. India's victory was decisive and led the two countries to sign the Simla Agreement in 1972, which transformed the ceasefire line into the Line of Control [commonly known as the LoC]. Pakistan's military was left weakened and, many Pakistani and Indians agree, humiliated by its decisive defeat and the loss of East Pakistan. One consequence was to reinforce the idea of using proxies in order to avoid directly engaging the Indian military. A second consequence was to leave Pakistan wanting revenge. The use of proxies later became not only a means of avoiding overt engagement with the Indian military, but also a tool to bleed India in retribution for the losses it had inflicted. However, in the short term the Civil War left Pakistan in a state of internal crisis and its military support to anti-India forces in Indian-administered Kashmir essentially ceased. A small number of indigenous actors kept the flame of liberation from being extinguished, prosecuting sporadic attacks.[12] Yet despite these activities, the number of people in Indian-administered Kashmir who reached for the gun or the bomb prior to 1989 was relatively low.

In 1987, the Muslim United Front, an umbrella party for Kashmiri Muslims seeking reform, was denied a victory in the State Legislative elections. These are considered to be the most compromised elections in Indian-administered Kashmir's history. Afterwards, an increasing number of Muslim men began crossing the LoC into

Pakistan-administered Kashmir for weapons and military training. The Jammu and Kashmir Liberation Front [JKLF], which already existed on both sides of the LoC, became the vehicle through which the insurgency initially mobilized.[13] In late July 1988 two bombs exploded in Srinagar, the summer capital of Indian-administered Kashmir: the first at the Central Telegraph Office, followed by a second at the Srinagar Club. Kashmiri youth executed the explosions, but the planner was a JKLF militant from Pakistani Poonch who had infiltrated across the LoC.[14] The following year was marked by mass demonstrations and protests, and the Kashmir Valley soon witnessed a JKLF-led revolt against Indian rule. New Delhi embarked on a heavy-handed response, which essentially turned the link between India and the population of the Kashmir Valley into an 'occupier-occupied relationship' that persists to this day.[15] The Kashmir conflict had begun.

The uprising was indigenous, but Pakistan moved quickly to exploit the situation. Its objectives were two-fold: to make Indian-administered Kashmir such a burden that India would abandon it; and to bleed India at little cost to Pakistan. The army and ISI quickly began moving to reorient the direction of the insurgency. The JKLF, which was leading the rebellion, was committed to independence for Kashmir and not accession to Pakistan. According to Amanullah Khan, one of the founders of the JKLF, the ISI requested the group stop calling for sovereignty and instead focus on self-determination. Khan rejected the request, putting it at odds with the Pakistani state. Not long after, the ISI cut off aid to the JKLF and undertook a dual approach to shape the insurgency.[16] First, it encouraged JKLF members to break away and form pro-Pakistani militant groups. Second, it built up Hizb-ul-Mujahideen [Party of Holy Warriors or HM]—the newly-founded militant wing of the Jamaat-e-Islami's branch in Indian-administered Kashmir—as a rival to the JKLF.[17] Because it was still the dominant insurgent group at the time, the JKLF remained the Indian security forces' main target. By roughly 1992 the JKLF was facing a three-front threat: from India, from splinter groups and from HM.[18]

HM's agenda met with resistance from the Kashmiri population for several reasons. First, HM's goal was accession to Pakistan and not independence. Second, the group was part of the Islamist Jamaat-e-Islami Jammu and Kashmir [JIJK] and was committed to establishing an Islamic state, which most Kashmiri Muslims had no interest in. However, HM also had several factors working in its favor. The Jamiat-e-Talaba [the JIJK's student wing] provided support to the HM, especially in the area of recruitment from the Kashmiri population. The appearance of anti-Muslim Hindu groups made the HM's Islamism more appealing to some of the local population. Rising anti-Muslim and Hindu nationalist sentiment in India helped too.[19] Ironically, the Indians did their part by arresting a number of JKLF leaders and killing others. On their own these factors might not have been enough to enable HM to predominate, but it had a trump card: Pakistan.

The Pakistani government increased its support for militancy in Indian-administered Kashmir and pumped a great amount of that support into HM.[20] In turn, HM devoted a significant portion of its resources and recruits to destroying the JKLF. Its operatives brutalized and murdered a number of JKLF members and led the Indian security forces to the hideouts of others.[21] The JKLF's capabilities were severely reduced by the end of 1991, and by 1993 HM was the dominant guerrilla organization in the field. India freed Yasin Malik, the head of the JKLF in Indian-administered Kashmir, from prison a year later. Malik called for demilitarization and unconditional talks following his release.[22] With the exit of the JKLF from the battlefield, all of the remaining major militant players aspired to accession.[23]

Pakistan was supporting a host of other smaller militant organizations as well as HM by this time. This accomplished two objectives. First, it ensured that all of Pakistan's eggs were not in one basket. If one group were infiltrated and destroyed, others could step in and fill the void. Second, supporting multiple groups meant no one organization grew so strong that it could threaten Pakistan's interests. A side effect of Pakistan's policy was that it naturally encouraged the country's myriad proxies to compete with one another. As is often the case, militants expended much effort fighting with one another rather than against the common enemy. To bring a degree of unity to the cause, the All Parties Hurriyat Conference [APHC] was established in 1993 and the United Jihad Council [UJC] formed in 1994. The former was an umbrella organization for the Kashmiri political parties opposed to Indian rule; the latter was a similar umbrella organization for militant groups fighting against India. HM dominated both organizations, but by this time its paramount status among militant groups was beginning to wane as was the boom period of the armed uprising in the Valley.[24] Although HM lost market share to non-indigenous groups, it remained the largest outfit operating in Indian-administered Kashmir and retained significant influence. However, HM's peak years were behind it by the mid-1990s.

Foreign militants, or 'guest mujahideen' as they were called, had been present in Indian-administered Kashmir as early as 1990.[25] At first they were often integrated into local groups and it was not until the communist Democratic Republic of Afghanistan fell in 1992 that they started appearing en masse. The ISI encouraged and supported the entrance of non-indigenous jihadi groups formed for the Afghan jihad into the Kashmir front for several reasons.[26] To begin with, India's counter-insurgency efforts had improved remarkably since the insurgency began. New Delhi greatly increased the number of troops and paramilitaries in Indian-administered Kashmir, and by 1993 they were beginning to get the better of HM and other local groups. The effects of attrition demanded more recruits. Indian counter-insurgency improvements had also made it more difficult to send militants from Indian-administered Kashmir across the LoC for training.[27] Further, beyond mere numbers, what the insurgency really needed were battle-hardened fighters of exactly the sort the Afghan jihad had produced.

In addition, the Indian government augmented the military aspects of its counter-insurgency with social and political reforms designed to win over the Kashmiris. These included steps such as increasing local autonomy, enhancing the legitimacy of local government, increasing spending for development and providing free medical services at military camps. Although the approach was somewhat ad hoc and the security forces continued to engage in brutality against segments of the populace, these measures did help to shrink local support for the insurgency. Shifting patronage to a non-indigenous recruitment base, whose membership would be immune to such reforms, was a means by which the Pakistan army could increase reliable manpower in the region.[28]

Indian forces were also raising local militias consisting of former militants—known as renegades—as well as fresh recruits. Some renegades were lured away by bribery after having lost the Darwinian struggle for funding and weapons. Others were frightened into betrayal by threats the Indian security forces made against them or their families. Still others left the armed struggle out of disillusionment with the militant groups involved in the conflict and their willingness to perpetrate violence against those Kashmiris who did not share their pro-accession or pro-Islamist sentiments.[29] HM, in particular, had acquired a bad reputation for killing members of smaller guerrilla groups in addition to the JKLF's pro-independence supporters. When the Indian army began using these renegades, HM suffered the brunt of this campaign.[30] In addition to killing some HM cadres and leading the Indian security forces to others, renegades also began targeting the families of HM militants, leading additional cadres to desert.[31] The ISI sought to mitigate this by introducing nonindigenous militants with no families or history in the region.

Husain Haqqani, Pakistan's Ambassador to the US at the time this book was written, has suggested that by introducing foreigners from outside the region Pakistan was also seeking to replicate the Afghan experience in terms of generating international attention. A key component of Pakistan's strategy has been to internationalize the Kashmir conflict. Haqqani asserted that Pakistan's rulers hoped the image of foreign fighters coming to the aid of their fellow Muslims in Kashmir would have a similar international impact as it did during the Afghan war against the Soviets.[32] According to Haqqani, in addition to the public relations advantages, Pakistan assumed nonindigenous Kashmiris would be easier to control as well. The thinking was that because these militants lacked local support structures, they would be more reliant on the ISI and thus more pliable. Further, some of the initial 'guest mujahideen' were not Pakistani, but rather foreigners who had come for the Afghan jihad against the Soviets. A good number of them were not welcome in their home countries, meaning they had nowhere else to turn.[33]

In 1993 the Harkat-ul-Mujahideen and Harkat-ul-Jihad-al-Islami, two Deobandi jihadi groups that had split from one another and were operating separately in Indian-administered Kashmir, reconciled to form Harkat-ul-Ansar [HuA]. The army and ISI directed more support to the newly formed group than to the other Pakistani proxies and, following the merger, HuA's militant activities greatly increased.[34] HuA initially served as the primary group through which 'guest mujahideen' fought in Kashmir. At first the foreign fighters' martial prowess won them the respect of the local populace. However, they were very abusive to the citizenry and soon their popularity was declining. Local support for the wider insurgency had already begun to wane by this time, and continued to slip over the next several years. By 1995 the insurgency had reached a stalemate and was entering a period of atrophy.[35] The army and ISI were looking to recapture the momentum, but HuA proved the wrong group for the job.

Control of its proxies was a very important factor for the ISI and with HuA it was lacking. To begin with, a number of HuA commanders in Indian-administered Kashmir exercised an uncomfortably high degree of autonomy from the group's leadership in Pakistan. This effectively meant that they enjoyed an uncomfortably high level of autonomy from their official handlers in the ISI, which also did not enjoy a satisfactory degree of leverage over the group as a whole. HuA drew a significant amount of its funding from outside of Pakistan at the time and also had strong ties to elements of the wider Deobandi infrastructure that existed inside Pakistan. While it received funding from the Pakistani intelligence service for the Kashmir jihad, these other means of support meant HuA could continue to operate independently, were official funding cut off.[36] Its ties to the Deobandi infrastructure also meant it was connected to the Jamiat Ulema-e-Islam [JUI], which had become a party in the ruling coalition after aligning itself with the victorious Pakistan People's Party [PPP] in the 1993 elections. This meant the HuA had a potential political patron, though the degree to which anyone within the JUI could influence the group's activities in Indian-administered Kashmir is unclear.

HuA's unreliability was borne out after the Indian security forces arrested HuA leaders Maulana Masood Azhar and Sajjad Afghani in February 1994. The group's Kashmir branch responded by embarking on a series of kidnappings with the intention of bartering hostages' lives for the release of its jailed leaders. After failing to secure their release by kidnapping an Indian major, the group snatched two British hostages who it later released under pressure from Islamabad, the APHC and other militant groups. Undeterred, HuA took another group of Westerners hostage in September 1994. This time Omar Saeed Sheikh, who was later convicted in Pakistan of involvement in *Wall Street Journal* reporter Daniel Pearl's murder, lured three Britons and one American away from Delhi to a farmhouse where they were held at gunpoint. The hostages were rescued, and Saeed Sheikh arrested, after one of the kidnappers inadvertently drew the attention of nearby policemen to the farmhouse where the hostages were held. Yet another kidnapping occurred in July 1995, when two Americans, two British citizens, a German and a Norwegian were abducted in Kashmir. A group called Al Faran, suspected at the time of being a front for HuA in Kashmir, claimed credit.[37]

It is unclear whether the HuA leadership in Pakistan sanctioned any of these kidnappings, and there is evidence to suggest that local actors were driving the final operation in 1995. Talks broke down to free those hostages when the Norwegian hostage was killed. Indian authorities later captured one of the militants involved, who asserted that by the time of the final kidnapping the group was fractured and the Kashmir-based leadership of the HuA had become 'anti-Pakistani.'[38] Regardless of where the breakdown in authority occurred, either the Pakistani security services were unable to control HuA or HuA's leaders were unable to control some of its commanders in Indian-administered Kashmir. The entire episode was a source of embarrassment for Pakistan internationally. A number of Western governments understandably got involved when their citizens went missing. In 1997 the US banned HuA, forcing the group to change its name back to Harkat-ul-Mujahideen [HuM] in an attempt to escape legal sanction.[39] It continued to play a role in the Kashmir jihad, but by this time was becoming increasingly Afghan focused as the Taliban rose to power. The HuJI faction, which had reunited with the group in 1993 to form HuA, split and re-established its independence. Its preoccupation with Afghanistan also deepened.

Beyond the possible risks associated with relying too heavily on HuA, the group was not operationally well-suited to the army's strategy in the mid-1990s either. The conflict was initially confined primarily to the Valley, but by 1995 militants there were meeting heavy resistance and the insurgency was stagnating. This contributed to the Pakistan army's desire to expand the fighting to Jammu in an effort to revive the conflict. The Valley remained the center of the conflict, but in 1996–1997 the Jammu districts of Rajouri and Poonch witnessed increased activity.[40] Although both are Muslim-majority districts, the town center for administration, commerce and education in each is predominately Hindu and Sikh. In addition to the fact the Indian counter-insurgency had made operations in the Kashmir Valley more difficult, the Pakistan army wanted to expand into Rajouri and Poonch in order to drive out the non-Muslim population. The aim was to increase the Muslim majority in the region for political purposes, and to make it easier for the insurgents to operate.[41]

Militants had made initial inroads into the Jammu district of Doda, but Rajouri and Poonch were relatively quiet during the early years of the insurgency despite being Muslim-dominated and lying alongside 250 kilometers of hilly border on the LoC. Sumantra Bose suggests three reasons why. First, unlike Doda, the Muslims in Rajouri and Poonch are ethno-linguistically different from the Valley's population. Instead, the population in both these districts shares ethnolinguistic ties with those living in Pakistan-administered Kashmir and Punjab province. This made operating there more difficult for the Valley Kashmiris who provided much of the manpower for the insurgency. Second, Muslims in Rajouri and Poonch suffered greatly during previous India-Pakistani conflicts, which made them wary of retribution from the Indian army. Third, the militants simply passed through Rajouri and Poonch after crossing the LoC because the high-priority areas originally were in the Valley.[42] HuA militants were not ethno-linguistically suited to operating in these areas and indigenous militants from these regions were unwilling to target Hindus civilians. Lashkar cadres, on the other hand, enthusiastically took to massacring non-Muslims. The group's recruitment patterns meant that many of its members shared the same ethnolinguistic characteristics as those in Rajouri and Poonch.[43] Lashkar's composition also matched that of the army, as the two recruited from similar areas in Pakistan. The army and ISI believed, correctly, that this would make the group easier to control. So too would the fact that it was an Ahl-e-Hadith outfit and lacked the type of infrastructure in Pakistan that HuA enjoyed.

Lashkar militants had been active in Indian-administered Kashmir since 1990, according to a report compiled by the group chronicling its activities there.[44] They often cooperated with other groups on operations during the early 1990s and at times served in a support capacity. Lashkar launched its first official operation in 1993 and increased its presence over the next several years; though it was in the latter years of the decade that its activities really accelerated. At one of the group's annual congregations, known as Ijtemas, its operational commander Zaki-ur Rehman Lakhvi claimed Lashkar militants had been 'engaged properly and striving hard' against Indian forces since 1995.[45] This aligns with the time period when state support for the group was increasing. By then a 'superficial normalcy' was returning to the urban areas. As the insurgency shifted to Rajouri and Poonch as well as remote areas of the Valley and Doda, Lashkar began paying greater attention to these regions.[46]

Having witnessed close to seven years of conflict, supporters of armed conflict in the Valley were plagued by 'exhaustion and loss of morale.' New Delhi moved to take advantage of this and complete its pacification campaign through continued repression combined with the reinstallation of a civilian government.[47] Elections for the State Legislature were held in September 1996 for the first time since the flawed 1987 round sparked the conflict. In addition to conflict fatigue and an increasingly sophisticated Indian counterinsurgency response, Lashkar faced the same hurdles as all of the other Pakistani groups. These included hostility to foreign fighters because of their pro-accession positions, their extremist views regarding Islam and resentment stemming from their poor treatment of the local populace. Foreign militants often arrived unannounced at people's homes and demanded shelter, extorted money and manpower for the insurgency, and made a practice of violently taking over mosques to preach their ideology.

Lashkar did not get off to a great start when it came to living up to is name as the 'Army of the Pure,' and was as guilty of these offenses as HuA and other 'guest mujahideen.' However, Lashkar was more capable—or perhaps more willing—to learn as an organization in terms of how its cadres engaged with the local populace. It is also possible that its sponsors in the army and ISI leaned on the group to do so. According to Lt. General Vinayak Patankar (Retd), who held a command post in the conflict zone, the Indian army intercepted communications telling Lashkar militants to pay for food, avoid theft or extortion and not to fraternize with local women.[48] One member of the group confirmed that such instructions were issued. He and several other interlocutors said that cadres began paying money to stay in people's homes, as well as bringing their own food and water in order not to impose.[49] The order to avoid fraternization with local women also made a difference, as there was a high prevalence of rape during the course of the Kashmiri conflict, committed by militants and Indian security forces.[50] In this environment, 'a group that does not touch your women was bound to gain some appreciation,' to quote one Indian expert who spent nearly a decade conducting field research on the conflict.[51] This does not mean Lashkar was entirely pure. Some of its members were implicated in mistreating Barelvi woman in Indian-administered Kashmir, including periodic rape. Nor did Lashkar's cadres entirely refrain from extortion. On the whole, however, its cadres were less involved in these types of negative incidents than those from other groups. According to one Kashmiri journalist who covered the conflict from its inception, Lashkar also sometimes intervened to stop other militants from disturbing the citizenry or to settle disputes, which were adjudicated based on sharia.[52]

However, despite its better manners, the group had no compunction about using fear and coercion to garner support, savagely punishing those who worked against it. Lashkar employed expressive violence to intimidate the local populace, mutilating informers and leaving them in the town square for all to see.[53] Although the group may have scaled back its open proselytizing, there were instances of Lashkar militants bullying others to adopt its interpretation of Islam. Sometimes this extended to taking over mosques belonging to other sects, primarily Barelvis, to preach the glories of the Ahl-e-Hadith creed. The group also engaged in violence to muscle its way onto the Ahl-e-Hadith scene in Indian-administered Kashmir.[54]

However, Lashkar mainly attacked Indian military targets, and often issued warnings to local Muslims to avoid Indian army camps and installations lest they be caught in the crossfire.[55] It attacked Hindu civilians as well, in some instances mutilating victims.[56] Gruesome attacks garnered publicity and intimidated the local non-Muslim populace, as well as disrupting peace negotiations and reigniting the conflict when it began to ebb. For example, Lashkar executed a massacre of Hindus in Doda one week after peace talks took place in 2001.[57] Over time the group had become infamous for these massacres. Despite its notorious reputation, Lashkar always maintained that killing civilians was against its religious beliefs. Hafiz Saeed declared doing so to be 'totally un-Islamic' and stated that 'Our policy in this regard is crystal clear. We don't want to target innocent civilians.'[58] In an attempt to avoid staining its reputation, Lashkar operated under different names. A Kashmiri who worked as a journalist in Indian-administered Kashmir and an Indian military officer who served there during the 1990s both noted that Lashkar used these assumed identities to take credit for operations in which it deliberately targeted civilians.[59]

A number of Indian experts who followed the Kashmir insurgency since its inception, as well as several former Indian military officers, suggested that Lashkar's rise beginning in the mid-1990s coincided with an increase in the quality of combat engagements from a tactical perspective. By the end of the decade Indian forces considered Lashkar to be the best trained of all the militant groups operating in Kashmir.[60] This is not surprising given the level and type of support the group received. Although a nucleus of militants already existed, the army and ISI essentially built Lashkar's military apparatus from the mid-1990s onward specifically for use against India. State support, which began around 1993 and increased significantly during the ensuing years, included: funding; assistance with organizing; combat training; campaign guidance; provision of weapons and kit, including sophisticated communications equipment; hides, launching pads and fire support for cadres crossing into Indian-administered Kashmir; assistance infiltrating into or exfiltrating out of India and other countries; intelligence on targets and threats; diplomatic support; and, of course, safe haven and protection in Pakistan.[61] The group's training primer reads as if the army co-authored it, which may not be too far from the case. That primer calls for a drawn-out war with India to deplete the country's manpower, exhaust its security forces and diminish their morale, and exploit weaknesses in the government's supply chain.[62] Army and ISI personnel were present at Lashkar's training camps, where they helped to develop the training regimen designed to realize these objectives and to train the group's trainers.[63] According to one former member who left the group in 1998, coordination was so close that representatives from the army, ISI and Lashkar would sit at the table together to plan attacks and strategy.[64]

With Pakistani assistance Lashkar was a recognized force in Indian-administered Kashmir by the late 1990s. According to the interrogation report of Abdul Razzak Masood, an Indian who joined Lashkar toward the end of the decade, when he went to join the Kashmir jihad he initially trained with HuM. However, he quickly moved to Lashkar. Masood explained this switch to his interrogators, saying 'the strength of Harkat group was very meager when compared to LeT.'[65] By this time the group was also becoming increasingly self-sufficient. This owed to the growth of its infrastructure, explored in the following chapter, as well as to its recruitment of army and ISI officers who joined the group following their retirement from active service.[66] In addition to those who joined full-time, there are reports of government and military officials taking leave for several months to fight with Lashkar.[67] These men increased Lashkar's self-sufficiency in terms of its decision-making capabilities, while also providing a boost to its organizational and operational capabilities.

While Lashkar was thriving by the end of the decade, then-Prime Minister of Pakistan Nawaz Sharif was ready to pursue a less militaristic approach toward India. The jihadi groups opposed this rapprochement vehemently.[68] When Sharif met Indian PM Atal Bihari Vajpayee on the sidelines of the South Asian Association for Regional Cooperation [SAARC] summit during the summer of 1998 he proposed reducing tensions. In November 1998 both countries agreed to resume passenger bus services across the border, with Vajpayee pledging to ride the first bus to Lahore. In February 1999 he made good on that pledge, and during his visit the two countries signed the Lahore Declaration. Among other things, this stipulated that the two countries would 'intensify their efforts to resolve all issues, including the issue of Jammu & Kashmir,' as well as 'reaffirm their condemnation of terrorism in all its forms and manifestations and their determination to combat this menace.'[69]

Three months later the burgeoning peace process crashed to a halt after Pakistani troops executed a daring incursion into Indian-controlled territory. The army's infiltration into the Kargil district high up in the Himalayas was already well advanced in terms of planning at the time the Lahore Declaration was signed.[70] The official Pakistani storyline about the Kargil conflict, which took place between May and July 1999, was that militants who were intent on liberating Indian-administered Kashmir launched the offensive. Numerous authors have since debunked this myth, including then Chief of Army Staff Pervez Musharraf who orchestrated what was very much a Pakistani military operation.[71] According to some estimates, militants only accounted for approximately 10 per cent of the forces that crossed the LoC and occupied the Kargil district.[72] Among the militant outfits that were involved, Lashkar claimed 'pride of place.'[73] Initially, the operation was a tactical success and the Indian army was caught off guard. But New Delhi soon responded with a massive counter-offensive. The third India-Pakistan war fought over Kashmir was underway. By the end of June 1999, the Pakistan army was looking for an exit strategy. Whether Sharif was aware of initial plans for the invasion remains a subject of debate, but in early July he traveled to Washington, DC to meet with US President Bill Clinton and agreed to a diplomatic solution. Though Clinton would not promise to mediate an end to the Kashmir conflict, he did pledge to take a personal interest in intensifying peace talks if the LoC could be respected.[74] This paved the way for a Pakistani withdrawal.

The Kargil operation had brought a great amount of positive publicity to the militants, who were presented in the Pakistani media as having taken this initiative to liberate Indian-administered Kashmir.[75] They were in no hurry to bring an end to the hostilities, and fought on for the next several weeks. Hafiz Saeed claimed the entire Pakistani population was with the militants who infiltrated Kargil, and issued a warning to Sharif saying no government in Pakistan can betray the Kashmir cause and survive.[76] Sharif's reign did not survive much longer, but it was General Pervez Musharraf who ended it via a military coup. The catalyst for the coup was not Kashmir, but Sharif's attempt to strip Musharraf of his position.[77] However, support for the Kashmir jihad, which had waned toward the end of Sharif's time in office, increased after Musharraf took power. Lashkar, in particular, benefited from a boost in support.[78] There was a concomitant increase in militant activity in Indian-administered Kashmir, reversing a three-year decline since 1996.[79]

Lashkar's introduction of fidayeen attacks was largely responsible for the escalation in violence. The group launched its first Ibn Taymiyyah Fidayeen mission on 12 July 1999, only eight days after Sharif signed the accord formally ending the Kargil Conflict. That day two fidayeen stormed an Indian Border Security Force camp in Bandipore, a town in the northern Valley, firing their automatic rifles indiscriminately and hurling grenades.[80] Additional attacks followed, and generally entailed groups of 3–5 men assaulting security camps where Indian soldiers or police were located. The objective of Lashkar's fidayeen attacks was not for the fighters to be martyred right away, but to inflict as much damage as possible on the enemy in order to inspire fear in others. These battles often lasted many hours and sometimes more than a day, which at times led security forces to employ heavy firepower that destroyed their own installations. According to Hafiz Abdul Rehman Makki, Saeed's cousin and brother-in-law as well as one of the group's founders, the aim was to terrify the enemy.[81] These attacks were also clearly intended to escalate violence and reignite the insurgency, which had continued to stagnate since the mid-1990s. The attacks succeeded, increasing the intensity of the conflict and diminishing the morale of the Indian security forces.[82]

The operations were criticized in some religious circles since Islam forbids suicide and fidayeen attacks are essentially suicide missions.[83] In response, Makki penned a three-part series entitled 'Fidayee Activities in Sharia' to dispel the 'common misconception that fidayee missions are suicide missions.'[84] Throughout the series, he attempted to ground these missions in Islamic history. Makki argued that:

A fidayee activity means attacking the enemy risking one's life, without taking necessary precautions, pouncing upon the enemy in the face of sure death, completing one's mission at every cost; If one embraces martyrdom in this course one feels it a divine blessing and if returns alive successfully one is jubilant over Allaah's bounty.[85]

The crucial distinction is that 'no fidayee ever killed himself' and if he is going to die then 'the fidayee would like to be killed by an infidel or unbeliever.'[86] In other words there are high prospects of martyrdom, but the fidayee tries to survive as long as possible during the attack. On a number of occasions fidayeen came back alive following a mission. The ultimate intention was typically martyrdom, however, and those who undertook fidayeen attacks often returned to combat repeatedly until they achieved it.[87] When the fidayee died it was because he fought to the death rather than dying by his own hand.

These direct and daring attacks against Indian forces cemented Lashkar's reputation as the premier militant group fighting in Kashmir and earned it the—at times grudging—respect of the local populace as well as other insurgents and the Indian military. Fidayeen attacks proved so effective that Jaish-e-Mohammad also adopted the tactic soon after it entered the Kashmir theater. Less doctrinally rigorous than Lashkar, JeM added a twist. It introduced suicide bombing to the Kashmir jihad. JeM was formed when Maulana Azhur, whose arrest along with several others triggered the wave of kidnappings in the mid-1990s, was freed following a HuM hijacking of Indian Airlines Flight 814 in 1999. He expressed his appreciation by promptly leaving to form his own outfit, taking many HuM cadres and resources with him. JeM quickly became one of the state's favored proxies and several experts on Pakistani militancy have suggested the ISI sponsored JeM's creation in order to check Lashkar's growing power.[88] Not surprisingly, the two groups had an uneasy relationship from the outset, sometimes cooperating and sometimes competing in the Kashmir theater.

Their combined activities helped to elevate the level of violence. Between mid-1999 and the end of 2002, at least fifty-five fidayeen attacks were staged against police, paramilitary and army camps, and government installations. Twenty-nine took place in 2001 alone, making that year the pinnacle of what Sumantra Bose termed the fidayeen stage of the insurgency. Indian military sources attributed the majority of them to Lashkar, which was the premier jihadi outfit fighting in Indian-administered Kashmir by this point.[89]

As Lashkar and other jihadi groups increased the tempo of the war, Islamabad again began talking about peace. On 25 March 2000 President Clinton visited India and Pakistan. Though his visit to Pakistan amounted to nothing more than a brief stop after a considerably longer time spent in India, he argued vociferously for a halt to state-sponsored militancy. After his visit, India and Pakistan initiated an 'informal, unannounced peace process.' Several months later, during a visit by US Under Secretary of State Thomas Pickering to Islamabad, Musharraf agreed to a unilateral ceasefire, bringing a halt to Pakistani artillery firing along the LoC. This practice had provided a shield to militants infiltrating into Indian-administered Kashmir, and once artillery fire ceased casualties among those trying to breach the LoC rose.[90]

However, the pace of the conflict did not abate. Rather than instructing its proxies to halt their activities, the ISI directed them to stop claiming responsibility for attacks in Indian-administered Kashmir. It also appealed to HM to honor the ceasefire on a short-term basis.[91] While HM was divided over negotiations with India, Lashkar wanted no part of peace. In an attempt to derail the process, the group launched its most brazen fidayeen attack yet. On the night of 22 December 2000 two Lashkar militants entered the historic Red Fort in Delhi, which at the time was being used as an army garrison, and killed two Indian soldiers and a guard before escaping. The low body count belies the large-scale significance of the attack. This was the first fidayeen assault conducted beyond the borders of Indian-administered Kashmir and took place in the heart of India's capital, illustrating Lashkar's reach and capabilities. After the attack, a Lashkar spokesman said, 'By attacking the Red Fort, we want to stress that India should stop this drama of cease-fire and talks; it should pull out its forces from Kashmir.'[92] New Delhi showed restraint and the ceasefire continued. Less than a month later, six Lashkar militants stormed Srinagar airport in a second audacious attack. All six militants were killed, as were four Indian paramilitaries and two civilians. Though a civilian airport, Lashkar claimed it was being used by the military and was thus a legitimate target. This attack also failed to end the ceasefire.

Although India and Pakistan continued to move forward, peace did not materialize. There was hope Musharraf and Vajpayee might settle on an agreement when they met at the Agra Summit in July 2001, but their two countries were unable to agree even on the wording for a joint communiqué. The process devolved further after 9/11 and hopes for peace broke down entirely after militants from JeM attacked the Indian Parliament in New Delhi in December 2001. Sporadic arrests aside, the Musharraf regime never seriously clamped down on the jihadi groups in Pakistan throughout the entirety of this peace effort. Meanwhile, after a three-year decline in militant fatalities from 1996–1999, the numbers steadily climbed from 1999 through 2002.[93] The majority of these remained indigenous fighters, which speaks to the fact that root grievances against India remained, with foreigners constituting approximately 30 per cent of those killed.[94] Using spectacularly violent attacks Lashkar and its fellow Pakistani jihadis had helped to spur another cycle of violence, which ultimately claimed mostly local casualties as a result.

The Red Fort and Srinagar airport attacks, though failing to halt the peace process, paid dividends at home. They not only boosted morale, but also Lashkar's recruitment and fundraising capabilities in Pakistan.[95] The Red Fort, in particular, had symbolic value. Moghul emperors had built and inhabited it. Thus, the attack was a symbolic re-conquest of the Hindu-occupied seat of the Moghul Empire. The militants specifically targeted an interrogation center the Indian army had created there; a site at which many captured mujahideen had died.[96] When interviewed by Pakistani journalist Zahid Hussain a month after the attack, Hafiz Saeed declared 'The action indicates that we have extended the jihad to India.'[97] In reality, Lashkar began exporting its jihad into India during the early 1990s; a time when it began building up its operations within Pakistan and its transnational networks abroad as well.

4

# THE LONG ARM OF THE LASHKAR

Lashkar's commitment to the Kashmir jihad and obedience as a proxy enabled the group to expand vastly its military apparatus with the help of the army and ISI. Military officials provided more than merely arms and ammunition. They developed the group's training regimen, fought alongside its members at times and some even retired to join Lashkar's ranks. However, Lashkar's leaders aspired to do more than merely build a militant outfit and so they leveraged official Pakistani support to create a robust domestic and international infrastructure. By examining how Lashkar built its foundation in Pakistan and constructed networks abroad during the 1990s, this chapter becomes the base for understanding many of the group's future activities. While the focus is on Lashkar's development in these areas prior to 2001, more recent examples are occasionally used when they are useful for clarifying a point. It is helpful to begin by briefly outlining the group's organizational structure as it took shape during the 1990s.

Technically, Lashkar was the militant wing of MDI, which was a hierarchical commander-cadre organization, rather than one composed of discrete cells. A shura council made up of different department heads and others in leadership positions was established to oversee all operations. This Pakistan-based policy-making body made all major decisions about the group's missionary and military activities, which were then relayed to cadres in the field who were organized hierarchically. Different units were established to manage activities in various geographical locations in Pakistan. For example, one commander was responsible for activities in Lahore, with sub-unit heads operating under him. The group's hierarchy in Indian-administered Kashmir was modeled along a military chain of command and a separate senior commander oversaw terrorist operations carried out against India. Zaki-ur Rehman Lakhvi was Lashkar's operational commander and responsible for all of its military activities. Until his arrest in the wake of the 2008 Mumbai attacks, Lakhvi operated primarily from Pakistan-administered Kashmir, from where he supervised training for recruits as well.[1] Hafiz Saeed was the amir of MDI, and in this capacity he also oversaw those militant activities carried out under Lashkar's banner. Saeed installed some of his relatives in top positions to ensure an added layer of control. Lashkar gained a deserved reputation during the 1990s as one of the most organized and disciplined jihadi groups. However, as is often the case, competition and personal rivalries existed, and some senior commanders were more apt to obey orders or inspired more loyalty from their men than others.

The group began seriously building its domestic infrastructure around 1994, a time when state support was increasing significantly. By the turn of the century it operated more than seventy district offices and a plethora of smaller ones. Its departments included: the Department of Construction of Masajid [the plural of Masjid, which means mosque] and Madaris; the Department of Dawa; the Department of Education; the Department of External Affairs; the Department of Finance; the Department of Media and Propagation; the Dar al-Andalus Department of Publishing; the Department of Social Welfare; the Doctors' Wing; the Farmers' and Workers' Wing; the Students' Wing; the Teachers' Wing; and the Women's Wing.[2] All of these departments technically came under the MDI umbrella.

Zafar Iqbal, who taught with Saeed at the University of Engineering and Technology and was another of the original MDI founders, oversaw the Departments of Education and Social Welfare. He also managed the Teachers' and Doctors' Wings that were respectively part of these departments. The Department of Education was the group's most profitable and powerful department, and contributed manpower for the organization. Many of those who passed through its schools went on to work in a non-martial capacity for MDI in Pakistan.[3] Iqbal had co-founded the Jamaat-ul-Dawa missionary group in 1985 with Saeed and saw himself as Saeed's equal. The decision that Saeed would head MDI after it was launched in 1986 therefore created some tension.[4] In 1999 Iqbal challenged Saeed's authority, accusing him of nepotism and campaigning to have him removed from power. The catalyst was Saeed's appointment of Hafiz Abdul Rehman Makki, his cousin and brother-in-law, to head the Department of External Affairs.[5] Iqbal believed that as the senior member of the group he deserved this post. A split was ultimately averted through internal negotiations and Makki assumed the position.[6]

The Department of External Affairs liaised with jihadi organizations inside and outside Pakistan. US and European officials believe that, through this department, Lashkar established close ties with more than a dozen jihadi groups in the Middle East, Southeast Asia and parts of the former Soviet Union.[7] Its operations wing also managed many of Lashkar's transnational operatives, overseeing activities ranging from reconnaissance for terrorist attacks to the provision of support or equipment for the group's military operations. In addition to liaising with jihadi outfits and operatives, this department also promoted the organization's agenda to foreign governments and political parties. Between 9/11 and March 2002 it sent off in excess of 3,000 letters and emails to 130 countries.[8]

Technically the group's headquarters is located at Jamiat al-Qadsia in Lahore, which is where its leadership has their offices. But the nerve center was built on a sprawling compound in Muridke. Its proper name is the Markaz-e-Taiba [Taiba Center]—meant to evoke the holy city of Medina, for which Taiba is an appellation—but it is commonly referred to simply as Muridke. Located about an hour's drive from Lahore, just off the Grand Trunk Road, Muridke is intended to be a beacon of the pure Islamic life. Sharia is enforced, all shops close during the call for prayer and music, television and smoking are forbidden.[9] Saeed has claimed affluent traders put up the money to buy the land on which it is built, and that two Saudis each contributed 10 million rupees for the early construction done there.[10] Mahmoud Mohammad Ahmed Bahaziq (one of MDI's founders) and Abdul Rahman al-Surayhi (Lakhvi's brother-in-law), two Saudis present at MDI's inception, provided a sizeable amount of the money for Muridke according to Noman Benotman who spent time working with Lashkar during the early 1990s and knew both men.[11] Open source evidence supports this assertion. A Pakistani lawyer alleged in the Lahore High Court in 2003 that interlocutors for Bahaziq approached his firm in the 1990s about constructing an educational complex at Murdike.[12] In their work on Islamist networks in Afghanistan and Pakistan, Mariam Abou Zahab and Olivier Roy also suggest Bahaziq [identified by his kunya Sheikh Abu Abdul Aziz] was among the Saudis who contributed to Muridke's construction.[13] Similarly, Pakistani media has reported al-Surayhi either contributed approximately 10 million rupees to Muridke's construction or helped to purchase the land on which the center was built.[14] Both men were acquainted with Osama bin Laden, who sometimes is rumored to have provided a portion of the seed money for Muridke. This is possible given bin Laden's efforts at the time to build his base through the distribution of largesse, but there is no definitive evidence he contributed funding and the group certainly had access to other Saudi donors at the time. In addition to whatever unofficial sources of funding received, state patronage also helped Lashkar to develop its expansive compound.

Muridke's palpable sense of ambition in terms of scale is unrivalled in the world of Pakistani jihadi organizations. The compound is surrounded by approximately 15 acres of agricultural land, with a vegetable farm where the staff grow all of their own vegetables, a children's playground, and a non-profit, subsidized grocery store. Over 100 staff members work there according to one of their number, including 20–25 farmers, 10–15 gardeners, 20–25 cooks, 60–70 madrasa instructors and 20 schoolteachers. The author visited in May 2009, at which point the Punjab provincial government had taken control of the facility in accordance with restrictions placed on the group following the 2008 Mumbai attacks. However, it continued to operate. The JuD administrator there, as well as the group's literature, attested to the fact that most of the services being offered in 2009 were in place by the beginning of the decade.[15]

Among the first buildings one sees upon entering the compound is the Abu Harrera mosque, which can hold 5,000 people along with a madrasa for 500. In addition to religious education, there is also the Dawa Model School and Science College providing instruction for students from primary school through university. The educational facilities include a computer lab, along with biology, chemistry and physics labs, each occupying one room. The school teaches math and instructs students in Urdu, Punjabi and English. Some of the students learn Arabic as well. As they progress students choose from one of two tracks, arts or sciences. The school charges 500–2,000 rupees per month depending on what a student's family can afford. Male students can live in a hostel, which has 100 rooms each accommodating four or five boys. Some additional pupils attend the school without living in the hostel. There is also a girls' school, which can teach up to 400 children, though there is no hostel on the compound for them.[16] As one high-ranking JuD official could not help but point out, while the Taliban banned education for girls his organization provided education to them.[17]

In addition to the educational complex, the other major facilities are health-related. The Al Aziz Hospital has been operating since 1999 and offers general medicine, dentistry, optometry, general surgery and tibb, or traditional medicine. All doctors are said to be Bachelor of Medicine, Bachelor of Surgery [MBBS] and Fellowship of the College of Physicians and Surgeons [FCPS] qualified and to donate their time gratis. Patients are given free care, a bed, food and medicine for up to one year and their relatives are allowed to stay at Muridke free of charge to be with them, according to the hospital administrator. He boasted there was no equivalent service offered in sixty-six surrounding towns and told the author that he ventured out every week to inform people of the medical care on offer at Muridke. The group also arranged medical camps for those unable to travel to the hospital, and provided an ambulance service as well.[18] By the end of the decade, its social welfare offerings reached well beyond the confines of Muridke.

Initially the group's offerings consisted primarily of health care and education, which fell under the auspices of the Departments of Social Welfare and Education respectively. According to MDI's now-defunct website, the Al-Dawa Medical Mission was 'devoted to the service of the sick and the wounded that deserve proper medical treatment.' By 2001 it offered a host of services all free of charge. These included ten dispensaries in Muzaffarabad, Lahore and Sindh Province, all of which offered medical check-ups and medication. Twelve medical camps were also set up in 'far-off places', which lacked dispensaries or hospitals. In addition to the Taiba Hospital at Muridke, another was built in Muzaffarabad, which is the capital of Pakistan-administered Kashmir.[19] In one example of the way in which Lashkar blended its social welfare offerings with its jihadi activities, the group proselytized to doctors in the hopes of convincing them to volunteer their time at Medical Mission facilities *and* as medics for the mujahideen in Indian-administered Kashmir. It also selected students from its schools who distinguished themselves in the sciences and trained them as paramedics who were then embedded with Lashkar militants fighting there.

As impressive as its medical services were, MDI's school system easily surpassed them. The first two Al-Dawa schools were established in 1994: one in Lahore and the other at Muridke.[20] More schools opened rapidly throughout the country. Their success was a result of the quality and breadth of instruction provided, as well as the group's willingness to subsidize tuition for those who could not afford it. According to a 2010 study by the Brookings Institute, Pakistan's education sector has been declining for several decades and access to quality education remains low. The primary barrier to education is a shortage of government or public schools, and many parents have turned to private schools rather than enroll their children in madaris where the curriculum is limited to predominantly Islamic studies.[21] Because private schools are often off limits for financial reasons, Al-Dawa schools can fill this void. MDI had established 127 schools with 15,000 students and 800 teachers across the country by 2001. There was even a procedure in place for non-MDI members to establish an Al-Dawa school in their area.[22]

Lashkar's provincial chief in Balochistan, Saeed Athar, summed up the rationale for focusing on education when he said, 'Children are like clean blackboards—whatever you write will leave a mark on them forever.'[23] According to its website, Al-Dawa Schools were set up to help realize the group's overarching mission as outlined earlier: 'Jihad in the way of Allah preaching the true religion and the training of [a] new generation on Islamic lines'. The group detailed the specific objectives and policies of Al-Dawa System of Schools as:

- To purify the society through the teachings of the Quran and the Sunnah;
- To prepare the individuals for the proclamation of the faith of Islam;
- To connect the religions and contemporary knowledge;
- To build up the students character to remove the destructive effects of secular education;
- To enable the students to play an active role in the society;
- To prepare sensible and responsible individuals; and
- To prepare the creative and independent minds.[24]

Lashkar's leaders are conscious of the fact that its students do not live in mosques or madaris and their goal is to prepare students to become productive members in society. Hence, as with the school at Muridke, all Al-Dawa schools taught subjects like mathematics and the hard sciences, with a particular emphasis on information technology.[25] This contributed to the group's technological prowess, which it used for military and missionary purposes, and also created a network of people within Pakistan's scientific community with ties to the organization. Despite secular aspects of the curriculum, Zafar Iqbal, who oversaw the education program, left little doubt that these schools had a missionary purpose when he said:

Christians have set up high quality schools in order to wean Muslim children away from Islam. These schools teach Christianity even to Muslim children. Christians are thus successful in their mission. We are setting up Islamic institutions along the lines of Christian missionary schools.[26]

A fair proportion of the curriculum also focused on jihad. For example, an Urdu textbook used by the classes in their second year of primary education featured the final testaments of mujahideen given before they went into battle.[27] Secondary school primers were modified such that 'c' is for cat and 'g' is for goat became 'c' is for cannon and 'g' is for gun. Teachers also had to have taken part in at least one jihad campaign or gone for military training.[28] Schooling entailed a significant physical element, including swimming, mountaineering, wrestling and martial arts. This curriculum was intended to prepare students for jihad, even though the group never intended to send all of them to fight.[29] The aim was to promote Lashkar's interpretation of jihad as an activity which all Muslims are obligated to participate in or support. It also stemmed from the belief that, according to Hafiz Saeed, when Muslims 'gave up jihad, science and technology also went into the hands of others.' This was natural, he said, since 'the one who possesses power also commands science, the economy and politics.'[30]

The group also opened madaris through the Department of Construction of Masajid and Madaris in order to promote its interpretation of Ahl-e-Hadith Islam. In addition to the madrasa at Muridke, two other prominent ones were Jamia Abu Bakr and Jamaat-ul-Dirasat-ul-Islamiyah. Both are located in the city of Karachi. The former followed the same curriculum as Medina University in Saudi Arabia and the latter educated approximately 500 students, many of whom came from South East Asia.[31] Military training was and remains separate from the group's schools and madaris. A student graduating from an MDI school or madrasa who wished to join the Kashmir jihad still needed to enter Lashkar's training program. Lashkar's four major training centers were the Muaskar-e-Taiba, Muaskar-e-Aqsa, Muaskar-e-Umm al-Qurra and Muaskar-e-Abdullah bin Masood. To process and house trainees, it opened the Bait-ul-Mujahideen [House of the Holy Warriors] in Pakistan-administered Kashmir.[32] In addition, Lashkar operated a host of smaller training centers elsewhere in Pakistan. The army and ISI greatly augmented Lashkar's training capacity, but its training program has changed little, with one exception: from 1998 Lashkar included additional religious training. Until that time its basic training regimen consisted of the Daura-e-Aama [General Session], which was essentially a three-week introductory course given to everyone and the Daura-e-Khasa [Special Session] consisting of three months of military training offered to select individuals. Additional specialized military courses were offered on an even more selective basis.

Training was intended to do more than prepare people to fight. Because Lashkar aimed to spread the Ahl-e-Hadith faith in Pakistan rather than merely to create a cadre of battle-ready militants, training was also used as a means to recruit and indoctrinate people in its interpretation of Islam. The Daura-e-Aama consisted primarily of prayer and physical training, with some introductory weapons drills. The main purpose was to teach the principles of its interpretation of the Ahl-e-Hadith school of thought, to convert those who belonged to other sects and motivate trainees to become involved in Lashkar's various activities.[33] Leaders, including Hafiz Saeed and Zaki-ur Rehman Lakhvi, made speeches to the recruits about the obligation to wage or otherwise support jihad and the need to prepare for it.[34]

The group's literature illustrates its organizational reach and the systematized nature of its training regimen during the 1990s. Regular classes for the Daura-e-Aama began every Monday and recruits were required to arrive at the training center on the previous Sunday. All trainees were instructed to bring a letter of authorization issued by their zonal or tehsil [sub-division] manager, a blanket, a jacket, and boots as well as money for their return trip home. Local managers were directed to apprise all prospective trainees of 'issues such as the situation at training centers, likely difficulties, the need for patience and fortitude, and the motivation for jihad.' Lashkar made clear to its recruiters that they should not refer 'biased activists from other organizations' for training. Once trainees completed the Daura-e-Aama and had returned home, local managers were instructed to keep them under surveillance so that they 'do not deviate from the right path.'[35]

To promote its missionary and reformist objectives, the organization created teams at the zonal, district, and divisional levels to proselytize. However, these were deemed insufficient, and in 1998 'it was decided that a short twenty-one day program called Daura-e-Suffa would be implemented to invite people to Islam.' The first such session was launched on 15 August under the supervision of Jamiat-ul-Dawa-al-Islamiyah [Institute for the Invitation to Islam] at Muridke to give students a crash course in dawa.[36] In short, the group began training an army of preachers. This new training was designed to cover Khitaab [oratory or readings of the Quran], information about the Hadith, Tarjumah [translation of the Quran], Salaat [prayers], Adhkar [remembrance] and calligraphy. The training session lasted fifteen days at Muridke after which participants were sent for a week of hands-on proselytizing to invite people to (Lashkar's interpretation of Ahl-e-Hadith) Islam. Preaching was carried out in places such as markets, bazaars, bus and railway stations, parks, hospitals, police stations and courts.[37]

To attend the Daura-e-Suffa potential trainees first had to complete the Daura-e-Aama and then obtain a letter of recommendation from their district or tehsil manager. They were instructed to arrive at Muridke at the end of each month, at which time all attendees were required to deposit money and other valuables at the Dar-ul-Amanat [Office for Safekeeping]. Participants were tested to determine their level of religious knowledge and advised to prepare in advance by studying a syllabus provided to them.[38] Local managers were requested to train illiterate participants in the syllabus in advance and not send anyone who had not completed the Daura-e-Aama unless they were educated and highly motivated. Once again, managers were directed to review graduated participants' performance at weekly or fortnightly meetings and to provide them a schedule of activities.[39]

Based on the testimony of captured operatives, it appears the Daura-e-Suffa soon became the first level of training followed by the Daura-e-Aama. It also seems that over time the focus became imbuing religious principals, including the obligatory nature of jihad, with less attention paid in some cases to sending trainees out to preach.[40] Lashkar offered the Daure-e-Aama and the Daura-e-Suffa to anyone regardless of sect and used them as an opportunity to convert people to the Ahl-e-Hadith faith. The group does not appear to have conducted background checks for either of these two training programs and it was possible to give a fake name if one wanted to. According to one former member and a researcher who tracked Lashkar's activities during the 1990s, more thorough vetting was done for those continuing on to the Daura-e-Khasa. Anyone actually sent into Indian-administered Kashmir received additional scrutiny.[41] Not everyone who completed the Daure-e-Aama and the Daura-e-Suffa advanced to the Daura-e-Khasa for military training. Some simply left and Lashkar assigned most who wished to join the organization to work for MDI (a practice continued with its successor, JuD) in various dawa capacities including raising funds, creating and disseminating propaganda or providing social services. Some recruits also chose this path, which the organization accepted. Both were considered essential to Lashkar's mission.[42]

Those who wished to receive serious military instruction needed a recommendation from a senior functionary and typically did not progress directly from the previous stage of training. Instead they often performed other supervised tasks that entailed proselytizing or performing khidmat [service] either at one of the group's offices or elsewhere. Often trainees were given time to return home to visit their families in between khidmat and the Daura-e-Khasa, during which time they might also be mentored by local Lashkar functionaries.[43] Lashkar's extensive organizational reach enabled it to monitor these trainees to ensure they comported themselves appropriately. Those selected to attend the Daura-e-Khasa were instructed to bring their Daura-e-Suffa card, a letter of recommendation and a deposit of 500 rupees, though managers were requested to cooperate with those who could not afford to pay. Numerous Pakistani interlocutors observed that Lashkar was considered stricter than other jihadi groups with regard to its requirements regarding the need to live by an Islamic code of life and the emphasis it placed on religious indoctrination. For example, would-be trainees needed to be prepared for Lashkar officials to conduct investigations into the state of the candidate's beard, his observance of prayers, and relevant family matters before issuing a recommendation.[44] Of course, personal relationships helped some recruits to access Lashkar's military training regimen more quickly than others.

The Daura-e-Khasa lasted three months and included physical training, small unit tactics, survival techniques, firing different types of light weapons and instruction on the use of hand grenades, rocket launchers and mortars. Lashkar disseminated a detailed primer outlining various aspects of guerrilla warfare and the specific requirements for conducting sustained attacks. It delineated the assets and capabilities an insurgent force needed as well as making recommendations in the areas of communications, medical aid, logistics and propaganda.[45] As already discussed, the army and ISI helped to design this training program, provided or oversaw military training and also trained Lashkar trainers. After completing this training the recruit adopted a kunya [nom de guerre] and was ready for battle. However, many were required to undertake additional proselytizing first. It has been suggested that recruits were also required to obtain their parents' consent to join the Kashmir jihad.[46] Anecdotal evidence based on interviews with current and former militants suggests this was not a hard and fast rule. Some obtained parental approval, while others did not and nor were they asked to get it. More important, according to several interlocutors, was that the recruit draft a letter or last will and testament, which stated he was not being coerced to wage jihad.[47] These letters were relatively uniform and, as detailed later in this chapter, often used for recruitment and fundraising purposes.[48]

Even after a recruit completed all of these requirements, some of those who were 'launched' [the term used for sending a militant across the LoC] received additional training before heading off to battle. This could include further training in guerrilla warfare, instruction in the use of heavy arms, or explosive training with a focus on making improvised explosive devices using locally available items or RDX [an explosive commonly used by jihadi groups in South Asia]. Some members, particularly those who might operate inside of India as recruiters or covert operatives, also went through Lashkar's Daura-e-Ribat. This program included training on how to collect intelligence, handle agents, engage in sabotage and surveillance, conduct briefings as well as debriefings, and communicate in code. It also featured lectures about India, its security agencies including the Research and Analysis Wing [RAW] and how to evade security personnel.[49] Finally, not all of those who went through these myriad training activities actually saw combat. Some were given management roles in the organization instead.

The group has claimed that 'the mujahideen trained by the Lashkar-e-Taiba are fighting the infidels everywhere.'[50] Most of the foreigners Lashkar trained returned to their respective countries to wage jihad; indeed the organization claims to have trained thousands of recruits from all over the world who went on to play leading combat roles in Afghanistan, Bosnia-Herzegovina, Chechnya, Kosovo, the southern Philippines, Kashmir and 'other areas where Muslims are fighting for freedom.'[51] As a group motivated by the desire to protect fellow members of the umma and one interested in developing transnational ties to other jihadi outfits, this readiness to train others is not surprising. According to one Pakistan-based Western diplomat who has tracked Lashkar's activities since the 1990s, it developed a reputation for being willing to train militants from other outfits.[52] However, its braggadocio aside, most of those who passed through Lashkar's camps came from Pakistan and fought in Indian-administered Kashmir.

Lashkar often exaggerated its exploits for propaganda purposes. Estranged from the other Ahl-e-Hadith organizations, and hence their networks, it had to maintain a healthy focus on propaganda in order to recruit and raise funds. In its early years, before the increase in state support, the group talked up its achievements prematurely and built a propaganda operation that was disproportionately large compared to its actual, on the ground, strength at the time. As one observer of the group's activities noted, 'people thought they were strong because they were so visible, but they were so visible because they had to build a network from nothing.' Image and presence were important, leading Lashkar to operate offices in areas where they had little hope of finding recruits.[53] It also produced an array of written material, the content of which was often exaggerated, a practice that continued even after the group's capacity increased. One former member admitted that, 'We used to make fun of the claims about the number of Indian soldiers killed. If you calculate the number Lashkar claimed to have killed from 1990 the Indian army should be gone by 2000.'[54] In addition to a penchant for hyperbole, the group sometimes claimed credit for other groups' operations as well.[55]

State support enabled many jihadi outfits to develop a powerful propaganda machinery that reflected aspects of the modern media. This 'jihadi journalism' employed the same printing systems, approaches to layout, and marketing strategies as normal newspapers in Pakistan. Their sales and circulation were comparable to competing mainstream publications, and low prices meant they

were easily affordable.[56] The MDI Department of Media and Propagation and its Dar-ul-Andalus Department of Publishing combined
to print the widest range of propaganda offerings of any jihadi
group in Pakistan, the flagship of which was a monthly magazine,
*Al-Dawa*, which Lashkar claimed enjoyed a circulation of 100,000 by
the end of the 1990s.[57] This was the highest circulation among jihadi
monthlies according to Amir Rana, who conducted an assessment
of jihadi propaganda in Pakistan. The group's weekly *Ghazwa
Times*, also in Urdu and later in Sindhi as well, gave the latest news
about Lashkar's jihad as well as national affairs and had the second
highest circulation among weeklies.[58] Both *Ghazwa Times* and *Al-
Dawa* magazine conveyed logistical information as well, such as
schedule changes for training courses.[59] The group published a
magazine for students called *Zarb-e-Taiba* and one for women called
*Taibat*, both also in Urdu. The media department also published
*Al-Ribat* in Arabic and *Voice of Islam* in English. By 2001, the Dar-ul-
Andalus Department of Publishing was printing over one hundred
booklets a year in Urdu, English, Arabic and Persian.[60]

The group also had a robust internet presence, maintaining websites in Urdu, Arabic and English. Its web presence kept pace with
the times and its sites became more interactive and sophisticated as
the 1990s drew to a close. By that time it had become the only jihadi
group in Pakistan with a web-based radio station, *Radio al-Jihad*,
which broadcast in Urdu, English, Arabic and Sindhi.[61] This boosted
the group's profile within Pakistan and abroad. At home, people
were able to tune in for live coverage of sermons given by Lashkar's
leadership. By broadcasting via the internet in English, the group
was able to reach members of the diaspora living abroad. In addition, the group also ran a 'News & Views' series in which it reported
on events throughout the Muslim world and offered commentary
pieces. In its 'Europe Under Muslim Rule' series, Lashkar offered
its own interpretation of the history of Muslim conquest throughout
Europe to support its irredentist ambitions.[62] Notably, the name of
its publishing department, Dar-ul-Andalus, is a reference to the
former Muslim empire of Al Andalus in today's Spain.

Propaganda naturally also covered all manner of jihadi activities
in Kashmir as well as glorifying the participation of its mujahideen

in sundry conflicts around the world. The group's website and several of its publications ran a 'Mujahideen Activities' series in which it reported on its fighters' exploits. The language used was often over-the-top, with headlines such as '30 Bodies Sent to Delhi,' and '12 [Indians] Sent Packing to Hell.' The body of the text was no less exaggerated. Lashkar's mujahideen were imbued with almost superhuman powers and, of course, a thirst for martyrdom.[63] Al-Dawa magazine also featured a special section with testaments and life stories of martyrs intended to inveigle other young men to follow in their footsteps. These testaments generally emphasized the redemptive value of joining Lashkar and becoming a martyr.[64]

The Department of Media and Propagation managed the group's public events as well as liaising with the media. In addition to the routine issuing of press releases, this department arranged programs and conferences at Murdike as well as at local offices. It also set up camps or stalls in different parts of the country to provide a venue for the general public to pose questions, gather information about Lashkar's activities, and hear its position on different issues. Some of these 'camps' offered 'civil defense training,' which combined lectures on the importance of jihad with the opportunity to fire off a few rounds from a Kalashnikov. The hope was to inspire young men to join the cause.[65] According to the group's Al-Dawa magazine, its media liaison team would arrange for the Pakistan press to attend. This included setting up press briefings and separate enclosures for the press corps.[66] In addition to inspiring recruits and gaining public notoriety, these events also were used to collect funds.

MDI held a number of Ijtemas, or congregations, of varying size each year. Many of these were small, local affairs, but its annual Ijtemas held at Muridke were reported to have drawn between 500,000 and 1 million people by the late 1990s.[67] In addition to facilitating social networking, these Ijtemas in Pakistan were also useful propaganda tools. Like any conference they acted as media events as well as illustrating the hosting body's strength, appeal and organizational abilities. They also provided a forum for disseminating key messages, and Lashkar used them to narrate success stories about its jihad campaigns to groups from different parts of the world.[68] Finally, these Ijtemas promoted the concept of the pan-Islamic umma and provided evidence of Lashkar's international appeal.[69] The Urdu publication *Jang* reported that mujahideen from over fifty countries attended Lashkar's 1998 Ijtema.[70] This may be an exaggeration, but even if it were half that number, that still demonstrates an impressive transnational appeal. According to Ahmed Rashid, the renowned Pakistani journalist and author who attended several of Lashkar's annual Ijtemas, the group was formidably well organized internationally. He noted that foreign attendees to these events came from locations including Chechnya, Tajikistan, China, Afghanistan, Sudan, Egypt, Saudi Arabia and the Middle East.[71] Boasting hyperbolically about its international presence, the invitation to the 1998 Ijtema proclaimed, 'That is to say, you can go to any jehadi front in the world and you will find Markazul Dawa Wal Irshad mujahideen crushing the infidels and destroying the fortresses of the devil, God willing.'[72] During the 1999 Ijtema speakers extolled jihad against India and America, while Taliban delegates from Afghanistan vowed never to hand over Osama bin Laden to the United States.[73] Current and retired members of the government and ISI attended as well, including former ISI Director General Hamid Gul.[74] Their presence spoke to Lashkar's close relationship with the ISI and growing presence within the country. It also represented a shift begun by the government during the mid 1990s, which was driven by the ISI, to stop apologizing for the Kashmir jihad.[75] By the end of the decade jihadi groups were more visible than ever before. In 1998 the Governor of Punjab Shahid Hamid visited Muridke to 'congratulate the Lashkar-e-Taiba on the martyrdom of their 418 mujahids in Indian-occupied Kashmir.' The Federal Minister for Information, the Provincial Law Minister and the Minister for Education accompanied him. Saeed told the press that the visit would help to dispel the impression that Lashkar was a terrorist organization.[76] Of course it was exactly that by this time, as well as a prolific social welfare provider. In addition to having multiple faces, by the end of the decade the group had an extensive reach domestically and transnationally.

Beyond serving missionary and training purposes, Lashkar used its infrastructure in Pakistan to recruit and raise money. It also developed networks abroad for the same purpose, in India, the Persian Gulf and the West. Its approach was based both on what the market would bear in each location as well as on what it endeavored to gain from each theater. Within Pakistan, the group sought fighters, support staff and donors. The overwhelming majority of Lashkar's fighters came from Pakistan, with the remainder drawn primarily from Afghanistan and Indian-administered Kashmir.[77] Before the 9/11 attacks no restrictions were placed on private Pakistani citizens joining militant groups or on those groups raising money for jihad.[78] By the end of the 1990s the group had little trouble attracting recruits, support staff or money in Pakistan.

Things were not always so easy for Lashkar. Jihadi organizations in Pakistan don't draw exclusively from their own sect, but they do rely on their own sectarian infrastructure. Here Lashkar was out of luck on two counts. First, the Ahl-e-Hadith movement's infrastructure in Pakistan was not as robust as that of the Deobandis'. Second, Lashkar was estranged from the other Ahl-e-Hadith organizations and so was unable to recruit in Ahl-e-Hadith madaris or mosques. One might expect that Lashkar relied heavily on its Al-Dawa schools as feeders for its militant jihad, but the group believed the quality of student produced at these schools was far too high to waste as cannon fodder. The group's founders wanted the MDI school system to be among Pakistan's best, and so did not wish to compromise access to potential students by using those schools as nothing more than a battlefield feeder. Of course, if students wanted to fight then Lashkar did not turn all of them away, though it did steer some toward further education and then into non-military roles in MDI. Many of its above-ground workers, first at MDI and later at JuD, were graduates of its school system. Other graduates went on to become productive members of society in various fields, which increased Lashkar's power and reach in Pakistan.

Even after opening new madaris, built by its Department of Construction of Masajid and Madaris, very few of Lashkar's recruits, percentage-wise, came from a madrasa.[79] In contrast, Deobandi jihadi groups relied much more heavily on madaris and mosque-based networks for recruiting.[80] Instead, most of Lashkar's recruits were educated at regular—or what are called 'government'—schools.[81] A sociological profile of 100 Lashkar martyrs found their background was similar to that of low-ranking officers in the army. Most came from lower middle class families and many of them were more educated than the average Pakistani, as well as than recruits to other militant groups, having completed at least secondary education and in some cases attended university.[82] According to its own records, as of 2001 the majority of its martyrs came from Punjab with the NWFP contributing the second highest number.[83] Over time Lashkar took advantage of the growing influence of Salafism among families in rural Sindh and Balochistan, as well as its own growing organizational reach, to begin attracting recruits from those provinces as well.[84]

Through its missionary activities Lashkar expanded the Ahl-e-Hadith pool from which recruits could be drawn and recruited some of those who attended its mosques. But the group sought to win over young men from among other sects too. When recruiting from government schools and universities Lashkar often sought to inveigle Barelvis and Deobandis rather than focusing exclusively on the Ahl-e-Hadith. In addition to casting its net wider, this was also a means of missionary work since Lashkar converted anyone who joined to its interpretation of Ahl-e-Hadith Islam. Amir Rana, a researcher who has studied jihadi recruitment in Pakistan, told the author that some Lashkar recruits whom he met were unsure of their sectarian affiliation at the time they joined, and only realized after beginning the religious indoctrination regimen that they were not adherents to Ahl-e-Hadith Islam. When this happened, some chose to stay while others left for a group representing their own school of thought.[85]

Lashkar was able to overcome its sectarian disadvantage in part because recruits were drawn to militant outfits 'mostly due to dynamics in the Indo-Pakistan security competition.'[86] As already illustrated, all Pakistanis are exposed from a young age to intense propaganda about Kashmir. This meant that for some would-be militants, a group's reputation vis-à-vis the Kashmir jihad was a major reason for joining. Lashkar's propaganda about its Kashmiri exploits, its growing prowess there and support from the ISI enabled the group to draw from beyond the Ahl-e-Hadith ranks. High profile operations, such as Lashkar's successful attacks against the

Red Fort and Srinagar airport, further boosted recruitment and fundraising.[87]

The group operated recruiting offices on university campuses, and often dispatched fighters to these locations to convince students either to join directly or to attend the annual Ijtema in Muridke after which many were inspired to sign up. Indian savagery was a common recruitment motif. One member told the author that Lashkar militants who had been fighting in the Kashmir Valley came to his college and described the 'butchery by the Indians.'[88] A number of Lashkar cadres captured by the Indian security forces said they were told during the recruitment process about the demolition of mosques in India.[89] Another common recruitment motif was the celebration of martyrdom.

Lashkar representatives gathered people in town centers and sports fields via loudspeaker to say prayers for its martyrs. During these public ceremonies Lashkar lauded the fallen mujahid's family and sometimes his entire village. The martyr's testament, which often exhorted others to join the cause, was then read. All of this inevitably prompted other volunteers to come forward.[90] Local officials from the group also visited martyrs' homes to congratulate the family, distribute sweets to celebrate the death and use the occasion to solicit new recruits.[91] In addition to these special occasions, Lashkar displayed banners and used graffiti as persistent reminders of the glory of jihad. Common slogans included: 'Neither cricket stars nor movie stars, but Islamic mujahideen,' 'Prolong jihad with your lives and property in the name of God,' and 'Break the necks and joints of non-Muslims.' The group's flag was—and remains—conspicuously graffiti'd on many walls throughout Pakistan.[92]

Money and identity mattered too. For many youths, especially those with few employment opportunities, the chance to join a respected outfit like Lashkar and fight the hated Indians to liberate Kashmir offered a means of boosting their self-esteem and identity. Through its dawa, social services and jihadi exploits Lashkar gained a positive reputation, making it an even more attractive jihadi group to join. According to an International Crisis Group report, in the Lashkar stronghold of Gondlanwala the group became so influential that villagers would accept its arbitration in local and familial disputes. The village came to be called Pind Shaheedan, meaning the village of martyrs, because almost every family had someone who fought or died in Indian-administered Kashmir, mainly with Lashkar.[93]

The group compensated its recruits well. Salaries are estimated to have ranged from Rs10,000 to Rs20,000 per month along with an end of tenure payment of between Rs300,000 to Rs500,000 for every year of 'active' service in the Kashmir jihad.[94] Lashkar also compensated a recruit's family if he died in combat. Through the Wurasa Shuhda-O-Ghazian [Kin of Martyrs and Fighters], the group offered assistance to the relatives of the martyrs of Kashmir. This included monthly stipends and other facilities.[95] It also cared for veterans and arranged jobs for those who could work.[96] Providing such financial support, along with maintaining the group's myriad training and social service networks, required a robust fundraising infrastructure. In the early 1990s, members of the group were forced to ask their friends to help finance the organization, but by the decade's end it had put those penurious days behind it.[97]

Lashkar received a fair amount of financial assistance from the army and ISI, but the group also developed a financial network of its own within the country. This network was managed by MDI's Department of Finance, which had a section devoted to collecting funds for the jihad in Kashmir. Every year the group solicited the hides of animals sacrificed for the Muslim holy festival of Eid al-Adha and then sold those hides for a large profit. Over time, the group developed a sophisticated collection strategy. One Pakistani citizen from whom the group solicited a hide described the process: he received a package several days before the holiday began containing a bag for a hide along with a brochure stating 'If you support the dominance of Islam then help us.' The bag came with the names and numbers of different functionaries responsible for collecting the hides from people in various zones in his city. This not only made for an orderly collection process, but also enabled the group to build a database of donors who responded.[98]

This was only one of many fundraising methods. Until its ban in 2002 Lashkar placed donation boxes to solicit funds in countless shops throughout Pakistan. Following a brief absence after the ban, these donation boxes returned, and were still present at the time of the author's last visit in May 2009. Staff members also collected money at MDI offices, through personal solicitations and at public gatherings to celebrate a fighter's martyrdom. Moreover the MDI website listed its address, phone number and bank details so that donors could deposit money directly.[99] In addition to collecting donations, the group collected taxes. MDI had, and JuD maintained, a Farmers' and Workers' Wing. Maqbul Ahmed initially ran this wing before Haji Muhammad Ashraf took over. Ashraf was one of four JuD leaders whose assets the US Treasury Department targeted in 2008, and he is the one who really developed the network. The Farmers and Labor Wing collected Ushr—an Islamic land tax that obligates farmers to donate 10 per cent of their harvest or income to charity for the provision of social services—from farmers in Pakistan.[100] Lashkar's leaders assert that, in the absence of a Caliph, it has the right to collect this tax.[101] According to one former member, people associated with the group who belonged to the business community also sometimes added an additional 5–10 rupees 'for the jihad' to the bill when selling various goods.[102]

Going beyond the gun to offer social services also won the group more than hearts and minds. It made Lashkar money. Al-Dawa Schools charged fees and although the group subsidized some students, overall it came out ahead. The administrator at Muridke claimed it never turned away students who were too poor to pay, and instead charged more from richer families and less from poorer ones.[103] Lashkar also charged a nominal fee for training, but could afford to waive that as well for those who could not afford it. Nor did it give away its propaganda for free. In one year alone, the Dar-ul-Andalus Publishing Department reportedly collected 80 lakhs [equivalent to 8 million rupees or approximately $150,000 in the late 1990s] from the sale of its jihadi publications.[104] The group invested some of the money it raised in legitimate enterprises, including factories and other businesses.[105] Fundraising for militant activities can be a volatile business, and these investments created another stream of reliable income. In making these investments Lashkar was increasing its territorialized infrastructure within Pakistan, but also making itself more vulnerable to state pressure since it now had assets that could be threatened. However, the group's footprint was by no means entirely Pakistan-centric.

In February 2000, Hafiz Saeed hinted that Lashkar had a presence in the Indian heartland. He explained that the Kargil incursion had been the first component of a new Lashkar campaign and the introduction of fidayeen attacks in Indian-administered Kashmir the second. Saeed promised that soon Lashkar would launch a third round.[106] Ten months later, the group executed its audacious fidayeen attack on the Red Fort in Delhi. A month after the attack Hafiz Saeed boasted, 'The action indicates that we have extended the jihad to India.'[107] Yet, while this was the first operation in India for which Lashkar took credit, in reality it had been involved in terrorist attacks there for almost a decade. According to one Indian security analyst, the Indian security services were arresting Pakistanis as early as 1992 who were tied to Lashkar, but at the time they did not know what Lashkar was since it was not big enough at the time to register clearly on their radar.[108] Thus, even before the state's decision to throw its support behind Lashkar and facilitate its expansion, the group was operating in India with the intention of building a network to execute or support terrorist attacks.

Initial recruitment and network-building took several forms. As in other countries with Muslim populations, Salafism was beginning to experience an upsurge in popularity in India during this time. Lashkar leveraged this surge in Salafi identity to inveigle recruits from Ahl-e-Hadith seminaries and other Salafi power centers, often relying on personal relationships forged via these seminaries and the Students' Islamic Movement of India [SIMI].[109] Very little open propagation was necessary, since SIMI and the various Ahl-e-Hadith seminaries in India provided a pool in which to fish for recruits. Above-ground Ahl-e-Hadith adherents, not necessarily or openly associated with Lashkar, helped to lay the groundwork and expand this recruiting pool through legitimate dawa operations intended to convert Indians to the Ahl-e-Hadith school of thought.[110]

More central to Lashkar's success was communal resentment in India, where the Muslim minority has suffered relative economic deprivation and some of whose members harbor a sense of political exclusion. In the words of the aforementioned analyst, the establishment has 'hammered Muslims quite badly' leading to significant disaffection.[111] Communal tension erupted into violence at times, such as in 1985 when pogroms targeting Muslims took place in the textile town of Bhiwandi. In response to this outbreak of violence, activists from the Jamaat Ghuraba Ahl-e-Hadith in India established a Muslim self-defense militia. Soon thereafter an obscure West Bengal-based cleric named Abu Masood announced the creation of Tanzim Islahul Muslimeen [Organization for the Improvement of Muslims or TIM]. Although announced by Abu Masood, the three key figures present at the meeting establishing TIM were Jalees Ansari, Azam Ghouri and Abdul Karim who was known as 'Tunda.'[112] During its early years, the TIM confined itself to parading recruits around the grounds of the Young Men's Christian Association [YMCA] and training with lathis.[113] Then, in December 1992, Hindu chauvinists demolished the Babri Masjid [Mosque of Babur], which had been constructed by the first Mughal Emperor of India [Babur] in the sixteenth century. Approximately two thousand people, mostly Muslims, were killed in the communal riots in Mumbai [Bombay at the time] and Gujarat which followed the demolition of the mosque. Not long before the riots, Hafiz Saeed had dispatched Mohammad Azam Cheema, a former colleague from the University of Engineering and Technology, to spearhead Lashkar's recruitment drive inside India. Thus Cheema, known as 'Baba' to his recruits, arrived just before these communal tensions erupted into violence.[114] After the demolition of the Babri Masjid, TIM's leaders decided the time for parade-ground drills was over and that it was time to fight what they saw as the threat from rising Hindu chauvinism. Ansari, Ghouri and Tunda subsequently joined Lashkar, contributing to its network in India during the 1990s and making TIM the initial block on which Lashkar's Indian operations were built.

A year to the day after the Babri Masjid's destruction, Ansari, Ghouri and Tunda executed the first Lashkar-supported attacks in mainland India: a series of coordinated bombings in several cities. Most of the explosions were small, but two people were killed and the ability to execute coordinated blasts illustrated the group's discipline and skill.[115] These bombings should not be confused with those perpetrated by Dawood Ibrahim, the Muslim leader of South Asia's largest crime syndicate known as D-company, who also was outraged by the destruction of the Babri Masjid. Ibrahim worked with the ISI to engineer a far more lethal series of bomb blasts in Bombay in March 1993, which killed hundreds of people.[116] Ibrahim relocated his organization's headquarters to Karachi following these attacks, where he is believed to have strengthened his alliance with the ISI and developed ties to Lashkar, some of whose activities he began financing. D-company operates primarily in Pakistan, India and the United Arab Emirates, and Ibrahim is also said to have begun providing Lashkar operatives with access to his smuggling routes as well as assisting Lashkar with the recruitment of Indian members.[117] This is particularly notable given that D-Company also had a presence in Bangladesh, Nepal and several Gulf countries, which were natural transit points for travel between India and Pakistan. In addition to smuggling people, D-Company's networks were also used to traffic weapons and move money via the hawala system.[118] Thus, although Lashkar was not involved in the blasts perpetrated by Ibrahim, it clearly benefited from his arrival in Pakistan. Even more important was the group's relationship with the army and ISI from the mid-1990s onwards. Military training in bombmaking and reconnaissance as well as ISI assistance infiltrating and exfiltrating operatives into and out of India subsequently played a major role in augmenting Lashkar's lethality. According to one Lashkar operative who operated extensively in India during the 2000s, the ISI provided him one-on-one instruction in surveillance techniques, which he considered much more scientific and effective than the instruction given to him during the Daura-e-Ribat.[119]

Not long after the initial wave of attacks, Ansari was captured in the midst of planning a second series of bombings scheduled to coincide with India's Republic Day celebrations in January 1994.[120] Tunda escaped to Bangladesh and Ghouri to Saudi Arabia, though both later came back to India. Tunda headed Lashkar's operations in Bangladesh during the mid-1990s, and became a conduit for recruits transiting from or through Bangladesh to its camps. Among those Tunda sent to Pakistan for training was Sheikh Abdur Rahman, who founded the Jamaat-ul-Mujahideen Bangladesh [JMB] in

1998. Rahman had previously been a member of Harkat-ul-Jihad-al-Islami Bangladesh [HUJI-B], the Bangladeshi branch of the Deobandi organization by the same name in Pakistan. He met Hafiz Saeed and other Lashkar leaders during his stay in Pakistan, where the group trained him on the use of small arms and explosives as well as instructing him on how to build a jihadi organization. Rahman wanted to wage a near enemy jihad against the government in Bangladesh, and after he returned there fell out with Tunda over the latter's insistence on using available jihadi assets in Bangladesh for the struggle against India.[121] Lashkar also began building networks in Nepal, which the group has since used to provide passports, cash and communications facilities for operatives transiting between Pakistan and India.[122]

With Lashkar's assistance, those Indians who had not fled or been arrested began a recruitment drive and also maintained a low-level bombing campaign.[123] SIMI provided many of the early recruits who, motivated by appeals to Muslim identity rather than the Kashmir conflict, sought out Pakistani jihadi groups. When stating that Lashkar recruited through SIMI it is important to be clear that SIMI was, and remained, independent of Lashkar. It had its own agenda, albeit one that linked local Indian grievances to the wider jihadi movement. No group had a monopoly on SIMI's operatives and it is not correct to say that SIMI provided operatives to Lashkar. A more precise explanation would be that Lashkar used some of SIMI's network as a recruiting pool, co-opting its cadres to provide manpower or support for operations. Lashkar sent many of those it recruited from 1993 onwards to its camps for training. During this stage, Lashkar was also providing funding, planning, direction and ideological support for its burgeoning Indian networks as well.

According to Praveen Swami, among the foremost experts on Indian jihadi networks, Indians were executing attacks, with Lashkar assigning Pakistani operatives to help build the bombs and provide other expertise.[124] By the mid-1990s, Cheema is believed to have been running over a dozen Pakistani Lashkar operatives across India.[125] As Indian actors became more capable, they assumed greater responsibility for operations. For example, when Tunda returned to India he became Lashkar's operational commander there as well as one of its premier bomb-makers and explosives trainers.[126] Ghouri came back to India in 1998, having spent considerable time based in Saudi Arabia, where he was in contact with several Lashkar operatives and helped to develop the group's Gulf networks.[127] According to statements made to the Indian security services by one captured Indian Lashkar operative, Ghouri had also traveled to Pakistan to train with the group since fleeing India in 1994.[128] When Ghouri did return to his native Hyderabad to build up Lashkar's networks, recruitment experienced a boost.[129] An attendant increase in bombings followed, mainly targeting civilian areas such as trains, buses and markets. Police finally caught up with and killed Ghouri in April 2000, but as subsequent chapters will indicate, since then bombing attacks by Lashkar-trained and supported Indians have only increased. Its ability to finance these and other operations as well as to support them logistically was partly a function of its presence in the Gulf.

Lashkar's relations to the Gulf region stretch back to the time of the anti-Soviet Afghan jihad, when several MDI founders studied in Saudi Arabia. Saudis associated with the group helped Lashkar to expand its networks in the Gulf during the ensuing decade, as did Pakistani and Indian operatives living there. For example, the US government asserts Mahmoud Mohammad Ahmed Bahaziq served as Lashkar's leader in Saudi Arabia at one point. From there he coordinated the group's efforts to raise money from NGOs and local businessmen, and also helped to extend its organizational reach in the Gulf. When the US Treasury Department froze Bahaziq's assets in 2008, it credited him with being 'the main financier behind the establishment of the LET and its activities in the 1980s and 1990s' and alleged that he remained an active contributor to the group's operations during this decade.[130] Several interlocutors with knowledge of Bahaziq's activities seconded this assertion, noting that he was well positioned to support the group's fundraising objectives in the region.[131] As the previous section highlighted, Azam Ghouri also played a role in supporting Lashkar's operations in the Gulf after fleeing to Saudi Arabia from India. The group's relationship with Dawood Ibrahim's criminal syndicate, which had a strong presence in the United Arab Emirates, helped too and brought with it access to smuggling routes and another source from which to acquire counterfeit documents for operatives transiting between different countries.[132]

Lashkar benefited from Gulf funding during the Afghan jihad against the Soviets, and continued to thereafter since its missionary ambitions continued to attract Arab donors interested in supporting the spread of Salafi Islam in South Asia. Exact figures are not available via open sources, but a number of Pakistani-based analysts and Western officials told the author that the largest source of Gulf funding comes from Wahhabi groups in Saudi Arabia. In addition to fundraising based on religious identity, Lashkar's donor base benefited from ethnic ties as well. According to some Lashkar sources, during the 1990s, the Pakistani diaspora in the Gulf contributed even more than their fellow ex-patriots in the United Kingdom.[133] This claim is questionable, and almost impossible to verify using only open source information, but it reinforces the proposition that Gulf funding was not limited to donors who backed the group for religious reasons. Lashkar's various funding networks were already quite robust by the end of the 1990s. According to the US Treasury Department, after Haji Muhammad Ashraf became Lashkar's chief of finance he assisted Lashkar's leadership in Saudi Arabia with 'expanding its organization and increasing its fundraising activities' during the following decade.[134]

A large portion of money came from charitable sources—legitimate and illegitimate—cultivated over the course of Lashkar's twenty-year existence.[135] For example, the group allegedly received financial assistance until 2007 from a Gulf-based charity organization which the US Treasury Department designated in 2008 as providing financial and material support to al-Qaeda and al-Qaeda affiliated organizations.[136] The group raised considerable amounts of money from private businessmen as well.[137] According to the interrogation report of Abdul Razzak Masood, an Indian who joined Lashkar in the late 1990s, this included well-known persons involved in business and the media in Dubai who donated large sums of money to support Lashkar's activities.[138] Funds often were donated to the group's above-ground wing, first MDI and then after 2002 to JuD. Until the United Nations blacklisted JuD in 2008 following the Mumbai attacks, contributing to it was perfectly legal in most countries. As is often the case when dealing with a group that has charitable and militant wings, some donors believed they were giving money to the former while others were aware that any funds donated were fungible. In addition to money donated directly to MDI or later JuD, cash was and continues to be transmitted using hawala or hundi networks, which is an alternative remittance system that operates beyond Western banking or financial channels and is therefore difficult to trace.[139] During a raid of a Lashkar operative's house in Mumbai in 2009 investigators discovered 37,000 Saudi riyals, which apparently were sent from Saudi Arabia via a hawala network.[140]

The Gulf also proved a fertile ground for recruitment. As in India, the recruitment process involved personal connections, often formed at mosques or other spiritual centers where so-called talent spotters aim to radicalize and indoctrinate potential recruits. The radicalization process is similar to that used by Lashkar in Pakistan and India. It includes showing would-be recruits footage of events such as communal rioting in India, the Babri Masjid demolition and violence in Indian-administered Kashmir. One Indian operative recruited in the Gulf described to police after his capture the speech that Hafiz Abdul Rehman Makki, Saeed's brother-in-law, gave when he visited Dubai. Makki told his audience about the need to liberate lands in India. In addition to hearing this information in person, the recruit also described the profusion of propaganda offerings such as *Voice of Islam, Tayyabba* and *Ghazwa Times* at various Lashkar offices in the Gulf.[141] Indian Muslims working in the region were, and continue to be, recruited for the very same reasons as Indian Muslims living in India: to assist with or prosecute terror attacks against their homeland. Some recruits were sent to Pakistan for training and then back to India to become part of an underground cell. Others joined Lashkar's support networks in the Gulf, Bangladesh or Nepal to help facilitate the movement of men, money and material. When recruits transited to Pakistan for training, the journey often was (and remains) a circuitous one. In some instances, Indians recruited in India were sent to the Gulf and from there began the journey to training camps in Pakistan or Pakistan-administered Kashmir. Although a more recent example, alleged statements made by another captured Indian operative, Fahim Ansari, to the Indian security services illustrates how these networks function.[142]

Ansari was born in Mumbai, India and claims to have openly expressed his desire to participate in jihad on several occasions, thus marking him out to recruiters. During a trip back to India from Dubai, where he had moved in 2005, Ansari was introduced to a Pakistani-trained member of Lashkar. This individual provided Ansari with false identity papers, told him to return to Dubai and to work there until he received further instructions. A second Lashkar member contacted Ansari following his return to Dubai and the two met a week later. After an initial attempt to leave Dubai en route to Pakistan failed, Ansari was given the phone number of a Karachi-based member named Mohammad Jassem [a.k.a. Tehsin] with whom he remained in contact thereafter. In December 2006, on Jassem's instructions, Ansari collected money from a shop and prepared to meet yet another Lashkar operative named Ilias who would arrange his illegal infiltration into Pakistan. After meeting Ilias the two crossed into Muscat, the capital of Oman, via Abu Dhabi, where Ansari lodged with a group of Pakistanis. He was brought to an Iranian who took him via ship to the port of Bandar Abbas in Iran, from where Ansari transited to Pakistan across the border and eventually reached Karachi. Upon doing so he contacted Jassem who took him the remainder of the way to the Bait-ul-Mujahideen office in Muzaffarabad.[143] Such a circuitous route was necessary for an Indian wishing to travel to Pakistan for training. For Westerners, especially during the 1990s, it was much easier.

One JuD member close to Lashkar's leaders admitted the group has long had a policy of training Westerners.[144] Some of those trainees have gone on to fight with Lashkar in Indian-administered Kashmir. Augmenting its ranks with large numbers of Western would-be jihadis was never a reasonable strategy, however, nor one the group seems to have considered seriously. Instead, recruiting and training Westerners appears to have served four main purposes: first, it enabled the group to develop a transnational network, which it used primarily for logistical and support purposes;

second, it promoted Lashkar's reputation as an organization with international reach and appeal; third it allowed the group to build its brand among the Kashmiri diaspora who contributed large amounts of money to the groups fighting in Indian-administered Kashmir; and fourth it was a means of promoting the concept of jihad and propagating Lashkar's version of Ahl-e-Hadith Islam. Historically, the majority of its Western trainees and operatives are believed to have come from the diaspora in the United Kingdom, though Americans and Europeans trained with the group as well. Estimates vary as to how many Westerners passed through Lashkar's camps, but it appears that few were actually sent to fight. Some were enlisted as operatives to support the group's activities in the West and many more were indoctrinated with Lashkar's extreme interpretation of jihad.[145]

The group took several steps to recruit Westerners. First, it propagated its views and ideology among diaspora youth when they visited relatives or friends in Pakistan and incited them to jihad in much the same way it did people who lived there. A disproportionate number of British Pakistanis are of Kashmiri descent and hail from the city and environs of Mirpur in Pakistan-administered Kashmir.[146] Because of the influence of the Kashmiri diaspora, most of the jihadi outfits and their above-ground organizations operated offices in Mirpur and proselytizing to visiting youth was common.[147] According to one Metropolitan Police Service source, at the time British Pakistanis with connections to Kotli [also in Pakistan-administered Kashmir] as well as Gujrat and Sialkot [in Punjab province] were also considered to be particularly well-suited to leverage familial connections in order to attain training.[148] To promote its image as a training provider Lashkar also advertised. For example, in 1999 the now-defunct London-based Global Jihad Fund trumpeted Lashkar-organized training courses held in Pakistan-administered Kashmir. The advert promised an introductory course of only twenty-one days offered at the beginner level with special courses afterward.[149] Until it was taken down in 2002 the MDI website also provided contact information for anyone looking to arrange training as well as listing its contact and bank details along with reminder messages about the importance of financially supporting the jihad.[150]

Finally, the group used agents to recruit youths and raise money. A brief tour through several countries illustrates the reach of Lashkar's transnational networks and the scope of its activities in the West.

The group did not have a significant presence in the US during the 1990s, but exploited the arrival of two Americans in 2000 to build up its footprint there. Both were part of a coterie of would-be jihadis that ultimately became known as the Virginia Jihad Network, which gained some notoriety because of its members' practice of preparing for jihad by playing paintball. Randall Todd Royer [a.k.a. Ismail Royer] traveled to Pakistan in April 2000 and spent several months training with the group.[151] Royer was an admirer even before arriving in Pakistan, and upon returning to Virginia he lauded Lashkar to his associates. Among them was Ibrahim Ahmed al-Hamdi, who earlier had attempted to wage jihad in Chechnya, but had been turned down due to his lack of military training. He hoped to rectify that and then to achieve martyrdom fighting in Indian-administered Kashmir. Before al-Hamdi left for Lashkar's camps in summer 2000 Royer reached out to a contact in Pakistan to ensure his confederate's acceptance once he arrived. Al-Hamdi trained with the group, but left after only a month. Approximately one year later another member of the network, Seifullah Chapman, also cut short his training. He was in Lashkar's camps on 9/11, and returned to the US soon after. By the time he arrived back home, additional members of the Virginia Jihad Network had already decided to train with Lashkar in preparation for defending Afghanistan against the expected American invasion.[152] As Chapter 6 will detail, none of them ever accessed the Afghan front, but the men from Virginia contributed to a small Lashkar network in the US. It was used primarily for logistical support, though several of those who trained with the group after 9/11 were also asked to conduct surveillance on possible targets in America.

During an inquiry into the possible support networks that the 'shoebomber' Richard Reid relied on in Paris, authorities 'confirmed the existence of channels for sending volunteers from France to the training camps in Pakistan aimed at international jihad.' At the center of those channels was Ghulam Mustafa Rama, a British citizen who undertook recruitment for Lashkar in France. He was president of the Chemin Droit Association, which French authorities asserted was the representative of the Jamiat Ahl-e-Hadith party in Paris, and had ties to the Jamiat Ahl-e-Hadith in the UK as well. In addition, he was affiliated with the Al Haramain Foundation, which was later declared an al-Qaeda front by the United Nations.[153] Authorities found Rama to be in possession of contact information for operatives in Europe who were connected to various other jihadi outfits and networks as well.[154] Hasan El Cheguer and Hakim Mokhfi, two of Rama's French recruits, were both known to the French security services because they 'hung out' with actors linked to the Salafi Group for Preaching and Combat [GSPC] and the Moroccan Islamic Combatant Group [GICM].[155] They described to authorities how Rama facilitated their training, first organizing and financing a trip to Pakistan in summer 2001. Once there, he drove them to Lashkar's offices in Lahore and introduced them to Hafiz Saeed, with whom he allegedly had a personal relationship. By vouching for them directly to Saeed, Rama apparently enabled the recruits to move directly on to receiving paramilitary training at one of Lashkar's camps in Pakistan-administered Kashmir. The two men were training with Lashkar on 9/11 and later told police 'there were cries of joy' and jubilation in the camp in response to al-Qaeda's attacks against America. Both left several days later and traveled to London, where they destroyed their passports before returning to Paris. Although they returned earlier than expected, Rama welcomed them home as mujahideen.[156]

Lashkar had a larger presence in the United Kingdom, where it fundraised and recruited actively from the Pakistani diaspora community as well as through Ahl-e-Hadith mosques. The UK was particularly lenient toward Islamist activism during the 1990s, which led many jihadi outfits to use it as a base for fundraising and recruitment. In January 2002, *The Sunday Times* quoted a senior Lashkar member explaining the scale and destination of money raised: 'We receive millions of pounds from Britain. British Kashmiris are very patriotic. Some is for charity, but the rest is used for attacks against [Indian] military targets.'[157] According to a 2002 report by the International Crisis Group, Lashkar and Jaish-e-Mohammed were collecting almost 5 million pounds annually in British mosques, mainly from the Kashmiri diaspora.[158] These estimates are impossible to verify, but even if Lashkar raised only one-fifth of the Crisis Group estimate, it would still constitute a substantial amount.

The case of Shafiq-ur Rehman illustrates the type of connections the group had to the United Kingdom through MDI in the mid- to late-1990s as well as the difficulty of separating support for MDI's social welfare operations from Lashkar's militant ones and the British government's evolving perception of the threat these activities posed. Rehman came to the UK in 1993 to work as a maulvi with the Jamiat Ahl-e-Hadith. In 1998 the authorities denied his application to remain indefinitely, meaning Rehman would be deported, on the grounds that he was 'involved with an Islamic terrorist organization Markaz Dawa Al Irshad' and hence represented 'a danger to national security.' Rehman appealed the decision via the Special Immigration Appeals Commission [SIAC]. During the ensuing proceedings in 1999, the government argued:

The Security Service assesses that while Ur Rehman and his United Kingdom-based followers are unlikely to carry out any acts of violence in this country, his activities directly support terrorism in the Indian subcontinent and are likely to continue unless he is deported. Ur Rehman has also been partly responsible for an increase in the number of Muslims in the United Kingdom who have undergone some form of militant training, including indoctrination into extremist beliefs and at least some basic weapons training. The Security Service is concerned that the presence of returned jihad trainees in the United Kingdom may encourage the radicalisation of the British Muslim community. His activities in the United Kingdom are intended to further the cause of a terrorist organisation abroad.

The Home Secretary also alleged Rehman was a 'personal contact of Mohammed Saeed, the worldwide leader of MDI and LT [Lashkar].'[159] Rehman admitted to attending an MDI conference in Pakistan and to raising funds, but argued the money was for educational and welfare projects in Pakistan and that he was not aware it was used for military operations. The SIAC noted Rehman's statement that he 'sympathised with [Lashkar's] aims' in Kashmir and recognized that he had 'provided sponsorship, information and advice to persons going to Pakistan for the forms of training which may have included militant or extremist training,' but found the authorities had not 'satisfactorily established' he 'knew of the militant content of such training.' It also construed threatening national security to mean promoting or encouraging violence '*targeted* at the United Kingdom, its system of government or its people,' and under such a rubric found that Rehman did not pose such a danger.[160] The SIAC therefore ruled against his deportation. The Home Office won the right to appeal in 2000, a decision which a second appellate court upheld in 2001. In both decisions the appellate courts found that the facts of Rehman's activities in support of MDI were not in dispute and that the SIAC had interpreted national security too narrowly. The case was remitted to the SIAC to determine on the basis of a broader concept of what constituted a threat to national security; one that took into account the ramifications of supporting a known terrorist organization, albeit an organization not targeting the UK directly.[161] However, after winning the right to reengage deportation proceedings against Rehman, the Home Office dropped the case a year later on the grounds that he had 'severed links with terrorist organisations' and thus no longer posed a threat to national security.[162]

When British authorities initially took an interest in Rehman, neither MDI nor Lashkar were illegal entities in the UK. The group was first banned under Britain's Terrorism Act of 2000, although that legislation was not passed until early 2001. Thereafter, the activities of those associated with MDI and Lashkar in the UK merited more serious scrutiny.[163] The British government banned Lashkar (and MDI) because of the group's fundraising operations and as a result of the fact that British Pakistanis were training with it. As one member of the British security services explained, by this time the authorities recognized to a greater degree than in the past that, while many British Pakistanis might only have been undergoing short stints with Lashkar, the connections and indoctrination to which they were exposed could have serious consequences.[164] These consequences are illustrated by briefly recounting details of just a few of the Westerners who passed through Lashkar's camps prior to 9/11.

Dhiren Barot [a.k.a. Abu Eissa al-Hindi], a convert to Islam of Indian origin, grew up in Britain. He trained and fought with Lashkar in Indian-administered Kashmir during the 1990s, and later wrote a book about his experiences.[165] Barot had graduated to al-Qaeda by the end of the decade, making the move primarily because he was enamored with bin Laden's focus on America and believed the ISI was wasting jihadis as cannon fodder in Kashmir. His transition from ISI-sponsored militancy to al-Qaeda would be repeated by a number of Pakistani militants after 9/11. By then Barot already had worked as a trainer in Afghanistan before becoming an overseas al-Qaeda operative, in which capacity he scouted targets in the US from 2000–2001. This reconnaissance was done before 9/11, but was not briefed to al-Qaeda leaders in Pakistan until 2004 by which time the US was a very different and more difficult operating environment.[166] Barot was in the UK by 2004, working on a plan to explode limousines in underground car parks using gas cylinders and to bomb the London underground. Soon after the discovery of his surveillance material in a Pakistani safe house, British police arrested Barot who admitted to conducting the surveillance and to involvement in terrorist plots against the UK.[167]

David Hicks's experience illustrates the ease with which Westerners were able to use Lashkar to connect with al-Qaeda and, once again, that connections existed between the two prior to 9/11. An Australian who traveled to Pakistan in 1999 in search of adventure, Hicks soon found himself among Lashkar recruiters in Lahore. Not long after that he was in the mountains training with the group. Hicks spent several months doing so, before moving on to a madrasa where he studied Arabic and the Quran. Hicks reportedly asked Lashkar for and received a letter of introduction to al-Qaeda. He crossed the border into Afghanistan in January 2001 and presented himself, along with his letter of introduction, to Ibn al-Sheikh al-Libi [born Ali Mohammad al-Fakheri], a senior al-Qaeda member who sent him to the al-Faruq camp.[168] His lawyer confirmed that, while in Afghanistan, Hicks attended three separate training camps and sat in on lectures given by Osama bin Laden.[169] Hicks was captured in Afghanistan after 9/11 and sent to Guantanamo Bay. In 2007 he plead guilty to providing material support for terrorism and was sentenced to a seven year jail term by a military tribunal, with all but nine months suspended. As part of his plea deal Hicks was repatriated to Australia to serve the remaining months of his sentence.[170]

Omar Khyam, a British national of Pakistani descent, also gravitated toward al-Qaeda, but not until after 9/11. He went to Pakistan in 2000 seeking training and soon found himself in Lashkar's camps.[171] There is no telling what role Khyam would have played with Lashkar had he completed the course. His family in Britain was anxious to secure his safe return and, through contacts in Pakistan's Military Intelligence, located him at a Lashkar camp in the mountains. Messages were relayed to commanders at the camp and Khyam agreed to meet his grandfather, who was waiting in the valley below to take him home.[172] His jihadi dreams were deferred, but not for long. Four years later Khyam was arrested for leading a group of homegrown British jihadis known as the 'Crevice Network,' who planned to explode a fertilizer bomb in the UK.[173] By that time he had graduated to working with al-Qaeda and was coordinating his attack plans with one of its high-level operatives in Pakistan.[174]

Lashkar's transnational networks spanned several continents by 9/11, but unlike al-Qaeda it was not using these overseas operatives to launch attacks against the US or its allies. The two outfits shared numerous connections and both embraced a pan-Islamist ideology, but had taken different paths. While al-Qaeda agitated for war against America, Lashkar embraced a jihad that prioritized war against Pakistan's rival, India. Although the reasons for Lashkar's focus on the Kashmir jihad and Pakistan's support for it were not the same, the group and the state found common cause in the fight against India. Lashkar benefited greatly from this arrangement as state assistance allowed it to construct a potent military apparatus and a powerful support infrastructure in Pakistan, including a vast social welfare infrastructure. Yet despite its robust operations in Pakistan and international reach, Lashkar had no significant interests in neighboring Afghanistan. Pakistan's Deobandi groups, on the other hand, had become more enmeshed in the Taliban-al-Qaeda nexus that developed during the 1990s. Al-Qaeda's attacks against America on September 11 irrevocably altered the future of the jihadi movement. The ensuing US counter-attack in Afghanistan also forced the Pakistani government, and hence its militant proxies, to navigate a much more complicated environment.

5

# AL-QAEDA QUEERS THE PITCH

September 11 began as just another day for Lashkar. As occurred with regularity, its militants were engaged in firefights with Indian security forces.[1] On the day al-Qaeda launched the deadliest ever terrorist attacks against America, Lt. Gen Mahmud Ahmed, the Director-General of the ISI, was on Capitol Hill in Washington, DC deflecting US entreaties to persuade the Taliban to hand over Osama bin Laden. The day after the attacks, US Deputy Secretary of State Richard Armitage summoned General Ahmed and Pakistani Ambassador Maleeha Lodhi. Foreshadowing the speech US President George W. Bush planned to give later that night, Armitage told General Ahmed and Ambassador Lodhi that Pakistan was either with America or with al-Qaeda.[2] Armitage and Secretary of State Colin Powell compiled a list of what the US demanded from Pakistan, which was presented to General Ahmed on 13 September. By the afternoon Pervez Musharraf, who had taken power in a bloodless military coup in 1999 and assumed the office of the presidency in summer 2001, had agreed to American demands. The US embassy in Islamabad reconfirmed Musharraf's agreement the following day, but added that Musharraf had indicated he would pay a domestic cost and needed to show Pakistan would benefit from the decision.[3] The Clinton Administration had taken a tough line with Pakistan throughout the 1990s, including the imposition of additional sanctions, and the country was in its fourth year of recession by 2001. Musharraf requested an end to sanctions as well as immediate economic relief. Within weeks the Bush Administration lifted sanctions on Pakistan and began channeling aid to the country.[4]

Backing the Taliban had been a cornerstone of Pakistan's regional security policy in the 1990s and was driven by the hope that it would provide a secure western border and strategic depth against India. Pakistan used Taliban-controlled territory in Afghanistan to run training camps for Deobandi militants fighting in Indian-administered Kashmir. Many of these militants were also fighting alongside the Taliban against the Northern Alliance for control of Afghanistan. When Musharraf gathered together his corps commanders to discuss the American ultimatum, several of them raised serious objections to aligning with the US. They argued that 'dumping the Taliban' would not only have dangerous domestic consequences, but would also send a 'negative message' to the jihadis fighting in Indian-administered Kashmir.[5] Their argument suggested that geopolitical and domestic concerns militated against abandoning the Taliban.

Musharraf countered that the consequences of allying against America overruled these concerns. He claims to have simulated a war game immediately after General Ahmed reported his conversation with Armitage. Even with its nuclear arsenal, there was no way Pakistan could prevail in a military conflict against the United States. Musharraf also argued India would be the major beneficiary of a Pakistani decision to stand by the Taliban since the US would accept help from New Delhi, which had already offered bases for an American counter-attack. An Indo-American alliance could result in Pakistan being declared a terrorist state and enable India to 'gain a golden opportunity with regard to Kashmir.' Musharraf feared this could lead the US to target Pakistan's nuclear arsenal, and he was loathe to lose the deterrent capability the country had achieved vis-à-vis India through its acquisition of nuclear weapons.[6] As Ahmed Rashid wrote, Pakistan's concept of national security at the time rested on three pillars: 'resisting Indian hegemony in the region and promoting the Kashmir cause; protecting and developing the nuclear program; and promoting a pro-Pakistan government in Afghanistan.'[7] Musharraf chose to sacrifice the Taliban in the hopes that doing so would protect the Kashmir jihad and Pakistan's nuclear deterrent. However, this 'sacrifice' was a temporary one. The Musharraf regime provided safe haven and other support to the Taliban after the successful American invasion, which contributed heavily to the latter's ability to mount an insurgency against US and Coalition forces during the ensuring years. No evidence suggests the US gave the Musharraf regime any guarantees with regards to the Kashmir jihad at the time. However, the cooperation Pakistan agreed to provide did not include action against those militants focused on fighting in Indian-administered Kashmir or attacking India, save to keep them from traveling to Afghanistan to support the Taliban.[8] America's focus in the near-term was on al-Qaeda and the Taliban, unless the latter agreed to hand over bin Laden and his associates. Musharraf claimed to have saved the Kashmir jihad from American interference and signaled that it would continue.[9] The Pakistani government distinguished the so-called freedom fighters of Kashmir from al-Qaeda and other foreign elements.[10] Although US President George W. Bush drew a rhetorical line in the sand between those who were with America and those aligned with al-Qaeda, the US did not immediately demand that Pakistan dismantle the militant groups it had nurtured. This was despite the fact that some of the same groups the Musharraf regime was protecting were deploying their fighters to battle US forces. Complicating matters was the fact that although the ISI had been directed to quit Afghanistan after 9/11, some of its officers also remained there to fight alongside the Taliban and the Pakistani jihadis allied with it.[11]

Lashkar's primary focus was Indian-administered Kashmir, and so Musharraf's decision to protect that front aligned with the group's priorities. The group also had no particular loyalty to the Taliban government or interests in Afghanistan. But, as detailed in the previous chapter, it did have significant interests in Pakistan that could be used as leverage against it. This contrasted with the Deobandi outfits, which had significant interests in Afghanistan and enjoyed robust relations with the Taliban. However, the US counter-attack understandably angered Lashkar's leaders and cadres, leading to debates within the group over how to respond.

Before examining Lashkar's response in greater detail, it is helpful to explore its pre-9/11 experiences in Afghanistan relative to the Deobandi groups, since this contributed to how these actors responded in the wake of al-Qaeda's attacks against America. Late in the autumn of 1991 the government of Pakistan began pressuring foreign fighters to leave the region, leading many of the Arab fighters who had come to wage jihad against Afghanistan to disperse. The degeneration of the Afghan jihad against the Soviets into infighting among the various mujahideen factions contributed to the exodus of foreign fighters, who had no desire to be party to Muslim-on-Muslim violence. Osama bin Laden decamped to Sudan where he established al-Qaeda's headquarters, though he continued to support militants in Afghanistan and Pakistan.[12] The Taliban movement had not yet activated when bin Laden left Afghanistan, hence he had no existing ties with its leadership when he returned in 1996. By this time the Taliban had already been fighting for almost two years against the Northern Alliance and various warlords, but had yet to conquer the capital city of Kabul. Osama initially found lodging in Jalalabad with one of the mujahideen factions, which was not a major contender for national power in Afghanistan. Yet the Taliban was clearly in the ascendancy, and after it took control of Jalalabad and then Kabul in September 1996 bin Laden sought to cement his ties with the movement. He was increasing his anti-American rhetoric by this time, and in March 1997 Taliban leader Mullah Mohammad Omar 'invited' bin Laden to relocate to Kandahar. This was done under the auspices of ensuring his security, but was more likely a means of keeping bin Laden close and under control.[13]

Following the Taliban's rise to power, it allowed numerous other jihadi outfits to establish training camps in Afghanistan as well. Many of the foreigners training in Afghanistan during late-1990s were rigid Salafis for whom Deobandi Islam was anathema and they looked upon their Taliban hosts with disdain. A split existed within the Salafi-jihadi movement based in Afghanistan at the time between doctrinaire Salafi ideologues unprepared to make theological compromises and pragmatists ready to overlook doctrinal differences in the interests of furthering the jihad.[14] Al-Qaeda's leadership was and remains in the pragmatists' camp. Although al-Qaeda's senior leadership was willing to overlook doctrinal dis-putes, relations with the Taliban were seriously strained owing to bin Laden's preoccupation with jihad against America. Interna-tional pressure and sanctions imposed on the Taliban led some of its leaders to argue for expelling bin Laden, or possibly handing him over to the Saudis.[15] While tensions remained through the end of the decade, many al-Qaeda-trained militants fought alongside the Tali-ban against the Northern Alliance and bin Laden's organization also contributed its own elite unit known as the 055 Brigade.

However, the largest collection of foreign fighters within the Tali-ban's ranks came from Pakistan, with estimates ranging as high as 7,000 by 2001.[16] A sizeable number came from Deobandi madaris in Pakistan, several of which had graduated the Taliban movement's leaders. Some madaris cancelled classes for extended periods of time and sent their entire student body into combat alongside the Taliban.[17] Some of these students were also connected to various Deobandi militant groups or the JUI, the Deobandi political party to which many of these militants groups traced their roots. A break-down of 109 Pakistani prisoners captured fighting with the Taliban by the Northern Alliance revealed that of those held between Octo-ber 1999 and March 2000, 51 were from the Harkat-ul-Mujahideen and 49 were from the JUI. Only 33 of 109 identified were Pashtun, indicating that support extended beyond ethnic solidarity.[18]

Fighting the Northern Alliance was a right of passage for many of the militants graduating from training camps in Taliban-con-trolled territory and doing so was compulsory for those belonging to Pakistan's Deobandi outfits according to several Pakistani inter-locutors. The ISI moved some training facilities for militants fight-ing in the Kashmir jihad to Afghanistan after the Taliban took power, and as mentioned a number of foreign jihadi groups estab-lished camps there as well. Al-Qaeda initially operated some camps while supporting others, which enabled bin Laden to build his base and cherry-pick the small number of recruits officially asked to join his organization.[19] For example, the ISI persuaded the Taliban to give al-Qaeda control of the al-Badr camps, which it earlier had handed over to Harkat-ul-Ansar [the group formed when Harkat-ul-Mujahideen and HuJI merged]. HuA militants as well as those from the sectarian Lashkar-e-Jhangvi continued to train there.[20] Some of the militants killed when the US launched cruise missile strikes against al-Badr in 1998 following al-Qaeda's attack against two US embassies in East Africa belonged to Harkat-ul-Ansar, which by this time was again calling itself Harkat-ul-Mujahideen.[21]

Bin Laden's relationship with Maulana Fazl-ur Rehman Khalil, who led HuM, stretched back to the war against the Soviets.[22] Despite their differing Islamic schools of thought, HuM became notoriously close with al-Qaeda because of their shared training experience.[23] After being displaced by Lashkar as the premier Pakistani proxy in Indian-administered Kashmir, HuM became even more enmeshed in the Taliban's war against the Northern Alliance and with al-Qaeda. Khalil was a founding member of bin Laden's International Islamic Front for Jihad Against the Jews and Crusaders. He was also one of the signatories to the 1998 fatwa issued by the International Islamic Front calling for attacks on Americans at home and abroad.[24] This affinity toward al-Qaeda carried over to Jaish-e-Mohammad after it split from HuM.[25] During its short lifespan before 9/11, JeM was very active in Afghanistan in addition to its activities in Indian-administered Kashmir. Because cadres moved back and forth among the Deobandi groups, this increased the personal connections among the groups themselves as well as between them and al-Qaeda.

Lashkar's cadres were never as portable as those from the Deobandi groups, meaning they did not move back and forth as frequently between different outfits, though some members did leave to join the Taliban. From an organizational leadership perspective, the group's leaders were less willing than al-Qaeda's to overlook doctrinal disputes. Several Lashkar members made clear to the author their disdain for adherents of Deobandi Islam and Zafar Iqbal, one of Lashkar's founders and the head of its education department, once referred to the Taliban as 'a group of misguided elements' and suggested his organization had 'higher ideal[s] than them.'[26] This does not mean that Lashkar had no relations with the Taliban, and its fighters did cooperate with those from the Deobandi groups on the ground in Indian-administered Kashmir. But these were ad hoc alliances. Outside of the Kashmir theater the sectarian divide between the Ahl-e-Hadith Lashkar and the Deobandis hindered close cooperation. Indeed Lashkar's cadres were training at the al-Badr camps when the Taliban originally handed them over to Harkat-ul-Ansar, but sectarian antagonism forced it to shift many of them elsewhere.[27] Further, Lashkar's strongest Afghan connections remained to Kunar and Nuristan provinces. Gulbuddin Hekmatyar's Hizb-e-Islami had driven Lashkar's former patron Jamil al-Rahman out of Kunar. In 1996 the Taliban defeated the Hizb-e-Islami and claimed dominion over Kunar province. However, the local Salafis did not recognize its right to rule and rejected the Deobandi Taliban on theological grounds. One scholar described Kunar as the place where 'the people resent the Qandahari ascendance [of the Taliban] almost as much as Uzbeks, Tajiks, and Shi'a Hazaras do.'[28] Many of the local Salafis in Kunar converged with some of the mujahideen factions in the Northern Alliance to fight against the Taliban. Ultimately an accommodation was reached whereby the Taliban kept a wali, or regional governor, nearby, but did not gain control of the province.[29]

Despite their animosity toward the Taliban, the Salafis in Kunar were on good terms with al-Qaeda, as was Lashkar. Bin Laden had helped some of the Saudis who came to Kunar during the Afghan jihad to establish bases in Kunar, and as mentioned in Chapter 1 some of these Arabs later joined al-Qaeda.[30] The Saudis in Kunar also worked with Jamiat al-Dawa al-Quran wal-Sunna, which gave early support to the Markaz al-Dawa wal-Irshad and helped to train Lashkar recruits in the early 1990s. Later in the decade al-Qaeda and Lashkar shared a logistician: Abu Zubayda vetted recruits for both organizations, and, it should be noted, for other Pakistani outfits too.[31] Zubayda was based in Peshawar where he screened trainees and made logistical arrangements for their travel to Afghanistan. According to the 9/11 Commission's report, he had an 'agreement with bin Laden to conduct reciprocal recruiting efforts whereby promising trainees at the camps could be invited to join al Qaeda.'[32] Lashkar militants trained at camps that were under al-Qaeda's control and which allegedly were run in cooperation with the ISI.[33]

Although Lashkar had good relations with al-Qaeda, it had no major assets in Afghanistan and was not particularly close to the Taliban. The Deobandi groups, however, had deep ties to the Taliban. In addition to historic relations forged via the same madaris, Deobandi militants from Pakistan spilled blood alongside their Taliban brethren on the Afghan battlefield against the Northern Alliance. The Taliban also protected various Deobandi militants from the Pakistani authorities at times. For example, when Sipah-e-Sahaba Pakistan experienced a crackdown in 1998 following its massacre of hundreds of Shia, some of the group's leaders fled to Kabul where the Taliban offered sanctuary.[34] Finally, the Deobandi groups had significant assets in Afghanistan. JeM's Maulana Azhar spent much of his time in Kandahar, while HuJI had its central secretariat in Kabul and Kandahar. In addition to contributing foot solders to the Taliban, the Deobandi groups also had members serving in the Taliban administration. HuJI contributed three government ministers and twenty-two judges to the Taliban's administration and its amir, Qari Saifullah Akhtar, served as an adviser to Mullah Mohammad Omar.[35] Given their deep ties to the Taliban and vested interests in the Islamic Emirate of Afghanistan, it is not surprising that militants from all of the Deobandi outfits fought against the US counter-attack in the wake of 9/11.

Scattered reports suggest some Lashkar militants may have been involved in battles against the US during the early days of the American invasion, though not necessarily as a Taliban ally. Circumstances surrounding many of the engagements at the time are opaque, but one Pakistani journalist who was covering the war believes skirmishes with US forces occurred as Lashkar fighters were withdrawing from Afghanistan.[36] A high-ranking JuD official told the author there was a division within Lashkar after 9/11 over how to respond, an assessment supported by several local interlocutors following the group at the time.[37] Some in the organization believed the Pakistani government was a puppet of the Americans and that Lashkar should wage a jihad against both. Others continued to prioritize the fight against India, and argued for maintaining a relationship with the state to wage jihad against their common enemy. Ultimately the leadership made the decision not to attack

Pakistan or commit cadres to the Afghan theater. However, the JuD official admitted that differences persisted within the organization regarding waging a jihad against America and Pakistan, and that the debate became polarized over time.[38] Further, some members did leave to fight alongside the Taliban, though they did not always break from the group completely and often were welcomed back into the Lashkar-fold. As ensuing chapters will illustrate, the practice of attempting to accommodate those who did not toe the leadership's line may have helped to keep the organization intact, but it also contributed to factionalization within it.

Lashkar's public communications in the wake of 9/11 evinced its inner conflict, though they also likely reflect an organization trying to have it both ways. The group actually issued a statement the day after the 9/11 attacks claiming, 'The attacks on the World Trade Centre and other places were not an act of terrorism but an Islamic duty.'[39] Lashkar backtracked almost immediately and later that day then-Lashkar spokesperson Abdullah Muntazir [the JuD spokesperson for international media at the time this book was written] categorically denied the group ever issued such a statement and refuted any report alleging it had.[40] The next day, Yahya Mujahid, who headed MDI's Public Relations Department and was Lashkar's lead spokesperson, said the report was part of a propaganda campaign by *Agence France-Presse* and *CNN* to malign the group. He asserted that not only was Lashkar exclusively focused on fighting to liberate Indian-administered Kashmir, but that it also never targeted civilians. Mujahid expressed Lashkar's regret for the loss of lives and property in the attacks.[41] Saeed reinforced this message two months later, stating 'We may differ with US policy, and that is our right, but we do not mean any harm to any US citizen or property.'[42]

Saeed was sending mixed messages however. He became a high profile spokesman in the public campaign against the US run by the Pak-Afghan Defence Council, which had been founded the previous December to protest UN-supported sanctions against the Taliban. Saeed warned the West that it would face the 'cohesive strength of the Muslims,' exhorted his countrymen to prepare for jihad against the enemy forces and saluted the Afghans for protecting bin Laden.[43] An MDI mufti, Abdur Rehman al-Rahmani, went further and issued a fatwa decreeing that the entire umma, especially Pakistan, was obliged to support bin Laden and Afghanistan against an American attack. It stated that a US invasion would be the beginning of a war between Islam and the kuffaar in which all Muslim states were required to fight. Asserting that Pakistan's raison d'être was the protection of Islam, it warned that if Pakistan's leaders sided with America then 'they would be treated as rebels of Allah.'[44] For all its impassioned rhetoric during the ensuing months, however, Lashkar's focus remained fighting against India. Three days after the 9/11 attacks Saeed pledged the Pakistani people would not abandon the Afghans in the 'present hour of trial and would fully stand behind them.'[45] Then, a week later, he denied Lashkar was shifting its fighters to Afghanistan and instead promised to carry the jihad further inside India.[46] As it turned out, JeM militants delivered the next strike to the Indian hinterland.

On 13 December 2001 gunmen infiltrated the grounds of Parliament House in New Delhi. Although the Rajya Sabha and Lok Sabha [the Upper and Lower Houses, respectively] were adjourned, many Members of Parliament and other government officials were still in the building. All of them escaped alive, but five policemen, a security guard and a gardener were killed, as were five Jaish militants. India initially accused JeM and Lashkar based on confessions obtained from several co-conspirators, but the Indian Supreme Court later ruled these confessions were inadmissible because they were obtained improperly.[47] All of those later convicted in India belonged to JeM, and in 2004 General Javed Ashraf Qazi (Retd), a former director-general of the ISI, publicly blamed it for the attack.[48] It is possible Lashkar or elements associated with the group provided assistance, but all of those known to be involved belonged to JeM and the attack is generally considered to be a Jaish-operation.

It does not appear that the leadership in the Pakistani government or military sanctioned the operation. Senior US officials who were interviewed several years later for a report on the crisis that developed following the Parliament attack doubted Musharraf would have risked war with India or complicating his burgeoning post-9/11 relationship with Washington.[49] Based on telephone calls made by the attackers prior to the assault, a senior level ISI official is believed to have authorized the operation.[50] One Pakistani reporter who investigated the attack asserted that the Brigadier General who handled militant groups in India-controlled Kashmir for the ISI gave the go-ahead.[51] Musharraf was reportedly furious about the attack because he knew it could mean a showdown either with India or the jihadi proxies he was working so hard to protect.[52] Because of a policy in which proxies and their ISI handlers operated without critical oversight in order to maintain plausible deniability, red lines could be crossed unintentionally. Thus, though Musharraf does not appear to have ordered the attacks, the policy of maintaining proxies and devolving decision-making created the conditions in which they occurred. Such a situation would repeat itself in later years.

The Parliament attack ruptured the peace process between India and Pakistan, and set the two countries on the path to war. They also cracked the wall that Musharraf had attempted to build between the Kashmir jihad and the global war on terrorism. Having been forced to contend with Pakistani jihadi groups for many years, India now sought to tie those outfits to America's 'War on Terror.' New Delhi moved to cast the Kashmir issue as solely one of combating terrorism, and argued it had just as much a right to pursue militants from Pakistan as the US did to pursue al-Qaeda. Further, it used the American response of strikes against al-Qaeda as well as its hosts to buttress its case against Pakistan. In a demarche to Pakistan's High Commissioner to India Ashraf Jehangir Qazi, New Delhi demanded that Pakistan crack down on all Lashkar and JeM activities, arrest the groups' leaders and freeze their financial assets.[53]

India also launched a massive military mobilization known as Operation Parakram. Skyrocketing India-Pakistan tensions threatened to escalate into a war between two nuclear powers, and immediately hampered American efforts in Afghanistan. The Taliban had formally surrendered the week prior to the attacks, but fighting raged on. In particular, the al-Qaeda leadership and hundreds of hardened militants were holed up at Tora Bora. The small number of US Special Forces operators on the ground were directing massive air assaults against the militants at Tora Bora, including Osama bin Laden. But the US did not have enough troops in the Afghan theater to head off militants fleeing across the Durand Line and so Pakistani soldiers were being called on to seal the border. Forces from the Pakistan Frontier Corps were near Tora Bora on the Pakistani side of the border, but not nearly in sufficient strength to carry out the job assigned to them.[54] The Parliament attack occurred just as additional troops from the Pakistan army were moving into position. As India went on a war footing and massed troops along the border, the additional Pakistani forces intended to reinforce the Pakistan-Afghan border were deployed instead to the eastern border with India. Musharraf has claimed that Pakistani forces arrested more than 200 militants retreating from Tora Bora.[55] Yet many more escaped in the days after the Parliament attack, possibly including Osama bin Laden.[56] According to the aforementioned report, which recounted US efforts to manage the crisis, substantial roundups of al-Qaeda operatives occurred along the Afghanistan border in late December. However, similar dragnets did not take place for another two years following the redeployment of Pakistani troops.[57]

Because India's war-fighting doctrine at the time called for a major troop build-up, this provided Pakistan time to respond in kind. A dangerous game of brinkmanship ensued as the two countries engaged in what became the biggest military concentration along their border in years. However, the time it took India to mass troops also provided a window of opportunity for the international community to become involved and push for a diplomatic solution. Whether or not this was New Delhi's intention remains an open question. US assessments at the time were divided between those who believed war was likely and those who viewed the respective mobilizations as intended to achieve a negotiated outcome. Neither country's leadership wanted war. But nor was India prepared to stand down without a public shift in Pakistan's policy of supporting militant proxies. Further, even a military mobilization launched for negotiating reasons brought with it the risk of unintended escalation. This was a major concern among US policymakers who sought to shape a diplomatic outcome that would avert war and enable Pakistan to refocus on assisting American efforts in Afghanistan.[58]

US officials began pressuring the Musharraf regime to take concrete steps toward affecting such a shift, including action against Lashkar and Jaish. The US government already had classified HuM as a terrorist group in the 1990s. Several weeks after 9/11 it froze HuM's financial assets in accordance with Executive Order 13224, which also prohibited transactions with those who commit, threaten or support terrorism.[59] Pakistan's central bank quickly followed suit, and Pakistan officially banned the group in November.[60] In October Washington implemented a similar freeze on Jaish's assets, in large measure because of its support for the Taliban and al-Qaeda. The US government finally took this same action against Lashkar on 20 December, a week after the Parliament attack.[61] In response, Pakistan's central bank also ordered Lashkar's assets frozen.[62] By this time, the government had technically banned all militant groups from collecting donations for jihad from the public as well.[63] Anticipating asset seizures by the Pakistani authorities, Lashkar, Jaish and HuM withdrew their funds and invested them in legal ventures. Sources within the militant outfits confirmed this action, and Pakistani intelligence officials admitted no money was in their respective bank accounts by the time each was frozen.[64] While Lashkar was not the only group whose assets slipped through the slow-moving hand of the state, it was the richest jihadi organization in Pakistan and invested on a wider scale than the others: in agricultural land and legal businesses, including commodity trading, real estate and the production of consumer goods.[65] Even had the asset freeze been successful, it was not going to diffuse the crisis and America pressured Musharraf to ban Lashkar and Jaish.[66] On 26 December the US designated both outfits as Foreign Terrorist Organizations, meaning that Pakistan's continued backing of them was tantamount to state support for terrorism.[67] The Musharraf regime accepted the need to take similar action, but Pakistan was not prepared to part with its proxies.

Lashkar was forewarned that it would soon be banned, and engineered a split with MDI. According to the press release issued the day after the split, Lashkar was now strictly a 'Kashmiri militant organization' and its newly elected leader was Maulana Abdul Wahid al-Kashmiri who would head the General Council with Zaki-ur Rehman Lakhvi as the Supreme Commander.[68] At a press conference announcing the split, Saeed declared that Lashkar was no longer active in Pakistan, having shifted all of its offices and activities to Pakistan-administered Kashmir.[69] In addition, MDI was dissolved and replaced by the Jamaat-ul-Dawa [JuD]. This was the organization Hafiz Saeed originally founded in 1985 and it still existed as a registered charity.[70] Saeed resigned as Lashkar's amir and assumed control of JuD, which the press release referred to as an 'organization for preaching of Islam, politics, [and] social work.' It promised to 'continue to work for the support of refugees and freedom fighters and countering Indian propaganda.'[71] Yahya Mujahid, who was one of the original founders of MDI and became a spokesman for JuD, asserted at the time, 'we handed Lashkar-e-Taiba over to the Kashmiris in December 2001. Now we have no contact with any jihadi organization. We, the Jamaat-ul-Dawa, are only preachers.'[72]

In reality, the separation was entirely cosmetic as was the name change. JuD's spokesperson for international media Abdullah Muntazir admitted that MDI and JuD were one and the same saying, 'only the word Markaz was replaced with Jamaat, otherwise it's the same organization.'[73] Hafiz Saeed, Zafar Iqbal, Hafiz Abdul Rehman Makki and Zaki-ur Rehman Lahkvi remained in charge, with al-Kashmiri as a quasi-figurehead. Further, Lakhvi and al-Kashmiri were both on the JuD 'executive board,' which met to decide high-level policy.[74] The departments and organizational structure remained unchanged. The purpose of the split and name change was to remove the state's legal ability, and hence its legal obligation, to go after the organization's assets. A high-ranking JuD official close to Saeed admitted the separation was undertaken at the ISI's direction in order to create this loophole.[75] Whereas MDI had been overtly geared toward supporting Lashkar's jihad, however, with JuD this was more covert. Although MDI had its own operations and networks, its identity was as Lashkar's political and social welfare wing. Despite playing essentially the same role, JuD constructed a more independent identity for itself. Much of this had to do with the fact that Hafiz Saeed, who had always been the public face of Lashkar, was ostensibly disconnected from it after 2002. Whenever he appeared in public or spoke to the press, which was quite often, it was as the leader of JuD. At many of these appearances Saeed connected JuD—sometimes tacitly and often overtly—to Lashkar's jihad against India as well as calling for jihad against the US and Israel at times.

President Musharraf formally proscribed Lashkar and Jaish on 12 January during a nationally televised address.[76] He pledged that Pakistan would not allow its territory to be used for any terrorist activity anywhere in the world, but used language that failed to include Pakistan-administered Kashmir, which had never been incorporated into the country and technically retained its own government. Musharraf also promised that henceforth his country would back only indigenous Kashmiri militant groups, which he stated must purge all non-Kashmiri members.[77] Recall that, only weeks earlier, JuD claimed—falsely—that Lashkar-e-Taiba had been handed over to the Kashmiris and its infrastructure moved to Pakistan-controlled Kashmir. During his speech, Musharraf also promised that no organization would be allowed to call itself Lashkar, Jaish or Sipah in Pakistan any longer. Technically, he was correct. Within a month, the ISI was quietly encouraging many of the banned groups to reconstitute themselves under new names.[78] Lashkar-e-Taiba became Pasban-e-Ahl-e-Hadith (also technically separate from the above-ground JuD), Jaish-e-Mohammad renamed itself Khuddam-ul-Islam and a JeM splinter faction emerged under the name Jamaat-ul-Furqan. Sipah-e-Sahaba Pakistan officially became Millat-e-Islamiyah Pakistan and Harkat-ul-Mujahideen changed its name to Jamiat ul-Ansar. All of these groups continued to operate and are generally still referred to by their original names, a practice this book follows.

Despite his ostensible separation from Lashkar, Pakistani police detained Saeed on 30 December, having done the same with JeM amir Maulana Azhar five days earlier. Pakistani authorities claimed both men were detained for making inflammatory speeches to incite people to violate law and order, though the actions clearly had been meant to mollify India.[79] Saeed was released in late March, when the Lahore High Court denied an appeal to extend his detention.[80] Following Musharraf's January speech, the police detained thousands more militants and closed hundreds of offices.[81] According to the author's Pakistani interlocutors, within several months almost all of those caught up in the post-ban dragnet were allowed to seep back out onto the street.[82] The federal government failed to bring charges against those detained and even pushed the provincial authorities to release anyone who agreed to dissociate himself from militancy.[83] By the time the government began sealing militant groups' offices, these outfits had already moved their official operations to Pakistan-administered Kashmir at the direction of the army and ISI.[84]

This was a potential inflection point. Many militant outfits lost fighters in Afghanistan, where the US routed the Taliban more quickly than expected. Pakistan had become a key US ally against al-Qaeda and was beginning to reap the rewards of this alliance in the form of aid and debt relief. If ever there was a time to demobilize its proxies, this was it. Instead, the Musharraf regime chose to divide its so-called good jihadis from the bad. Pakistan would crack down on al-Qaeda and sectarian groups engaged in domestic terrorism, but maintain jihadi groups like Lashkar as assets for the country's regional strategy against India. Islamabad's double game had begun. However, Pakistan's proxies were not prepared to play by its rules.

# PART III

6

# GOOD JIHADI/BAD JIHADI

Al-Qaeda's attack against America altered the militant landscape in Pakistan and the subsequent assault against India's Parliament in December 2001 allowed New Delhi to invoke the US response to 9/11, arguing it had a similar right to pursue any terrorist outfits that had attacked it and to hold their state sponsors accountable. As India massed troops along the border, Pakistan responded by doing the same. This created immediate complications for US efforts in Afghanistan, while war threatened to destabilize South Asia. American and Indian pressure on Pakistan was severe, and the Musharraf regime was forced to ban Lashkar and several other outfits in January 2002. The Markaz al-Dawa wal-Irshad was renamed Jamaat-ul-Dawa, which was technically separated from the now banned Lashkar. This enabled the group to protect its assets, but the operating environment it faced was nonetheless a more challenging one than it had enjoyed only months earlier.

Life after the ban was not as easy for any of Pakistan's jihadi groups as it had been beforehand. Fundraising, recruitment and training were restricted to different degrees for different outfits, but none got off scot-free if only because these activities could no longer be carried out as overtly as hitherto. However, the Musharraf regime had no plans to dismantle all of Pakistan's proxies. As part of what has become known as Pakistan's 'double game,' militant outfits were categorized as 'good jihadis' that were covertly supported for continued use as proxies and 'bad jihadis' that were cracked down on more harshly. This was not a purely binomial division. Assessments and treatment existed on a spectrum, meaning some 'good jihadis' were treated better than others and some 'bad jihadis' cracked down on more harshly. Categorization was based on the threats that a group posed to the state and the utility it continued to offer. The focus here is on Pakistani militant outfits. Treatment of and support for the Taliban is discussed in the following chapter. However, it is important to note that although the Musharraf regime helped to rehabilitate the Taliban, its willingness to side with the US was viewed as a betrayal of it by many of Pakistan's jihadis. Thus, the Deobandi groups, which had close ties to the Taliban, were suspect as a result of these relationships.

In addition to targeting al-Qaeda and other foreign militants aligned with it, the Musharraf regime cracked down forcefully on the sectarian Lashkar-e-Jhangvi. It had become a serious challenge to domestic order as well as an embarrassment to the state and the security services employed various measures against LeJ, including arrests, assassinations, and aggravated inter-group massacres.[1] Not surprisingly, this pressure fractured the organization. Many of its members turned against the state, strengthened their ties with al-Qaeda and became involved in many terrorist plots in Pakistan. Some outfits that had been active in Indian-administered Kashmir also came under state pressure, though not to the same degree as al-Qaeda or LeJ. Harkat-ul-Jihad-al-Islami, which was particularly close to the Taliban regime, was put under strict surveillance and many of its cadres were detained at various times. While HuJI's Azad Kashmir chapter was allowed to remain active in Indian-administered Kashmir, its camps were raided on numerous occasions and some of its militants turned against the state.

The 'good jihadis' included Lashkar, Jaish-e-Mohammad and Harkat-ul-Mujahideen as well as other smaller Kashmir-centric groups. JeM and HuM were suspect because of their ties to the Taliban and were not allowed to be as active as they had been, but nor were they cracked down on too harshly. However, Pakistan's selectivity with regard to JeM and HuM overlooked the fact that Deobandi cadres were portable owing to their common history. While the leaders of both outfits did not break with the state, their continued relationship with a government that had betrayed the Taliban to side with the US led many members to break ranks and form their own more extreme outfits.

HuM was already weakened by the time of the 9/11 attacks, having lost much of its infrastructure and manpower to JeM. It was weakened further after 9/11 when the group lost its infrastructure in Afghanistan along with a number of its remaining cadres during the US counter-attack. The organization split when some members left to form Harkat-ul-Mujahideen-al-Alami (Alami means 'international') in response to the leadership's unwillingness to break ties with the state. JeM was the largest and best-funded Deobandi group fighting in Indian-administered Kashmir by the time of the 9/11 attacks. But it was a new group, organizationally fractious, with a weak ideological foundation. As early as October 2001, JeM gunmen were targeting Westerners and Christians inside Pakistan in retaliation for the US counter-attack in Afghanistan.[2] Its leader, Maulana Azhar, is believed to have expelled some of those who were involved in the October 2001 attacks in order to avoid his own arrest.[3] In response to this action, as well as Azhar's general willingness to continue working with the army and ISI, many Jaish members left and joined those who were expelled to form the splinter group Jamaat-ul-Furqan. Both the HuM and JeM splinters suffered harsh reprisals at the hands of the security services.

Lashkar was the most reliable in Islamabad's eyes and fared the best. To begin with, it benefited from stronger connections to Pakistan's army, ISI and civil service than other groups. Several journalists pointed out that, in addition to having recruited retired army and ISI officers into its ranks, Lashkar members had family in the middle ranks of the army and various civilian security agencies. Thus, the group was better connected than any other militant outfit.[4] It also had no strong allegiance to the Taliban and therefore was viewed as less of a threat to the state. According to one former senior official in the Intelligence Bureau, the government ordered Lashkar not to side with the Taliban in the immediate aftermath of 9/11. When it complied, this reinforced the perception that it was an obedient and reliable proxy.[5] Finally, Lashkar's leadership shared Musharraf's India-centric priorities and the group remained

Pakistan's most potent proxy. One Western diplomat stationed in Pakistan went so far as to suggest the Musharraf regime would have sacrificed the other outfits if necessary in order to protect Lashkar because of its utility against India.[6] The result was that, as a former high-ranking ISI official explained, 'because Lashkar responded differently [than the Deobandi groups] in the post-9/11 environment it was treated differently,'[7] But Lashkar was playing a double game of its own.

Just as the Musharraf regime's policy vis-à-vis militancy was nuanced after 9/11, so too was Lashkar's. The group's leadership continued to prioritize India as the main enemy, making it easier to reconcile the decision to maintain a relationship with the state. This also provided the group an opportunity to expand its own influence over the long term; an approach that argued for patience. But impulses within the organization to contribute to the jihad against America and its allies were impossible to ignore.

This chapter examines Lashkar's behavior from 2002–2005, looking at its 'good jihadi' and 'bad jihadi' activities respectively. A note on this choice of terminology is warranted. Though typically used to denote Pakistan's preferences regarding its various proxies, the terms 'good jihadi' and 'bad jihadi' are used here to denote those aspects of Lashkar's behavior that aligned with state interests (providing social services and waging a controlled jihad against India) and those that were anti-statist (contributing to the jihad against America and its allies as well as possibly participating in attacks against Pakistani officials). Before assessing Lashkar's behavior, it is important to explore in greater detail the evolving environment in which it was operating at the time.

In addition to banning several outfits after the Parliament attack, the Musharraf regime also temporarily clamped down on cross-LoC activity. Heavy US pressure contributed to these steps and helped to avert a war between India and Pakistan. According to one Indian account, New Delhi pulled back forces preparing to launch a limited incursion into Pakistan-administered Kashmir in early January after US officials provided evidence of Pakistan's efforts along the LoC.[8] The redeployment of Pakistani troops from the Afghan front to the border with India during this time period also closed the window that existed for a low-cost incursion. American officials also sought to persuade India of the importance of Musharraf's January 2002 speech. Although Indian Prime Minister Vajpayee remained reluctant to initiate a wider conflict, New Delhi remained skeptical and the Indian military continued to prepare for war with Pakistan.[9] The Indian government rebuffed Musharraf's proposal to resume talks on Kashmir, insisting that Pakistan cease its support for militancy as a precondition for any resumption of dialogue.[10] Because infiltrations typically increased in the spring when the snow melted, New Delhi was intent on waiting to see whether Musharraf's early efforts had staying power.[11] Meanwhile, both sides maintained troop deployments along the border.

US officials understood that it would take time for Musharraf to fulfill his promises vis-à-vis decreasing support for militancy in Kashmir.[12] However, an incremental approach hinged upon Pakistan's actual willingness to make forward progress. Instead, those groups that were banned after the Parliament attack had quickly reinvented themselves under new names. The ISI had directed Lashkar and other outfits on the steps they should take in order to protect their assets. It also encouraged attacks in Indian-administered Kashmir in order to 'resuscitate morale among the jihadi groups and to show that the army had not abandoned them.'[13] Indian officials asserted that the number of militants infiltrating across the LoC in March and April was roughly the same as in the previous two years. According to a *New York Times* report filed on 13 May, Indian officials also alleged that approximately 2,000 militants remained spread out along the Pakistani side of the LoC. Despite the prospect of a rise in infiltration, the Indian defense minister said at the time that India did not foresee taking military action in the near-term.[14]

A day after that report was filed, Lashkar launched an attack against a passenger bus and an Indian army barracks in the town of Kaluchak, reigniting the crisis. The barracks housed not only Indian military personnel, but also their families. Many of those killed were wives and children of Indian soldiers.[15] New Delhi responded by expelling Pakistan's ambassador and moving its forces to forward positions. Amidst intense exchanges of fire across the LoC, the two countries also redeployed fighter aircraft and began making public statements about their nuclear readiness. Once again the US sought to mediate a solution. Deputy Secretary of State Armitage met President Musharraf in Pakistan in early June, and the latter insisted that 'nothing is happening' along the Line of Control. He had used this language, artfully articulated in the present tense, before and Armitage sought a guarantee that cross-LoC activity would not resume once the crisis had cleared. He secured a pledge from President Musharraf to halt cross-LoC infiltration permanently and, after privately apprising Indian officials of this promise, announced it publicly while in India. It is questionable whether American or Indian officials believed Musharraf would make good on his promise, but it provided a means to de-escalate the situation once again.[16]

Despite the danger Pakistan's proxies posed to regionally stability, the US continued to view tackling the Kashmir jihad as too difficult in the near term. Instead it remained committed to an incremental approach designed to pressure Pakistan to reduce support for militancy over time. Yet a month after making his pledge to Armitage, President Musharraf made clear during an interview with *Newsweek* that his commitment came with an expiration date:

I've told President Bush nothing is happening across the Line of Control. This is the assurance I've given. I'm not going to give you an assurance that for years nothing will happen. We have to have a response from India, a discussion about Kashmir. If you want a guarantee of peace in this region, there are three ways: (1) denuclearize South Asia; (2) ensure a conventional deterrence so that war never takes place in the Subcontinent; (3) find a solution to the Kashmir problem.[17]

In 2003 the government of Pakistan decided to keep alive its strategic assets for use against India and the 'good jihadis' were told they would not be dismantled provided they calibrate their activity in Indian-administered Kashmir per the direction of the state, remove fighting America from their agendas and abstain from attacks within Pakistan.[18] Ambassador to Pakistan Nancy Powell complained publicly in November that jihadi groups were reconstituting themselves under new names. Singling out Lashkar and JeM, Powell said 'These groups pose a serious threat to Pakistan, to the region and to the United States.' Lashkar was widely understood to be operating openly under the JuD banner, while Jaish had reemerged as Khuddam-ul-Islam. In response to US pressure, President Musharraf banned Khuddam-ul-Islam [formerly JeM] along with two sectarian groups, which had reemerged under new names: Millat-e-Islamiyah Pakistan [formerly SSP] and Islami Tehrik Pakistan [formerly Tehrik-e-Jafria, a Shia Party].[19] Several days later Musharraf also banned Jamaat-ul-Furqan [a JeM splinter group], Jamiat-ul-Ansar [formerly HuM] and Hizb-ul-Tahrir, which was previously legal.[20] JuD escaped this second round of bans and was only placed on a government watch list, leaving Lashkar with a legitimate front organization in Pakistan. One member of Pakistan's Anti-Terrorism Force told the author that this owed to its leadership's commitment to adhere to the state's guidelines in exchange for the group being able to 'keep its supply lines open.'[21] A source inside the organization admitted as much, saying the government decided not to ban JuD after the group agreed to keep a low profile 'in line with Pakistan's needs.'[22] Open source accounts support the assertion that Lashkar's willingness to remain India-centric, stay low-key and calibrate its activities in the Kashmir jihad in accordance with ISI direction enabled it to survive the new round of bans.[23] The ISI also reportedly gave Saeed a substantial amount of money in the form of 'severance pay' for agreeing to temper Lashkar's activities in accordance with official directives.[24]

In December 2003 militants from a coterie of outfits, along with rogue members of the Pakistani military, made two attempts on Musharraf's life within the span of a fortnight. Details of the attacks are discussed in the final section of this book. Relevant here is the degree to which the government had lost control over many of its former proxies as well as elements within the armed forces by this time. Several weeks after he escaped assassination, Musharraf met Indian Prime Minister Atal Bihari Vajpayee who visited Islamabad in January to attend the seven-nation South Asian Association for Regional Cooperation summit. At what was intended to be only a courtesy visit with Musharraf, the two men agreed to begin a new round of formal negotiations geared toward achieving peace between their countries. To this end India and Pakistan initiated a composite dialogue process [hereafter the composite dialogue] to settle bilateral issues between them. Afterwards, Musharraf pledged 'not [to] permit any territory under Pakistan's control to be used to support terrorism in any manner.'[25] This was a step beyond his declamation in 2002 when he banned Lashkar, Jaish and others, since the words 'any territory under Pakistan's control' also included Pakistan-administered Kashmir.

Pakistan attempted to demobilize some militants as a means of thinning their ranks in accordance with the country's needs, while others were kept in reserve. By early 2004 many jihadi leaders in Muzaffarabad were 'idling away their time in their, almost empty, offices.' Yet some outfits remained active. According to one HuJI commander, 'Lashkar-e-Taiba, Hizb-ul-Mujahideen and some other [smaller] groups are still busy with their business as usual. But on a smaller scale, and these are being imposed on us as the role models.'[26] Lashkar was not only far more active in Indian-administered Kashmir than any other Pakistani militant outfit by this time, it also retained a greater militant infrastructure. Under US pressure the ISI reportedly closed down many of the training camps in Pakistan-administered Kashmir in 2003, though some of them were relocated elsewhere. Lashkar was the only outfit operating large, territorially-rooted camps in Pakistan-administered Kashmir by 2004.[27]

Most of the militants not allowed to fight in Indian-administered Kashmir were confined to their camps, but rather than remain idle many joined splinter groups or began freelancing. Some of them began making their way to North and South Waziristan in FATA to link up with al-Qaeda and the Taliban, which were regrouping there. This accelerated the process of fragmentation and decentralization among the Deobandi groups that began after 9/11. Over time, their group names—JeM, HuM, HuJI and LeJ—came to mean less from an organizational perspective. These names maintained utility as identity-markers and alerted others to a person's background, but stating someone was from JeM no longer meant he necessarily belonged to the group. This phenomenon was less pronounced for Lashkar. As many interlocutors pointed out, its name still meant something in the way that those of the Deobandi groups no longer did by the middle of the decade.

Lashkar did split briefly in spring 2004, though not because of disagreements over policy as happened with the Deobandi outfits. Rather, the issue was Hafiz Saeed's nepotism, specifically accusations that he was selectively promoting members of his Gujjar caste. Tension over how money was being distributed also factored in the dispute. When Saeed married a woman thirty years his junior who was the widow of a Lashkar martyr, Zafar Iqbal and other members of the leadership council objected, suggesting it was unsuitable for the head of the organization.[28] Iqbal was one of the initial founders of the organization and viewed himself as Saeed's equal. Friction between them was nothing new and Saeed responded by criticizing Iqbal's second marriage to a young Baltistani girl.[29] Tensions escalated and several top leaders, including Iqbal and Lakhvi, split to form Khairun Naas [People's Welfare] taking some of Lashkar's senior commanders with them.[30] Because the heads of the Al-Dawa Schools, seminaries, hospitals, and health centers had joined Khairun Naas, the new organization laid claim to all of those institutions. Lakhvi also claimed the centre at Muridke because of his familial relation to Abdur Rahman al-Surayhi, who contributed to the construction of Lashkar's compound there.[31] Salafi religious scholars and other elders (and possibly the ISI) intervened to resolve the dispute, and the two sides soon reconciled.[32]

This was a temporary split, driven by personal animosity and internal power dynamics. In the years after 9/11, Lashkar did not fragment and nor did it birth any major splinters of note, like Jaish's Jamaat ul-Furqan. The fact that Lashkar was allowed to be more active in Indian-administered Kashmir than other groups helped. So too did its Ahl-e-Hadith identity, which meant many of its members did not share the same connections to other groups and therefore were less portable. In addition, several Lashkar members told the author that militants who were no longer participating in the Kashmir jihad for any number of reasons could 'go into the reserves.' Some of them might assume support roles for Lashkar's militant activities, but others maintained their connection to the organization via above-ground social work or preaching done through JuD.[33] This enabled the group to keep these men under its control. Lashkar's ideological focus on dawa and jihad contributed to this dynamic since it allowed some militants to maintain a sense of mission even when not fighting.

However, while Lashkar's organizational cohesion was strong relative to other outfits, it was not absolute. The group inevitably 'threw off' some small splinters to quote one member of the security services.[34] Individuals also took leave, or in some cases quit the organization, to work with other outfits or fight alongside the Taliban. This process accelerated after the leadership reaffirmed its willingness to submit to state control in 2003 and slowed its activities in the Kashmir jihad following the 2004 peace accord. Some of those who left maintained links with the organization and sometimes returned to the Lashkar-fold. Others remained part of Lashkar and engaged in occasional freelance activities or agitated for policy changes from within the organization. Three notable trends developed as a result. First, from an analytical perspective it is not always clear who was in and who was out, thereby making it difficult to assess sanctioned from unsanctioned activities at times. Second, the number of connections to the other networks and outfits that were less amenable to the state's agenda increased, since Lashkar members did not necessarily break all ties with the group to work with these other entities. Third, some of those with a broader agenda retained influence within the organization, which contributed to debates about whether to remain obedient to Lashkar's official patrons or join the jihad against America and its allies.

It is useful to introduce several new characters at this stage, since following their stories through the ensuing chapters provides one means of charting these trends as they accelerated in the latter years of the decade. The first is Abdur Rehman Syed. He was a major in the Pakistan army, whose unit was stationed on the Pakistani side of the Durand Line in early 2002. Ordered to fight the Taliban fleeing across the border following the US counter-attack in Afghanistan he refused, and was subsequently demoted to the rank of captain. Although Syed was soon reinstated as a major, he quit the army that year and began working for Lashkar. Major Haroon Ashiq and his brother Captain Khurram, who served in the elite Special Services Group, also took early retirement. Both had met Zaki-ur Rehman Lakhvi and joined Lashkar after leaving the army.

Abdur Rehman and Haroon became trainers, providing combat instruction to operatives and especially to those charged with executing fidayeen attacks. However, Haroon and his brother began distancing themselves from Lashkar in late 2003 as a result of the leadership's conservative and India-centric posture. They kept in contact with various members of the group, including Abdur Rehman, and attempted to influence their former colleagues—in one instance distributing pamphlets impugning Lakhvi. Although Abdur Rehman remained with the group until later in the decade, by the 2004–2005 time period he was developing differences with the senior leadership; leaving for extended periods of time to fight alongside the Taliban and beginning to leverage Lashkar's infrastructure to build his own networks at home and abroad.[35]

All three men became part of a wider network of current and former Lashkar members who challenged the leadership and, in some cases, the Pakistani state as well. They also all eventually gravitated toward Ilyas Kashmiri, who headed the Azad Kashmir chapter of HuJI at the time. He was detained in connection with the December 2003 attempts on Musharraf's life, but released several months later only to be detained again in 2005 after refusing to close down his operations in Indian-administered Kashmir. Upon his release, Kashmiri shifted his operations to FATA.[36] His outfit, known as the 313 Brigade, became responsible for a number of attacks in Pakistan during the latter years of the decade.[37] It was linked to al-Qaeda as well as various pro-Taliban militants, and comprised of anti-statist members from a number of different outfits.

Despite the advent of desertions and internal disputes, Lashkar remained the most organizationally intact and coherent jihadi outfit in Pakistan in the years after 9/11. This meant that in addition to receiving better treatment by the state than any other outfit, it was also better positioned to maximize its freedom of movement. Lashkar not only shared the Musharraf regime's focus on India, its leaders also surmised that remaining close to the state was the best means of maintaining influence in the long term. Because JuD remained legal, this provided a means to augment its strength and resources as well as to increase its societal standing. As JuD consolidated and expanded its support base among the populace, this strengthened the government's case for refusing to ban it, even as the group leveraged its legality to support militant activities against India as well as the West. Yet, although Lashkar's behavior after 9/11 was Janus-like, it was careful to show only one face publicly.

*Good Jihadi*

The group gave even greater weight to the provision of social services after Lashkar's ban in early 2002 and the cosmetic separation from JuD that immediately preceded it. JuD's departments essentially mirrored those that existed as part of the prodigious MDI infrastructure, but post-2002 they became even more robust and the scope as well as the scale of their offerings increased.[38] So too did the group's reputation as an organization that 'looks out for you not only with money, but with education, health, house-building, dispute arbitration, whatever you need' according to one prominent Pakistani journalist.[39] Increasingly, what Pakistanis saw in terms of its public behavior was not militancy as much as social work and religious activism and when the group did promote jihad, it was mainly against India. One former member claimed that despite 'belonging to the Salafi sect, Lashkar has [the] sympathies of people from all sects [in Pakistan] because of its social work and because it has focused on jihad against India and does not kill innocent people in Pakistan.'[40]

A Full-Service Provider

The group's medical mission was greatly expanded and by the middle of the decade had more than 140 dispensaries discharging medical care for a nominal fee; six hospitals; and sixty-six ambulances.[41] According to the Amir of JuD for Rawalpindi, whose job it was to oversee all of the group's operations in that area, by 2009 it had the second largest ambulance fleet in the country.[42] The group also held hundreds of medical camps from 2003 onwards, and claimed to have served over 30,000 by 2006.[43] JuD also started a 'Self Supporting Program' that provided widows who had no income with items like a sewing machine and unemployed or uneducated men with those such as a bicycle so they could earn money on their own. It developed religious-specific programs as well, including the 'Taiba Qurbani [Sacrificial] Program' that collected donated animals for destitute families to sacrifice on Eid al-Adha and an 'Arrangement for Breaking Fasts Program' that arranged food for people to break fast during the month of Ramadan.[44]

The organization's Social Welfare Department was renamed the Humanitarian Relief Department, or Idarah Khidmat-e-Khalq [IKK], and introduced a host of new service offerings, including an 'Emergency Aid Program,' which provided resettlement and relief aid to the victims of natural disasters; a 'Water Provision Program' to dig water wells and provide hand pumps where clean drinking water was not available; and a 'Refugees Rehabilitation Program' in Pakistan-administered Kashmir. The latter proffered food and other essential items on a monthly basis to Kashmiri refugees who fled across the LoC.[45] According to one former senior officer in the Intelligence Bureau this program also provided Lashkar with a good cover to carry out recruiting activities.[46] IKK also worked internationally, providing relief aid following a major earthquake in the Iranian city of Bam in 2003 and sending 20 million rupees worth of relief goods to Sri Lanka when the Asian tsunami hit that country in December 2004. Amir Hamza, one of the group's founders, also traveled to the Maldives to distribute money among the victims there.[47] Separately from its relief work, JuD claims to have provided clothes to over 75,000 people across the provinces of Pakistan as well as to approximately 2,000 others in Sri Lanka, the Maldives and Indonesia through its 'Dress Provision Program.'[48] Once again, this altruism also brought operational benefits: the Maldives was one of a number of nodes in the networks the group used to support terrorist operations against India.[49]

The Al-Dawa System of Schools expanded and by the latter part of the decade boasted over 170 educational institutions at which approximately 20,000 students were receiving an education annually. It also began offering two different educational tracks: a 'Sharia Based Education Program' and a 'Modern Education in Accordance with Islamic Values Program.' The former provided Islamic education only, though the aim was to 'produce religious scholars—

rather than just imams—who can provide ideological leadership to the nation.' The latter taught the same 'c' is for cannon and 'g' is for gun curriculum as during the 1990s. By this point JuD had published close to fifty books for use in its schools, and developed a teacher training course that covered its curriculum.[50] The group continued to charge for its schools (though it also continued to subsidize students in need) and for its propaganda offerings, as well as raising large sums of money by selling the donated hides from animals sacrificed during Eid al-Adha. All of this was in addition to its investments in subsidiary organizations, agricultural land and other businesses.[51]

Lashkar, along with some other groups, still received cash from the ISI, but funding could be frozen and there is anecdotal evidence to suggest this happened at times.[52] Most of the other jihadi outfits suffered financially, since the state's crackdown made their efforts to raise money from private donors in Pakistan and abroad more difficult.[53] The fact that JuD remained legal meant it could continue to fundraise openly, and it did so aggressively. The group still asked for people's sons for jihad, but it increasingly said 'If you want to save the Islamic umma then give us money.'[54] This is not to suggest Lashkar ceased recruiting, but rather that at the time there was a strong enough recruitment stream to satisfy its militant demands. As the group expanded its social services offerings many people who never previously gave money to finance the jihad began donating to the group to support its welfare activities.[55] Because JuD was a legal entity in Pakistan, its bank accounts also remained secure. As late as 2008, the group was directing domestic and international donors to deposit money into a JuD account.[56] As already mentioned, it was not until the UN Security Council proscribed JuD following the 2008 Mumbai attacks that this loophole was closed.

Fundraising was not the only area in which JuD's legality made a difference in terms of the type of operating environment the group enjoyed versus what other outfits had to contend with. At various times, the Musharraf regime ordered all of the groups to close their liaison offices in Pakistan, making open recruitment more difficult. Not only were most of the Deobandi groups banned, meaning they had to disguise their activities in some way, but their charitable wings and hence those offices were scrutinized more heavily than those official belonging to JuD.[57] This meant that Lashkar could continue to use its infrastructure for missionary purposes in order to build a support base as well as to recruit more openly.[58] The group purchased real estate throughout the country in order to open up new offices and had more than 1,500 full time offices operating across Pakistan by the middle of the decade.[59]

The group's propaganda operations also remained intact. Although other outfits continued to put out propaganda, they could not do so as overtly or on such a grand scale because what they were doing was technically illegal. Once again, everything done under the JuD umbrella was legit. All of the group's existing propaganda offerings migrated from MDI to JuD, and ultimately increased to nine print publications as well as enhanced virtual offerings.[60] Its *Al-Dawa* magazine continued to claim the highest monthly circulation among jihadi monthlies; *Ghazwa Times*, which previously had the second highest circulation among weeklies, jumped to the top spot.[61] JuD's website and publications still detailed Lashkar attacks in Indian-administered Kashmir despite the ostensible separation of the two groups.[62] A number of the author's Pakistani interlocutors also pointed out that Saeed and other JuD preachers enjoyed far more freedom of movement than leaders of other organizations. This enabled them to travel around, promote Lashkar's jihad and raise money. A number of Pakistani journalists told the author the ISI also warned members of the media it was acceptable to write critically about other outfits, but to lay off Lashkar. Several of them reported receiving threatening phone calls from the security services directing them to cease publishing negative stories about the group.[63]

Its reputation experienced an additional boost following its response to the South Asia Earthquake, as it is now known, which struck Pakistan, India and Afghanistan on the morning of 8 October 2005. The quake registered a magnitude of 7.6 on the Richter Scale and its epicenter was located near Muzaffarabad; Pakistan-administered Kashmir, the NWFP, northern Punjab and Indian-administered Kashmir were the areas most affected. Delivery of humanitarian assistance was constrained by the mountainous terrain, cold weather and damaged or destroyed civilian infrastructure. Over 73,000 people died, an additional 69,000 were injured and 2.8 million left homeless in Pakistan. Another 1,300 people were killed in Indian-administered Kashmir, with more than 6,000 injured and over 150,000 made homeless.[64]

Although the army officially took the lead in relief efforts, in some areas jihadi groups were among the first on the scene. Years spent training in the area meant they were familiar with the terrain and also had grassroots networks in place that enabled them to reach victims quickly. It also meant they had well-equipped facilities near the quake site.[65] A number of their own cadres were killed, and approximately fifteen training camps were buried by landslides or otherwise destroyed by the earthquake.[66] The militants who survived quickly laid down their arms and picked up relief goods, carrying them to the remote areas they had come to know so well. The army provided logistical support, including helicopters, to help jihadi outfits engaged in the relief efforts. At least seventeen banned outfits were involved in either the immediate relief effort or reconstruction work later undertaken. A number of these operated under the banner of, or in coordination with, above-ground NGOs. Together they managed thirty-seven of the seventy-three camps operating either in or around Muzaffarabad and had a presence in every affected district of Pakistan-administered Kashmir.[67] Owing to the need to deliver aid as rapidly as possible, the UN and international NGOs worked with militants who were already in place.

JuD channeled considerable resources toward providing assistance through its relief wing Idarah Khidmat-e-Khalq: in Muzaffarabad it was treating patients within thirty minutes of the quake. Within thirty-six hours, the group had opened a fully functioning field hospital there and a second one in the Mansehra District [in the NWFP] where training camps have been located for a number of years. It also set up surgical centers, mobile dispensaries, mobilized its ambulance service (claimed to be the second largest in the country) and flew in extra doctors from Indonesia and Turkey. In addition to this outpouring of medical aid, it built approximately 1,000 shelters and brought in generators to provide electricity.[68] Because JuD's response was so quick and comprehensive, the Pakistani state relied heavily on it to carry out aspects of the relief work. That Lashkar was considered the most reliable jihadi outfit did not hurt either, especially considering the government's desire to exercise strict control over the militants involved in the relief effort.

One consequence was to marginalize local, secular NGOs, which international organizations bypassed given the government-approved contributions Islamist outfits were already making. According to JuD communiqués, and confirmed by independent reports, it worked closely with the World Food Program [WFP], World Health Organization [WHO], United Nations Children's Fund [UNICEF], United Nations High Commissioner for Refugees [UNHCR], and the Red Cross [ICRC]. These organizations had copious relief materials, but JuD provided the manpower to help deliver them.[69] For example, it distributed US relief aid and ran some of the camps where UNHCR supplies were distributed.[70] Some of the group's members even ferried NATO soldiers across rivers when the need arose.[71]

These efforts enhanced the group's reputation as a premier social welfare organization. In return, it received accolades from the population as well as members of the government, including Musharraf.[72] In a typical example of the kind of praise offered by survivors, one woman who was rescued said, 'If Dawa people hadn't helped us, we would have died. Nobody else came to help us. We are grateful to them and we offer them our support back.'[73] Pakistan-administered Kashmir's President Lt.-General (Retd) Sardar Mohammad Anwar Khan visited Lashkar's camp in the city of Muzaffarabad to express his gratitude. On the same day, the Prime Minister of Pakistan-administered Kashmir, Sikandar Hayat Khan received Hafiz Saeed at his official residence in Muzaffarabad and thanked him on behalf of his government.[74] The Prime Minister later attended a JuD conference in Muzaffarabad, where he praised the organization for its public welfare work and for being the first on the scene after the earthquake. He told those assembled 'nobody could do what you did' and donated 100,000 rupees from his own pocket to 'help them in their work.' Notably, he also lauded the group's efforts to liberate Kashmir.[75]

JuD got more than pocket money, however, as the government channeled funds to it for reconstruction in Pakistan-administered

Kashmir.[76] This enabled the group to expand its footprint there and to operate a number of relief camps, some of which doubled as recruiting grounds.[77] Lashkar also received huge charitable donations, much of which mysteriously disappeared. According to the US Department of Treasury, JuD used its relief wing Idara Khidmat-e-Khalq as well as its network of offices, madaris, mosques and other fundraising mechanisms to exploit the earthquake in order to raise money to support its militant activities.[78] Six months after the earthquake the US designated JuD and Idara Khidmat-e-Khalq as terrorist organizations. It stated that to evade sanctions Lashkar-e-Taiba had renamed itself Jamaat-ul-Dawa, which had established Idara Khidmat-e-Khalq as a 'public welfare organization that it utilizes to collect funds and undertake other activities.'[79] JuD responded by posting on its website a letter to then US Treasury Secretary Henry Paulson refuting claims it had used earthquake donations to support terrorist operations.[80] The group need not have worried too much. Unlike in 2002 when Islamabad followed Washington's ban of Lashkar, this time none was forthcoming. Some analysts believed Musharraf sent a dangerous message by refusing to follow Washington's lead, and ascribed his reluctance to do so to the extensive aid work JuD undertook following the earthquake.[81] In reality, the group was already heavily insinuated into Pakistani society and the earthquake provided the Musharraf regime with an opportunity to identify its relief work as a reason not to ban it. Certainly, JuD's utility and reputation as a service provider contributed to the state's unwillingness to act against it, but this was also a function of Lashkar's efficacy as a proxy against India.

Fighting the 'Good Fight'

The Musharraf regime had clamped down on cross-LoC infiltrations after the December 2001 attack on India's Parliament, but by early spring it had once again begun encouraging militant activity in Indian-administered Kashmir. A second pause followed after Lashkar militants executed the Kaluchak massacre in May 2002. Although cross-LoC infiltration soon resumed, violence measured in terms of fatalities and the number of violent incidents began declining after 2002.[82] There were several reasons for this. A key driver was Pakistan's efforts to calibrate the tempo of operations in response to pressure from New Delhi and Washington. In addition, the Deobandi groups were also no longer as robust and many of their militants were no longer as focused on the Kashmir jihad. JeM had been the second most active Pakistani group after Lashkar at the turn of the century, but it was pulled in different directions after 9/11 and its footprint in Indian-administered Kashmir shrank significantly over the years. The 2002 elections in Indian-administered Kashmir were also seen to be mostly free and fair. This contributed to the normalizing of politics within the region, though it must be said that the expected improvements in governance did not materialize. Finally, the introduction of fencing along the LoC in 2003 made infiltration more difficult, while India's counter-insurgency capabilities also continued to improve.

Lashkar was already the most powerful Pakistani militant outfit in Indian-administered Kashmir by 2001 and remained focused on that front thereafter, in contradistinction to the Deobandi groups. It was also more amenable to state control and thus more willing to abide by directives to increase or decrease the tempo of operations. Thus it became the primary, though not the only, vehicle for waging a 'controlled jihad.' The ISI began sending smaller groups of fighters across the LoC and became more selective about the militants with whom it worked.[83] This favored Lashkar, which was the state's most reliable proxy, and its militants are reported to have begun operating in smaller groups as befit a more calibrated jihad.[84] The group also relied on cadres already in Indian-administered Kashmir, where by one estimate it had approximately 1,500 militants by 2002. This amounted to roughly half of the total number of militants from Pakistani jihadi groups in the Kashmir theater at the time.[85] This meant it could maintain a level of militant activity inside Indian-administered Kashmir even during those periods when the ISI was directing it to reduce infiltrations across the LoC.

Lashkar also increased its focus on indigenous recruitment in Indian-administered Kashmir. Enhancing its local network enabled Lashkar to reduce its practice of contracting out logistics. Most non-Kashmiri groups paid locals to serve as guides and porters, but such cash transactions meant they were essentially hiring logistical mercenaries, and, like most mercenaries, these actors were unreliable. They often dumped the jihadis' gear at the first sign of trouble, and at times turned them in to the authorities. By developing a network of its own Lashkar increased its operational capabilities and its internal security, thereby enabling it to step into the breach throughout the region when other groups' capacity to carry out attacks declined.[86] In addition, these local actors helped Lashkar to find new routes across which to launch their operatives when fencing was installed along the LoC in 2003. Bringing more Kashmiris into its ranks had also become important following Musharraf's edict in 2002 that only Kashmiri groups would wage the Kashmir jihad. Most of its fighters continued to be Pakistani, but increasing the presence of locals in support roles gave Lashkar more of a Kashmiri face and helped to promote the fiction that it was no longer a Pakistani outfit. To this end, Lashkar and two other Pakistani groups also joined the Kashmir Resistance Force and, through it, the United Jihad Council in October 2003.[87] This appears to have been done at the ISI's behest as a way to buttress their credentials as purely indigenous outfits.[88]

While Lashkar brought more Kashmir Muslims into its ranks to play non-military roles, it also increased its focus on attacking 'soft' targets in Indian-administered Kashmir. In part this owed to the improved efficacy of the Indian security forces, but it was also a way to foment communal tensions and keep India-Pakistan relations in limbo. So too was the group's involvement in terrorism directed against the Indian heartland, which increased during this decade. According to one member of the Indian security services, based on intelligence gathering and information provided by captured operatives, Lashkar leaders are believed to have met in 2002 or early 2003 and determined it was necessary to accelerate the pace of attacks inside India.[89] The Indian economy had begun to grow more quickly after 2002 and the group also increased its focus on economic targets. The terror campaign against India continued to include bombing attacks launched in concert with indigenous actors as well as fidayeen assaults, for which Lashkar dispatched its own highly trained operatives. The former were intended to bleed

India through a consistent campaign of coercion, while the latter were higher-profile operations staged to draw attention.

An increasing supply of would-be Indian jihadis meant the group could rely more heavily on indigenous actors. The destruction of the Babri Masjid in 1992 and communal violence that accompanied it had contributed to an initial wave of Indian volunteers who joined the group or trained with it. Muslim grievances continued to fester as a result of e ʾnomic and political injustices, and were exacerbated by the rise of the Hindu nationalist movement in India. A decade after the Babri Masjid's demolition, riots in the state of Gujarat in early 2002 claimed the lives of 790 Muslims and 254 Hindus, according to official statistics.[90] Unofficial estimates put the death toll as high as 2,000. It was widely alleged that officials from the state government, led at the time by the pro-Hindu Bharatiya Janata Party encouraged and assisted Hindus who were involved in the violence.[91] The Gujarat riots mobilized a section of India's Muslim population already prone to radicalization as a result of relative deprivation and a sense of political alienation. More young men began seeking military training in Pakistan.[92] Because Lashkar had been building its Indian networks since the 1990s, and maintained the most robust training infrastructure in Pakistan, it was well placed to take advantage of this situation.

A terrorist network that became known as the Indian Mujahideen became the primary, though by no means the only, vehicle through which Lashkar escalated its involvement in terrorist attacks against India. The key players in the Indian Mujahideen network became active during the early years of the decade. They did not coalesce until 2004, however, and the network did not identify itself as the Indian Mujahideen until November 2007 when it issued the first of five manifestoes. The men who led this terrorist network came together through familial connections, personal ties often formed via association with the Student Islamic Movement of India [SIMI] and shared connections to Muslim members of the Indian criminal underworld.[93] SIMI was not launching terrorist attacks in India as an organization, but it had been a recruiting pool for Lashkar since the 1990 and remained a place where some of those who became involved in Indian jihadism rubbed elbows with one another. Muslim members of Indian organized crime had also played a role in promoting the growth of indigenous terrorism since the 1990s, the most notorious example being Dawood Ibrahim who was responsible for the bombing of the Bombay Stock Exchange, among other targets, in 1993. Ibrahim fled to Karachi following the attack, which was intended to avenge the destruction of the Babri Masjid, and after arriving in Pakistan began providing financial as well as logistical support to Lashkar. Criminals still based in India made important contributions too; connecting indigenous militants to one another and to Lashkar, while also funding and directing attacks themselves. Before exploring the nature of Lashkar's support to the expanding Indian jihadi movement, it is important to discuss briefly how it took shape during the early 2000s.

Two former SIMI activists, Mohammad Sadiq Israr Sheikh and Riyaz Ismail Shahbandri [a.k.a. Riyaz Bhatkal], went on to lead the Indian Mujahideen. Together they make a useful lodestar for navigating the growth of that network. Sheikh had been drawn to SIMI in the wake of the riots that accompanied the Babri Masjid's destruction in 1992, but by 2001 had grown frustrated with its inactivity and left the organization. A family member introduced him to Aftab Ansari, a ganglord who served time in prison during the mid-to-late 1990s alongside Pakistani militants.[94] Ansari connected Sheikh to Asif Khan, another well-established figure in Indian organized crime, who arranged for him to train with Lashkar.[95] Shahbandri also knew Asif Khan, from whom he sought funding for terrorist operations in India.

Shahbandri and Sheikh appear to have been working on separate tracks and though they knew one another through SIMI, it was their shared connection to Asif Khan that helped bring them together.[96] After Khan was killed in a shootout with police in December 2001, his brother Amir Khan set up an Indian jihadi outfit named the Asif Raza Commando Force. The following month, motorcycle-borne militants, operating under its banner, fired at policemen outside of the US Government's information center near the American consulate in Calcutta. Six policemen were killed and another fourteen injured.[97] Aftab Ansari was the alleged mastermind. The attackers were reportedly linked to his gang and to HuJI. Given the overlapping networks in India at the time, it is possible they shared ties to Lashkar as well.[98]

Amir allegedly began providing money to Shahbandri to send operatives to Pakistan for terrorist training and directed Sheikh, who returned to India in late 2002, to begin recruiting cadres for training there as well.[99] Once back in India, these men quickly became involved in launching bomb attacks.[100] However, Shahbandri and Sheikh were not the only two men building jihadi networks in India at the time. Other indigenous operators were active too and much of the terrorist activity remained relatively uncoordinated. Indian prosecutors allege that Riyaz Shahbandri brought various operators from the atomized jihadi movement together for a retreat in the south Indian town of Bhatkal in 2004. A year later Sheikh, Shahbandri and another Indian jihadi entrepreneur named Abdul Subhan Qureshi, who also trained with Lashkar and was present at the retreat, are believed to have formed the Indian Mujahideen network. Indian officials assert Sheikh's cadres who had trained in Pakistan provided the manpower for attacks and that he acted as the IM's Mumbai-based leadership liaison to these operatives. Shahbandri's cell was responsible for procuring explosives and bomb components, while his brother Iqbal recruited operatives to provide specialized IT support. Qureshi recruited SIMI activists for logistical support.[101] In 2005 the Indian Mujahideen network announced its presence with a bomb attack against a Hindu temple in the north Indian city of Varanasi.[102]

Lashkar is suspected of playing a key role in planning or otherwise supporting a number of the bombing attacks launched by Indian militants. It is often difficult to ascertain Lashkar's precise role in these attacks because the group deliberately obscured its involvement. Sometimes Indian militants were acting at its behest, at other times they were acting semi-autonomously with the group's assistance. Two things are clear: first, the Indian jihadi movement remained motivated primarily by domestic grievances rather than by India-Pakistan dynamics; and second, that movement became far more lethal than it otherwise would have been without external support. However, just as Lashkar does not view itself as an instrument of the state, even though it often acts in this capacity, most Indian militants did not perceive themselves as proxies for either Lashkar or Pakistan. To quote Praveen Swami, a journalist and expert on Indian jihadi networks, the wave of bombings that took place during this decade was 'homegrown terrorism, watered and fertilized by Lashkar.'[103] In other words, the group was a force multiplier for Indian militancy, rather than a key driver of it. Further, while Lashkar was the chief external outfit providing support for Indian jihadism, it was not the only one. It is to the nature of this assistance that we now turn.

External support was fluid. Lashkar was considered the primary training provider and financier. It was also the most active in terms of transiting operatives between India and Pakistan via third countries such as Bangladesh, Nepal or those in the Gulf, often supplying false documents for these trips.[104] ISI agents are suspected of abetting these efforts, as well as with providing explosives training.[105] The Bangladeshi branch of Harkat-ul-Jihad-al-Islami [HuJI-B] is known to have furnished local actors with explosive material as well as facilitating the transit of weapons and other material across the Bangladesh border.[106] Sometimes Lashkar and HuJI-B worked in tandem, other times they worked independently. As Lashkar expanded its presence in Bangladesh over the course of the decade, the development of surrogate bases there and in Nepal enabled it to act more independently in terms of moving men, money and material into and out of India.

According to information provided by captured Lashkar operative David Headley, a Pakistani-American who performed reconnaissance on all of the targets hit during the 2008 Mumbai attacks, Karachi became a base in Pakistan for supporting Indian jihadism.[107] The sprawling port city is a natural entry and exit point for Indians traveling to and from Pakistan. In particular, it has traditional commercial links with Maharashtra (of which Mumbai is the capital) and Gujarat (where the 2002 pogroms occurred). It is also home to various organized criminal networks, including Dawood Ibrahim's D-Company. When the US Department of Treasury designated Ibrahim as a Specially Designated Global Terrorist in October 2003 it specifically noted his financial support for Lashkar-directed attacks in Gujarat.[108] His syndicate, along with other criminal networks, also would have continued to provide another means for smuggling guns, explosives and recruits into and out of India. Amir Khan is also believed to have fled to Karachi via Bangladesh in roughly 2003, and continued to contribute to coordinating attacks in India from there.[109] Notably, Lashkar worked with other criminal syndicates located elsewhere in Pakistan as well to move arms and explosives into India.[110]

Headley told investigators that at least two separate Lashkar units existed in Karachi for the purpose of launching or supporting attacks against India. Abdur Rehman Syed, the major who took early retirement and joined Lashkar in 2003, controlled one of them. Sajid Mir [a.k.a. Sajid Majid] oversaw the other. Sajid's personal history is murky. According to Headley, Sajid joined Lashkar in roughly 1994 when he was eighteen years old. After heading the Lahore unit, he graduated to a position in the External Affairs department where he became responsible for handling overseas operatives. In this capacity, he allegedly visited numerous countries on 'business trips' including Canada, Dubai, India, Qatar, Syria and Thailand. Numerous references to Sajid Mir suggest he is a former army officer. Headley made no reference to this in his testimony when detailing Sajid's rise in the organization, though it is possible he served in the army at some stage. Also unclear is the degree of coordination between the two units or when each was launched. Notably, Syed finally split from Lashkar in 2008, but kept control over his unit in Karachi. Two things are clear from Headley's testimony. First, the purpose of each unit in Karachi was to launch operations in India using indigenous actors. Second, Lashkar members were in contact with and received assistance from ISI officers for these operations.[111]

In addition to supporting and promoting attacks by indigenous militants, Lashkar continued to launch its own fidayeen assaults. In September 2002, approximately six months after the Gujarat riots, two Lashkar fidayeen stormed the Akshardham Temple in Gandhinagar, the Gujarat state capital.[112] Approximately 600 worshippers and tourists were inside at the time, over thirty of whom were killed in the attack. This was the first fidayeen attack Lashkar executed beyond Indian-administered Kashmir since its inaugural raid on the

Red Fort. The Akshardham assault was intended to avenge the pogroms that took place in Gujarat, though at roughly this time the group was also beginning to increase its focus on economic targets in order to slow India's burgeoning economy by hitting the country where it hurt financially. The story of Sabauddin Ahmed and his involvement in a Lashkar assault on the Indian Institute of Science [IISc] in Bangalore is worth briefly exploring because of what it demonstrates about the group's target selection, the role of its regional networks and the continued support provided by the ISI.

Ahmed, who was arrested in 2008 and described to investigators his experiences with Lashkar, was among those who flocked to the group after the Gujarat riots in 2002.[113] That year, one of his fellow students at university convinced him of the need to 'fight against the injustice meted out to Muslims' and soon introduced him to a Lashkar recruiter tasked with sending Indian youths for training in Pakistan.[114] Not long after, Sabauddin crossed the LoC into Pakistan-administered Kashmir and enrolled in his first Lashkar training program. Upon completion of the initial program, Sabauddin and others were taken to a camp in Punjab province for additional training with weapons and explosives. Lashkar's operational commander, Zaki-ur Rehman Lakhvi, then directed him to work with the ISI who Sabauddin told investigators prepared a Pakistani passport and other documents for him. He used these to travel to Bangalore via Kathmandu, Dhaka, Colombo and the United Arab Emirates.[115]

Sabauddin arrived in Bangalore in 2004 and, at Lashkar's direction, began to survey possible targets for a terrorist attack. He told police the group chose Bangalore because it was enjoying an economic boom. This fact, coupled with the city's growing reputation as a global hub for the IT industry, meant an attack would harm India economically and attract international attention. Working with a Pakistani commander known as Abu Hamza [an alias], for whom Sabauddin also provided safe haven, the two identified four possible targets. According to police they zeroed in on the Indian Institute of Science [IISc], which Sabauddin confessed to reconnoitering a day prior to the attack, because it was hosting an international conference. On 28 December 2005 the two men launched a fidayeen assault, storming the auditorium where a seminar was in progress and killing a professor who was visiting from Delhi. Abu Hamza escaped to Pakistan while Sabauddin fled to Nepal, where he went on to become a top Lashkar commander and allegedly oversaw the movement of operatives transiting between India and Pakistan. On 31 December 2007 he became the first Indian operative to command Pakistani fighters during a Lashkar fidayeen attack, when a team of militants assaulted a Central Reserve Police Force [CRPF] camp in Rampur in the Indian state of Uttar Pradesh.[116]

The outcome of Sabauddin's journey was exceptional. Most Indian jihadis were not used to support, much less lead, fidayeen assaults. Rather they were part of a loosely knit movement responsible for a host of bombing attacks, executed with varying degrees of external direction and support. These bombings increased in terms of frequency and scale during the early years of the decade, a result of an expanded pool of would-be recruits as well as an escalation of external support from Lashkar as well as other actors. Even after indigenous elements came together to form the Indian Mujahideen, that terrorist network remained part of a larger jihadi project. Sabauddin's experience was also atypical since fidayeen assaults constituted the exception rather than the rule in terms of Lashkar's involvement in terrorist attacks against India. These were intermittent and high profile operations, in contrast to the consistent drumbeat of bombing attacks designed to bleed India. They were also relatively small-scale affairs; the Akshardham Temple and Bangalore operations each involved only two fidayeen. This made the Mumbai attacks in 2008, executed by a ten-man attack squad, all the more striking. So too did the inclusion of Western and Jewish targets, since many continued to view Lashkar as a purely India-centric outfit. Yet in reality the group began participating in the jihad against America and its allies almost immediately after 9/11. It is to these activities that we now turn.

## Bad Jihadi

Lashkar was wary of associating too closely with al-Qaeda after 9/11, lest this draw the unwelcome attention of the United States or upset its Pakistani sponsors. Al-Qaeda operatives, in turn, were wary of working too closely with the group because it remained close to the

ISI. They sometimes suspected unfamiliar Lashkar foot soldiers of being ISI agents or informants.[117] Nevertheless, several Pakistan-based Western diplomats and one senior officer in the Pakistan security services confirmed reports that senior leaders within the organization were involved in al-Qaeda led meetings with the Taliban and other jihadi organizations after 9/11.[118] Lashkar's contributions to the jihad against America and its allies during the 2001–2005 time period primarily entailed the provision of facilitation, training and support to other actors, though on several occasions the group or elements within it undertook direct actions to kill Westerners. For organizational purposes it is helpful to develop a rough typology of Lashkar's activities in the global jihad against America and its allies. These are divided into the following categories: the provision of safe haven and protection for other jihadi outfits; participation in the open fronts in Iraq and Afghanistan; the provision of training to non-Lashkar recruits and the facilitation of access to al-Qaeda's networks and training camps; and participation in terrorist attacks at home and abroad (beyond the provision of training or facilitation of access to al-Qaeda). There are two main drawbacks to such a typology. First, rigid categorization obviously misses the degree to which one form of activity may elide into another. Second, grouping activities by type obscures the chronology of Lashkar's participation in the global jihad in the years immediately after 9/11. However, this is offset by the fact that a thematic representation enables drawing out the extent of the group's various activities during the first half of the decade, which in turn provides a baseline for comparison in terms of their escalation in later years. The examples that follow are intended to illustrate the group's capabilities, reach and motivations, and do not claim to offer an exhaustive account of its activities in 2002–2005. Further, Lashkar's precise connection to various operations and motivation are not always clear. It is sometimes difficult to determine when elements in the group were acting quasi-independently or factions were pursuing their own agendas. Where possible, these distinctions are explicated. Finally, it is notable that in some instances activities associated with Lashkar's participation in the jihad against America and its allies were also used to support operations against India.

## Lending a Logistical Hand

There is little indication al-Qaeda believed it would lose its Afghan sanctuary following the 9/11 attacks, but within months its members were fleeing across the border along with other jihadis who also lost their sanctuary when the US invaded. Pashtun tribesman brought the Taliban safely out of Afghanistan into the border regions in Pakistan, and also escorted out between 600–800 Arabs, for which they were well compensated.[119] Most of the major Pakistani outfits also assisted with the exfiltration of al-Qaeda cadres and other Arab jihadis from Afghanistan where possible as well as with facilitating safe haven in Pakistan or safe passage through and out of the country.[120] Of all of these groups, Lashkar had the best network in the country. Its cadres are urbane, able to navigate the cities and ports, and so Lashkar played a major role in moving Arabs, from al-Qaeda and other groups, through the country. It provided safe haven in Pakistan to some. For others, Lashkar facilitated their emigration to the Middle East or other safe destinations despite international watch lists and US naval patrols. In doing so, Lashkar displayed enormous clout in terms of its ability to produce fake passports, safe houses, guards and fixers.[121] One captured Lashkar operative alleged that the group also provided medical support to Arabs wounded during the US counter-attack.[122] This support was not ad hoc, according to an interrogation report of foreign and Pakistani nationals arrested in Punjab in March 2002. Lashkar operatives admitted they were directed to facilitate safe haven and safe passage for al-Qaeda cadres and other fugitive Arabs.[123] Tariq Pervez, the former Director General of Pakistan's Federal Investigation Agency, reaffirmed the belief that this was an organizational directive.[124]

Lashkar has a history of proffering safe havens to jihadi fugitives from justice. It is reported to have given refuge to Mir Aimal Kansi, who was ultimately caught and convicted for murdering two and wounding three employees of the US Central Intelligence Agency in a shooting outside its headquarters in Langley, VA. The group also allegedly allowed Ramzi Yusuf, the mastermind behind the 1993 World Trade Center attack and nephew of Khalid Sheikh Mohammed, to hide in one of its Muridke guesthouses in order to avoid a police dragnet.[125] This hospitality continued after 9/11. Gary Schroen, who led the first CIA team into Afghanistan after 9/11, stated that local jihadi groups, and primarily Lashkar, were running most of the safe houses in which al-Qaeda members were caught in the early years of the decade in Pakistan.[126] According to Ahmed Rashid, who was covering the story at the time and has written extensively about the post-9/11 environment in the region, the government suppressed most of the evidence regarding these arrests and the Pakistan army exerted heavy pressure on the local media not to report them. This was particularly the case when Lashkar was involved.[127]

Abu Zubaydah [born Zayn al-Abidin Muhammad Hussein] remains the most notable operative captured at a Lashkar safe house. In his pre-9/11 role as a logistician, Abu Zubayda had worked closely with Lashkar and it was in one of the group's safe houses that he was captured in March 2002. The CIA station in Islamabad had learned the previous month that Zubayda was in either Lahore or Faisalabad, and US officials sought to narrow the search by tracking Zubayda via his mobile phone. They were able to identify fourteen possible locations in both cities, all of which were put under surveillance. On 28 March the Punjab Police's Elite Force led simultaneous raids on each location, with Americans waiting outside. One of the teams captured Zubayda in an upscale house in Faisalabad, where they also found bomb-making equipment and $100,000 in cash.[128] The central Punjab city has long been a Lashkar stronghold and it appears that Zubayda chose Faisalabad as the location in which to establish his new operational headquarters.[129] A number of suspected Lashkar members were also captured during the raid, but according to media reports the Pakistani authorities released sixteen of them a month later, despite American protests.[130]

## Dabbling in Open Fronts

Lashkar's historical connections to Afghanistan lay in Kunar and Nuristan provinces, which are located in the northeast of the country. The Afghan Salafis there had provided early support to Lashkar's parent, Markaz al-Dawa wal-Irshad, and one of the group's first training camps was based in Kunar. Lashkar members maintained a relationship with the Afghan Salafis there during the 1990s, some of whom fought with the Northern Alliance against the Taliban prior to 9/11. Following the destruction of the Taliban government in 2001 there was an intense rivalry among various factions to gain control of Kunar province. The organization that had aided Saeed and Lakhvi when they first launched MDI, Jamiat al-Dawa al-Quran wal-Sunna [JuDQS], emerged from a scrum of competing factions as one of the most functional political entities in the area. Haji Rohullah who led JuDQS and was the most prominent Salafi leader in Kunar was chosen as a delegate to the Emergency Loya Jirga that elected Hamid Karzai as the new head of state.. However, he was arrested in August 2002 for allegedly collaborating with the Taliban and al-Qaeda, though several observers noted the possibility that a rival engineered his arrest.[131] This episode contributed to disaffection among Rohullah's followers and coincided with a series of other incidents that angered locals, leaving some of them open to insurgent recruitment.[132]

Sporadic fighting began in late 2002 when the US army's 82nd Airborne arrived in the Korengal Valley, though according to one expert the Americans were 'chasing ghosts' because insurgent activity amounted to low-level hit-and-run affairs.[133] Those associated with JuDQS appear to have needed some time to reorganize following Rohullah's arrest, and the local Hizb-e-Islami commander along with foreign fighters associated with al-Qaeda were the ones believed to be leading the revolt at the time.[134] In 2003 insurgents from the Baujur Agency in Pakistan, where JuDQS and a host of other militant actors had a presence, increased raiding on positions close to the border. They linked up with Afghan fighters in the Korengal Valley, which in later years became the site of some of the bloodiest battles that US forces faced in Afghanistan. This brought a greater American presence and in November 2003 the US launched Operation Mountain Resolve, which contributed to making this a more active front. Lashkar had been working with JuDQS to transit weapons and other materials across the border to the Afghan Salafis in Kunar prior to 9/11, and stepped up its efforts afterwards to support them logistically.[135]

The consensus among the author's interlocutors is that it was not until roughly 2004–2005 that Lashkar entered the Afghan theater, a move that is explored in the following chapter. However, some of its members either took leave or split from the group to enter the Afghan front during the early years of the decade. For example, after 9/11 a commander known as Abu Shoaib argued for prioritizing the Afghan front over the jihad in Kashmir and when Lashkar's leaders demurred he formed a small outfit to fight there.[136] According to the interrogation by the Indian security services of a captured Indian operative named Abdul Razzak Masood, a Lashkar financier and facilitator called Arif Qasmani along with several other members of the group floated a militant outfit in 2003 for the purpose of supporting the insurgency in Afghanistan. One of those members was also known as Abu Shoaib.[137] It is not uncommon for different commanders to use the same kunya [nom de guerre] and so it is unclear whether this was the same commander or the same outfit. In either case, the US government alleges that Qasmani acted as a liaison for Lashkar with other militant outfits, was close to members of the Taliban and proffered financial as well as other support to al-Qaeda, including the provision of supplies and weapons as well.[138] Masood's testimony supports these assertions; in it he recounts Qasmani detailing his connections with the Taliban and al-Qaeda. He asserted that members of the new group, which Qasmani and others from Lashkar formed, fought alongside Arabs and other foreigners as well as Pakistanis against Coalition forces near Kunar province in 2003. Masood said he then spent the next two years transporting money and militants from Lashkar, JeM and HuM sent by Qasnami from Karachi to Afghanistan. Masood claims that Qasmani offered to help him reach the Iraqi front in 2005, but he appears to have gotten side-tracked and was arrested that year while recruiting Muslims in India for military training.[139] Notably, Qasmani remained connected to Lashkar while Masood's arrest suggests he returned to work with the group against India after fighting in Afghanistan. This raises questions as to whether the outfit Masood described was a true splinter or something more akin to a spin-off formed by a faction within Lashkar as a means for those militants who prioritized the Afghan jihad to fight there without breaking their ties to the group.

Masood was not the only Lashkar recruit interested in fighting in Iraq. The US invasion of Iraq caused anger throughout Pakistan, as it did in many Muslim countries as well as among Muslims living in Western countries. Not long after American military operations commenced in Iraq, the group held its Defense of the Umma Conference in Islamabad. Hafiz Saeed proclaimed: 'The powerful Western world is terrorizing the Muslims. We are being invaded, humiliated, manipulated and looted. How else can we respond but through jihad?' He declared, 'We must fight against the evil trio, America, Israel and India' and urged militants to fight in Iraq.[140] Lashkar is alleged to have played a role in recruiting jihadis to fight there, a charge that even the ISI did not entirely discount.[141] Lashkar internet postings spoke of an army of fighters bound for Iraq from different countries while an Indian newspaper reported in June 2004 that up to 2,000 Pakistanis had volunteered to fight for the group there.[142] That number is wildly exaggerated, but Lashkar was indeed recruiting for Iraq through JuD offices in 2003 and 2004.[143] Many of those enlisted under the auspices of fighting in Iraq were later steered toward the Kashmir jihad. According to one Pakistani researcher who interviewed recruits at the time, after completing training these recruits were told 'You can volunteer to go to Iraq, but you are obligated to go to Kashmir.' Some of them agreed; others split from the group.[144]

Fighting in Iraq fit with Lashkar's classical jihadi ideology. It was, after all, a Muslim land under occupation. However, Lashkar leaders argued that jihad in Indian-administered Kashmir took priority for the group because of its proximity to that front.[145] Further, ideological preference was not the only factor that kept a significant number of Lashkar recruits from fighting in Iraq. The overwhelming majority of foreign fighters there were from elsewhere in the Middle East, North Africa and Saudi Arabia.[146] Even many of these men found operating in Iraq difficult because they spoke a different Arabic dialect and were not familiar with the terrain. Given that Lashkar recruits were South Asian, they had even less hope of navigating the Iraq theater. Nor were there robust networks in place for fighters to travel from South Asia to the Iraq theater, compared with the numerous channels for would-be jihadis from the Arab-speaking world. Meanwhile, for those members of the group who did want to fight against the US, Afghanistan was next door. Thus, it is not surprising that despite Lashkar's hyperbolic announcements, few of its fighters actually turned up in Iraq.

Lashkar's operational commander Zaki-ur Rehman Lakhvi is believed to have directed a small number of operatives to travel to Iraq in 2003 and followed up by dispatching additional cadres as well as funds to attack American forces in Iraq in 2004.[147] In the spring of 2004 British forces captured two Lashkar militants there. Both of them were handed over to the US, which sent them to a prison in Afghanistan.[148] One of those captured reportedly had been Lashkar's operational commander in charge of the forward camps from which cadres were launched across the LoC, a position he held from 1997–2001.[149] The Pakistani security services reportedly came down hard on the group once the presence of its cadres in Iraq was brought to Musharraf's attention. The British Foreign Office also alerted Musharraf to the fact that the captured Lashkar cadres had the phone numbers of ISI agents in their mobile phones. According to the senior British Foreign Office official who provided this information, Musharraf dealt with the specific ISI agents involved.[150] Whatever the consequences for Lashkar, its domestic operations were not seriously affected.

## A Training Provider and Gateway Organization

The US counter-attack had destroyed the training infrastructure in Afghanistan. The major Pakistani groups were able to maintain some instruction capacity within Pakistan, but their capabilities varied. Lashkar continued operating larger camps more overtly than other groups in Mansehra and Pakistan-administered Kashmir; it also ran smaller ones in FATA, mainly in the Waziristan and Mohmand agencies, not far from where al-Qaeda was establishing some of its training bases.[151] In the early years after 9/11, while al-Qaeda and the Taliban were re-establishing their training capacity, Lashkar picked up some of the slack. This included training local militants as well as foreigners who pre-9/11 would have trained in al-Qaeda camps, but now were looking for other avenues of instruction. For example, a stream of militants from Indonesian militant groups began passing through Lashkar's induction program after 9/11. Some of them belonged to Jemaah Islamiyah [Islamic Group or JI], which was responsible for the 2002 Bali bombings, and others to Lashkar Jihad, a group dedicated to fighting Christians in Indonesia.[152] In September 2003, Indonesian and Malaysian students linked to JI were arrested in Karachi from the JuD-affiliated madrasa Jamaat-ul-Dirasat-ul-Islamiyah.[153] Among those arrested was a student alleged to be the brother of Nurjaman Riduan Ismuddin [a.k.a. Hambali], the mastermind behind the 2002 Bali bombings.[154] In addition to trainees looking for new venues of instruction, the closing of al-Qaeda's camps also meant that its freelance trainers needed to find new places to set up shop, and some of them gravitated to Lashkar. This cut both ways and as al-Qaeda re-established its infrastructure in Pakistan, some Lashkar trainers began working at its camps as well.[155]

Lashkar was an appealing outfit for would-be Western jihadis because it maintained a more robust training apparatus and received less scrutiny than other groups. Some Westerners who sought training in Pakistan after 9/11 were looking to fight in Afghanistan or Indian-administered Kashmir, though the latter was a less attractive option and sometimes viewed merely as a means of gaining combat experience. Others were looking for training in urban terrorism, which they intended to employ to prosecute attacks back in Europe or North America. Notably, there were instances in which Westerners sought training in order to fight on open fronts, but were reoriented toward participating in terrorist plots abroad or providing logistical support to established outfits. Lacking in combat experience and familiarity with the local language or terrain, often their most useful assets were a passport from a Western country and perhaps a 'clean skin,' meaning they did not feature on terrorist watch lists.

Although the Musharraf regime directed Lashkar not to host foreigners in its camps, attempts at enforcing this directive were lax and easily evaded. The group was also easy to access because its above-ground JuD infrastructure remained legal, enabling Westerners to use its offices, mosques or madaris as initial entry points. The days of 'walk-ins' were over after 9/11, but Lashkar's transnational networks, particularly among the Pakistani diaspora, enabled those seeking to train with it to make contact before arriving in Pakistan. For all of these reasons, it not only served as an appealing training provider, but also as a gateway organization to reach al-Qaeda. The examples that follow are not an exhaustive accounting of all those Westerners known to have trained with Lashkar after 9/11. Rather they are intended to illustrate the aforementioned attributes of those seeking training as well as of Lashkar as a training provider and gateway to al-Qaeda.

The case of Willie Brigitte demonstrates the impunity with which Lashkar operated after 9/11 and the degree to which this enabled it to provide training to a host of foreign recruits. Brigitte, a French convert to Islam, trained with the group for several months from late 2001 through early 2002. He was arrested in Australia in 2003, where he was involved in a terrorist plot connected to Lashkar. The details of this operation are discussed in the final section of this chapter. Relevant here is the information Brigitte provided during his interrogation in France, where he was deported to following his arrest in Australia. According to French authorities, when Brigitte presented himself to Lashkar for training he was debriefed for more than two weeks and asked to give names of fellow jihadis known to the group who could guarantee his bona fides. Once this initial round of vetting was complete, he was taken to a second camp where instructors debriefed him further for another fortnight. It was only after the group had confirmed he was not a French or American spy that Brigitte was introduced to the camp's amir and allowed to commence training.[156]

When French magistrate Jean-Louis Bruguière interrogated Brigitte in 2003 the latter explained that he first underwent training in a camp near Lahore. He then was taken, along with two British and two American recruits, to the Bait-ul-Mujahideen in Pakistan-administered Kashmir. This road trip entailed crossing four army checkpoints 'without any problems and without any identity checks.' Brigitte testified to Bruguière that from there he went to a camp higher up in the mountains where he estimated several thousand Pakistanis and Afghans were training. He further testified that some of his instructors were soldiers on detachment and that Gulf Arabs, Tunisians, Somalis as well as British and American jihadis trained alongside him.[157] His training lasted two and a half months, during which time Brigitte alleged military materials were air-dropped by army helicopters and collected by the new recruits.[158] Notably, he also asserted that the group was forewarned in advance of swoops designed to ensure foreigners were not present in its camps. Brigitte says he witnessed such inspections on four occasions during his ten weeks in the mountains, each time from the woods skirting the camp, where he was directed to hide by Lashkar members who were forewarned that the inspectors were coming.[159]

Lashkar was training Westerners, including Americans, prior to 9/11. Some of those who went through its camps later facilitated entrance for others who sought to wage jihad against the US. The case of the Virginia Jihad Network, introduced in Chapter 4, exemplifies the role that these pre-existing networks played in promoting Lashkar as a training provider. It is also illustrates the manner in which the group continued to leverage these networks for its own logistical purposes. Three men from the Virginia Jihad Network traveled to Pakistan to train with Lashkar before 9/11: Randall Todd Royer, Ibrahim Ahmed al-Hamdi and Seifullah Chapman. The latter was at one of Lashkar's camps on 9/11. As he was making his way back to America in the days following the attacks, Ali Al-Timimi, a native US citizen and leader at a mosque in Northern Virginia, gathered together others from the Virginia Jihad Network. He encouraged the group to answer Mullah Omar's call to defend Afghanistan against the anticipated US invasion. Four men agreed to do so: Mohammed Aatique; Khwaja Mahmood Hasan; Masoud Ahmad Khan; and Yong Ki Kwon. Al-Timimi and Royer advised them that Lashkar would be the best group with which to train in preparation for fighting against American forces in Afghanistan. Royer also phoned his Lashkar contacts to smooth the way and provided contact information to the four men, all of whom made the trip to Lashkar's Masada camp near Muzaffarabad in Pakistan-administered Kashmir.[160] A month after the initial meeting in Northern Virginia, Ali Asad Chandia also traveled to Pakistan at al-Timimi's urging and presented himself at the Lashkar office in Lahore.[161]

The US invasion of Afghanistan made American forces legitimate targets in their eyes, just as were Russian soldiers in Chechnya or Indian soldiers in Indian-administered Kashmir. However, none of these aspiring jihadis ever reached the Afghan front. They did not train with Lashkar for very long either and the instruction they received was limited to practicing with small arms, anti-aircraft guns and rocket-propelled grenades at Lashkar's Masada and bin Masood camps.[162] In other words, the available evidence does not suggest they received instruction specifically for urban terrorism. Nor does Lashkar appear to have made any effort to deploy them to Indian-administered Kashmir or to Afghanistan. Instead, several of the men from Virginia became nodes in a logistical network, working with Mohammed Ajmal Khan [a.k.a. Abu Khalid], a British Lashkar operative who was later convicted of using money raised in the UK to provide all manner of military kit for the group. This included Kevlar body armor, firearms and hi-tech surveillance equipment.[163] He is believed to have undertaken this procurement mission at the behest of Sajid Mir, the Lashkar commander in charge of overseeing transnational operatives. Ajmal Khan made multiple visits to the US in 2002 and 2003, where Chandia, Masoud Khan and Seifullah Chapman assisted him in his efforts to acquire equipment for Lashkar.[164] Most of the men involved in the Virginia Jihad Network were convicted on or plead guilty to various charges relating to their preparation for jihad, training with Lashkar and support given to the group.[165]

Although the men from Virginia were used in a support capacity, one concern about such networks is that their purpose can change over time. In addition to using the Virginia network for procurement, Sajid Mir also asked two of the trainees to undertake missions involving information gathering as well as the dissemination of propaganda.[166] This suggests Mir was interested in expanding Lashkar's networks in the US. Masoud Khan told the US Federal Bureau of Investigation in 2004 that at one point the group also asked him to perform surveillance on a chemical plant in Maryland.[167] Precisely what Lashkar or elements within it planned to do with this information is unclear, but it highlights the potential risk that such transnational networks pose. When authorities arrested

Khan in May 2003, they found him in possession of automatic weapons, a document entitled 'The Terrorist's Handbook,' containing instructions for the manufacture and use of explosives, as well as a photograph of the FBI's Washington headquarters.[168]

Jihadi networks are often self-perpetuating and, thus, not self-contained; nodes within them either have ties to or may be seeking to connect with other outfits or networks. As a network grows, this is more likely to be the case. For example, Seifullah Chapman was in touch with another American named Mahmud Faruq Brent al-Mutazzim. Brent was not part of the Virginia Jihad Network (he lived in New York), but had also attended a Lashkar camp in 2002. Once back in the US, Brent introduced Chapman to his roommate, Tarik Shah. Notably, Brent described Chapman as a recruiter for training camps overseas.[169] Shah and another Brent associate, Rafiq Sabir, were aspiring jihadis interested in making contact with al-Qaeda. The two of them later pledged bayat, an oath of allegiance, to Osama bin Laden during what they believed was a meeting with an al-Qaeda recruiter, but who turned out to be an undercover FBI agent.[170] By the time Shah helped the FBI to bust Brent in a sting operation in 2005, the latter no longer maintained strong connections to Lashkar. Nevertheless, he pleaded guilty to providing material support to Lashkar, while Shah and Sabir were sentenced to prison terms for proffering material support to al-Qaeda.[171]

The growth of the internet during the early years of the decade contributed to the proliferation of networks among established and would-be jihadis, facilitating virtual connections across countries and continents. In addition to connecting the worldwide jihadi community, it also served as a vehicle for radicalizing a new generation. The growth of online jihadi forums and the explosion of accessible propaganda enabled established actors to reach a greater audience than ever before. The internet also provided aspirant jihadis with a seemingly anonymous space in which they could engage in 'risky behavior,' which in turn led to the rising threat of homegrown terrorism in Western countries. Yet although the threat of online radicalization was real, it often took contact with established activists or militants to give virtual recruits the final push toward violent action. Further, despite the profusion of instruction materials that could be found online, there was no substitute for training with professional militants, a function Lashkar remained ideally placed to offer as a result of its protected position in Pakistan. Its physical networks also meant that online recruits could contact established activists in the West who in turn facilitated access to the group.

Aabid Hussain Khan [a.k.a. Abu Omar] was one such activist. He was at the center of an 'online network that connected extremists in North America, Europe and South Asia.'[172] Using various online sobriquets, he indoctrinated recruits via secure internet forums after inveigling them from open discussion websites.[173] According to the US government, Khan was a 'facilitator' for Lashkar and Jaish-e-Mohammad, and the British security services believe he may have talent-spotted for one or both of them. During his trial in the United Kingdom, where he held citizenship, Khan testified to having connections with both groups.[174] He is also known to have visited Pakistan several times, and on one occasion went to the NWFP where he shot footage of himself with other 'American-sounding individuals in an area where LeT posters were prominently displayed on public walls.'[175] Khan was arrested as he flew back to Britain from Pakistan in 2006 and convicted two years later on counts relating to the possession of information useful for terrorism.[176] Among those with whom he was in contact were: two Americans from the state of Georgia, later convicted of providing material support to Lashkar; a Serbian militant in Bosnia-Herzegovina named Mirsad Bektasevic, later found in possession of over 20 pounds of plastic explosives, detonators, a suicide belt and a manifesto promising an attack on Western interests; and a number of Canadians who were part of what became known as the 'Toronto 18.'[177]

The two men from Georgia were Ehsanul Islam Sadequee and Syed Haris Ahmed, both of whom were in touch with Khan via various jihadi web fora on which they had become active by late 2004.[178] Sadequee and Ahmed, along with others in Khan's virtual network, determined they needed military training. Khan later admitted to making contact with Lashkar and JeM for this purpose. Sadequee thought Lashkar the better option, writing over email:

I was thinking, we should be with LT, due to them being same 'Aqeedah [ideology or belief], and they fighting against Hindus, so the Murtaddeen [the Pakistani government] shouldn't bother us as opposed to if we go to other apostates-haters.[179]

In other words, Lashkar's special status vis-à-vis the state continued to make it a safe bet for foreign jihadis. Khan believed a covert staging point was needed since, as he wrote to others in the network, the group was growing and 'we cant have like 12 bearded people just go together to Pakistan.'[180] He aimed to use Toronto for this purpose.[181] Ahmed and Sadequee went there from Atlanta, Georgia for a week in March 2005 to meet with others from the online network. At least one of them was part of the 'Toronto 18,' a group of fourteen adults and four youths arrested in 2006 by the Royal Canadian Mounted Police on suspicion of plotting to attack the Parliament Buildings in Ottawa and detonate truck bombs in Toronto.[182]

During the meeting in Toronto, Ahmed and Sadequee not only discussed training in Pakistan, but also identified possible targets for a terrorist attack in the US.[183] A month later the duo traveled to Washington, DC, where they shot video recordings of possible targets, including the US Capitol, the headquarters building of the World Bank, the Masonic Temple in Alexandria, Virginia and a group of large fuel storage tanks near a highway in northern Virginia.[184] Sadequee then sent those video clips to Khan as well as to Younis Tsouli, a British man known online as Irhabi 007 [Terrorist 007] who acted as a propagandist for al-Qaeda in Iraq [AQI].[185] While Ahmed and Sadequee were clearly ready to contribute to terrorist attacks in the US, Ahmed was also open to fighting alongside Lashkar in Indian-administered Kashmir or elsewhere if directed to do so by the group. On 17 July 2005 he traveled to Pakistan, intending to study in a madrasa and then train with Lashkar.[186] While there he met with Aabid Khan in an attempt to actualize his ambition of training with Lashkar, but failed to gain entrance to the group's camps and returned to Atlanta in late August 2005. Sadequee also left the US in mid-July and traveled to Bangladesh, where he began working more closely with Tsouli and Bektasevic, the Serbian militant arrested in Bosnia-Herzegovina, to launch what he hoped would be a European affiliate of al-Qaeda. Both Ahmed and Sadequee were later arrested by US authorities and convicted on multiple counts, including the provision of material support to Lashkar.[187]

The threat from homegrown terrorists radicalized in Western countries and trained in Pakistan was brought into stark relief on 7 July 2005 when four young British men blew themselves up on three London underground trains and a bus. The 7/7 attacks, as they are commonly known, killed fifty-two civilians and injured hundreds more. They occurred ten days before Syed Haris Ahmed arrived in Pakistan hoping to train with Lashkar, and may have contributed to his difficulty accessing the group's camps.

Mohammad Siddique Khan and Shehzad Tanweer, two of the men responsible for the 7/7 attacks, made multiple trips to Pakistan in the years prior and evidence suggested they had connections to Lashkar and Jaish-e-Mohammad. The two men were connected to a wider network in the UK, which included Omar Khyam, the British Pakistani introduced in Chapter 4 who trained with Lashkar in 2000.[188]

Conversations between Mohammad Siddique Khan and Khyam recorded in Britain in early 2004 indicate that the two of them, along with Tanweer, were planning to travel to Pakistan together. During those conversations, they discussed training in the Tribal Areas and waging jihad in Afghanistan. By this point, Khyam had graduated from training with Lashkar to working with an al-Qaeda operative in Pakistan on a plot to explode a fertilizer bomb in the UK and so for him the trip was partly a means of fleeing the country. His arrest thwarted any plan for the three men to travel together, but Siddique Khan and Tanweer went ahead with the trip. When they departed for Pakistan it appears to have been with the intention to wage jihad on an open front—Siddique Khan made a farewell video for his daughter before departing, which suggests he did not expect to return.[189] It is not uncommon for aspiring jihadis to go for training with the hopes of fighting (and dying) on an open front only to be convinced they can do more for the cause by engaging in terrorism back home.

Siddique Khan had already trained in Pakistan and possibly Afghanistan on at least one occasion in the late 1990s or early 2000s, and again in Pakistan in 2003.[190] Tanweer had previous exposure to militants in Pakistan as well, having met members of Jaish-e-Mohammad during a prior trip.[191] Western intelligence officials believe that he, and possibly Siddique Khan too, had also earlier attended Lashkar training sessions focused primarily on indoctrination, which suggests the Daura-e-Suffa, Daura-e-Aama or both.[192] In advance of this final trip, Tanweer reportedly placed an unknown number of phone calls from his home in Britain to Lashkar's compound at Muridke and spent several days there at some point after his arrival.[193] The aforementioned intelligence officials assert he met with members of the senior leadership while at Muridke and believe that both he and Siddique Khan availed themselves of Lashkar safe houses enroute to al-Qaeda's camps in the Tribal Areas.[194]

It is an article of faith among the American and British security establishments that Lashkar has acted as a gateway to al-Qaeda on numerous occasions, providing indoctrination, networking opportunities, safe haven or other forms of facilitation to aspiring jihadis like Siddique Khan and Tanweer. However, it must be noted that the group was viewed as a partner in a consortium with al-Qaeda rather than a contractor which made potentially valuable operatives available.[195] Members of the Pakistani diaspora were (and remain) particularly well placed to use what has been termed the 'Kashmir Escalator,' namely the process by which members of the diaspora were radicalized at home and then traveled to Pakistan, where they initially connected with current or previously Kashmir-centric militant groups—primarily Lashkar or Jaish. Some exploited familial and friendship ties in Pakistan to make these initial contacts; others took advantage of the international networks both groups initially built to support the Kashmir jihad. Once in Pakistan, would-be jihadis exploited grassroots connections among foot soldiers as well as organizational linkages to access al-Qaeda operatives in the Tribal Areas. Some of them later reappeared in the West to launch terrorist attacks while others stayed in Pakistan planning or otherwise supporting such attacks.[196]

Those arriving in Pakistan often took advantage of Lashkar's above-ground infrastructure, which remained legal. The group's offices and madaris are considered to have become a first port of call after 9/11, though these were not the only entry point. For example, several of the British men involved in the thwarted al-Qaeda plot to use liquid explosives to bomb transatlantic airlines flights en route from the UK to North America in 2006 worked in JuD relief camps after the October 2005 earthquake. From there they are believed to have moved on to training camps in Waziristan.[197] British investigators also suspected that Lashkar funneled some of the money raised for earthquake relief to plotters of the attempted attack.[198] Its operatives in Britain reportedly provided money for the plane tickets used to conduct a practice run as well as for the attacks themselves.[199] This use of Lashkar's networks to provide direct financial or operational support for terrorist attacks constitutes yet another means by which it contributed to the global jihad after 9/11. It is to these activities that we now turn.

Participating in Terrorist Attacks

In December 2001 the al-Qaeda-directed 'Shoe Bomber,' as Richard Reid is now known, attempted to blow up American Airlines Flight #63 midway between Paris and Miami in December 2001. When interrogated by the FBI after being taken into custody in Boston, where the flight diverted following the failed attempt, Reid told investigators he had acted alone. Yet he was found to lack the technical knowledge necessary to construct the explosive device. Unemployed and with no fixed domicile, Reid also refused to explain how he paid for the ticket for flight #63 or the extensive international airline travel he undertook prior to the failed attack.[200] Clearly there was a support network behind him. Khalid Sheikh Mohammed, the mastermind behind the 9/11 attacks, has since taken responsibility for the operation.[201] Reid is also known to have trained with al-Qaeda in Afghanistan prior to 9/11 and to have fought alongside the Taliban.[202] Moreover, this was not meant to be a one-man operation. A second shoe bomber, Saajid Badat, was slated to blow up a flight from Amsterdam to the US, but pulled out at the last minute.[203] Given these facts, much of the support presumably came from al-Qaeda. However, as the former French magistrate Jean-Louis Bruguière observed, Reid had no historical ties to Paris and therefore no means of subsisting there without a support network.[204]

A French prosecutor asserted that Lashkar's representative in Paris, Ghulam Mustafa Rama, served as Reid's 'compass' in France.[205] As discussed earlier, it was the investigation into support networks for Reid in France that shed light on Lashkar's recruiting networks there. Rama was determined to have recruited Hasan El Cheguer and Hakim Mokhfi, and then facilitated their access to a Lashkar training camp. French authorities suspected, but were never able to prove, that Rama met Reid during the latter's time in Paris, supported him while there and provided him with contact information for a person or persons in Pakistan. Reid traveled to Pakistan in November 2001, not long after this alleged meeting, and is known to have visited Lahore and Karachi. As mentioned, investigators later determined he did not have the technical knowledge to assemble the explosive devices found in his shoes, and it is believed that during this trip Reid had it done for him.[206] This was an al-Qaeda plot, but at the time Reid might have received this technical support the US counter-attack in Afghanistan was in full swing. It is possible he sought assistance from other militants with the requisite knowledge, or perhaps simply needed help connecting with al-Qaeda operatives already in Pakistan.

Rama offered multiple and conflicting stories about this meeting in which the person he met was/was not Reid, El Cheguer and Mokhfi were/were not present and the meeting did/did not happen. Witnesses, to whom Rama confided, said the meeting took place, and French authorities uncovered other circumstantial evidence linking Rama to Reid and suggesting on-the-ground support as well. But none of this was concrete and in the end Rama, El Cheguer and Mokhfi were convicted, for 'participation in an association of criminals with a view toward the preparation of an act of terrorism.'[207] This charge is quite broad and a person can be convicted of this crime even if unaware the people with whom he was associating, and perhaps supporting, were criminals or terrorists. It is an umbrella charge under which various different activities could fall. In this case, the French authorities were unable to prove support to

Reid occurred, and instead the convictions of Rama, El Cheguer and Mokhfi resulted from their association with Lashkar.[208]

So why mention this episode? First, the nebulous nature of the case illustrates the complexities inherent in unraveling terrorist facilitation. Lashkar's transnational networks are dangerous, in part, because of the spectrum of opportunities they offer for facilitation, the difficulty to prove that this has occurred and the possibilities for elements within the organization to make use of these networks without official sanction. Providing such facilitation is also a subtle means by which Lashkar can contribute to the global jihad, and hence one that enables deniability. Second, the permutations of possible Lashkar support for an al-Qaeda attack against America must be viewed within the context of the discussions taking place within the group after 9/11 about how involved to become in the global jihad. In particular, numerous interlocutors believe there were debates over whether to continue using transnational cells only to support local operations or to expand and also use them for attacks abroad. These debates take on added resonance in light of the involvement of Lashkar operatives in attempted terrorist strikes against Australia in 2003, an operation in which the group's French connections were also involved.

On 22 September 2003 France's domestic intelligence agency, the Direction de la Surveillance du Territoire [DST], sent a cable to Australia's national security service, known as the Australian Security Intelligence Organization [ASIO]. The subject was Willie Brigitte, who, as mentioned earlier, began training with Lashkar soon after 9/11.

French authorities had been searching for him under an alias for almost a year by September 2003, and after determining he had left France on a one-way ticket to Australia sent the initial cable to confirm his presence there. Less than two weeks later the DST sent a second cable to the ASIO. It was not intended simply to confirm Brigitte's location; instead, it said, 'Brigitte is possibly dangerous.'[209] Australian Federal Police arrested Brigitte not long after the second cable arrived. ASIO had been granted coercive powers to detain and interrogate suspects several months before Brigitte's arrest, but Australian investigators knew far less about him than their French counterparts. After eight days in detention, Brigitte was sent back to France where the law was far harsher toward suspected terrorists.[210] When DST notified the Australians it was based on the belief that he was involved in a plot to attack targets in Australia, a suspicion that subsequent interrogations of Brigitte in France and investigations in Australia confirmed. Like Rama, El Cheguer and Mokhfi, Brigitte was convicted in France of participation in an association of criminals with a view toward the preparation of an act of terrorism. However, unlike them, the authorities were able to bring evidence of his involvement in a terrorist plot. This, coupled with the fact that he trained in Pakistan with Lashkar, figured in his conviction.[211]

Brigitte was dispatched by his Lashkar handler to assist Faheem Khalid Lodhi, an Australia-based operative of Pakistani descent, with launching attacks there. After the French alerted ASIO, the Australian security services put Brigitte under surveillance, which in turn led them to Lodhi who was arrested and later convicted of planning to blow up the Sydney electricity grid.[212] Lodhi was born in Australia and emigrated to Pakistan in 1999, where he trained with Lashkar before returning home. He again traveled to Pakistan in late 2001 and linked up with the group.[213] Other trainees there at the time have testified that Lodhi appeared to have a middle management role.[214] He returned to Sydney in 2002 and maintained regular contact with Lashkar according to one security official familiar with the case.[215]

The genesis of Brigitte's involvement in the plot can be traced to the time he spent training with Lashkar from late 2001 through early 2002. Sajid Mir, the Lashkar member responsible for managing its overseas operatives, was one of the men who debriefed Brigitte after his arrival and became his handler.[216] Brigitte told Bruguière during an interrogation that in 2002 Sajid directed him to leave Pakistan and return to Paris, where he was to act as a point of contact for any Lashkar operative transiting through France. Mir gave Brigitte his contact details, telling him to check in often. Brigitte kept in touch as directed, making at least forty phone calls to Sajid from Paris, not including calls possibly made from phone booths or emails sent from internet cafes.[217] During one of those communications, Sajid ordered Brigitte to travel to Australia and arranged financing for his trip. Brigitte detailed the process through which this was accomplished. He told French authorities that Sajid directed a Britain-based operative to instruct contacts in Paris to retrieve the money designated for financing the operation via the hawala system described in Chapter 4. According to Bruguière, the Lashkar operative in Britain was responsible for overseeing the recruitment of foreigners in Europe.[218] The latter arranged for two Paris-based colleagues to collect 3,500 Euros and provide the cash to Brigitte for his mission in Australia.[219] French police crosschecked this information, which Brigitte provided, with mobile phone and email traffic. Investigators confirmed there were a flurry of phone calls prior to Brigitte's departure for Australia between him, Sajid and Ashraf.[220]

Sajid also arranged for Lodhi to meet him upon arrival in Australia, providing the latter's phone number to Brigitte as well as giving his description to Lodhi.[221] An Australian court found that 'Sajid was endeavoring to co-ordinate a liaison between the offender [Lodhi] and Willie Brigitte in Sydney so that, in general terms, the prospect of terrorist actions in Australia could be explored.'[222] When Brigitte arrived at the airport in May 2003 Lodhi was there to greet him, as well as to help him obtain a flat and a phone purchased under a false identity.[223] Lodhi remained a persistent presence, but Brigitte's circle quickly grew beyond only him. In addition to building relationships with several other men suspected of involvement in jihadi activities by the ASIO, Brigitte soon found a wife.[224] He married a Muslim convert who also happened to be a former member of the Australian military. Brigitte's now ex-wife has claimed that during their brief union he repeatedly pressed her about her knowledge of the joint US-Australia Pine Gap electronic surveillance base near Alice Springs.[225] Brigitte also remained in contact with his Lashkar handlers and it appears that both he and Lodhi were calling Sajid Mir in Pakistan during this time.[226]

When the Australian police raided Brigitte's apartment, they found internet downloads of chemical compositions that could be used to create explosives. They also found downloads of the Lucas Heights nuclear reactor along with map references to the Garden Island naval base, the nearby Maritime Headquarters and the Victoria Barracks.[227] During a raid of Lodhi's home, they discovered he possessed a map of the Electricity Supply System, was in the process of ordering chemicals to make explosives and also had recorded the ingredients for making various types of bombs.[228] Australian security officials believe that Brigitte and Lodhi intended to select a suitable target and purchase the chemicals necessary to build a large bomb, but that they were planning to bring in a foreign explosives expert to assemble it. Brigitte told French investigators that Lodhi wanted him to host an unnamed guest, and that when he inquired as to the identity of this mystery man, Lodhi 'made it clear, through gestures, that he [the guest] was an explosives expert.'[229] There were reports that this explosives expert worked in Lashkar's camps, but whether he was a member of the group or a freelancer who contracted out his services is unknown.[230]

Australia's contribution to the invasions of Afghanistan and Iraq is believed to have been the motive factor, but it is unclear who generated the plot. According to the French dossier on Brigitte, and confirmed by a former Australian security official, Lodhi was the head of a clandestine cell that was preparing attacks in several countries. This cell was not homogeneous, however, meaning a number of its members were not linked to Lashkar.[231] It is possible Lodhi was directed to launch the attack in Australia, though equally plausible is that he developed the idea and that Lashkar acted as a force multiplier by deploying Brigitte and possibly the explosives expert. Sajid Mir worked directly for Abdul Rehman Makki, who was the head of the External Affairs Department as well as Hafiz Saeed's cousin (and brother-in-law), and so it is questionable whether he could or would have deployed Brigitte without the senior leadership's sanction. Nevertheless, it is possible Sajid was acting on behalf of a faction within the group or that there was disunity about the decision to support this operation. In either case, the operation illustrates Lashkar's capacity to project power far beyond South Asia as well as its direct involvement in terrorism directed against a Western target years prior to the Mumbai attacks.

Domestically, the group's policy remained to abjure violence against the state. However, there are indications Lashkar, or at least operatives associated with it, provided logistical support for one and possibly both of the assassination attempts against President Musharraf that took place within a fortnight in 2003. On 14 December would-be assassins exploded a bomb under a bridge in Rawalpindi less than a minute after Musharraf's motorcade had crossed it. The bridge was roughly a mile away from the general headquarters of the Pakistan army, and several air force personnel were later found to have been involved in the plot. Eleven days later there was a second attack, not far from the bridge where the first attempt occurred. This time two suicide bombers each drove a vehicle full of explosives into Musharraf's convoy. One of them turned out to have been a member of Jaish-e-Mohammad, the other formerly belonged to Harkat-ul-Jihad-al-Islami. Both had fought in Afghanistan alongside the Taliban. At least two commandos from Pakistan's Special Services Group were involved as was a police officer who provided information about when Musharraf's motorcade would arrive at the pre-selected attack location. Al-Qaeda is believed to have provided the explosives training and contributed to the attack planning as well.[232]

Additional manpower, resources and other logistical support came from a mix of several Pakistani militant groups, including Lashkar, according to three of the author's interlocutors. One is a Western diplomat based in Pakistan at the time of writing and another a former US intelligence officer. Both were stationed in Pakistan at the time of the attempts on Musharraf's life. Each, independently and unprompted by mention of the other, recounted a similar version of events; they stated that members from Lashkar were part of a congeries of actors involved in the December 2003 attacks against Musharraf. Both believe that members of the group provided reconnaissance and possibly other logistical support for the attempts.[233] A Pakistani journalist, who was well acquainted with several of the group's leaders and mid-level commanders at the time, supports this version of events.[234] David Headley's testimony to investigators also suggests that Lashkar members were at least aware of the plot. He recounts discussing the assassination plan with Abdur Rehman Syed, Haroon and others. Haroon is the army major who, like Syed, took early retirement to join the group. He split from Lashkar in 2003 and later went to work for Ilyas Kashmiri, who was among those arrested for attempting to kill Musharraf, though he later was released for lack of evidence.[235] Notably, Headley stated that Lashkar's operational commander, Zaki-ur Rehman Lakhvi, knew members of the group had discussed the assassination plot. If true, this would indicate Lashkar's leadership was aware of the plan.[236]

It must be noted that no open source evidence exists to confirm Lashkar's involvement or the participation of any of its members. When asked independently about this lack of public evidence, both the US intelligence officer and the Western diplomat responded almost identically. They each stated that the Pakistani government had the evidence and that they had seen it, but that the government did not allow it to become public because it did not want to have to deal with the repercussions of what that would mean. Notably, the six air force officers along with other military personnel and civilians were tried in a secret court-martial for the two assassination attempts. The number of accused was never made public, though twelve people were found guilty and sentenced to death in 2006.[237]

The Musharraf regime's double game after 9/11 created a situation in which it was cooperating with the US against al-Qaeda while simultaneously supporting militant outfits participating in the jihad against America and its allies. Lashkar was not the only militant group that continued to receive state support, but it was viewed as more reliable and less of a threat to Pakistan than the Deobandi groups, a proposition that proved accurate. In return for keeping a lower profile, Lashkar was granted more freedom of maneuver and allowed to remain more active than other outfits. This enabled the group to build up its martial and social welfare capabilities, and to put itself on the path toward increasing financial independence. It focused the majority of its energies on the Kashmir jihad and on launching or supporting terrorist attacks against India. However, although ordered to remain completely focused on India, the jihad against America and its allies was impossible to ignore. A series of events from mid-decade onwards led to increased integration with the global jihadi nexus developing in Pakistan, even as leaders like Hafiz Saeed and Zaki-ur Rehman Lakhvi continued to prioritize the fight against India.

7

# EXPANSION AND INTEGRATION

India and Pakistan came close to war after the Parliament attack in December 2001 when the two countries massed troops along their shared border. The Musharraf regime clamped down on cross-LoC infiltration immediately afterwards and banned several militant outfits, including Lashkar, but neither side demobilized and relations between the two remained fraught with tension. Infiltrations resumed and, despite the ban, Pakistan took no steps to dismantle the militant infrastructure on its territory. The Kaluchak massacre in May 2002 threatened to catalyze war, once again leading to a temporary clampdown in infiltrations. Within several weeks of Musharraf's pledge to US Deputy Secretary of State Richard Armitage to halt cross-border terrorism, Indian officials reported an approximately 90 per cent drop in shelling by Pakistani troops in Kashmir and a significant decline in cross-LoC infiltration. This was another tactical pause rather than a strategic shift, and by August infiltrations were rising.[1] Nevertheless, state assembly elections in Indian-administered Kashmir were held in September and October 2002. The successful election process provided New Delhi with an opportunity to pull its troops back and Operation Parakram, launched in the wake of the Parliament attack, was officially called off after the elections. War between India and Pakistan had been averted and relations between the two were normalizing. In late 2003 the two countries agreed to a ceasefire along the LoC and in 2004 they initiated the composite dialogue to address the bilateral issues between them.

According to one Indian analyst close to the security establishment in New Delhi at the time, the Indian government was surprised when Pakistan agreed to the composite dialogue because it meant discussion on terrorism and political issues, rather than only focusing on territorial disputes.[2] Simultaneously, the view in Pakistan was that this meant Kashmir was a legitimate topic for bilateral dialogue.[3] Thus, it is fair to say that from the outset each side was focused on different outcomes. Pakistan officials and others close to the security establishment with whom the author spoke in 2008 suggest the country had little to show in practice for its participation in the peace process. In their eyes, movement on Kashmir, as well as on other smaller territorial issues like the resolution of Sir Creek and the Siachen Glacier, was to take place along a parallel track with the rollback of Pakistani support for militancy. They assert that beginning in 2004 Musharraf pushed to contain militancy, even if he did not fully dismantle the infrastructure supporting it, and that over time increased his efforts. Yet, they argue, this brought no substantive reward from India. As the ruling power in Indian-administered Kashmir, it benefited from the status quo and there was a sense in Pakistan that 'New Delhi was going through the motions without actually going anywhere.'[4] This assessment is not without merit, even according to Indian interlocutors. As Rahul Roy-Chaudhury, the aforementioned Indian analyst, explained, India was aware that Pakistan viewed confidence-building as a path to conflict resolution, particularly with regard to Kashmir, and did not openly dispute this notion. No timeline was put in place, however, and India was happy to engage in confidence-building for its own sake.[5]

The composite dialogue was a formal process and took place in public view. In 2004 India and Pakistan also initiated back channel negotiations to address territorial disputes directly. These negotiations consisted of clandestine contacts between representatives from India and Pakistan, who held a series of secret meetings in third countries. The primary agenda item was finding a solution to the dispute over the status of Kashmir. While it was not the only stumbling block to peace between India and Pakistan, a resolution to the Kashmir dispute had the potential to enable the two countries to redefine their relationship and thus make peace easier to attain.

According to a report by Steve Coll, which shed significant light on the back channel negotiations, the two main envoys were charged with developing a 'non-paper.' This was a document with no signatures on it, thus providing each side with deniability, but intended to be detailed enough to serve as the basis for a formal agreement.[6] The solution mooted during the back channel was based on three immutable propositions: India could not accept the de-accession of Indian-administered Kashmir; Pakistan could not accept the LoC as an international border; and the Kashmiris wanted self-rule and would not submit to partition. The answer was to make the borders irrelevant, de facto reuniting the princely state of Jammu and Kashmir. Proposals were put forward to turn the LoC into a 'soft border,' grant significant autonomy to the Kashmiris living on either side of it and eventually demilitarize the former princely state. This signaled a major policy shift by Islamabad, since it denoted Pakistani recognition that India would not relinquish control over its part of Kashmir. A joint-body comprised of Indians, Pakistanis and Kashmiris would be formed to deal with issues affecting people living on both sides of the 'soft border.'[7] As is often the case, the devil was in the details and the joint body was among the most difficult issues to resolve. Pakistan argued for shared governance, with Kashmiris in the lead role, while India pushed for far less in terms of power sharing. It is unclear how far along the two sides were in terms of hammering out how this would work. Those involved in the secret negotiations claim they were close to a deal by early 2007.[8] Indian interlocutors debate this, and suggest that New Delhi did not view back channel negotiations as being as advanced as some suggest. They assert there was a vision and negotiators were filling in the blanks, but the sense was a deal was not imminent.

Some within the Indian security establishment had pushed to reach agreement because they believed that Musharraf, as head of the army as well as the country, was their best bet in terms of a Pakistani partner who could deliver on any deal made.[9] But he was forced to resign his position as Chief of Army Staff in late 2007 and by August 2008 had lost his grip on power completely. His resignation ushered in a civilian government, which led the army to re-exert control over foreign policy, a typical occurrence when civilians were in power. Absent Musharraf, the army was not predisposed toward peace in general, and this was compounded by the view that India aimed to maintain the status quo on Kashmir. The details of the back channel negotiations, which remain a matter of debate, did not come to light until after Musharraf's tenure ended. By that time the subject was moot. This contributed to the sense among many in Pakistan during and after Musharraf's reign that the country got nothing in return for its efforts against militancy.

Musharraf's efforts to rein in the Kashmir jihad became more strenuous beginning in the middle of the decade, but did not extend to dismantling fully the militant infrastructure on Pakistan's soil. His government had decided to keep alive some of its militant assets in 2003, despite the fact that pockets among Pakistan's jihadis had begun turning against the state soon after 9/11. After initiating the composite dialogue and back channel talks in 2004 the Musharraf regime began making a more consistent effort to curtail militant infiltration across the LoC. However, the security services continued to clamp down more robustly on some outfits than on others. Lashkar's activities in Indian-administered Kashmir slowed as a result, but the group faired better than its jihadi brethren and it continued to wage a controlled jihad. In July 2004, US Deputy Secretary of State Armitage affirmed 'the infrastructure, the camps, still have not been entirely dismantled' adding that 'there is indeed cross Line of Control violence.'[10] Further, the state's efforts were not only incremental, but also reversible. Training camps outside of FATA, and therefore in areas under state control, reportedly reopened in May and early June of 2005.[11] Two Western officials who were tracking cross-LoC infiltrations at the time assert these were rising, as they normally did during the spring and summer months.[12] Then in July 2005 came the suicide bombings in London, the shock waves of which reached all the way to Pakistan, where two of the bombers had trained. In their aftermath the Musharraf regime faced enormous international pressure to show that it was really cracking down on the terrorist infrastructure in Pakistan.

All of Musharraf's efforts against Lashkar to this point had been 'more about PR' to quote one Western diplomat who witnessed them first-hand.[13] After the 7/7 attacks the army and ISI put pressure on all of the jihadi groups, including Lashkar, to scale back their activities further. The security services closed down several Lashkar camps, though not all of them, and threw some of the foreigners attempting to train in them out of the country.[14] But the most visible indicator of official action, and hence the easiest way to show results to the international community, was to reduce militant activity in Indian-administered Kashmir to a greater degree than hitherto. Lashkar was not the only group that had its operations curtailed, but it was much more active than any other outfit and so this had a far greater impact on it. The security services pressured Lashkar to reduce cross-LOC infiltrations more so than before and also directed Lashkar operatives in Indian-administered Kashmir to scale back the level of violence still further.[15] According to several Pakistani-based journalists with sources in the ISI and Lashkar, the group was told that support for the Kashmir jihad would return to previous levels and pressed the group to remain patient.[16] Instead, militancy continued to decline in the Kashmir theater and by 2006 even the Indian Defence Minister acknowledged Pakistan's contribution to the reduction in violence there.[17] Jihadi outfits exist to fight, but many Lashkar militants no longer had the opportunity to do so on the Kashmir front. Worse, this was a direct result of state pressure, to which the leadership appeared to submit. The group had agreed to government oversight in order to keep its supplies open. It had a steady flow of resources and recruits, but was under orders to limit their use in Indian-controlled Kashmir. The leadership's control over some of its members weakened as a result.

Meanwhile, attacks against Coalition forces in Afghanistan jumped to over 5,000 in 2006, more than a three-fold increase from the previous year.[18] This rapid escalation had been building since at least 2003.[19] Significant recruiting efforts directed toward Pakistani volunteers began in 2004 and these recruits were playing an important role in the Afghan insurgency by 2005.[20] Many of them were pro-Taliban Pashtuns from the Tribal Areas, but an increasing number of men from a variety of Punjab-based outfits, as well as their splinter cells, also began heading for the Afghan front. Most were from the Deobandi outfits, but militants from Lashkar were among them. Small Lashkar splinters (or spinoffs) had been active in Afghanistan since 2002 and by 2004 the leadership was beginning to pay more attention to that front. Lashkar had no hope of leading the jihad being waged there and its core leaders, who remained India-centric, still viewed liberating Kashmir as the most legitimate front on which to fight. But Lashkar was a pan-Islamist organization and there was an occupation in Afghanistan that was becoming more difficult to ignore. Further, the group was being forced to hold back more of its militants in accordance with ISI pressure to reduce activities in Indian-administered Kashmir. A small number of Lashkar operatives began appearing in Kunar and Nuristan provinces in 2004, though they kept a relatively low profile at the time.[21] As the Kashmir jihad continued to decelerate and the Afghan insurgency to gain momentum from 2005–2006 onwards, the group increased its efforts to recruit and deploy fighters to Afghanistan. Over time an increasing number of its members and potential recruits also became motivated more by anti-Americanism than jihad against India.[22] This contributed to debates within the group about how involved it should become on the Afghan front.

Fighting in Afghanistan necessitated an expanded presence in the Tribal Areas and NWFP, where a proto-insurgency against Pakistan was developing. Pro-Taliban Pashtun tribesmen who ultimately coalesced to form the Tehrik-e-Taliban Pakistan [TTP or Pakistani Taliban] were in the vanguard of attacks against the Pakistani military, working alongside al-Qaeda and a cast of actors from various Deobandi outfits. By 2007 a full-blown insurgency had erupted, heralding the advent of an unprecedented revolutionary jihad in Pakistan. Thus, Lashkar militants were increasing their presence in FATA at a time when the dominant actors in the region were pro-Taliban tribesmen aligned with the Deobandi school of thought, many of whom were at war with the state. Given Lashkar's Ahl-e-Hadith identity and close relationship with the ISI, this sometimes sparked conflict. These episodes were the exception, not the rule, and collaboration with these and other militants increased. The result was that by 2008, this was 'not your mother's LeT' to quote one Pakistan-based Western diplomat.[23] Before exploring Lashkar's operations in Afghanistan and attendant collaboration with other outfits based in FATA, let us first turn to its India-centric activities.

## Pakistan's Gas Stove

Although Pakistan was clamping down on militancy, eliminating its proxy capability would rob the state of what some in the army and ISI perceived to be a necessary auxiliary force in the event of war with India, which they continued to view as an existential threat. Further, if the Musharraf regime completely discontinued the use of proxies, then it would be much more difficult for it to resume support for militancy in the event a political payoff from India did not materialize. Pakistan therefore sought to reduce militant activities, while keeping strategic assets like Lashkar intact and thus maintaining the option of increasing pressure if necessary. Interlocutors in both countries have likened this approach to an old gas stove: Pakistan could lower or raise the temperature, but if the pilot light was extinguished then the stove could not be turned back on automatically. The idea was no longer to bleed India via Kashmir, but simply to send a message that Pakistan was in control and could turn the temperature up or down, increasing or decreasing the flow of militants and tempo of operations. Lashkar was the predominant player on the Kashmiri pitch by this time. But the group's mandate was to maintain a presence inside Indian-administered Kashmir through low-level attacks, nothing more.

To ensure its dictums were met, the security services threatened retribution against those militants who disobeyed the directive to reduce their militant activities in Indian-administered Kashmir. According to one Pakistani journalist who reported from Pakistan-administered Kashmir at the time, Lashkar cadres who infiltrated across the LoC without permission risked arrest upon their return as well as physical harm to themselves and their families.[24] A member of the Pakistan Anti-Terrorism Force confirmed this based on his own interrogation of Lashkar cadres. Militants were told that if they did not toe the line as directed then when they returned from Indian-administered Kashmir they would find their families dead.[25] Both interlocutors agreed the ISI put significant pressure on

Lashkar's leadership to keep its cadres in line as well. The ISI also put pressure on the guides and porters who helped militants to infiltrate.[26] Coupled with the reduction in ceasefire violations, this made it harder to move weapons and supplies across the LoC to support fighters there. According to one Lashkar militant who had been the District Commander in Srinagar, the group was forced to rely more heavily on the support infrastructure it had built in Indian-administered Kashmir after 2005.[27]

Violent incidents dropped 16 per cent from 2005–2006, 34 per cent from 2006–2007 and 35 per cent from 2007–2008, according to the Indian Ministry of Home Affairs.[28] Indian counter-insurgency efforts contributed to this decline, and by this time security forces were having significant success breaking up Lashkar's cells and killing its cadres. The population's appetite for conflict also remained low. Money was pumped into the region for reconstruction following the earthquake that occurred in 2005, further reducing the number of ready recruits or supporters of the ongoing insurgency. Many Kashmiris were already disenchanted with the conflict, and as the populace became increasingly concerned with local political issues they became even less interested in waging a bloody liberation struggle. Several interlocutors from Indian-administered Kashmir also observed that while anger at India remained potent, many people were simply fed up with the militants by this point. That local factors contributed to stability does not nullify Pakistani attempts to decrease violence there. Most Indian interlocutors agreed that Musharraf's efforts were a major driver in the reduction of violence. As one Indian analyst said, 'to give the devil his due, he was making a real effort.'[29] Indeed, by 2006 Pakistan's efforts were deemed significant enough to merit considering reciprocity. A modest troop withdrawal from Indian-administered Kashmir was mooted that year, but it was not to the scale Islamabad sought. The Indian government also wanted to handle the issue via private negotiations and balked when Pakistan pushed publicly for major demilitarization.[30]

Meanwhile Pakistan remained unprepared to abandon the Kashmir jihad entirely: first, because doing so would rob the country of leverage; and second, because closing down the Kashmir jihad completely would have internal repercussions in terms of Pakistan's relations with those militants who remained committed to this front. The army and ISI continued to encourage small numbers of militants to cross the LoC and directed others to use alternative routes to reach Indian-administered Kashmir. The aforementioned journalist who was reporting from Pakistan-administered Kashmir at the time asserted that Brigadier-rank officers were sent to the LoC to make sure launchings stayed low, but not to end them entirely.[31] Current and former Lashkar sources confirm the army allowed small numbers of militants to attempt to cross the LoC. Soldiers and ISI officers also sometimes provided necessary intelligence, including identifying locations conducive to infiltration.[32] According to one civil servant in Indian-administered Kashmir, controllers operating on the Pakistani side of the LoC also continued to dictate targeting instructions to their commanders in the field.[33] Most of those infiltrating still came across the LoC, but Indian sources assert that Lashkar infiltrated small numbers of militants into India via Nepal, Bangladesh or by sea, after which they would attempt to make their way to Indian-administered Kashmir.[34] The fact that Lashkar cadres went to this trouble is notable not only in light of the alleged directive to use alternative routes. It also illustrates the depth of Lashkar's commitment to the Kashmir jihad. However, it should be noted that some of those who made this journey might have done so to retrieve weapons or explosives for use against targets in India's heartland.

In addition to using Indian-administered Kashmir as a staging or transit point, or simply hunkering down and contenting themselves with low-level operations there, Lashkar also increased its non-violent activities. The group sought to 'rebuild the foundation of Kashmir' by providing money for the construction of mosques and dispensaries. As in Pakistan, one aim was to make its interpretation of the Ahl-e-Hadith faith acceptable to the people. To this end, Lashkar began steering more money and manpower toward non-militant activities in order to do it.[35] This included providing funding for some NGOs and members of Kashmiri civil society in the hopes they would act as its public face in the region. These people did not proclaim their support for Lashkar, but indirectly

181

worked to influence the environment in its favor. One Indian analyst asserted that this included attempting to stoke grassroots protests and political violence.[36] However, because protests were, and remain, a response to poor governance and the Indian security forces' heavy-handedness, it is questionable whether Lashkar's agitation was necessary or counted for much. Further, despite local frustration with the status quo and anger at many aspects of Indian rule, the populace remained largely unenthused about both Lashkar's interpretation of Islam and its desire to regenerate the conflict.

Indian jihadis were more enthusiastic, and Lashkar continued to assist the indigenous terrorist movement it had helped to build. The Musharraf regime, which made a real effort to curtail the Kashmir jihad, never dismantled the infrastructure on its soil used to execute and support terrorist attacks against India. On 7 July 2006, militants bombed seven commuter trains running on Mumbai's suburban railway. The explosions occurred over the course of approximately ten minutes and killed more than 200 people. Indian Prime Minister Manmohan Singh stated he was 'certain that the terrorist modules responsible for the Mumbai blasts are instigated from across the border.'[37] Lashkar is suspected of recruiting some of the operatives responsible for the 2006 strikes, facilitating their transit into Pakistan for training and providing some of the financing.[38] Abdur Rehman Syed, the army Major who joined Lashkar in 2003 and had his own unit in Karachi, claimed to know the Indian militants responsible for the blasts.[39] Lashkar is believed to have directed its Indian affiliates to execute the attacks, but whether this included targeting guidance or simply instructions to 'do something big' is unclear. Among the Indian security establishment, there was confusion regarding both who ordered the attacks and the nature of their objectives. Indian militants were undoubtedly involved in executing the operation, but at the time there were some in New Delhi who believed members of the ISI in Pakistan who wanted to scupper the peace process had pulled the strings.[40]

Whether or not ISI officers were actively seeking to spoil the peace process, the agents tasked with handling those Lashkar operatives who coordinated operations against India would have known about the attacks. These line officers enjoyed significant operational latitude, in part to provide their leaders with plausible deniability, and often acted upon their own initiative when it came to managing relations with the militants they handled. This remained the case at the time of writing. As one observer has noted, ISI operations were (and still are) typically regulated by 'directive control' rather than 'detailed control' meaning field officers were empowered to act without prior approval from their superiors.[41] The Musharraf regime's decision to maintain Lashkar as an asset with which to apply calibrated pressure also meant directives from Islamabad were relative rather than absolute. In other words, they were open to interpretation. Out of loyalty to Lashkar, ideological inclinations or their own sense of what served Pakistan's interests, some field officers took advantage of the ambivalent nature of Musharraf's policies. Thus, even if the attacks were not sanctioned at the highest levels, this does not absolve the Musharraf regime of responsibility. Regardless of who ordered the attacks, one thing was certain: talk about peace could not continue.

New Delhi publicly terminated the public dialogue with Pakistan that had been moving steadily forward since 2004. Under international pressure, Hafiz Saeed was placed under house arrest on 10 August.[42] He was released on 29 August after the Lahore High Court ruled that the government had failed to provide evidence for his detention, but detained once again only hours later for a two-month period.[43] This appears to have been done in anticipation of a meeting between Musharraf and Singh on the sidelines of the Non-Aligned Movement summit in September. Dialogue between the two leaders during that summit helped to forge an agreement the following March [2007] to establish the Anti-Terrorism Mechanism to coordinate an exchange of information between India and Pakistan on terrorist threats. Although the foreign ministries, rather than intelligence agencies, led this effort it was still doomed to fail operationally because lack of trust between the two countries made real intelligence sharing almost impossible. However, its true intention does not appear to have been operational according to interlocutors close to the respective security establishments in India and Pakistan. Rather, the move was intended to show progress on the problem of Pakistani support for terrorism against India and thus enable a resumption of dialogue, which it did.

One Indian analyst asserted that, following the 2006 attacks, Lashkar worked hard to put a firewall between its own operations and those of its Indian affiliates.[44] By this time the Indian Mujahideen was a potent force, even if it was to be another year before the movement began claiming attacks using that moniker. However, it was also a fluid network in which, despite increased coordination, cells often operated clandestinely from one another. Nor was every jihadi cell connected to the Indian Mujahideen—other outfits existed and operated independently.[45] What many of these actors shared was continued access to external support, of which Lashkar remained the primary provider. The case of Ali Abdul Aziz al-Hooti is useful for understanding how extensive Lashkar's transnational support for Indian militancy was by this point. The child of an Indian mother, al-Hooti was radicalized during visits to his home near Mumbai where he heard about atrocities visited upon Indian Muslims. Al-Hooti is alleged to have trained twice with Lashkar by the time he had turned thirty, and became one of its top organizers in the Gulf and a key interface with the Indian Mujahideen. He transited money and weapons into India and helped to send dozens of recruits to Pakistan from his base of operations in Muscat, the capital of Oman.

However, Al-Hooti's recruitment efforts were not limited to the Gulf. He is believed to have recruited operatives from across the Indian Ocean, and his efforts reached all the way to the Maldives.[46] Some of the funding he supplied is believed to have enabled Lashkar to establish networks used to transit weapons into India by sea. These networks were employed in an unsuccessful attempt at a seaborne infiltration of eight Lashkar fidayeen into Mumbai in 2007. According to the Omani authorities, al-Hooti also considered launching operations within the Sultanate itself. In June 2007, he and Lashkar sympathizers in Oman discussed targeting prominent landmarks in Muscat, including the Golden Tulip Hotel and a British Broadcasting Corporation [BBC] office. No final plans were ever put in place, but the Omani authorities were able to gather enough evidence to convict al-Hooti in 2009.[47] His case illustrates the degree to which Lashkar's networks, intended primarily to support operations against India, could be used against other countries as well.

Al-Hooti's case was also part of a developing trend in which operatives pursued attacks against both Indian and foreign targets. Riyazuddin Nasir, alias Mohammad Ghouse, sought to blend the two by launching attacks in India that would kill Westerners, Jews and Indians. A resident of Hyderabad, India, Nasir is believed to have trained with Lashkar for 12–18 months between October 2005 and July 2007.[48] He belonged to a cell headed by Mohammad Abdul Shahid, one of the men recruited by the group in the wake of the Gujarat pogrom of 2002. The cell was linked to Lashkar and HuJI-B, on which it relied for logistical support.[49] As with the Indian Mujahideen, these men saw themselves as independent operators even though in reality their ability to function effectively without support from groups such as Lashkar or HuJI-B was limited. Nasir broke contact with his handlers in Pakistan soon after returning to India, and began planning a series of bomb attacks targeting American and Israeli tourists on Goa's crowded beaches over the Christmas-New Year period.[50] He and an accomplice later told police that, in addition to targeting Israeli and Western tourists, they also planed to strike against American and other foreign information technologies [IT] companies in Bangalore.[51] Nasir at one point claimed to an Indian journalist that he had discussed the Goa operation with Zaki-ur-Rehman Lakhvi, but Indian security officials believe he was acting independently of Lashkar by this time.[52] Nasir's case, to an even greater degree than al-Hooti's, highlights the degree to which the fight against India was overlapping with the global jihad by the latter half of the decade.

The emerging focus on foreign targets is notable, but we should not forget that Indians remained the ones dying by the hundreds in attacks perpetrated by their own countrymen. The bombing campaign, led by the Indian Mujahideen and supported by Lashkar operatives like al-Hooti, reached its apex from 2007–2008. Although the IM network had existed since the middle of the decade, it first announced its presence on 23 November 2007. That day it sent emails to media outlets immediately prior to executing a series of bomb blasts in three cities in the North Indian state of Uttar

Pradesh.[53] Additional emails and attacks followed: nine bomb blasts in busy markets in the city of Jaipur on 13 May 2008; eight low-intensity blasts in India's IT capital of Bangalore on 25 July 2008; sixteen synchronized explosions in Ahmedabad in the state of Gujarat the following day; and five bomb blasts in the capital, New Delhi, on 13 September 2008.[54] The Indian Mujahideen released a 14-page manifesto prior to the Ahmedabad bombings, which stated these attacks were in retaliation for the injustices meted out against Indian Muslims and made specific mention of the 2002 Gujarat riots.[55]

For many years, Lashkar's aim had been to recruit indigenous actors capable of launching terrorist attacks against India, while sending Pakistani foot soldiers to fight in Indian-administered Kashmir. As is evident, from 2005–2008 it was having more success with the former than the latter. By mid-2008 the Indian security services were getting to grips with the threat from homegrown jihadis, breaking up cells and capturing or killing operatives. Despite successful counter-terrorism measures, only one of the Indian Mujahideen founders, Mohammad Sadiq Israr Sheikh who was introduced in the previous chapter, was in custody at the time of writing. Most of the key commanders were fugitives and Indian officials alleged they were hiding in Pakistan and Bangladesh. Several captured operatives reportedly confirmed the presence of Indian commanders in Karachi, where they were believed to play a role in coordinating with Lashkar, South Asian criminal syndicates (some of whose members also remain based in Karachi) and operatives in India.[56] Meanwhile, the number of Pakistani militants the group was successfully sending across the LoC had dwindled, and many of those in Indian-administered Kashmir were laying low. The group was born in 1986 during the anti-Soviet jihad in Afghanistan. Twenty years later, more of its members were returning there to wage war against America and its allies.

## Separateness and Togetherness

Musharraf's decision to side with the US in the wake of the 9/11 attacks necessitated forsaking the Taliban in Afghanistan. However, this did not extend to vigorously pursuing the movement in Pakistan, where Taliban leaders were allowed to resettle in the Tribal Areas and Quetta (the capital of Balochistan province). During its subsequent counter-terrorism campaign the Musharraf regime spared the Taliban, which in turn followed a policy of abjuring attacks in Pakistan. Nor did the US, after demanding that Pakistan abandon support for the Taliban in Afghanistan, force the issue. Pakistan was making an effort to capture or kill al-Qaeda operatives on its soil in the early years after 9/11, which was then America's top priority. The overriding primacy the US gave to al-Qaeda allowed the Taliban space to regenerate. It began redeveloping its networks in Afghanistan and laying the foundation in 2003 for a future escalation.[57] The insurgency there was showing signs of growth in 2004, but even as late as 2005 the political and security situation had not yet deteriorated. Raiding into Afghanistan from Pakistan began in earnest that year. According to Ashley Tellis, an expert on the region who has advised the US government, it was at this point that pressure on Musharraf to interdict the Taliban became the subject of high-level US demarches to Pakistan.[58] By this time Islamabad's calculus favored increasing support for the Taliban, rather than cracking down on it.

Pakistan had supported the Taliban during the 1990s in the hopes of securing strategic depth in Afghanistan, partially as a place to train militants for operations against India and primarily for use in the event of a war with India. Doing so was also a means of negating Indian influence in Afghanistan, which stoked Pakistani fears of encirclement. Nor was Pakistan alone in supporting a proxy force in Afghanistan, where India had supported the Northern Alliance, though not nearly to the same extent. India not only maintained relations with some former Northern Alliance commanders, but in the decade following the Taliban's overthrow in 2001 it also poured in close to 1 billion dollars in development aid.[59] This reinforced Pakistan's already high fear of encirclement and stoked suspicions that India's intelligence agency, RAW, was bent on stirring up trouble. In addition to concerns that India was using its Afghan consulates as listening posts to gather intelligence, it was an article of faith among the Pakistani security establishment that RAW used Afghanistan as a base from which to support separatists waging a low level insurgency in Balochistan; an allegation Western interlocutors agreed was not unfounded. A former member of the British intelligence community and a British academic who undertook extensive fieldwork in Balochistan in 2009 both agreed that RAW had provided financial support, though there was no definitive evidence that its assistance extended to providing weapons or training to Baloch separatists.[60] Minor though support may have been, however, Baloch separatism was and remains a neuralgic issue for Pakistan. So too is India's overall presence in Afghanistan. As its economic and diplomatic footprint there grew, the Taliban's utility as an instrument to secure Pakistan's interests increased.

This expansion of Indian influence coincided with increasing uncertainty about US staying power in Afghanistan. In summer 2005 Washington announced that it would hand over control of the Afghan mission to NATO, and later said that it would withdraw more than 1,000 troops. Because of the escalating insurgency the order was reversed, but Lt. Gen. David Barno (Retd), who had been the US commander in Afghanistan at the time, testified two years later that the message sent by the initial order caused 'both friends and enemies to re-calculate their options—with a view toward the US no longer being a lead actor in Afghanistan.' He specified that in mid-2005 Pakistan 're-calculated its position vis-à-vis Afghanistan in light of concerns for a diminished and less aggressive U.S. presence.'[61] Former US Deputy Secretary of State Richard Armitage offered a similar assessment, suggesting that the ISI became more heavily involved in Afghanistan in late 2005–early 2006.[62] A trove of US military field reports from Afghanistan in 2004–2009 were leaked in 2010 and reconfirmed the already common assessment that the ISI was abetting, and at times possibly guiding, militants fighting Coalition forces in Afghanistan. This reportedly included all manner of support, including direct assistance to the Taliban with organizing military offensives.[63] In other words, just when Musharraf's regime was reducing the tempo of operations in Indian-administered Kashmir, the ISI was simultaneously expanding support to insurgents in Afghanistan. Yet its alliance with

America also forced Pakistan to take steps against some militants, for which its military and citizenry paid in blood.

The development of the insurgency in Pakistan that sprang forth from the Tribal Areas is worthy of its own book-length study. Briefly stated, the Tehrik-e-Taliban Pakistan [TTP], a consortium of pro-Taliban tribal militants that officially united in 2007 and spearheaded the insurgency, coalesced in the early years of the decade in response to military interventions into the Tribal Areas. Al-Qaeda's growing presence in South Waziristan and escalating raids into Afghanistan led to US pressure on Pakistan to take action. The government initially tried to negotiate the handover of foreign fighters present in the Tribal Areas, but after attempts at diplomacy and bribery failed, Pakistan launched a series of incursions into South Waziristan. These efforts resulted in significant losses for the military and failed to halt cross-border activity or permanently dislodge al-Qaeda militants, many of whom relocated to North Waziristan where they were welcomed by the Haqqani Network.[64] It is named for its leader Jalaluddin Haqqani, a legendary commander during the anti-Soviet jihad in Afghanistan who was also a favorite of the US at the time. His network is closely aligned with the Taliban and is one of the main insurgent groups active in the Afghan insurgency against Coalition forces. Its leadership is close to both the ISI, which has supported its efforts across the Durand Line, as well as to al-Qaeda.

The first significant military incursion into South Waziristan began in March 2004 and was followed by a peace agreement with tribal militants in late April. More fighting ensued from June through January 2005, with yet another peace agreement signed in February. The accord was intended to spare the army further losses and to restore the status quo, whereby the tribes were held responsible for maintaining security in FATA. The militants with whom the state was dealing, however, had no intention of returning to the status quo and the state's willingness to cut deals only emboldened them to expand their writ. Meanwhile, al-Qaeda members and other foreign fighters migrated to North Waziristan, which became their main base for operations. Pro-Taliban militias were emerging in other tribal agencies, as well as in parts of the NWFP, during this time too. In January 2006, Hellfire missiles fired from an American CIA-operated drone obliterated three buildings, described as safe houses, in Damadola village in Bajaur. The strike was intended to kill Ayman al-Zawahiri, al-Qaeda's number 2, but he had left hours earlier. Instead, the strike claimed the lives of eighteen civilians, including five women and five children. This fueled anti-American sentiment across the country and especially in the Tribal Areas where approximately 8,000 Pashtun tribesmen protested, sparking an acceleration of violence.[65] Militants came out in the open in FATA that year, ambushing army convoys, attacking military and government installations as well as abducting and executing various officials.[66] They also began employing suicide attacks against security forces there and in the NWFP. Yet another peace agreement followed in September 2006. Known as the Waziristan Accord, and signed in North Waziristan, it was intended to end all fighting between pro-Taliban militants and the government. This brought a momentary calm to North and South Waziristan, but also enabled the burgeoning TTP movement to expand further. Their growing strength, coupled with the Taliban's resurgence in Afghanistan, invigorated the wider Pakistani jihadi community. In the years immediately prior, the security services were coming down particularly hard on those who openly affiliated with al-Qaeda and many militants from various groups had gone underground. Now there was a sense the tide was shifting, and militants were once again letting their jihadi flag fly.

A proto-insurgency was clearly extant by this time. The event that precipitated its extension beyond the Tribal Areas and severed any remaining ties between Pakistan and many of its former proxies took place in Islamabad. The leadership of the pro-Taliban Lal Masjid [Red Mosque] located there had been challenging the government over a host of issues, including implementing sharia in Pakistan and ending support for the US. The Lal Masjid included a male madrassa [Jamia Faridia] and a female madrassa [Jamia Hafsa], and the army had used it since the 1980s to recruit fighters for proxy jihads in Afghanistan and Kashmir. However, its leaders also had strong ties to the militants in FATA who were a war with the state and by 2007 the Lal Masjid was considered a potential threat to Pakistan's capital city. Fearing government action against their alma mata, former students who had earlier joined various Deobandi outfits began holing up in the mosque in spring of that year.[67] Meanwhile, the leadership continued to agitate for sharia while their students harassed local businesses deemed un-Islamic. Lashkar's leaders initially supported the call by clerics at the Lal Masjid for sharia, but as the situation devolved they distanced themselves from the agitation, claiming no group had the right forcibly to implement sharia in Pakistan.[68] On 3 July 2007 a series of provocations led to a gun battle between members of the Lal Masjid and Pakistan security forces. Soldiers surrounded the mosque and imposed a curfew, but also offered amnesty to those who surrendered. The siege lasted a week. Then, on the morning of 10 July, Pakistani commandos launched an assault. Casualty figures vary and conspiracy theories abound regarding how many died during the fighting, which lasted two days. Among those killed was Maulana Abdul Rashid Ghazi, one of the two leaders of the Lal Masjid. The other leader, his brother Maulana Abdul Aziz Ghazi, was arrested while trying to escape disguised in a burqa.

FATA erupted and over 300 people were killed in the weeks following the storming of the Lal Masjid.[69] Within a year the insurgency, in the form of high-profile terrorist attacks, had spread to Punjab province. However, FATA and the NWFP continued to absorb the lion's share of the violence. The TTP officially united in December 2007 under the leadership of Baitullah Mehsud, with commanders operating in each of Pakistan's seven tribal agencies as well as a number of districts in the NWFP. It was an umbrella organization rather than a hierarchical one, and disputes continued to exist among the various actors operating under its banner. Nonetheless, Baitullah succeeded in bringing greater unity to the movement before he was killed by a US drone strike in August 2009. His death created temporary confusion and competition among TTP commanders, but did little to slow the insurgency. Nor was the military able to dislodge permanently militants from their strongholds in the region. After launching an incursion into the Swat Valley in spring 2008 to clear it of militants and another into the Bajaur tribal agency, the army deployed over 40,000 troops into South

Waziristan in October 2009. Although it proved able to clear these areas in the short term, consolidating gains and keeping insurgents at bay proved far more challenging. This contributed to the army's reluctance to expand counter-insurgency efforts into North Waziristan, as did the fact that the Haqqani Network based there remained a useful proxy in Afghanistan.

Pakistan's policy of separating good jihadis from bad meant that it was both a supporter and victim of jihadism. On one end of the spectrum were Lashkar, the Haqqani Network and the Taliban. They did not attack the state and instead directed their violence beyond Pakistan's borders. In return, they continued to receive preferential treatment. Al-Qaeda, the TTP, Ilyas Kashmiri's 313 Brigade and the Punjabi Taliban [a network of militants who formerly belonged to JeM, LeJ and SSP] were on the other end, actively at war with the state, with a mélange of other actors at various points in the middle. However, what all of these outfits shared in common was involvement in Afghanistan, which created the conditions for increased collaboration and cross-pollination. Thus, the state was actively supporting actors aligned with those militants with which it was at war. Further, although the ISI retained strong influence over many of Lashkar's senior leaders, these leaders did not always exercise control over the group's commanders or its rank-and-file. In other words, selectivity also failed to take account of internal group dynamics, since the state was supporting outfits whose own militants were sometimes involved in attacks against Pakistan.

The schizophrenia of this macro policy was amplified at the ground level by elements within the ISI who sometimes worked at cross-purposes. For example, David Headley's impression, according to his interrogators, was that the ISI felt tremendous pressure to stop the integration of Kashmir-centric outfits with those based in the Tribal Areas.[70] Yet one Pakistani researcher alleged that ISI operatives arranged meetings between previously Kashmir-centric groups and the Taliban in spring 2007 for the purpose of enhancing cooperation in Afghanistan to counter Indian influence.[71] According to that researcher, Abdul Rehman Makki, Lashkar's head of External Affairs responsible for liaising with other jihadi groups, attended.[72]

EXPANSION AND INTEGRATION

It is possible Headley's interpretation was incorrect or that the ISI's calculus changed after the insurgency gained steam following the storming of the Lal Masjid in summer 2007. But it is equally plausible that one hand did not know what the other was doing or that different line officers were pursuing their own tactical objectives without due consideration of the wider strategic ramifications.

The questions of how much to contribute to the insurgency in Afghanistan and, to lesser degree, whether to fight against Pakistan drew different answers from various factions within Lashkar. Interviews with some of the group's leaders revealed fury at America's perceived occupation of Afghanistan and the belief that current policies in Pakistan had been imposed on the country by the US. This overlapped with anger about India's presence in Afghanistan and its perceived desire to destabilize Pakistan from across the Durand Line.[73] Entering the Afghan front presented an opportunity to fight the US *and* another avenue for harming India. Yet these leaders also made clear that liberating Kashmir remained the priority. According to several Lashkar members, the leadership continued to insist this was a more legitimate jihad, making some of the same arguments they had made since the 1990s: the number of security forces per capita in Indian-administered Kashmir remained one of the highest in the world; and Lashkar's main base was closer to Indian-administered Kashmir than Afghanistan, making it imperative to fight there first.[74] Zaki-ur Rehman Lakhvi also made the point that Lashkar had built its reputation in Indian-administered Kashmir and remained close to the population there, meaning it could perform jihad better than in Afghanistan where it would be difficult to replicate its success.[75] Yet this did not stop him from steering a small, but steady, flow of fighters toward Afghanistan once the decision was made to open a second front there.[76]

Several factors likely influenced this decision. First, although Lashkar was not facing mass desertion, joining the insurgency in Afghanistan was a means to keep its cadres on side. The Kashmir jihad was flagging, in part because the state was restraining it, and even some Lashkar members who favored this cause over fighting against America and its allies began leaving for want of an open front. Others were drawn to the Afghan jihad because of the success

193

other actors were having there. Just as Lashkar's reputation as the most aggressive and committed group fighting in Indian-administered Kashmir had swelled its ranks during that conflict's heyday, it now risked losing current and potential members for the same reason. Still others had become motivated more by waging jihad against the 'Crusaders' in Afghanistan than the Hindu occupiers in Indian-administered Kashmir.[77] The issue of preserving personnel was particularly important in terms of Lashkar's commanders, who were more difficult to replace than rank-and-file recruits. For example, a senior commander and one of the group's founders, known as Abdul Qadir, left to fight with the Taliban in 2005 in part because Lashkar was not prioritizing the Afghan jihad. (He was also a rival of Lakhvi's and hoped to replace him as Lashkar's top commander, suggesting personal dynamics also may have played a role.)[78] Second, in addition to the issue of manpower, some donors, particularly those in the Gulf, were more interested in funding jihad against America and its allies than they were in liberating Indian-administered Kashmir. Third, although it made no secret of prioritizing the Kashmir jihad, Lashkar was a pan-Islamist organization. Fighting on the Afghan front was not only ideologically appealing to some of its leaders; it was also difficult to justify abstaining from for others who might have preferred an ongoing exclusive focus on Kashmir. Finally, as already mentioned, growing Indian influence in Afghanistan meant fighting there provided an opportunity to wage jihad against the Hindus and the Crusaders.

Lashkar's entrance into the Afghan front was the result of a policy decision taken by the senior leadership to launch a jihad there, after which a commander was designated to oversee operations. It is difficult to quantify how many people Lashkar deployed or recruited to fight in Afghanistan. Estimates suggest the number remained small through 2009–2010, when the group's footprint there appears to have expanded.[79] Although it was no secret that its militants were participating in the insurgency, for the purposes of deniability they did not fight openly under the Lashkar banner and nor did the group publicize their activities as prolifically as it did for those fighting in Kashmir. Instead, many fought with Lashkar-linked groups based in Kunar province or the Tribal Areas. Several interlocutors believe that Hafiz Saeed used his connections to help facilitate this development, setting up a logistical line that directed financial support and fighters to like-minded outfits.[80] In addition to those members Lashkar deployed to Afghanistan or recruited specifically to fight there, some within the organization continued to take what essentially amounted to a sabbatical and to imbed on their own with other outfits. For example, Abdur Rehman Syed spent much of 2005 and 2006 fighting alongside the Taliban, periodically returning to Lahore and working with Lashkar.[81] Allowing members to take leave or exploiting connections with other groups to channel fighters to the Afghan front contributed to the intermingling of Lashkar members with other militants. At times, it also limited the senior leadership's command and control.

Jamiat al-Dawa al-Quran wal-Sunna [JuDQS], which supported the nascent MDI after its inception in 1986, was one of the outfits Lashkar worked with to channel fighters to the Afghan front.[82] JuDQS had a presence in Kunar province, where the majority of Lashkar fighters were active, as well as a base in the Bajaur tribal agency from which militants raided across the border. Arab fighters who either settled in Kunar following the anti-Soviet jihad, or had links to people who did, provided another connection for Lashkar militants fighting there.[83] The Shah Sahib Group in Mohmand Tribal Agency provided yet another means for members of the group to access the Afghan front. Muslim Khan [a.k.a. Khalid Shah Sahib], who had been a member of Lashkar before 9/11, founded it to provide infrastructure for people from his former organization to fight in Afghanistan. Despite being a stand-alone outfit and receiving support from al-Qaeda, Shah Sahib was known on the ground as a Lashkar group.[84] However, according to one Pakistani researcher familiar with the group, it was actually closer to people who officially worked on the JuD-side of the organization.[85]

Fighting in Afghanistan necessitated an increased presence in the Tribal Areas and greater integration with the mélange of jihadi outfits located there, rather than just those few that were directly connected to Lashkar. Its group identity remained that of an India-centric, Ahl-e-Hadith outfit whose leadership and top operatives were close to the ISI. Yet its members were now operating amidst

Pashtun tribesmen and Deobandi militants, some of whom were at war with the state. During conversations with high-ranking members of JuD and Lashkar militants, they made clear their anger at Pakistan's rulers and admitted that some of their members were motivated to join the insurgency. However, they also criticized the jihad being waged against the country and made clear their ideological disdain for those actors responsible.[86] These tensions existed not only within the organization, but also between Lashkar's leaders and the outfits with which they were collaborating. Lashkar's relationship with the ISI, which sometimes used the group to eliminate militants threatening the state, led some in the TTP, al-Qaeda and among the various Deobandi militants to question the group's loyalty even after it entered the Afghan theater.[87] Thus, different cliques co-existed within Lashkar, which in turn now existed in a space where various outfits with overlapping and competing agendas were present. Being a distinct faction, inside a group or space where multiple factions are present, includes both separateness and togetherness. As a result of Lashkar's expanding presence in FATA, opportunities for collaboration and conflict increased.

Collaboration with other outfits included: working together to recruit and infiltrate fighters into Afghanistan; sharing safe houses and resources including weapons, explosives and information; joint training; and fighting together in Afghanistan.[88]

Joint training took place at the organizational level and some of Lashkar's instructors worked in camps belonging to other outfits, though at times this may have been done in a freelance capacity. Although Lashkar members did not have a substantial footprint in terms of manpower in Afghanistan, their acumen with regard to small unit tactics and explosives meant even a small number of men could have significant influence. The group's bomb-makers are also known to be among the best in the region, according to Western diplomats and security officials. They assert Lashkar's 'bomb jockeys' (to steal the term one of them used) became responsible for building some of the improvised explosive devices used in Afghanistan as well as instructing others on how to do so.[89] Notably, there was an influx of Western recruits into the Tribal Areas beginning in mid-2006.[90] Some of Lashkar's trainers and explosives experts are believed to have begun working with al-Qaeda to instruct would-be Western terrorists, though whether they were always doing so with the blessing of the leadership or were occasionally working in a freelance capacity remains unclear.[91]

Joint training signaled an expanding Lashkar presence in North and South Waziristan, where al-Qaeda and the Haqqani Network were based. The group also had a strong presence in Bajaur, thanks to historical relationships with JuDQS and Jamaat-ul-Mujahideen, and Mohmand, where the Shah Sahib group operated. These two tribal agencies constituted a recruiting ground, as well as a base for housing recruits before infiltrating them across the border. Its members developed a high-degree of integration and cooperation with other actors operating in these agencies as well, including the TTP, the Taliban, and operatives from al-Qaeda.[92] Along with growing its presence in the Tribal Areas, JuD established additional mosques, madaris, schools and offices throughout the NWFP and built up its relief efforts in the region.[93] This infrastructure was used for missionary work, the provision of social services, and to recruit for the Afghan jihad. For example, the group is known to have recruited in the Lower Dir and Swat districts of the NWFP, where local interlocutors assert those who joined were sent primarily to Kunar province.[94] Lashkar also reclaimed a foothold in the Peshawar scene where its members were able to link up with Afghan Salafis connected to JuDQS who were moving men across the border, via Bajaur and Mohmand, to fight in Kunar.[95] Outside of the NWFP and FATA, Southern Punjab was by this time becoming a feeder for the fight in Afghanistan, and Lashkar recruiters stepped up efforts there too.[96]

Several specific examples of Lashkar recruitment are notable because they illustrate its members' integration with al-Qaeda, the Haqqani Network and the TTP, which were running camps in the Waziristan agencies to indoctrinate and train young Pakistanis to become suicide bombers. Lashkar members recruited men from the Ahl-e-Hadith mosque in the Jalozai refugee camp in Peshawar, promising they would be given training and their expenses paid in return for joining the jihad in Afghanistan. According to the accounts given to a Pakistan-based journalist by relatives of those recruited, some of the men were sent to the aforementioned camps to become suicide bombers in Afghanistan.[97] In another instance, a Lashkar operative recruited two youths from Buner in the NWFP and brought them to Muridke where they were given the option of becoming suicide bombers. He promised them two weeks of training at Muridke, after which they would be taken to Peshawar and introduced to other militants. After tribal elders intervened and brought both of them home, one of the boys explained that at Muridke, 'We were told it is our choice to become a freedom fighter or a suicide bomber. But we should never fight against Pakistan.'[98] To put these recruitment activities in perspective, suicide bombings in Afghanistan jumped from 17 in 2005 to 123 in 2006, and some of the US military reports leaked in 2010 detailed efforts by ISI officers to run networks of suicide bombers recruited from Pakistan.[99]

The bulk of Lashkar members who participated in the Afghan jihad during this time fought in and around Kunar and Nuristan provinces. A few of them had already begun turning up in the area earlier in the decade, and by 2005 the Korengal Valley in Kunar province was a place where insurgents were guaranteed combat if they wanted it. This was not strictly, or even primarily, a Lashkar front; multiple outfits were active in the area. Because the group had historical ties to Afghan Salafis there, this was the natural place for its members to engage the enemy. Others fighting there included the Afghan Taliban, local Salafis, Kashmir Khan's Hizb-e-Islami faction, Jaish-e-Mohammad, the Tehrik-e-Taliban Pakistan and Jamiat al-Dawa al-Quran wal-Sunna, which included some Arab fighters from the first Afghan jihad in its ranks. Additional Arab veterans, who had settled in Pakistan after the Soviet withdrawal, also returned to fight, while other foreign fighters and some al-Qaeda operatives appeared as well.[100] Lashkar members shared a commonality of interests with these other actors and were part of the complex insurgency there.

According to a senior US defense official, the militants Lashkar deployed to Eastern Afghanistan were, along with militants from JeM, among the most effective fighters in the region.[101] An ISAF official said that when there was a particularly well-organized attack Lashkar was their default suspect since 'they are top notch fighters, a cut above what we normally see.'[102] An attack on US Combat Outpost (COP) Wanat in mid-July 2008 is among the most notable operations in which Lashkar cadres are known to have participated since entering the Afghan theater. They were part of a force consisting of almost 200 militants from several different outfits who assaulted and nearly overran the combat outpost, which was located in the village of Wanat in Nuristan near the border with neighboring Kunar province. Nine US soldiers were killed and another fifteen US soldiers and four Afghan soldiers were wounded during four hours of fighting.[103] The insurgents were advanced enough to warn the villagers to leave beforehand, gather undetected and mount the operation without breaking radio silence, which would have alerted the allied force.[104]

Six days earlier, on 7 July 2008, Hamza Shakoor drove an explosives-laden vehicle into the Indian embassy in Kabul. The Haqqani Network planned the operation, but Shakoor had entered the world of militancy when JuD's Gujranwala chapter recruited him in 2006.[105] The attack reportedly was supposed to be a fidayeen assault, but the embassy had upgraded its security after the Riyasat-e-Amniyat-e-Milli [Afghanistan's security service, known as RAM] alerted India. This made such an attack more operationally challenging, which presumably led Shakoor to execute the vehicle-born suicide bombing operation.[106] American officials later accused the ISI of helping to plan the attack.[107] This was not an isolated incident. According to US intelligence, the ISI used the Haqqani Network to strike Indian targets in Afghanistan on other occasions.[108] In addition to attacking Indian targets, Haqqani militants were also responsible for a host of assaults against high-profile coalition targets. It is unclear whether Shakoor was dispatched to take part in the operation against the Indian embassy, volunteered for the assignment or was already fighting alongside the Haqqanis by this time. It is also worth highlighting that collaboration between Lashkar and the Haqqani Network was fueled partially by the fact that both functioned as proxies for the ISI, which at times coordinated cooperation between the two.[109]

As Lashkar's footprint grew in the NWFP and FATA, so too did the opportunity for occasional conflict with local rivals. For example, according to one former senior officer in the Intelligence

Bureau, and confirmed by a high-ranking JuD official, the TTP killed approximately fifteen JuD members in Swat in 2008 and another three members in Bajaur in April 2009.[110] Both sources claimed these cadres were doing relief work, though it is possible they also were engaged in recruitment or other activities. Given the organization's missionary zeal, they almost certainly were promoting the Ahl-e-Hadith school of thought in areas where Deobandi militants were the most powerful actors. In addition to the sectarian divide, because Lashkar (and JuD) members were sometimes suspected of working with the ISI against those militants at war with the state, it is possible this contributed to the clashes.

One of the most striking examples of factional infighting occurred in the Mohmand tribal agency when the Lashkar-linked Shah Sahib group clashed with the Omar Khalid group during the summer of 2008. The latter was led by Abdul Wali Raghib [a.k.a. Omar Khalid] and operated under the TTP umbrella.[111] It fought in Afghanistan as well as against the Pakistani state and was considered more powerful than the Shah Sahib group, which abjured fighting in Pakistan.[112] The two groups managed to coexist for some time, running separate training camps and roadside checkpoints. That changed in mid July 2008 when militants from the Shah Sahib group ambushed a local TTP commander. Omar Khalid lost little time in responding, first storming Shah Sahib's shelters and later that day attacking one of its training camps. During the clash approximately ten members of the Shah Sahib group were killed and many more reportedly captured. Omar Khalid quickly had Shah Sahib and his deputy tried in a Taliban court, which ordered their executions.[113] Lashkar leaders intervened to secure their release, but despite these efforts both were killed.[114] The two outfits continued to clash for several days, while local security forces looked on passively.[115] Omar Khalid said he would release the other captives only after Lashkar's leaders assured Baitullah Mehsud that the Shah Sahib group would leave the Mohmand tribal agency. He also took over the Shah Sahib headquarters and warned that any group operating in Mohmand must show allegiance to the TTP.[116] Local commander rivalry appears to have been one driver of the altercation. However, some sources have suggested Omar Khalid's response was fueled partly by suspicions that the

Lashkar-linked Shah Sahib group was collaborating with the security services, hence the initial attack. Baitullah sought to smooth things out and his spokesman at the time, Qari Hussain Mehsud, stated that Shah group is our ally and his death is a big loss for all of us.[117] The situation was resolved soon after and the Shah Sahib group continued operating in Mohmand agency and working with the TTP.

Collaboration with the TTP and other actors was centered on the jihad in Afghanistan. Lashkar's leaders drew the line at fighting against Pakistan. However, because of the interconnectedness of groups fighting on both sides of the Durand Line, collaboration in Afghanistan sometimes elided into action against Pakistan. Increased integration with other actors launching attacks in Pakistan inevitably led some Lashkar members to become involved in anti-state violence. This included: facilitating the movement of suicide bombers and other terrorists from the NWFP and FATA to the Punjab; building or supplying explosive material for attacks and helping to move this material through the country; providing safe houses and false identity papers to would-be terrorists; and conducting target surveillance.[118] It is difficult to decipher when this cooperation took place at the organizational level and when individuals were freelancing. Moreover, because debates existed within the group about whether to cooperate on attacks against the state, organizational involvement could amount to factions deciding to collaborate with the leadership looking the other way. Most interlocutors believed that those Lashkar members who provided manpower (as opposed to facilitation) to the TTP or other actors for anti-state violence were freelancing. This did not mean that they had split from the group, though in addition to those who engaged in freelancing there were small fissiparous units believed to be active in the Tribal Areas by this point too.[119] Finally, operating in the Tribal Areas meant that even those Lashkar members who were not part of the insurgency in Pakistan or engaged in freelance activities ran the risk of coming under fire from the army. Sometimes the concept of self-defense mutated, prompting militants previously opposed to anti-state violence to engage in it. For example, one Pakistan-based journalist recounted the case of a Lashkar commander who was killed during a military offensive in Bajaur.

He had played no part in the insurgency against Pakistan, but some of his comrades engaged the military following his death.[120]

Lashkar remained more cohesive than other militant groups and its cadres more disciplined, but freelancing increased in 2006–2007.[121] Whether as trainers, explosives experts or tacticians, Lashkar's members were considered among the best in Pakistan. Some began selling their expertise or skills, either on a consistent basis as 'consultants' or in an ad hoc manner for specific attacks.[122] Others were motivated more by ideological conviction and frustration at the leadership's willingness to toe the state's line despite a series of perceived betrayals: Musharraf's willingness to ally with America in 2001; the crackdown [albeit selective] on jihadi outfits thereafter; the army's entrance into the Tribal Areas to root out al-Qaeda and other foreign fighters; and the decision to scale back the Kashmir jihad. The storming of the Lal Masjid was viewed as the final betrayal. This event had an even greater impact on Deobandi militants because of their connection to the Lal Masjid, but Lashkar's cadres were not immune. For example, David Headley suggests this episode contributed to his becoming 'distanced' from the leadership. He saw current colleagues, such as Abdur Rehman Syed, and former ones, like Haroon and his brother Khurram, fighting a clear battle against 'the Crusaders' in Afghanistan. Meanwhile the Pakistani government appeared confused and compromised. As he described it, Headley began to understand that Syed, Haroon and Khurram were engaged in a different type of battle from Lashkar leaders, who continued to prioritize Kashmir, abjure attacks against the state and work with the ISI.[123] Haroon and Khurram had split from Lashkar in 2003, and by the latter years of the decade were working with Ilyas Kashmiri, whose 313 Brigade was close to al-Qaeda and responsible for several attacks in Pakistan from 2007 onwards. But they also kept in touch with members of their former organization, thereby influencing some Lashkar cadres, as well as serving as yet another nodal point for those who wished to access Kashmiri's outfit or through it al-Qaeda.

Lashkar was thriving as a social welfare provider and remained Pakistan's most reliable proxy against India, which continued to be the group's primary enemy. Its leadership was committed to the cause and retained influence in the organization, despite their close ties with the ISI. However, although the leadership still viewed Kashmir as the most important front and it remained the one on which Lashkar focused above all else, that jihad was a shadow of what it once had been. There was internal debate about how deeply involved it should become in the Afghan insurgency and to what degree Lashkar should cooperate with other outfits, particularly those attacking the Pakistani state. Yet, in reality, there was only so much the group could do to halt its members from moving in that direction if they chose to do so. The jihadi milieu in which Lashkar operated by this time was protean, characterized by a mélange of networks that existed alongside, and were interwoven with, institutional outfits. The intensifying integration of established groups and the rise of new ones brought a concomitant atomization, since the burgeoning array of opportunities for collaboration meant actors could shop around for like-minded allies. Militancy in Pakistan had become a buyer's market.

As collaboration increased between Lashkar members and the Taliban, TTP, the Haqqani Network and other Deobandi militants, the sectarian divide shrank, though it did not disappear. Lashkar leaders still viewed Deobandis with a fair degree of disdain, but this mattered less than before. The old loci of activity continued to hold some utility, but new ones had emerged and all of these now overlapped to a greater extent than hitherto. First, Afghanistan had become a focal point for every major militant outfit as well as a host of smaller networks and splinter groups. Second, India continued to receive significant attention from Lashkar. In a sign of the atomization and integration that was taking place, Abdur Rehman Syed, who had been distancing himself from Lashkar for several years, finally quit the group in 2008. He launched his own outfit called Jund-ul-Fida [Army of Fidayeen], which incorporated the Lashkar unit he had overseen in Karachi for attacks against India. It operated under Ilyas Kashmiri's 313 Brigade and was intended to carry out operations primarily in India, though Syed aspired to attack other non-Islamic countries as well.[124] The Haqqani Network also contributed to the jihad against India by attacking that country's interests in Afghanistan. Third, sectarian attacks continued in Pakistan. Not only did a number of the insurgents bring with them their viciously sectarian agendas, but exacerbating sectarian tensions also constituted another means of destabilizing the state.

This highlights the introduction of a new locus of activity: revolutionary jihad against the state. Historically militants had been motivated either by pan-Islamism or sectarianism, and successive regimes—martial and civilian—had encouraged these impulses. Some of Pakistan's militants had turned on their former masters not long after 9/11. By the latter years of the decade a revolutionary ideology had fully taken hold among many established jihadis and a new generation of militants who had little if any affiliation with recognized outfits. Those belonging to this new generation often were more extreme and less nationalistic than the old guard, sometimes competing to outdo one another when it came to attacks in Pakistan in an attempt to build their reputations. The issue of waging war against the state became a major dividing line within the jihadi universe—cutting not only between outfits, but through some of them too. Lashkar's policy vis-à-vis attacking Pakistan remained at the opposite end of the spectrum from a host of other actors who were engaging in revolutionary jihad. But it was close to them geographically and operationally, which contributed to fluidity between them. Thus, Lashkar militants could be active in the revolutionary locus even if the group's formal policy was to avoid it.

Al-Qaeda promoted revolutionary jihad in Pakistan, a decision influenced by its ideology as well as the understanding that destabilizing the country would protect its own safe haven and create difficulties for America. It also focussed significant energies on the insurgency in Afghanistan. The US presence there blurred the lines between a classical jihad to liberate Muslim land and al-Qaeda's American-centric global jihad. This latter approach entailed not only fighting the US and its allies on open fronts like Afghanistan or Iraq, but also striking targets belonging to them wherever they may be found. By the latter years of this decade, al-Qaeda's global view of warfare was infusing an increasing number of militants who were looking to launch out-of-area attacks against American and allied interests. This signified the emergence of a global locus of activity among Pakistan's jihadis. Lashkar's fidayeen assault in Mumbai integrated the Indian and global loci. After several years during which the group's relevance as a militant outfit appeared in decline, despite its limited expansion in Afghanistan, the attacks also launched Lashkar onto the world stage.

weeks and consisted of running, climbing and weapons instruction. Like many trainees before him, Kasab then had to do khidmat, the performance of supervised service at a Lashkar office or camp.[2] After three months of service, Kasab enrolled in the Daura-e-Khasa at the beginning of summer 2008. He traveled, along with the remaining recruits, to Lashkar's office in Okara district's Model Town and then on to the Bait-ul-Mujahideen outside of Muzaffarabad. The camp where they trained was located in the mountains, and once the recruits arrived they were not allowed to leave without their trainers' permission. The Daura-e-Khasa consisted of advanced weapons training as well as further religious indoctrination. The physical element was strenuous, and ten recruits deserted during the two-and-a-half month long training program.[3]

Kasab and the remaining recruits then returned to Muridke for additional classroom instruction, after which they traveled to Karachi for maritime training.[4] They lodged in a house in Azizabad, where Pakistani investigators later found a treasure trove of evidence at the house, which they documented in a dossier delivered to Indian authorities the summer after the Mumbai attacks. Evidence included 'militant literature, two inflatable life boats, different maps including [a] detailed map of [the] Indian coastline, hand-written literature on navigational training, [and a] manual of [an] intelligence course meant for operation[s].'[5] Indian and Pakistani dossiers on the Mumbai investigations state that Lashkar made use of a total of four houses and two training camps in Karachi while preparing for the attacks.[6] From Azizabad the recruits traveled to the coast and then out to sea where they learned to navigate using maps and GPS devices. After completing this initial maritime training they returned to the Bait-ul-Mujahideen near Muzaffarabad, at which point six of the remaining thirteen men were deployed to Indian-administered Kashmir.[7] Three new members were added to the group a day later, and soon after the ten-man squad was told they would be attacking Mumbai. They were divided into five two-person teams, with each team assigned a target: the Chhatrapati Shivaji Terminus [CST]; the Leopold Restaurant and Café; the Taj Mahal Hotel; the Trident-Oberoi Hotel; and a Chabad House [previously known as Nariman House].[8]

All of the men studied maps as well as photographs and video footage of their targets. Lashkar handlers also equipped the recruits with cover identities. The men were given false identification cards with Hindu names, showing them to be students at Indian colleges. Following his arrest police found Kasab to be in the possession of an identification card showing him as a student at Arunodaya Degree College in Hyderabad.[9] Kasab said during one interrogation session the purpose was to fool the Indian coast guard or other law enforcement officers in case they stopped the gunmen prior to the attacks.[10] However, the choice of Hyderabad is also notable given its location in the Deccan Plateau and the fact that Lashkar invented a fictitious group called the Deccan Mujahideen to take credit for the assault on Mumbai. In addition to their fake identities, the men were instructed to tie thread around their wrists, a common practice among Hindus.[11] An Indian national who was working as a Lashkar trainer also taught them Hindi.[12]

The would-be fidayeen then set off once more for Karachi for another day at sea, during which they were taught how to operate the inflatable dingy that would take them the final leg of their seaborne journey. The men also learned how to open the sea valve on a boat so they could sink the ship that would take them most of the way there. It was September and the men were ready for their mission. They set out to sea with their handlers, but the boat purchased for their journey hit a rock. The attackers bound for a martyrdom operation in Mumbai almost drowned. Another boat brought them back to shore and Lashkar planned a second attempt. In October the squad set off once again with several handlers, this time in a rented vessel. They intended to capture an Indian ship to sail them into Indian waters, but as they approached their target its crew became aware of the impending danger, there was an exchange of gunfire and the Indian vessel evaded them.[13] Lashkar made its third attempt on 21 November. The ten-man fidayeen squad left Azizabad for a house by the seashore, and set out from there the following morning for the Arabian Sea, along with their handlers. Each of the ten men was equipped with a rucksack, an assault rifle, eight magazines with thirty rounds each, a 9mm pistol with three clips of ammunition, eight hand grenades, materials to make an improvised explosive device (IED), a knife, a water bottle, dried fruit and a mobile phone pre-programmed with their handlers' contact details. Every two-man team was given a GPS device. Kasab's partner, Ismail Khan, was chosen to lead the fidayeen squad and he received a satellite phone as well.[14]

The men boarded a small launch and set off to rendezvous with a ship named the *Al-Husseini*, which they boarded on 23 November along with other Lashkar members. Later that day, having entered Indian waters, the *Al-Husseini* took control of an Indian fishing vessel named the MV *Kuber*. The ten fidayeen boarded the fishing trawler. Four members of the *Kuber*'s crew were transferred to the *Al-Husseini* and killed not long after. Amar Singh Solanki, the *Kuber*'s captain, was kept on board to help guide the attackers the remaining 550 nautical miles to the Indian coast.[15] The terrorists also made use of their GPS, which was programmed with the coordinates from Karachi to Mumbai, and kept in contact with their handlers in Pakistan via the satellite phone given to Khan.[16] According to a log the attackers kept, the trawler reached a point 4 nautical miles off Mumbai's coast at approximately 16:00 hours on 26 November.[17] They waited until nightfall and then slit Captain Solanki's throat.[18] The fidayeen then abandoned the MV *Kuber* for an inflatable dingy. While they were in the process of doing so, another boat came close to theirs'. Believing it was the Indian navy, all of the men jumped quickly into the dingy. Crucially for investigators, they left the satellite phone behind and forgot to open the sea valve, which would have scuttled the *Kuber* and with it much of the evidence eventually used to prove Lashkar's involvement.[19] Once on board the dingy, the attackers traveled to Badhwar Park Jetty, where they had been instructed to dock. On the night of 26 November they moored in Mumbai.

After alighting the ten men broke into five pre-arranged teams, one of which pushed back out to sea for the short journey by boat to the Trident-Oberoi Hotel at Nariman point. The other four teams split up and took taxis to different locations. Two of the teams planted IEDs, timed to explode later in the evening, inside their taxis. Another three IEDs were planted at locations along the routes taken from Badhwar Park to various targets. These too were timed to explode later in the evening, but either failed to detonate or were rendered inoperative by the Indian bomb squad.[20] Causing multiple explosions at various locations was intended to create confusion and give the impression of a larger strike force.[21]

Mohammed Ajmal Amir Kasab [a.k.a. Abu Mujahid] from Faridkot and Ismail Khan [a.k.a. Abu Ismail] from Dera Ismail Khan traveled to the Chhatrapati Shivaji Terminus, headquarters of India's Central Railways. The two removed their weapons from the bags they carried, began firing indiscriminately and lobbing grenades. When Kasab was later asked by police at the hospital who he was meant to kill, he replied, 'Whoever was there.'[22] One boy who survived the carnage said that when a Muslim man began praying out loud the gunmen promptly shot him down.[23] The two terrorists rampaged relatively unchallenged for almost ninety minutes. A police officer present at the time has since stated that he and his poorly-armed colleagues initially hid for cover. When three of them decided to challenge the gunmen, they did so with only one bolt-action rifle and one pistol among them. Several were gunned down and the killing continued until better-armed police arrived.[24] By the time Kasab and Khan fled the railway station they had murdered fifty-two people and wounded more than 100, making this team responsible for approximately one third of the total deaths during the close to sixty hour siege of Mumbai.[25]

The two men fled the terminus as additional police arrived, rather than holding their ground and fighting to the death. They looked for a taxi or car to commandeer outside the CST, but under fire from police arriving on the scene instead made their way to the Cama & Albless Hospital for woman and children. Finding many of the rooms locked, they abandoned the hospital. Meanwhile more police were speeding to the scene. Among them was Anti-Terrorism Squad chief Hemant Karkare and two other senior commanders. They had four additional policemen with them. The commanders had made repeated calls for backup, but it never came and the seven men drove to the hospital alone hoping to cut off the terrorists' escape. As they neared the hospital, their vehicle suddenly came under heavy fire from the two fidayeen. None of the seven escaped the fusillade of bullets. Kasab and Khan pulled the three wounded commanders from the front, and drove off with the four wounded or dead policemen still in the rear. Karkare and his two colleagues lay dying near the hospital—200 yards from police headquarters. All three were dead by the time additional police reached the scene.[26] Following another vehicle-born gunfight, the fidayeen hijacked a civilian vehicle, but soon confronted a police barricade where Khan was killed in an exchange of gunfire. A wounded Kasab pretended to surrender, before pulling out his rifle and killing another policeman. Several other officers overpowered Kasab and beat him unconscious.

Not long after Kasab and Khan commenced their killing spree at the Chhatrapati Shivaji Terminus, Shoaib [a.k.a. Abu Shoheb] from Sialkot and Nazir Ahmad [a.k.a. Abu Umer] from Faisalabad walked into the Leopold Café and Bar. It is one of Mumbai's best-known bars, and a popular hangout for foreigners. The two-man team confirmed with the staff that they were in the right place, and spent the next several minutes laughing with one another. Suddenly one of them pulled a grenade from his bag and threw it toward a table of patrons.[27] Several minutes of indiscriminate firing followed, during which time the gunmen stopped only to reload. After killing eleven people and wounding another twenty-eight the two left and ran toward the Taj Mahal Hotel located several hundred yards away.[28]

A Mumbai icon, the Taj Hotel has two wings: the Heritage Wing and the Taj Towers. At approximately the same time as the attack on the Leopold Café commenced, Hafiz Arshad [a.k.a. Abdul Rehman Bada or Hayaji] from Multan Road and Javed [a.k.a. Abu Ali] from Okara entered the main lobby of the Taj Hotel. The two opened fire immediately and indiscriminately, killing close to twenty people within the first few minutes.[29] The attackers from the Leopold arrived soon thereafter. The two teams linked up and together they moved to the sixth floor of the Heritage Wing. The terrorists at the Taj, as well as those who attacked the Trident-Oberoi and the Chabad House, were in touch with handlers in Pakistan via their own cell phones as well as those taken from hostages and victims. At the Taj, the fidayeen contacted Lashkar handlers in Pakistan as soon as the two teams had linked up. They were directed to start a fire immediately. Video shows that instead of doing so the fidayeen spent several minutes wandering around the luxury hotel in awe. During a follow-up call to check on the status of the fire, one of the Lashkar fidayeen responded with non-sequiturs about their palatial surroundings: 'There are computers here with thirty inch screens' and 'The windows are huge. It's got two kitchens, a bath and a little shop.'[30] Their Lashkar handler kept pushing for a fire, which was intended to propel potential hostages from their rooms. It would also draw media to the scene and make for great theater. One handler told the gunmen that the Taj was the most important target, and pictures of the iconic hotel engulfed in flames have since become an enduring image of the Mumbai attacks.[31]

As with the Trident-Oberoi and Chabad House, each discussed below, a hostage situation developed at the Taj. Most of the thirty-six people who were killed throughout the course of what became a three-day siege died during the initial onslaught.[32] Many guests locked themselves in their own or other people's rooms; others hid along with hotel staff in common areas. The attackers phoned random hotel rooms to narrow their search, while hotel staff did the same, warning guests to lock their doors, switch off the lights and not to flush the toilet or make any other sounds. One guest recounted receiving received three calls, which he did not answer, and subsequently discovered two came from terrorists checking to see if the room was occupied.[33]

The Trident-Oberoi Hotel also has two wings. Immediately after entering the Trident wing, Abdul Rehman Chhota [a.k.a. Saakib] from Multan Road and Fahadullah from Kasoor Road began firing indiscriminately before detonating an IED in the hotel's tea lounge.[34] The two gunmen killed or wounded a number of people in the hotel's Tiffin restaurant, before rounding up hostages and heading to the Oberoi wing of the hotel. Among their hostages were two Muslims, a husband and wife from Turkey. Obeying instructions not to kill Muslims at the hotels, the gunmen spared the Turks telling them 'No kill. You brothers.' A Lashkar handler later instructed the fidayeen to kill their remaining hostages, all of whom were women.[35] One of the attackers at the Trident-Oberoi also phoned the news media and, claiming there were seven terrorists in the building, demanded that India release all the imprisoned mujahideen in return for the hostages.[36] This contributed to confusion among the authorities about the number of terrorists they faced and the nature of the operation; i.e. whether it was a hostage situation or a mass casualty attack. Seventeen hours elapsed before Indian forces retook control of the hotel and killed the two terrorists who, by then, had murdered thirty-five people.[37] Fahadullah took refuge in a bathroom after his partner was killed. It took several phone calls from a Lashkar handler before he was ready to emerge for a final showdown. During those conversations, recorded by Indian intelligence, Fahadullah was told he mustn't allow himself to be arrested. 'For your mission to end successfully,' his handler sternly reminded him, 'you must be killed.'[38]

The Chabad House is as obscure as the Taj Mahal and Trident-Oberoi hotels are famous. Formerly known as Nariman House, it was purchased in 2006 by the Chabad Liberation Movement of Hasidic Jews and subsequently renamed. A rabbi lived there along with his family and the building generally accommodated Jewish tourists, especially Americans and Israelis, visiting India. One of Lashkar's handlers in Pakistan told the attackers that because this was a Jewish target, every person killed there was equal to fifty killed at the other targets.[39] Immediately after breaching the building, Nasir [a.k.a. Abu Omar] from Faisalabad and Imran Babar [a.k.a. Abu Aakasha] from Multan killed Rabbi Gavriel Holtzberg and his wife Rivka, who together managed the Chabad House. The fidayeen also killed two guests. Imran took Rabbi Holtzberg's mobile phone and called an Indian television channel. He claimed credit for the attacks on behalf of the Deccan Mujahideen, a phony group ostensibly comprised of Indian Muslims and concocted to hide Lashkar's involvement.[40] A Lashkar communications specialist also sent an email from Pakistan on behalf of the fictitious group warning the government to 'stop the continuing injustice against the Muslims' and demanding it 'return all the states seized from the Muslims.'[41]

The fidayeen kept two women as hostages, and once news of Kasab's arrest was reported their potential value increased. From a

Lashkar command center in Pakistan Sajid Mir directed the terrorists to force one of the women to call the Israeli consulate in the hopes that the Israeli government could secure Kasab's release.[42] She was also made to give a status update directly to Sajid who, speaking in fluent English, promised he would release her and the other hostage in exchange for Kasab. He even suggested she might be free by the beginning of the weekend, in time to 'celebrate your Sabbath with your family.'[43] However, by the night of the second day, it was becoming apparent that India was not about to release Kasab and Lashkar handlers in Pakistan did not want to risk the chance that the hostages might get away should the fidayeen come under attack. The gunmen were ordered to kill the hostages, all of whom were dead by the time Indian forces assaulted the building. The Holtzbergs' maidservant, who managed to hide from the attackers, escaped with the couple's two-year old son.

In total, 166 civilians and security personnel were killed and 304 were injured.[44] The attacks dragged on for almost three days, prolonging Lashkar's moment in the spotlight and embarrassing the Indian security forces. Dividing their forces and moving from target to target had created the impression of a larger strike force, which the fidayeen fed by inflating their numbers in calls to the press. Erroneous media reporting subsequently overestimated the actual size of the fidayeen squad. The one major cost associated with the use of multiple strike teams was that the small size of each limited their capacity when engaged by well-armed Indian forces. This also helped minimize the body count in the hotels where potential victims were able to disperse and hide. The number of dead easily could have been much higher at the hotels considering the length of the operation and large number of potential victims present. Because terrorism is a form of expressive violence intended to induce repercussions far beyond those immediately victimized by it, the operational success of the Mumbai attacks cannot be measured by body account alone. The fact that they were so successful owed partly to a seriously flawed Indian counter-terrorism response.

US officials issued several warnings to their Indian counterparts about various aspects of the attack. The first came in early 2008 and contained general intelligence regarding Lashkar's ambition to strike Mumbai. A second, more specific, warning followed in May 2008 and included information that the Taj might be a target. A third alert regarding the Taj was issued in September, at approximately the time when the attacks initially were intended to take place. Finally, on 18 November, days before the fidayeen finally set sail, US officials issued a warning to India about a suspicious vessel believed to pose a potential maritime threat.[45] RAW immediately disseminated a specific advisory to the coast guard requesting it intensify patrols and look out for suspicious vessels, most likely of Pakistani origin. However, the MV *Kuber* blended in with the thousands of other Indian-registered fishing vessels.[46] Monitoring an expansive coastline is a challenge facing many littoral states, but this was compounded by a dearth of resources necessary for coastal surveillance. The committee that investigated the attacks found the Maharashtra government took no significant measures to improve coastal security despite repeated alerts.[47] There were fewer than 100 boats guarding over 5,000 miles of shoreline at the time of the attacks, and Maharashtra State had refused money set aside by the central government for the purchase of twenty-six additional vessels because it lacked the funds necessary for maintenance.[48]

India was hardly the first country to have prior warning of a terrorist attack and yet remain powerless to stop it. Connecting the dots is always easier in hindsight. More troubling was the degree to which the various security forces in India were unprepared to respond to the attacks once they began. After the September warning, hotel security and the police implemented limited security measures at the Taj. However, no significant steps were taken to harden its perimeter or increase police vigilance and the temporary security enhancements were lifted weeks before the attacks. The police admitted they did not have the overall manpower to maintain a presence, nor were the personnel they could have posted at the hotels trained to deal with a terrorist attack.[49] This was borne out during the assault. As first responders, the Mumbai police were wholly unprepared to deal with the situation. To begin with, there simply were not enough of them. Ajai Sahni, a terrorism analyst based in Delhi, had been criticizing India's low police-to-population ratio since well before the 2008 attacks. The United Nations recommends, on average, 250 police per 100,000 citizens for normal, peacetime policing. India, which is forced to contend with numerous active insurgencies, had approximately 125 police per 100,000 people as of 2007, or half of the recommended number. Most police officers did not have the proper weaponry or body armor to contend with the threat posed by well-trained and well-armed commandos. Many of them were unarmed and some of those who initially responded to the attacks were equipped with 0.303 bolt-action rifles, similar to those the British army used in the 1950s. Most officers also had only a 5mm plastic protector—useful as riot gear—rather than bullet-resistant vests.[50]

Local army units arrived five hours after the attacks began. The Marine Commandos [Marcos], who were the first special response team on site, got there soon afterwards. However, they pulled out before engaging. An Indian cabinet minister proclaimed that 200 National Security Guard Commandos [known as the NSG, or Black Cats because of their uniforms] would be deployed in the next two hours. Because Lashkar handlers were monitoring the news from Pakistan and communicating with the attackers in Mumbai, this enabled them to provide two key pieces of information to the fidayeen.[51] The terrorists were now aware that no special operators were active in the area and, based on those operators' scheduled arrival, they also knew when to expect a rescue mission to begin.

The NSG, modeled on the British Special Air Service [SAS] and created for this type of counter-terrorism operation, did not arrive until 08:50 the next day. Their tardiness exposed inadequate planning and logistical capabilities. First, the NSG were headquartered in Delhi and at the time of the attacks had no bases anywhere else in the country.[52] Nor did they have an aircraft dedicated to round-the-clock transport in the event of an attack. The only plane available that night was a Russian transport carrier located 165 miles north of Delhi. Additional time was lost because the pilot needed to be woken, the crew assembled and the plane fueled before it could even take off. By the time it arrived in Delhi to take the NSG to Mumbai it was already 02:00. Despite the fact that a commercial flight takes 2 hours from Delhi to Mumbai, the NSG transport took 3.5 hours.[53]

Most counter-terrorism experts assert that a rapid-reaction force must be on site within thirty minutes. The NSG arrived almost a full twelve hours after the first shots were fired. It was almost another hour before they were able to begin search-and-rescue activities. By the time they engaged, most of the hostages who were killed at the two hotels and the Chabad House had been dead for hours.[54] The standoff, however, continued. This owed in part to poor operational planning. Despite all of the time it took the NSG commandos to travel to Mumbai, they reportedly were never informed at any point during the trip that two hotels were under attack. The commandos arrived believing it was only one. Nor were they told that the floors at the Oberoi encircled an atrium, enabling the terrorists to assume vantage points on higher floors and fire on those entering the building. Yet the Mumbai police, army and Marcos were all on the ground and so could have transmitted this information to the NSG commandos in advance of their arrival.[55] The army had even established an operations hub, which should have facilitated information sharing, but it was never converted into a joint operations center. Nor did the NSG set up an operational command center of its own to coordinate the rescue mission, leaving commandos to storm the hotels without adequate real-time intelligence. Inadequate equipment also constrained their operational choices, as the lack of night vision goggles and thermal-imaging systems meant they could only operate during daylight hours.[56] The NSG commandos charged with securing the Taj also had only one electronic-swipe master key, and it took NSG teams up to five minutes to open or force there way into each room.[57]

Before they could even begin an assault on the Chabad House surrounding buildings had to be cleared. The NSG did not have the authority to do this and so the Mumbai Police were called in. Local residents opened their homes to those being temporarily displaced, but the process took almost an entire day.[58] When operations did begin at the Chabad House none of the authorities involved stopped the television media from broadcasting the assault live. This was despite the fact that the NSG, intelligence agencies and Mumbai police all knew that the terrorists were in contact with Lashkar handlers who were watching Indian television and relaying operationally useful information. When an Indian air force heli-copter air-dropped NSG commandos on the roof of the Chabad House, the terrorists inside were ready for it. They waited patiently on the fourth floor and opened fire as the commandos descended, killing one of them.[59]

Yet, as confused as the Indian counter-terrorism response was, the investigative pieces of this savage puzzle fell quickly into place. Despite the communications claiming credit on behalf of the Deccan Mujahideen, the attacks had all the hallmarks of a Lashkar operation. Even as many Western pundits reflexively pointed the finger at al-Qaeda during the first days of the attacks, Indian investigators were compiling a strong case against Lashkar. Evidence came to light over a period of time, but it did not take long before India could credibly claim that the attacks originated on Pakistani soil and that Lashkar was the most likely culprit. A thoroughly pre-planned attack would have required no contact, but Lashkar's leaders may have foreseen the need to provide guidance and encouragement to the fidayeen. The group has a history of using electronic communications to increase command-and-control, stretching back to the 1990s when commanders in Pakistan directed foot soldiers in their attacks on security forces in Indian-administered Kashmir. Lashkar's leadership may have wagered that the benefits of maintaining contact with the fidayeen, some of who did waver once in the midst of battle, outweighed the potential costs. Lashkar handlers in Pakistan were speaking with the fidayeen via a VoIP (Voice over Internet Protocol) service, which uses the internet as a medium of communication and is difficult to trace. However, Indian intelligence was able to lock onto the VoIP number, at which point they could listen to all of the calls being made. Some 284 calls were recorded totaling almost 1,000 minutes of conversation among Lashkar's handlers and the terrorists at the Taj, Trident-Oberoi and Chabad House.[60] Within hours of the attacks' commencement, those listening heard one of the Lashkar fidayeen describe how they failed to scuttle the MV *Kuber*.[61] The coast guard found the abandoned trawler the next morning, and with it a wealth of information including the forgotten satellite phone, which contained contact numbers for several Lashkar leaders.[62]

Capturing Kasab alive was another breakthrough, and it enabled Indian authorities quickly to build a compelling case. A video filmed by Indian police shows him lying on a hospital trolley on the first night of the attacks, confessing to his membership of Lashkar and to the group's responsibility for the attacks.[63] In addition to identifying the operational masterminds, Kasab provided an in depth description of how the team prepared for the attacks and the instructions they were given. Kasab later retracted his confession, only to reaffirm it unsolicited and in more detail before a magistrate.[64] Rama Vijay Sawant Vagule, the magistrate to whom Kasab confessed, testified that he volunteered his confession and was given several days to reconsider before doing so.[65] Kasab also offered a verbal confession in open court, speaking for several hours about his training with Lashkar and role in the attacks. The media published parts of this verbal confession, which were strikingly similar in detail to the account Kasab gave to the magistrate.[66] He later retracted these confessions too, but in May 2010 the court in Mumbai found him guilty on all charges, sentencing him to death on multiple counts and awarding life in prison on several more.[67]

The government of Pakistan initially denied that Lashkar or any other Pakistani played a role in the attacks, despite the mounting evidence. This position became particularly tenuous when a journalist in Pakistan broke the story within weeks of the attacks that proved Kasab was from Faridkot. The report also alleged that the security services had spirited away his parents from their village and were feeding misinformation to reporters looking for evidence of his origins.[68] Despite this report and subsequent new stories reconfirming Kasab's identity, Pakistani officials continued to stonewall.[69] In early January, India handed over to Pakistan the first of numerous dossiers containing evidence of the involvement of Pakistanis. The dossier included information on interrogations, weapons and data gleaned from satellite phones used by the suspects. India said the material proved Pakistan-based militants had plotted and executed the attacks.[70] Pakistani Interior Minister Rehman Malik admitted that part of the planning occurred in Pakistan. He also confirmed Kasab was a Pakistani national, but initially declined to confirm the identities of the other nine terrorists. Malik announced Pakistan was seeking additional information from India and said all the accused who were in Pakistan would be tried there, rather than extradited.[71] Six months after receiving India's first dossier and only days before the prime ministers of the two countries met at a summit of non-aligned countries in Sharm el-Sheikh, Egypt, Pakistan presented its own dossier to India. It contained the first official admission that Pakistani nationals from Lashkar were responsible for planning and executing the Mumbai attacks.[72] The group had undertaken or supported many attacks against India over the years, but the target selection and operational theatrics meant that Mumbai was like no other it ever perpetrated. What still remained unanswered was what led Lashkar to stage such a terrorist spectacular.

## Making Sense of Mumbai

The Director General of the ISI, Shuja Pasha, reportedly sought to answer this question when he visited Zaki-ur Rehman Lakhvi in jail following the latter's detention in the wake of the attacks.[73] The picture that emerges is one of a more modest operation in the works for some time, which rapidly expanded at the end as a result of internal dynamics. David Headley, the Pakistani-American who conducted surveillance for the Mumbai attacks, has provided the most thorough accounting to date of how the plan developed. US authorities arrested Headley in October 2009 in connection with another terrorist plot, and he agreed to cooperate in order to avoid the death penalty in America and extradition to India.[74] Investigators from India's National Investigation Agency interrogated Headley for thirty-four hours in the presence of his lawyers and officials from the US Federal Bureau of Investigation in early June 2010. This section draws heavily on the testimony he gave to them, which places significant explanatory power in the hands of one witness. Nevertheless, it is a thorough insider account of how Lashkar planned the Mumbai attacks and one which US and Indian officials told the author they have corroborated through other evidence, including Headley's travel records, Kasab's testimony, communications intercepts and various intelligence sources. In addition, the

following makes use of additional open source material for corrobo-
rative purposes wherever possible.

According to Headley, Lashkar's leadership was involved heavily in selecting the targets. He also confirmed Kasab's statement to
an Indian magistrate that Hafiz Saeed participated in early indoctrination sessions, visited the men to check in on their training and
motivated them to undertake the attacks, adding that every major
operation was undertaken only after receiving his approval.[75]
Headley identified Sajid Mir, who oversaw all transnational operatives, and two Lashkar commanders known as Abu Al-Qama and
Abu Qahafa as three of the handlers on the phone.[76] He also told
investigators that every major Lashkar operation is done in coordination with the ISI and that all of the group's major operatives
have ISI handlers. His was Major Iqbal, who provided him with
money for surveillance trips to India and, Headley believes, funding to Lashkar for the boat that sank during the first attempt in
September 2008. Notably, Iqbal often directed Headley to carry out
surveillance of other targets and to gather intelligence information
unrelated to the Mumbai attacks. Sajid, Headley's Lashkar handler,
was the person instructing him to survey the targets struck in
November 2008. However, Headley briefed Iqbal on his activities
for Lashkar and so the latter was aware of all the targets hit during
the attacks.[77] If every major Lashkar member had a handler, as
Headley claimed, then it is reasonable to assume others in the ISI
were also aware of the operational details. This is reinforced by the
fact that at times Headley met with Iqbal to brief him on information, which the latter already had. Western security officials familiar with the case believe a small coterie of serving and retired
officers played a role in or had knowledge of the attacks, though
that knowledge may not have been uniform.[78] It is also important
to reiterate that Headley stated the purpose of Pasha's visit to
Lakhvi was to 'understand the Mumbai attack conspiracy.'[79] Pasha
had become the Director General of the ISI in late September, after
the initial attempted maritime infiltration and two months prior to
the attacks. His visit, as Headley describes it, suggests that the ISI
leadership was out of the loop, at least with regard to the scope of
the plot. If so, this may have resulted from Lashkar's handlers not

passing information all the way up the chain of command or from the turnover taking place among the ISI leadership at the time.

Because Headley's testimony provides a useful vehicle for unraveling the attack planning process, it is important to address briefly his own back-story. He was born Daood Gilani and took the name David Headley in 2006 to facilitate his reconnaissance for Lashkar. For the purposes of clarity, this section refers to him as David Headley. Headley was the child of a Pakistani father and an American mother. His father raised him in Pakistan, where he was enrolled in the Hasan Abdal Cadet College. It is an elite military boarding school, many of whose graduates become high-ranking officers in the army. His mother withdrew David from Hasan Abdal in 1977 when he was seventeen and brought him back to the US where she was living.[80] In adulthood he became a heroin addict and some-time drug smuggler. He was arrested in 1988 for smuggling heroin from Pakistan, cooperated with authorities and received a four-year sentence while his co-defendant got ten. The US Drug Enforcement Agency [DEA] arrested him again in 1997 and he was convicted for conspiracy to import and possess heroin with the intent to distribute it.[81] After his second arrest in 1997 he began working as an informant for the DEA, and according to a 1998 letter sent by prosecutors recommending a lenient sentence 'helped the DEA infiltrate the very close-knit Pakistani narcotics dealing community in New York.' He also 'traveled to Pakistan...to develop intelligence on Pakistani heroin traffickers.'[82] Headley received an early release from prison and was allowed to travel to Pakistan in 1999 for an arranged marriage while still on probation. His probation also ended ahead of schedule; intended to last through 2004, a court agreed to discharge him in December 2001.[83]

When in Pakistan he sometimes visited the mosque at Jamiat al-Qadsia, Lashkar's headquarters in Lahore, to offer prayers. During one trip he saw a Lashkar poster soliciting money for the jihad against India and phoned a number given for the group's office in Model Town, Lahore. Two people came to his home to collect money and asked him to attend a lecture Hafiz Saeed was giving. He agreed and met Saeed for the first time. The two met again several weeks later at an Ijtema at Muridke. In 2001 Headley 'firmly decided' to join Lashkar and in February 2002, two months after his probation ended early, he attended the three-week Daura-e-Suffa at Muridke. In August 2002 he participated in the Daura-e-Aama in Muzaffarabad and then the Daura-e-Khasa in April 2003. Headley expressed his desire to Lakhvi to join the Kashmir jihad, but was told he was too old. Instead, he was directed to the Daura-e-Ribat, which focuses on surveillance, counter-intelligence and recruitment and is primarily intended for members who will operate in India. In December 2003 he spent another four months learning un-armed combat and close-quarter battle techniques in a course taught by a non-commissioned officer from the Pakistan army.[84] In 2004, he was assigned to the wing responsible for Lashkar's Indian operations. It was at this point that he met Sajid Mir, who Headley knew as Sajid Majid and to whom he began reporting in January 2005. Headley made an ideal cover operative, thanks to his US passport and fluency in English, and it was decided he would work in India, though at this stage what he would do or where he would go had not yet been determined. Upon learning of his general assignment, he suggested changing his name and using a friend's immigration business as a cover for his activities in India. In September 2005 he returned to the US to put this process in motion.[85] On 15 February 2006 in Philadelphia, Daood Gilani became David Coleman Headley, though his confederates in Pakistan continued to know him by his given name.[86]

Through at least 2003, and possibly as late as 2005, Headley remained a DEA informant, according to one US official familiar with his case.[87] In August 2005 the Joint Terrorism Task Force [JTTF], a multi-agency unit led by the FBI, received a tip from one of his wives [he had a total of three, none of whom appears to have known about the others, as well as one ex-wife] that her husband was involved with Lashkar. His wife reportedly phoned in the tip following an altercation the previous day and she later met with several investigators, providing information about her husband's affiliation with Lashkar, including his training activities and attempts to procure equipment such as night vision goggles for the group.[88] Two years later, another wife met twice with officials at the US Embassy in Islamabad. She too spoke about her husband's involvement with

Lashkar and frequent trips to India.[89] A diplomatic security officer who met with her sent a written report about the allegations to the FBI, CIA and DEA.[90] However, US officials asserted that she offered no information about specific attack planning and spoke only of her husband's general involvement with Lashkar.[91]

Shortly before this book went to press, the US Director of National Intelligence initiated a review of how Headley's case was handled. At the time of writing, it was unclear what action was taken in response to either the JTTF investigation or the US embassy report. Also unknown was the degree to which the DEA was aware of their charge's involvement in militant activities or what type of information he was providing to them while still an informant. Some US and Indian officials believe that by 2008 American agencies were monitoring Headley and that intelligence they gathered led to the warnings issued to India regarding the Mumbai plot.[92] If so, this would suggest investigators put him under surveillance following either the 2005 or 2007 warnings, or perhaps that his former US handlers began tracking him because they suspected foul play. However, it is also possible that information regarding the attacks was gathered through communications intercepts or other sources on the ground in Pakistan or Afghanistan.

Headley did not begin performing surveillance for Lashkar until the end of 2006 and the Mumbai attack plot did not take shape until 2008. Indeed, five years after joining Lashkar the group had made little use of Headley and it appears to have taken a misadventure in the Tribal Areas to bring him into contact with his handler Major Iqbal. In January 2006 Headley and his friend Abdur Rehman Syed, the retired army major who joined Lashkar in 2003, were detained in the Khyber tribal agency. The two were there on what appears to have been an unsanctioned mission to solicit Headley's old drug smuggling contacts to bring weapons into India. When interviewed by an ISI officer known as Major Samir Ali, Headley told him about his association with Lashkar and the likelihood that he eventually would be deployed to work in India. Ali suggested he knew some people who could be useful to this mission and said they would be in touch.[93] The following day the two Lashkar men were released and returned to Lahore. Major

Iqbal contacted Headley not long afterwards. Iqbal's boss was also present at their initial meeting and promised Headley financial support as well as directing him to report to Iqbal henceforth. After his trip back to the US in February 2006 to formalize his name-change, Headley again met with Iqbal who assigned an NCO to train him on the basics of intelligence. This included how to create sources and operate covertly, and after proffering instruction the NCO often took Headley onto the streets of Lahore to practice. Headley returned to the US again in June 2006 where he claimed to have solicited the assistance of a friend, Tahawwur Hussain Rana, who owned the First World Immigration business. He too was a graduate of the Hasan Abdal Cadet College, and Headley alleged Rana gave him permission to open an immigration office in Mumbai as a cover for his surveillance activities.[94]

Headley returned to Pakistan and in August Major Iqbal visited him at home, bringing $25,000 to be used for surveillance work. A separate meeting with his Lashkar handler, Sajid Mir, followed in Muzaffarabad and in September Headley departed on his first trip to India. Using the money given to him by Iqbal, he opened an immigration office and even hired a secretary. Headley also began taking photographs of various potential targets, including the Taj. He returned to Pakistan in December and met separately with Iqbal in Lahore and Sajid in Muzaffarabad to brief them. This pattern repeated itself on numerous occasions and it is notable that Headley always met his ISI and Lashkar handlers separately, delivering to each their own customized photographs or video recordings.[95] Sajid was very interested in the Taj Hotel, and particularly in an annual conference of software professionals held there. However, there was no specific discussion of targeting the hotel at this point and Headley did not perceive any immediate plans for a strike. Rather, Lashkar seems to have been at the information gathering stage. Meanwhile, Headley continued training with the NCO detailed to him by Iqbal.[96]

Following another round of meetings with his ISI and Lashkar handlers respectively, Headley returned to Mumbai in February 2007. He continued photographing various sites and making video recordings, while also making unscheduled trips to Pakistan on one occasion and to Dubai on another without telling his handlers. He made a scheduled return to Pakistan in June, and met first with Iqbal and then Sajid, giving each a memory stick with surveillance footage. Headley met with them again before traveling back to India in September. By this stage he was receiving more specific instructions from each, but his marching orders did not overlap. Major Iqbal provided him with counterfeit Indian currency and directed him to conduct surveillance in the city of Pune. Sajid was 'very clear in his mind': he wanted extensive reconnaissance of the Taj, which had become a potential target for attack. Headley said that, during his time in Pakistan, he and Sajid often discussed striking the hotel during the aforementioned annual conference of software professionals. Lashkar had focused on economic targets since the early years of the decade, and this fit neatly within those confines. The aim was to infiltrate one or two fidayeen into India via Nepal or Bangladesh, strike the Taj and then exfiltrate them somehow; a plan not dissimilar in motive or operational scope from the 2005 attack on the Indian Institute of Science in Bangalore.[97]

Headley's return visit to Pakistan in summer 2007 coincided with the storming of the Lal Masjid. He contrasted the devotion of those waging jihad against the Crusader forces in Afghanistan, and their supporters at the Red Mosque, with the confused priorities of the Pakistani government, to which Lashkar's leadership still gave allegiance in his view. Although he continued working for the group and remained close with his ISI handler, Major Iqbal, Headley's testimony suggests a man pulled in different directions—an inner struggle that is reflective of the tensions extant within Lashkar at the time. Abdur Rehman Syed had distanced himself from the group by this point and asked Headley to undertake reconnaissance for him of the National Defence College in Delhi, to which the latter agreed. Thus, by the time he departed for India in September 2007, Headley was surveying different targets for Iqbal, Sajid and Syed. He flew into Delhi and did a brief, initial reconnaissance for Syed before traveling on to Mumbai and conducting extensive reconnaissance of the Taj as well as other targets that were not included in the final attack plan. Headley also visited Pune during this trip, and surveyed army installations for Major Iqbal.[98]

When Headley returned to Pakistan in late 2007 he met first with Major Iqbal to deliver videos of Indian troop movements taken in Pune, and also with Syed to whom Headley gave a briefing about the National Defence College in Delhi. Notably, the two also discussed the Taj and other potential targets, meaning Headley was keeping his friend and former Lashkar colleague up-to-date on the group's attack plans. Sajid showed no interest in Headley's surveillance in Pune. He remained fixated on the Taj, though the two also discussed the National Defence College. By this time, the surging jihad in Afghanistan and eruption of violence in the Tribal Areas had created an 'identity crisis' for Pakistan in Headley's opinion. He described fierce ideological debates within militant outfits regarding where to focus their violence and disillusionment among some Lashkar militants with the leadership's decision not to devote greater attention to the Afghan jihad or to become involved in the revolutionary struggle taking place in Pakistan.[99] It was amidst this atmosphere that Lashkar's leaders began considering a spectacular strike against multiple targets in Mumbai.

Several of the key architects of the Mumbai attacks met at a house in Muzaffarabad in March 2008. A clean-shaven man with a crew cut joined them. Headley understood him to be a 'frogman' from the Pakistan navy. As the plan expanded to include multiple attackers, Lashkar veered away from infiltrating them by land and was exploring the viability of a maritime insertion. The men examined nautical charts and discussed various landing options. The frogman directed Headley to explore the position of naval vessels in order to avoid a gunfight before entering Indian waters, and in the days following this meeting Sajid taught him how to plot locations on a GPS. In a sign of the coordination in place, Major Iqbal was already aware of the planned maritime insertion by the time Headley returned to Lahore and met with him. Because this was an atypical mode of infiltration, Iqbal wanted to maximize the opportunity and use the ship to smuggle weapons into India as well. Further, while attack planning was accelerating, Iqbal also had other instructions. He directed Headley to explore the Bhabba Atomic Research Centre [BARC] in Mumbai during his next trip, and to pay particular attention to its staff colony as a potential target. India and Pakistan have a bilateral agreement not to attack one another's nuclear installations, and Iqbal's interest in the BARC as a potential target suggests he was among those in the ISI prepared to push the boundaries.[100]

After returning to Mumbai in April 2008 and conducting surveillance in the residential area surrounding the BARC, Headley took a series of boat rides around the harbor. The first two and the fourth did not amount to much, save for the fish he caught and gave to his landlady. But the third proved quite helpful and Headley plotted the coordinates for this landing site into the GPS he had been given.[101] Despite the expansion to include multiple attackers, Sajid and others remained intent on exfiltrating them from Mumbai after the operation. To this end, Headley surveyed the Chhatrapati Shivaji Terminus and a nearby bus station to assess their feasibility as an egress point. Back in Pakistan later that month Lakhvi was becoming convinced that he could 'see this thing happening.' But Headley did not perceive the same sense of urgency he saw before his last trip to India. Then in early June Sajid called him to another meeting. The attacks had been scheduled for September. The fidayeen would infiltrate by sea, but the plan remained for them to flee in the aftermath. Sajid continued to view the Chhatrapati Shivaji Terminus as a viable egress option and directed Headley to take note of the train timings at the terminus during his next trip.[102]

Headley received another call from Sajid in late June, telling him it was urgent that he return to Mumbai. A host of targets was now on the table: many were economic, political or military. But some were foreign, specifically Jewish or Israeli. The Chabad House was one of them, and this was the first time it was discussed. Headley was very pleased and told Abdur Rehman Syed, who expressed his satisfaction and told his friend to insist upon its inclusion. Iqbal was also 'very happy to know that Chabad House had been chosen as a target,' according to Headley who traveled back to Mumbai for the month of July. He surveyed numerous targets, including all of those struck several months later.[103] Notably, Headley assessed other possible Jewish targets during this time as well, but at least one was deemed less appealing because only Indian Jews frequented it.[104] Conversely, American and Israeli Jews patronized the Chabad House. The primary aim was to enhance Lashkar's jihadi credibility, but its choice also may have presented the group with what was perceived to be an opportunity to damage India's strong civil and military relationship with Israel.[105]

Upon returning to Pakistan in August 2008, Headley first met with Iqbal and briefed him on the various targets. He then traveled to Muzaffarabad, where Sajid informed him the attackers were being trained. Lashkar had settled on a ten-man fidayeen squad and was preparing two sets of targets depending on when the gunmen landed. Although the attacks were slated to take place within a month's time, questions still remained. Major Iqbal expressed concern about the battle-readiness of the attackers given that most only began the Daura-e-Khasa two months prior and none had any combat experience.[106] Debates were also ongoing with regard to the choice of targets. Zaki-ur Rehman Lakhvi called a meeting of Lashkar's hierarchy to discuss the operation, and though Headley did not attend he learned that at least one of the group's leaders expressed reservations about striking the Chabad House. The man in question argued that doing so would create another enemy for Lashkar and could cause additional problems for the group in the future.[107] It is difficult to determine how vehement the opposition to striking the Chabad House was. Once it was promoted as a possible target, however, arguing against it almost certainly would have been an uphill battle. With its attack on the Chabad House, Lashkar became the first Pakistani jihadi group to actualize the fulminating 'Hindu-Zionist-Crusader' rhetoric common to many of them.

Although the target selection was settled, the question remained of how to extract the fidayeen. In his meetings with Iqbal and Sajid in late June, Headley found that both continued to view the egress option as viable. The plan was for the fidayeen to take a bus or train to Indian-administered Kashmir, where they would remain following the attacks. However, when Headley traveled back to Mumbai for the month of July he assessed potential attack venues from the perspective of a 'strong-hold option,' and by August most agreed the egress option would be difficult. Later that month, with only a short window of time before the attacks were supposed to be launched, Lashkar's leaders embraced the idea of executing a martyrdom operation. Kasab and his fellow would-be fidayeen were shifted back to Muridke after completing the Daura-e-Khasa program.[108] According to Headley's testimony, the purpose was to indoctrinate them further on the importance of martyrdom. Hafiz Saeed, Abdul Rehman Makki and others lectured to them during this time.[109]

Executing an operation in which the fidayeen fought to the death, rather than a series of hit-and-run strikes, contributed to the duration of the attacks and hence their spectacular nature. But the decision to do so was driven partly by operational necessity, and its last-minute nature may help to explain the need for Lashkar handlers to communicate electronically to the fidayeen throughout the course of the attacks. Another consequence of dropping the egress option was to shift the Chhatrapati Shivaji Terminus from an exfiltration point to a target, from which Kasab and Abu Ismail fled. Notably, they were the only ones not in touch with Lashkar handlers during the course of the Mumbai attacks. The interception of Lashkar's electronic communications coupled with Kasab's capture robbed it of plausible deniability. However, neither the group, nor its ISI handlers, could have reasonably assumed their involvement would not be presumed even if the operation had gone according to plan. The difference lay in what the Indian government knew or suspected and what it could prove. This meant that in an ideal scenario it was conceivable to deny involvement, as Lashkar had in previous instances, while still sending a message to the Indian government and, in doing so, possibly spoil the peace process. Further, the group never had any intention of hiding its involvement from the jihadi community.

According to Kasab, one of Lashkar's leaders motivated them by declaiming that for fifteen years the group had been fighting for Kashmir, but the Indian occupation continued. The fidayeen were told they could help to liberate Indian-administered Kashmir by bleeding India. Because the country's financial strength was in Mumbai, which was also a tourist destination, it was imperative to strike targets that would make India a less attractive venue for businesses and tourists alike.[110] In this regard, Lashkar's calculus was no different than if it had adhered to the original, and more modest, plan to strike the Taj hotel. The attacks were intended to punish and coerce India, a long-standing Lashkar objective. Their spectacular nature and the inclusion of foreign targets served an additional purpose. The group had been playing a double game since the beginning of the decade: India-centric proxy on the one hand, participant in the global jihad against America and its allies on other. Mumbai was intended to reconcile the two and to enhance Lashkar's credibility in the eyes of the jihadi community in Pakistan.

A number of interlocutors remarked that the attacks came as a surprise. Not only because the group had never before launched such a bold operation or deliberately targeted Westerners and Jews in India, but also because in recent years it had kept a low profile to the point of being overshadowed by other jihadi groups in Pakistan. Headley affirmed this assessment in his testimony, in which he described how the aggression and commitment of those fighting against the Crusader forces in Afghanistan (and in certain cases against Pakistan as well) influenced some committed fighters to leave Kashmir-centric groups. In his words, this 'compelled the LeT to consider a spectacular terrorist strike in India.' He also suggested that Lashkar's ISI handlers approved the Mumbai attacks as a result of their awareness that the group needed to show results in order for the leadership to retain control over elements within the organization.[111] Once the determination was made to stage a terrorist spectacular, the process took over. Operational necessity was a major factor in shifting to a martyrdom attack, a decision that contributed to Mumbai's duration and hence to its sensational nature. Another consequence of dropping the egress option was the late inclusion of the railway terminus, where one third of the fatalities occurred. It was also the scene of the most indiscriminate killing, in contrast to the hotels where the fidayeen took some steps to avoid murdering Muslims. Thus, two of the most notable aspects of the attacks—their duration and the high body count—were attributable to the operational demands of staging a ten-person, multi-target assault. This does not detract from the obvious global jihadi influences and nor should it alter our perceptions of the overarching objectives. Rather it merely suggests the attacks were perhaps even more operationally successful than they were intended to be.

After Mumbai India quickly suspended the composite dialogue with Pakistan. Meanwhile, Lashkar experienced a boost in the influx of money and men.[112] Its popularity also surged on jihadi forums as a result of the group's target selection and operational sophistication. For example, the Al-Yaqeen Media Center issued a report assessing the gains achieved including striking a blow against the crusaders, 'creating a new crusader enemy' in an area with a large Muslim population and illustrating the mujahideen's power, intelligence and fighting abilities. It opined that because the operations were so successful they could contribute to copycat attacks.[113] Security and counter-terrorism officials in many Western countries also took note of this possibility, and began increasing their vigilance against this type of low-tech assault. The fear was not only that Mumbai might inspire other jihadis to prosecute such an attacks, but also that Lashkar might launch an assault in a Western country or train others to do so. The New York Police Department was concerned enough about the possibility of similar strikes in New York City that it sent three officers to Mumbai to study the attacks in detail in order to take the necessary precautions to prevent their repeat.[114] The fear of copycats was not unfounded, as subsequent fidayeen-style assaults in Afghanistan and Pakistan proved. Nor was the concern that Lashkar might attempt attacks outside of India, as the next chapter will detail. Indeed, the attacks not only marked Lashkar's return to the South Asian limelight, but also its emergence as a significant player in the global jihad.

9

# DAYS OF RECKONING

The Mumbai attacks were the most successful terrorist spectacular since 9/11 and brought Lashkar-e-Taiba to the attention of the world. Yet the speed with which Lashkar was found culpable also led to heavy pressure on Pakistan to take action against the group, including: dismantle the militant infrastructure that made Mumbai possible; outlaw JuD, which was clearly the group's above-ground wing; and either extradite or take serious legal action against those involved in the plot. There was a flurry of initial activity in the weeks after Mumbai as the government and army took steps to show they were serious about cracking down on the group. The security services raided a Lashkar camp outside Muzaffarabad on 7 December 2008, the same day a journalist revealed Kasab's Pakistani origins. They took approximately ten to twenty members, including Zaki-ur Rehman Lakhvi, into custody and sealed the offices there.[1] This was the first concrete step taken against the group, but Pakistani officials took pains to avoid appearing as though they were acquiescing to Indian pressure and asserted the state would go at its own pace in terms of taking action against Lashkar.[2] Indeed, these initial raids took place even as Pakistani officials continued to deny that any of the country's citizens were involved in the Mumbai attacks.[3]

The UN Al-Qaeda and Taliban Sanctions Committee labeled JuD a front organization for Lashkar-e-Taiba and declared it a terrorist organization in early December. It also designated Lakhvi, Saeed,

235

and two other top officials as terrorists subject to a freeze of assets, travel ban and arms embargo.[4] In response, the government promised to take 'consequential actions, as required, including the freezing of assets.'[5] Pakistan also sealed some JuD offices, ostensibly banned it from fundraising as well as distributing propaganda and detained Hafiz Saeed along with a handful of other high-ranking JuD officials.[6] By the end of January, the security services had rounded up close to 100 members of Lashkar and JuD, while putting over 100 more under surveillance. The government also announced it had assumed control over Muridke as well as other JuD infrastructure in Pakistan and shut down numerous relief camps, some of which were suspected of doubling as recruiting or training centers.[7] However, despite these initial steps, JuD was not banned under Pakistan's Anti-Terrorism Act and it remained a legal organization in Pakistan at the time of writing.

Pakistan had a history of executing mass detentions in the wake of an attack against India, only to release militants once pressure abated. Nor was this the first time the government had seized Lashkar's offices, closed down some of its camps and restricted its activities in the short-term in order to be seen to be doing something. The 2001–2002 experience, in which the group was banned and then allowed to reinvent itself as JuD illustrated the degree to which efforts made in response to US and Indian pressure were reversible. At the height of Pakistani action against Lashkar and the above-ground JuD, there was widespread suspicion that this latest crackdown would prove as cosmetic as those in the past. One Pakistani journalist told the author this would be just like the movie *Groundhog Day*, in which the lead character repeatedly awoke to the same day over and over again, to drive home the point that any crackdown would turn out just like 2001. This proved an accurate assessment. When exploring Pakistan's treatment of Lashkar it is important to remember the country is not monolithic. The civilian government in power at the federal level was more predisposed toward peace with India and action against the country's militants than the army or ISI, which sought to preserve Lashkar as an instrument for proxy war. Meanwhile, the two political parties in power at the federal level and in Punjab province were fierce adversaries, which hampered coordination between the two. Thus, it was possible for some actors to pursue action against Lashkar, while others sought to protect the group either for strategic or political interests. Of the approximately 100 Lashkar members rounded up in December 2008 and January 2009, most were never charged and instead bled back out onto the streets over the next several months. Pakistan's Federal Investigative Agency [FIA] registered a case in early February 2009 against five Lashkar members who were arrested and in custody, including Lakhvi who was identified as the mastermind of the plot; Mazhar Iqbal [a.k.a. Abu al-Qama] who was identified as one of the handlers; Abdul Wajid [a.k.a. Zarar Shah] who was identified as a facilitator and expert of computer networks; Hammad Amin Sadiq who was identified as a facilitator of funds and hideouts; and Shahid Jamil Riaz who was identified as a facilitator of funds as well as a crew member aboard the *Al Husseini*. An additional thirteen low-level functionaries not in custody were also named as proclaimed offenders.[8] It took almost a year to issue an indictment. One day ahead of the first anniversary of Mumbai, seven Lashkar members were indicted for their involvement in the attacks. The Islamabad Bureau of the BBC obtained a copy of the 10-page charge sheet filed on 25 November 2009. It listed the case as the State versus Hammad Amin Sadiq etc., whom it described along with Lakhvi and five others as 'active members of defunct proscribed organization Lashkar-e-Taiba.' The seven were accused of training, instructing and providing funds as well as hideouts for the ten gunmen.[9] All pleaded not guilty.[10]

This was the first time in the country's history that criminal charges were levied against the perpetrators of a terrorist attack on foreign soil, and was a significant step forward. However, it is notable that several of the architects of the attacks were absent from the indictment, as was Hafiz Saeed. Pakistani officials continued to claim they were serious about cracking down, but argued not enough evidence existed to put Saeed on trial for the Mumbai attacks.[11] India repeatedly challenged this assertion, insisting that Kasab's confession and Headley's testimony confirmed his involvement. Indian officials claimed to have shared this and other information with their Pakistani counterparts, but to no avail.[12] New Delhi also produced a list of additional suspects and requested that Pakistan extradite Majors Iqbal and Samir Ali.[13] In response the government of Pakistan announced in July 2010 that it was investigating both men as well as four additional militants identified by India as playing important parts in the Mumbai attacks.[14] The outcome of these investigations and of the trial against the seven indicted Lashkar members remained uncertain at the time of writing.

The authorities in Pakistan had put Hafiz Saeed under house arrest within weeks of the Mumbai attacks. They did so in response to intense US pressure, and immediately following a visit from Deputy Secretary of State John D. Negroponte who issued a stern warning that Pakistan must take action against Lashkar. However, placing Saeed under house arrest was a tactic that had been used in the past: in winter 2001 following the Parliament attack; in spring 2002 following the Lashkar attack on Indian security forces and their families in Kaluchak; and again in 2006 after the Mumbai train blasts. It was a temporary action, designed to show Pakistan was doing something as well as a means of lowering Saeed's profile, and thereby JuD's as well, in the short-term until pressure subsided. He was always released and allowed to resume addressing rallies, recruiting and fundraising. In this instance, his detention was extended twice after the initial orders expired. When pressed by the courts to provide grounds for these extended detentions, however, the government referred primarily to the UN designation of JuD as a terrorist organization. While the inclusion of JuD on the UN Al-Qaeda and Taliban Sanctions Committee list brought with it a travel ban as well as an assets freeze and arms embargo, it did not demand the arrest or detention of the organization's leaders. When Saeed mounted a legal challenge, a court ruled his detention was illegal and ordered him released.[15] Later, a Lahore court threw out an additional two anti-terrorism cases against Saeed, ruling that the prosecution had presented no evidence that JuD was involved in terrorism. Both of the cases had been registered under Pakistan's Anti-Terrorism Act and Saeed's defense argued, correctly, that he could not be charged under this law since Pakistan had not proscribed JuD.

JuD's headquarters at Jamiat al-Qadsia in Lahore also remained open for business. The author was repeatedly denied access in spring 2009, but two Pakistani colleagues who offered Friday prayers at the Jamia Masjid al-Qadsia, the mosque attached to JuD's headquarters, described what they saw upon entering the complex. At least five men armed with submachine guns and dressed in camouflage commando jackets were present, three between the entry gate and the courtyard, and another two on the roof. Two people were collecting money for Lashkar's jihad and urged all who were attending to contribute. The bookstore had posters advertising jihadi literature, and the offices remained open. Hafiz Saeed's son, Hafiz Talha Saeed, led the prayers and during his sermon preached that because Jews and Christians were united against Muslims, it was the responsibility of all Muslims to wage jihad against them. This jihad was compulsory and he urged Muslims to fight Jews and Christians wherever they were or, if they could not physically fight, then to support the jihad in other ways. Sermons such as this one are not uncommon, and nor was the continued practice of fundraising for the jihad or sale of jihadi propaganda. The author and several interlocutors saw collection boxes for Lashkar, JuD and other banned organizations in various locales. Fundraising at other mosques and door-to-door drives continued as well, while Lashkar's jihadi propaganda continued to be sold at shops visited by the author and several colleagues. One told the author that the JuD-owned bookstore near his home in Lahore simply took down the Jamaat-ul-Dawa sign and put up one naming it the Islamic Library, while continuing to sell the same publications as in the past. These activities belied government claims that JuD publications had been banned along with the group's right to raise money. Yet even if authorities wanted to prosecute such activities, doing so would prove difficult for the same reason that holding Seed indefinitely was impossible: JuD was not a banned organization.

Technically, JuD was prohibited from collecting donations or maintaining accounts and funds in public banks. However, two days after JuD's accounts supposedly were closed, *Wall Street Journal* reporters discovered some remained open for deposits. According to one of the journalists who broke the story, a local stringer phoned JuD's offices in Lahore at the *Wall Street Journal's* behest and asked to donate money. He was told to contact a Lahore branch of another bank, where an account remained open in the name of Markaz Jamaat-ul-Dawa.[16] The bank details for the Lahore branch given to the *Wall Street Journal* match those on a flyer produced by the group soliciting money during the Muslim festival of Eid, which ended not long before the ban was instituted. The banner headline stated 'Don't forget mujahideen and refugees of Kashmir & Afghanistan during your Eid delights.' The appeal continued, 'The Lashker-e-Taiba mujahideen fighting against the tyrannical forces occupying the Islamic world, the heirs of more than 1500 martyrs and hapless refugees of Kashmir and Afghanistan are the most deserving of your alms, Zakat and other donations.' Notably, this appeal for funds on behalf of Lashkar's martyrs directed supporters to donate money into a JuD account.[17]

After this initial oversight the authorities did close those remaining public accounts listed under JuD's name according to Western diplomats monitoring the situation at the time.[18] They had less success seizing the group's existing financial assets, and there is little doubt the group knew an asset freeze was coming. A former official in the Punjab provincial government involved in executing the crackdown told the author that the authorities did not want to come down too hard for fear of creating a backlash. Instead, they sought to exploit Lashkar's history of avoiding violence against the state and took the JuD leadership into their confidence. The official said this extended to briefing senior leaders in advance about activities that would be taken against them. He recounted that they were told, 'Don't panic. We're not going to crack down too hard. We will tell you in advance what we will do.'[19] To be fair, it's questionable whether such a warning was even necessary. The public lead-up to the initial UN resolution gave the group plenty of time to move money out of its public accounts and stash that cash elsewhere. One Pakistani finance ministry official estimated that JuD transferred at least hundreds of thousands of dollars and possibly millions in the days leading up to the ban. He expressed skepticism that Pakistan would ever find those funds.[20]

Indian officials alleged that at least some of this money was transferred into the accounts of the Falah-e-Insaniat Foundation [FIF].[21] This was the new name for Idara Khidmat-e-Khalq [IKK], JuD's relief wing that played such a big role in rescue operations following the 2005 earthquake. In addition to using it as a repository for funds transferred to avoid the asset freeze, the group also raised money under the FIF banner.[22] Only two months after the restrictions were put in place, members marched through the streets of Lahore waving the JuD flag, soliciting donations and handing out receipts in the name of the FIF.[23] The group launched an FIF web site to promote its relief efforts. The site featured a prominent link urging people to 'Join Hands With FIF' by making a donation.[24] As it had done with the JuD name after Lashkar was banned in 2001, the group also began using the FIF label to keep some of its offices open for business.[25] By the time of the attacks, JuD was estimated to have approximately 2,000 offices in towns and villages throughout Pakistan.

However, FIF was more than just a JuD front. When heavy fighting broke out in the Swat Valley between the Pakistan army and pro-Taliban elements during the spring of 2009, it created an enormous refugee crisis inside Pakistan. The government was still pressuring the group to keep a low profile at this point and shut down its initial attempts to establish relief camps because JuD was operating openly under its own banner. The government had recently done the same in Balochistan, where the group had been providing earthquake relief using its own name.[26] In response, the group operated under the FIF banner. It established 24-hour kitchens, which fed over 50,000 refugees fleeing the fighting in Swat according to Hafiz Abdul Rauf, who previously headed IKK and was overseeing FIF relief operations there. A fleet of minibuses transported victims from the battle zone, and ambulances ferried the injured to a hospital. FIF also paid bus fares for refugees fleeing the area, as well as organizing lodging at madaris for those who could not make the trip.[27] Although FIF employees claimed no connection to JuD, the black-and-white Jamaat-ul-Dawa flag flying over the FIF's makeshift headquarters signaled the group's true identity.[28]

When monsoon rain caused massive flooding in Pakistan the following summer, FIF was again on the scene, though its officials were no longer reticent about belonging to JuD. The magnitude of the disaster dwarfed anything Pakistan had previously experienced, and left millions of people in urgent need of potable water, shelter and food. Experts predicted the ramifications in terms of economic hardship, loss of property and disease would be worse, and longer-lasting, than those that followed the 2005 earthquake. FIF claimed that it had deployed 2,000 volunteers and a fleet of ambulances within a week of the flooding.[29] It also opened refugee camps and provided foodstuffs to those in need in Northwest Pakistan and parts of Punjab.[30] The chaos and confusion made it difficult to determine how big a role the group was playing in comparison to other local and international aid agencies, though once again the army took the lead. While it has always been the primary institution responsible for disaster relief, the inability to reach many flood-effected areas without helicopter-transport meant the army played an even bigger role relative to other aid providers than in the past.

The main thrust of the post-Mumbai efforts against JuD took place in Punjab, where the provincial government sought to gain oversight over some of its activities. This oversight was nominal-based, meaning any organization with Jamaat-ul-Dawa in its name came under the provincial government's control. Money raised as well as spent by these organizations was supposed to flow through the government's coffers. The provincial government in Punjab appointed an administrator from the Education Department to oversee schools, one from the Department of Health to oversee hospitals and dispensaries and one from the Religious Affairs and Auqaf Department to oversee JuD mosques and madaris. Certain key staff were fired, but rank-and-file JuD members were allowed to remain in place. Those charities, schools, dispensaries, health clinics, mosques and madaris that operated under the JuD umbrella using their own names remained independent and were allowed to continue operating unmolested.[31]

The Punjab government also formally took control of Muridke, along with all of its assets, on 25 January 2009 and appointed an administrator to supervise all of the social, charitable and welfare projects at the facility.[32] Although a government administrator arranged the author's visit to Muridke in May 2009, no provincial officials were present. Abu Ehsan, the JuD administrator at Muridke, told the author they oversaw operations from Lahore and only made weekly visits. He said that since the ban the government was collecting money from the schools as well as the hospital, and was paying everyone's salary and funding all other provisions such as food and upkeep.[33] In June 2010 it emerged that the Punjab provincial government issued a grant of approximately 79 million rupees to the Markaz-e-Taiba compound at Muridke along with another 3 million rupees for JuD schools. Rana Sanaullah, the law minister in Punjab at the time, maintained the money allocated to Muridke was for the two schools and hospital located there.[34] Yet, even he had acknowledged publicly several months prior that JuD and Lashkar were simply different wings of the same group.[35] Further, while Sanaullah made a point of highlighting the restrictions in place when announcing the funds for Muridke, Hafiz Abdul Rehman Makki claimed these had been lifted and that 'now everything is running exactly the way it was running under the Jamaat's system.'[36] When the Punjab Home Department banned or re-banned many organizations in July 2010 in response to a series of terrorist attacks in the province, JuD once again escaped legal sanction.[37]

The decision to keep JuD schools and welfare organizations running, some with a modicum of oversight and many others without any, was driven by two factors according to local and Western officials: first, authorities wanted to avoid a revolt among the rank-and-file were they to be summarily dismissed; and second, these schools and welfare organizations provided important services. The federal and provincial governments did not have enough people to staff every position on their own. However, the decision to overlook those organizations operating under the JuD umbrella, but using different names, suggests that outward appearances were more important than actually reining in the group. Further, the oversight that did exist was never rigorous, and by most indications it became less so over time. JuD's continued legal status complicated matters, but so did its power in Punjab. It was not a political party, but JuD was and remains a political player. Its vast social welfare offerings and high public profile translated into influence with the population and some politicians depended on it to help deliver the vote banks they needed to remain in office. Beyond the ballot box, JuD intimidated politicians and police because of the well-trained and well-armed men at its disposal.

The security services made no attempt to dismantle the military apparatus that produced Lashkar's militants and which made the Mumbai attacks possible. Lashkar's infrastructure in Manserha, where some of the training for the Mumbai attacks took place, remained intact according to local journalists and interlocutors who arranged meetings for the author with Lashkar militants.[38] Authorities raided one of Lashkar's main camps outside of Muzaffarabad, which the army then occupied. However, according to one former fighter who remained in touch with the group, 'They sit there for the sake of the media, to show that Pakistan is acting against the LeT. But it's all just a game.' The camp had not really closed, only moved to a more discreet location, some 25 miles from Muzaffarabad. A sign pointed to a JuD-run school, but militants confirmed they were using the camp as a jumping off point for the Kashmir jihad. According to a journalist who visited it, police at a checkpoint nearby evinced a clear awareness of its location.[39] According to a government report seen by the Islamabad bureau of the BBC, the opening of this new camp was only part of a wider militant expansion in the months after Mumbai. A copy of the report, submitted by local police to Pakistan-administered Kashmir's cabinet on 25 March 2009, detailed militant activity by Lashkar, JeM and HuM in the city of Muzaffarabad and elsewhere in the region. When militants killed some of the locals it led to a stand-off that was resolved only when a local administrator and senior army officials intervened. The report recommended authorities take up the matter with 'the intelligence agency responsible for the militants.' Notably, it did not advocate any additional action other than continuing to observe the militants and possibly relocating them to avoid further clashes.[40]

The degree to which Lashkar continued to operate openly was captured in spring 2010 when the government suspended access to the social networking website Facebook after some of its users (outside Pakistan) started a contest called 'Everybody Draw Muhammad Day.' Not long after a joke began making the rounds in Pakistan: What do Facebook and Lashkar-e-Taiba have in common? Both are technically banned in Pakistan, but still easy to join. Ironically, by this time the group was using Facebook to maintain an internet presence after the JuD web page was taken down following Mumbai in order to lower its profile. Pictures on its Facebook page captured the duality of Lashkar's continued Indo-centric and expanding global jihadi impulses. The image of the Taj Mahal Hotel in flames appeared with slogans that read 'free Kashmir, Pakistan's lifeline, from the enemy' and 'freedom of the Muslims of Gujarat, Hyderabad, Ahmedabad and the rest of India.' Alongside it were several images of Osama bin Laden, including one showing him riding away on horseback from the White House, which was engulfed in flames.[41] The group also launched a JuD Youtube page, which included videos of Lashkar militants and other outfits waging jihad across the globe. The page made no attempt to separate JuD and Lashkar, instead listing their names along with relevant links side-by-side.[42] Its Facebook and Youtube pages were part of a larger online presence for which the group produced many videos in the two years after the Mumbai attacks. While many of these focused on India, others included footage of attacks in Afghanistan, Iraq and elsewhere, though not necessarily by Lashkar militants.

Lashkar's social welfare infrastructure as well as part of its military apparatus used for jihad in Kashmir and terrorist attacks against India remained intact. But the jihad in Indian-administered Kashmir remained moribund and the group was under pressure by the ISI to keep a low profile in the wake of Mumbai.[43] Meanwhile the insurgency in Afghanistan was going from strength to strength. Soon the number of Lashkar members fighting there was expanding and collaboration with other outfits in the Tribal Areas increasing to an even greater degree than pre-Mumbai. Thus, the trends that contributed to the Mumbai attacks—a stagnating jihad in Kashmir, a surging one in Afghanistan and the effect of increased integration with other outfits—accelerated in their aftermath. The conflation of the Indian locus with the jihad against America and its allies, which was among the defining features of Mumbai, also continued. Finally, as was the case at the time of those attacks, Lashkar members who still found their leaders too conservative or India-centric had other options to choose from.

*Amalgamated Jihad*

In March 2009 Lashkar launched its first major offensive inside Indian-administered Kashmir since the Mumbai attacks. Claiming credit for the ensuing firefight with Indian forces that killed twenty-five soldiers, Lashkar spokesman Abdullah Ghaznavi (believed to be an alias) warned, 'The gun battles should serve as a message to India that the struggle for Kashmir's freedom is on with full vigor.'[44] In reality the insurgency remained torpid. When Lashkar fidayeen attacked a police post in Srinagar in January 2010 before besieging a five star hotel, the attack was notable primarily because these assaults had become such a rarity.[45] Indeed civilian fatalities and terrorist incidents continued to decline.[46] According to one count, 375 people were killed in 2009, the last year for which such data was available at the time of writing. That is still more than one per day, but must be viewed within the context of a conflict that since 1989 has cost the lives of somewhere between 40–50,000 people (by the Indian army's count) and approximately 100,000 (according to the separatists).[47]

Although the number of infiltration attempts across the LoC increased over the previous year in 2009 for the first time since 2005, they also remained far lower than during the peak years of the insurgency.[48] According to Indian security officials, attempts remained at roughly the same level through mid-2010, but met with even less success. However, they also insisted that, despite these low numbers, the Pakistan army was continuing to allow this militant infiltration.[49] Most of those attempting to cross the LoC belonged to either Lashkar or Hizb-ul-Mujahideen, with the latter acting primarily in a support capacity for the former.[50]

Despite the fact that the Kashmir insurgency was moribund, India continued to maintain a heavy security presence. As a 2010 report by the International Crisis Group observed, the population was still 'subject to curfews, security checks, arbitrary arrests, torture, rape and extra-judicial killings.'[51] Protests remained a regular occurrence in the Kashmir Valley, and major demonstrations had erupted every summer since 2008. This cycle continued in 2010 when, during clashes with protestors, police fired a teargas shell that struck and killed a seventeen-year old boy on his way home from school. Separatists immediately called for a strike to protest his death, and more clashes soon erupted between demonstrators and the security forces.[52] Additional strikes and protests ensued, but in addition to these there was also a grassroots uprising by Kashmiri youth. Their weapon of choice was not the gun or the bomb, but rather the rock. Stone-throwing throngs of young people confronted the security forces on an almost daily basis throughout the summer. Local police, who were not equipped to control large crowds, repeatedly fired into them, killing unarmed protesters and fueling additional unrest.[53] Unlike the 1990s when unarmed civilians demonstrated against Indian rule *and* militants fought the security forces, there was virtually no militant activity this time. By summer's end some Indian analysts had begun referring to the street violence as the 'Kashmir Intifada,' highlighting the degree to which the unrest was led by rock-throwing youth as opposed to militant outfits or separatist leaders.[54] These boys had not trained in Pakistan, were not tainted by association with the ISI and many disliked the militants. But they viewed the Indian security forces as a brutal occupying force.[55] In short, the political grievances that sparked the insurgency in 1989 were still present, even while the Kashmir jihad they sparked had waned.

Meanwhile the insurgency in Afghanistan remained robust and Lashkar's members were fighting there in greater numbers in Afghanistan by late 2009—early 2010. The flow of Lashkar fighters increased into Kunar and Nuristan provinces in eastern Afghanistan, which remained the primary focal point for the group's operations.[56] The integration of the group's members with the Taliban and Haqqani Network also accelerated, enabling Lashkar fighters to expand their presence.[57] For example, in summer 2010 a joint Afghan-international security force operation led to the capture of a Taliban commander who ISAF claims assisted with the 'recent influx' of Lashkar militants into Nangarhar province, which is located in eastern Afghanistan south of Kunar.[58] According to the top US military intelligence official in Afghanistan at the time, some Lashkar fighters were also heading to the south in search of combat there. Southern Afghanistan was a Taliban front, and it would be almost impossible for Lashkar militants to operate there unless they were integrated into Taliban units.[59]

Lashkar members are also suspected of participating in several joint attacks on Indian targets since autumn 2009. The first was a strike against the Indian Embassy in Kabul, which took place in early October of that year and killed seventeen people.[60] Two months later came an attack at the Heetal Hotel in Kabul, which was located next to a guest house in which approximately forty Indians were staying at the time. Lashkar members are believed to have helped orchestrate the operation, in which eight people were killed.[61] In February 2010 militants believed to belong to Lashkar and the Haqqani Network launched a complex attack against two guest houses in Kabul frequented by Indians. Eighteen people were killed, among them nine Indian nationals of which two were army doctors.[62] According to Afghan intelligence officials, some of the attackers spoke Urdu and searched specifically for Indians during the assault, including specifically demanding to know 'Where is the head Indian doctor?'. As with Mumbai, handlers outside of Afghanistan coordinated the attack via cellphone.[63]

Less than two weeks prior to the assault on the two guest houses in Kabul, homegrown jihadis executed the first successful terrorist attack in India since Mumbai. On 13 February 2010, they used a mobile phone alarm to set off a bomb, which ripped apart the German Bakery in the city of Pune killing seventeen people and injuring many more. The city hosts a diverse population as well as a growing IT sector, and the German Bakery was known as a frequent haunt for foreigners living there. It was also among those sites that David Headley had scouted for Abdur Rehman Syed. However, Indian authorities alleged that Mirza Himayat Baig was the mastermind behind the attack, hatching the plot and surveying the site himself. Baig was reputed to be Lashkar's top operative in the state of Maharashtra, in which the cities of Pune and Mumbai are located.[64] Officials from India's Anti-Terrorism Squad contend that he was in constant contact with Lashkar handlers while planning and preparing for the attack and that he relied upon operatives associated with the Indian Mujahideen for help executing the operation.[65] Indian officials viewed the Pune bombing as evidence that networks belonging to Lashkar and the Indian Mujahideen were being reengaged to execute a fresh round of terrorist attacks.[66] Circumstantial evidence supports this. According to another two arrested Indian operatives, their handlers in Pakistan were trying to engineer serial bomb attacks in Delhi, Mumbai and Bangalore. They said that operatives were being instructed to include foreigners in their target sets when plotting attacks in India.[67]

The Pune attack and the growing number of operations in Afghanistan against Indian interests shared a common characteristic: both were indicative of a trend toward hybridized target selection. This suggested that Lashkar was more inclined than it had been in the past to include US and allied interests in its target set, a proposition reinforced by the fact that in late 2008 Lashkar began plotting a terrorist attack in Denmark in concert with David Headley, the operative responsible for surveillance in Mumbai. There is little doubt that this began as a Lashkar-led enterprise or that the group was prepared to use a highly valuable operative for an out-of-area operation. As the Danish plot reveals, however, the leadership remained susceptible to ISI pressure and preoccupied with India. Yet this did not stop Headley from moving forward independently from Lashkar after his handler postponed the operation. Thanks to the interconnectedness of jihadi networks in Pakistan by this point, he was able to find operational support elsewhere. Indeed, as the following will demonstrate, Lashkar remained a gateway to al-Qaeda, even if it did not always want to be. It also remained an opportunistic outfit, unprepared to let go of a valuable transnational operative despite his freelancing or to shut the door on the Danish plot completely.

Initial discussions regarding a possible attack in Denmark began in October 2008. With the assault on Mumbai looming, David Headley received a visit from his Lashkar and ISI handlers, Sajid Mir and Major Iqbal. Headley had always met each one separately and this was the first time all three were together. They discussed launching an attack against *Morgenavisen Jyllands-Posten*, the Danish newspaper responsible for printing cartoons in 2005 that depicted the Prophet Mohammad. Sajid codenamed it Northern Project, overruling Headley's suggested 'Mickey Mouse Project [MPP].'[68] Major Iqbal's presence at a meeting in which Lashkar operatives discussed plans for a terrorist attack in a Western country is a significant event. It is unclear whether he approved of the plot or if his attendance was a means of keeping tabs on possible future operations in order to rein in the group if necessary. Even if it was the latter, that such a discussion could take place is a testament to the relationship between Lashkar's operatives and their ISI handlers. Moreover, the fact that planning for the attack was allowed to progress is indicative of the latitude some of Lashkar's handlers were prepared to provide the group.

Not long after this visit from Mir and Iqbal, Headley met separately with Abdur Rehman Syed. The latter had moved away completely from Lashkar by this time and indicated that if Lashkar did not go through with the attack then he knew someone else who would.[69] Although Syed did not reveal this person's identity at the time, he did indicate the person was close to al-Qaeda and asked if Headley would be interested in working with them. The person in question was Ilyas Kashmiri, the former HuJI commander who moved his infrastructure to North Waziristan in 2007 and led the 313 Brigade. Syed had floated his own outfit, Jund-al-Fida, which operated under Kashmiri's command.[70] Headley accepted Syed's invitation, but also continued moving forward with Sajid on preparations for the Northern Project. The two met again in early November, at which point Sajid gave Headley a memory stick containing information about Denmark as well as pictures of the editor and cartoonist at *Morgenavisen Jyllands-Posten*. Sajid instructed him to conduct surveillance on the newspaper's offices in Copenhagen and Aarhus, and provided 3,000 euros to cover his travel and expenses.[71] Headley claims to have met with Sajid again in December before making his first reconnaissance trip, at which time the latter directed him to survey a synagogue in Denmark in addition to the newspaper's offices.[72]

Headley returned briefly to the US in December and once against turned to his friend Tahawwur Hussain Rana about using First World Immigration as a cover. He alleges that Rana agreed, and thereafter Headley presented himself as a First World representative interested in placing advertisements in the *Jyllands-Posten*'s newspaper as a means to gain entry to its offices. He used this ruse twice during his first trip to Denmark: first in Copenhagen where he accessed the newspaper's offices and took extensive video surveillance of the surrounding areas, and then several days later to obtain access to the *Jyllands-Posten* office in Aarhus. As he had in Copenhagen, Headley surveyed the surrounding area as well. Headley then returned to Pakistan, where he met separately with Sajid and Abdur Rehman Syed in late January, providing video surveillance to each of them. Syed passed the surveillance footage on to Kashmiri, and took Headley to meet him in North Waziristan the following month. Kashmiri said he could provide the manpower for the operation and therefore Lashkar's participation was unnecessary.[73] According to Headley's testimony to Indian investigators, he was also tasked with doing reconnaissance of targets in India. Headley asserts he did not tell Sajid about his meeting with Kashmiri, suggesting this was not a case of sharing resources.[74] Rather, Kashmiri was attempting to poach Lashkar's operative and its operation.

This was not the first time Syed had asked Headley to undertake surveillance independent of Lashkar's direction; he had done so once before in 2007 and Headley obliged by doing a quick survey of the National Defense College in Delhi. This time the mission was more extensive, and Headley spent several weeks in India during the month of March conducting surveillance for Syed who funded the trip. In Headley's estimation, Abdur Rehman was more interested in attacks against India than in the Northern Project at this point. However, it is worth noting that in addition to tasking him with reconnaissance of traditional Indian targets, including thorough surveillance of the National Defense College, Syed specifically directed Headley to survey additional Chabad Houses as well as other sites at which Israelis or other foreigners were present. After returning to Pakistan, Headley discussed with Syed all of the targets he had surveyed in detail. The latter had established a setup in Nepal during previous trips there while still working with Lashkar and suggested this network could help with launching attacks. Syed also operated a setup in Karachi dedicated to operations against India, for which Headley believes he coordinated with an ISI handler; a relationship Headley alleges continued despite the fact that Syed was working closely with Ilyas Kashmiri (responsible for a host of attacks in Pakistan) and by extension al-Qaeda.[75]

A transnational operative with an American passport was a valuable asset, and upon learning of his reconnaissance in India both Sajid and Lakhvi instructed Headley not to work with Abdur Rehman.[76] Exacerbating concerns about Headley's freelancing was the fact that the group was under heavy pressure from the ISI to lay low following the Mumbai attacks.[77] Mir informed Headley of the need to postpone the Northern Project in response to this pressure.[78] The result was to push him deeper into Kashmiri's orbit, and, through him, into al-Qaeda's orbit as well. Headley told investigators that he had doubts about Lashkar's leaders as a result, describing them as 'coward[s] and pliable.'[79] Yet, Headley did not break his ties with Lashkar. Instead, like other members troubled by the leadership's conservatism, he kept one foot inside and the other outside of the group. Meanwhile, Sajid continued to rely on Headley even after it became clear he was pursing the Northern Project in concert with Syed, and through him with Kashmiri, in direct contravention of Lashkar's instructions.

Abdur Rehman took Headley to North Waziristan once again in May. Kashmiri was much more enthusiastic, telling him the 'elders', whom Headley understood to be al-Qaeda's leadership, were anxious for the attack to take place as soon as possible. He was given $1,500, told to return to Denmark post-haste and take more videos. Kashmiri also provided contact details for several operatives in Europe, directing Headley to inform them the operation should be a suicide attack for which the terrorists needed to prepare martyrdom videos.[80] Headley first returned to the US, where he continued to correspond with Abdur Rehman and Sajid. By this time Lashkar had 'got clearance to launch another attack' against what Headley believed was an economic target in Gujarat.[81] Sajid wanted him to travel to India immediately, but he demurred. The Northern Project came first. In late summer Headley visited Denmark once more, conducting a second round of surveillance, as well as traveling to the United Kingdom and Sweden to meet with Kashmiri's contacts.[82] Unbeknownst to Headley, the British security services were keeping the operatives whom he met under surveillance. 'David the American,' as he was known, was now on their radar.[83]

Headley's detection by the British security services ultimately led to his downfall, and to the wealth of information he provided regarding Lashkar's operations. Sajid seems to have known Headley was playing with fire, and in doing so exposing the group to potential risks. This became apparent when Syed was detained in Pakistan in late spring, two months before Headley exposed himself to British intelligence. When Sajid corresponded with Headley following the latter's trip to Denmark, he warned that Abdur Rehman might be 'singing,' but lamented that his advice was futile 'coz you do what you feel like.' Yet he also inquired as to whether Headley had carried out surveillance in Denmark that Lashkar could use.[84] It appears that, having resigned himself to the fact that Headley could not be controlled, Sajid opportunistically sought to make use of his unsanctioned efforts. But Lashkar also continued to prioritize another attack against India–in his correspondence Sajid alerted Headley to the fact that Lakhvi and Seed had cleared his trip there.[85] It is not insignificant that the former was in prison and the latter under house arrest at the time.

Headley also remained opportunistic, as did Abdur Rehman who by summer's end had been released from jail. The latter lost contact with Kashmiri, who was believed to have been killed by a US drone strike.[86] Records of the communications that followed reveal that Headley suggested that, in light of Kashmiri's apparent death, Syed should reach out to Sajid Mir and re-solicit Lashkar's support. Neither held the group's leadership in the highest esteem. Headley complained they were perpetually focused on India, had 'rotten guts' and were too risk averse, to which Syed agreed, saying 'They do not want to take risk and [yet] they want to be praised also.' Nevertheless, in a separate coded conversation with his friend Tahawwur Hussain Rana, Headley made clear that what he wanted most was to carry through with the operation: 'I don't care that if I am working for Microsoft or I am working for a ...any...GE or Philips. I don't care. As long as I am making money, I don't give a shit.'[87] In other words, he would work with whoever helped him, whether it was Kashmiri or Lashkar. Such a decision never became necessary. On 30 September Syed reported that Kashmiri was alive. Headley stated that he would return to Pakistan in early October to meet with both of them. US authorities arrested him three days later at O'Hare Airport in Chicago. He had approximately thirteen surveillance videos in his possession.[88] Soon after detaining Headley, US authorities arrested Rana as well and later indicted him for his alleged role in the Danish plot and the Mumbai attacks.[89] He pleaded not guilty and was awaiting trial at the time this book went to press. The US government also indicted both Syed and Kashmiri, though neither was in American custody at the time of writing.

A month later, police in Bangladesh took three men into custody.[90] Two of them were Indian nationals and all three confessed to being Lashkar operatives. Local authorities alleged they were planning attacks on the US Embassy and the Indian High Commission in Dhaka, the Bangladeshi capital.[91] Acting on information stemming from these initial arrests, the Bangladeshi and Indian police quickly detained additional suspects, including several more Lashkar members as well as other Pakistani militants.[92] By summer 2010, they had arrested over a dozen Lashkar operatives, including four Pakistanis and six Indians. Several of these men had been in Bangladesh for years, building Lashkar's network there, and they told authorities that many more operatives were still in the country. Police allege that some of the suspects confessed to having been taken to Pakistan for training and said that ISI agents helped to prepare their passports, though when this occurred is unclear.[93] Most were in Bangladesh to organize attacks against India, which raises questions about whether the attack in Dhaka was a sanctioned Lashkar operation.

Western and Bangladeshi officials suggested these developments came amidst what they viewed as an expansion of Lashkar activity in Bangladesh and indications the group was considering opening up an active front there.[94] However, according to another Western intelligence analyst who tracks the group and is familiar with the case, evidence suggests a faction within the group or loosely connected to it may have been responsible for the attempted attacks.[95] Police in Bangladesh said the arrests were made based on information gained from Headley and Indian intelligence reportedly intercepted phone conversations linking those detained to Abdur Rehman Syed, who is believed to have provided money as well as issued the directive to launch the attack.[96] It is possible Abdul Rehman was working with Lashkar in Pakistan to execute the operation, but equally plausible that he leveraged his connections to the group's network for an unsanctioned attack. As mentioned above, Syed controlled his own unit in Karachi and built up networks in Bangladesh and Nepal while with Lashkar. He took this 'Lashkar infrastructure' with him when he floated his own outfit.[97] Whether sanctioned or unsanctioned, the episode provided additional evidence of four trends that characterized Lashkar post-Mumbai: the expansion of its jihad; the versatile and protean nature of its networks; the possibility that personal connections might enable individuals or factions to use these networks for freelance operations; and, finally, the integration of Indian targets with the jihad against America and its allies.

# CONCLUSION

For many years after 9/11 the US did not push Pakistan on Lashkar, instead focusing mainly on eliciting support for the fight against al-Qaeda. That changed after the Mumbai attacks and since then concerns about the group have grown in concert with its expansion in Afghanistan and the wider South Asian region. Approximately one year after Mumbai, US President Barack Obama wrote a letter to his Pakistani counterpart, President Asif Ali Zardari, in which he specifically mentioned Lashkar as one of the militant groups against which the government should act.[1] A chorus of US diplomats, security officials and military officers reiterated this call for action, pressuring Pakistan publicly as well as privately to move against Lashkar. Yet the group's position remains relatively secure. There are two main reasons for this state of affairs. First, despite collaboration with other actors waging war against state and the involvement of some of its members in anti-state violence, Lashkar's policy remains to abjure launching attacks in Pakistan. The security establishment has determined that in order to avoid additional instability it must not take any action that could lead Lashkar to change this position. Second, the group still provides much needed leverage vis-à-vis India. The civilian government is more amenable to cracking down on militant outfits that provide utility against India, but has no real control over the army or ISI, which continue to determine the country's policies in this regard. Thus, while Pakistan has made efforts to battle some of the militant groups operating from its soil, selectivity with regard to which outfits to take action against remains the order of the day. A former high-ranking

ISI officer put it bluntly, saying, 'Pakistan is being expected to hit Lashkar to prove we are treating every jihadi group equally when it is other groups that are hitting us while Lashkar is not.' For this reason, he said 'they are not equal to us and of course Pakistan favors Lashkar.'[2]

Pointing to ongoing military operations in FATA and terrorist violence savaging the country, one senior official in the security services asserted that Pakistan did not have the capacity to deal with Lashkar at present. He said that first al-Qaeda and the Pakistani Taliban must be eliminated. Although he admitted Lashkar shared their extremist ideology, he indicated dealing with it would have to wait because it was not an immediate threat to the state.[3] Numerous other interlocutors inside or close to the Pakistani security establishment echoed this argument for triage, and asserted that in the short-term Pakistan must avoid taking any action that would lead Lashkar as an organization to become more involved in the insurgency against the state. Members of the security services are particularly concerned about opening up a second front in Punjab province, where Lashkar is based. They believe doing so would lead the group to intensify its collaboration with other militants, including al-Qaeda and the Pakistani Taliban, to help them escalate the tempo and scale of attacks in that province. There is a strong sense, which is not entirely unfounded, that the police are ill-equipped to deal with the ramifications were this to occur and that the army might need to be called in. The army is not only overstretched, but its ranks also draw heavily from Punjab province and so initiating operations there could destabilize it as an institution as well as the country.

It would be naïve to suggest Pakistan should not first focus on the militants currently attacking its people. But fear of acting against Lashkar is not the only reason it is still allowed to operate. The group continues to be used as a proxy against India and elements within the army and ISI clearly wish to maintain this capability. In a moment of candor, an ISI officer asked rhetorically, 'Who benefits if we go after the Lashkar? And who pays?' His response: 'India and Pakistan.'[4] Members of the Pakistani security establishment remain convinced that India poses an existential threat.

Indeed, the army is overstretched partly because many of its troops are deployed to counter possible Indian aggression, making them unavailable to take on Pakistan's own militants. The disparity between the two countries in terms of size and economic strength creates an attendant variation in their respective conventional military capacity, which may only grow with time. Developing a nuclear capability was one means of redressing this imbalance; reliance on irregular outfits like Lashkar is another. It is therefore impossible to de-link the issue of support for the group from any process designed to forge peace between India and Pakistan. The issue of Kashmir, over which India and Pakistan have fought three wars, is not the only stumbling block to peace or to dealing with Lashkar. But it does play a major part in Pakistan's calculus. The predominant view appears to be that dismantling Lashkar without extracting some concessions from India would remove a valuable, and one of the few, sources of leverage Pakistan has at its disposal. Irrespective of what one feels about the use of terrorism as a bargaining chip, it is unrealistic to assume support for Lashkar will cease without a political payoff in return.

The group understands its utility too. One member very close to the leadership asserted that 'the ISI cannot stop its support because Lashkar has the ability to inflict the biggest losses on India.' Thus, it will not be dismantled so long as the Pakistani security establishment needs leverage against the country's rival.[5] It is not at all certain that Lashkar could be stopped from launching an attack to upset relations with India should they begin to improve. Complicating the situation is the fact that spoilers exist in both countries. Lashkar remains among the best instruments to sabotage any burgeoning peace process, and particularly one that hardliners in Pakistan believe gives away too much to India. This geopolitical reality suggests the group will remain intact for the foreseeable future. So too does Pakistan's domestic political reality, where the army and ISI wield disproportionate power. In addition to Lashkar's strategic value and the possibility of a backlash that could result from attempting to dismantle it, the group's members have forged relationships with personnel in these institutions. A number of former officers joined its ranks, which further strengthens these bonds.

Because Lashkar and the army both recruit heavily from Punjab, familial and friendship ties compound and complicate matters. Lashkar's provision of social services and relief aid has also enabled it to forge relationships with people in the national as well as provincial governments. As a result, sympathizers exist in the army and ISI, as well as among the police and officials in the national and provincial bureaucracies, albeit to a lesser extent. Further, JuD has developed into a formidable political-religious force. Even those officials who may not sympathize with the group nevertheless fear its political clout, with some politicians depending on it to deliver needed vote banks. All of these domestic factors are in addition to the aforementioned security concerns that accompany any considered action against the group.

How did Lashkar grow so powerful? It began as a small band of men who joined forces with the ambition to unite the Pakistani Ahl-e-Hadith movement and purify society through dawa and jihad. This jihad was not nation-centric, but rather pan-Islamist, and members fought on multiple fronts during the group's early years of operation. Jihad was also obligatory according to Lashkar's interpretation, a view that estranged it from the small Ahl-e-Hadith movement in Pakistan. The group had major ambitions inside the country and abroad, but the nature of those ambitions closed off avenues of support among its primary audience. The offer of state sponsorship to promote the scale and lethality of Lashkar's participation in the Kashmir jihad was a significant opportunity, and the group seized it. Fighting there also aligned with the group's ideological preferences. It was the closest Muslim land under perceived occupation and therefore deemed the most important one for Lashkar. However, the group did not view this simply as territory in need of liberation. The Kashmir jihad was part of a larger battle against Hindus, which its leaders believe has existed since the inception of Islam. Increased focus on and participation in the conflict in Indian-administered Kashmir have reinforced Lashkar's extreme anti-Hindu convictions.

Pakistan's reliance on proxies dates back to the days of Partition. Since then successive governments, civilian and military, have instrumentalized Islam to promote cohesion at home and foreign policy aims abroad. As Husain Haqqani, Pakistan's Ambassador to the US at the time of writing, observed, these policies evolved into a 'strategic commitment to jihadi ideology.'[6] Lashkar is among the most fruitful results of these policies. The army and ISI initially supported the group as a result of its small size and lack of natural allies in Pakistan, the assumption being that Lashkar could become powerful externally without building up a significant support base or threating the state domestically. This assumption proved only partly correct. State support enabled the group to develop a powerful military apparatus, but because of its commitment to dawa, Lashkar also channeled a significant portion of the resources it received into the provision of social services as a means of missionary outreach. Thus, by the late 1990s it controlled a robust social welfare as well as a powerful military apparatus. In addition to its infrastructure in Pakistan, Lashkar wove together transnational networks which were used for fundraising and logistics to support its non-violent activism in Pakistan, military operations in Kashmir and terrorism in India. Its domestic infrastructure was also mobilized to support Lashkar's jihad in Indian-administered Kashmir, where its growing reputation simultaneously drew recruits from beyond the Ahl-e-Hadith faith to the group. Thus, its missionary and military activities became self-reinforcing. Meanwhile, because Lashkar's ideological priorities vis-à-vis liberating Indian-administered aligned with state objectives, the group's pan-Islamist identity and its role as a Pakistani proxy were aligned.

Debates took place within Lashkar after 9/11, as they did in other jihadi organizations, about whether to alter its priorities or relationship with the state. Ultimately the group agreed to continue submitting to state oversight. The leadership's readiness to do so stemmed from a committment to the Kashmir jihad as well as a desire to protect the organization's position and robust infrastructure in Pakistan. In exchange for adhering to the Musharraf regime's agenda, Lashkar was given greater freedom of maneuvre than any other outfit in the country. JuD remained legal, enabling the group to keep its supply lines open. Its local and international fundraising surged, while recruitment remained steady. With its safe haven in Pakistan secure, the group also broadened its already robust transnational networks while maintaining a healthy level of militant activity in Indian-administered Kashmir. The Musharraf regime periodically scaled back militant activities there during the first years after 9/11, but these were periodic interuptions. Lashkar remained the most prolific Pakistani outfit fighting on the Kashmir front, and also began devoting greater attention to executing and supporting terrorist attacks against India. The group had been involved in terrorist violence within India since the early 1990s, where communal grievances fueled the growth of a nascent jihadi movement. A greater number of Indian Muslims were drawn to jihadism after the Gujarat riots in 2002, and Lashkar's support augmented the lethality of this indigenous movement.

Although it prioritized the fight against India, Lashkar began playing its own double game after 9/11, using its infrastructure in Pakistan and transnational networks to contribute to the global jihad against America and its allies. This included the provision of training and logistical support to established outfits as well as aspiring Western jihadis, for whom the group sometimes facilitated access to al-Qaeda. Lashkar operatives were directly involved in an attempted terrorist attack against Australia and are suspected of pitching in to support other operations directed at the US and its allies. Some members left to fight in Afghanistan while others distanced themselves from the group as a result of the leadership's willingness to submit to state oversight. But Lashkar remained relatively cohesive, and desertions and splintering were minimal compared to other outfits in Pakistan. Some of those who left were later welcomed back into the Lashkar-fold and others maintained connections to, as well as influence on, members in the organization. This later contributed to tensions within the group and facilitated the integration of Lashkar members with other outfits.

President Musharraf's decision to make a concerted effort to reduce militant activities in Indian-administered Kashmir had significant consequences for Lashkar. After Pakistan initiated the composite dialogue with India in 2004 it took limited steps to curtail militancy, sidelining some outfits. Lashkar sent smaller numbers of militants across the LoC, calibrating its activities in line with state directives. This enabled it to remain active in Indian-administered

Kashmir, but less so than in the past. Pressure mounted on the group to slow its activities further after 2005 as the Musharraf regime sought to show results in the wake of the 7/7 London attacks. As a negotiated solution began to appear possible, Pakistan strengthened its efforts to scale back the Kashmir jihad and by 2006 even Indian officials admitted they were having an impact. The environment in Indian-administered Kashmir had also become less conducive to militancy by this time, which factored into the reduction in violence there. The leadership's decision to adhere to state directives weakened its internal credibility among pockets within the organization, at a time when overall control was attenuating as a result of the group' inability to maintain a high level of activity in Indian-administered Kashmir. Some Lashkar militants were willing to lay low, to edge toward non-violent activism in JuD or to return to their lives outside of the group. Others made their way to the Tribal Areas in order to join the insurgency in Afghanistan. Lashkar was a pan-Islamist outfit and so liberating Indian-administered Kashmir was never intended to be the apotheosis of its jihad. But senior leaders, as well as many of its rank-and-file, continued to view this as the most important front. Lashkar was closer to it and to the population, the group had built its reputation there and the proportion of 'occupiers' to 'occupied' remained high. Yet even if members were obligated to fight there, doing so had become far more difficult. Meanwhile, the Afghan jihad was thriving and thus impossible to ignore for a pan-Islamist outfit like Lashkar.

A small number of Lashkar members already were active in the Afghan insurgency by the middle of the decade when the group's organizational footprint on that front grew. Entrance into the Afghan theater necessitated a greater presence in the Tribal Areas and heightened collaboration with other militant outfits active there. Many of these actors were considerably more involved in Afghanistan than Lashkar while some were also at war with the Pakistani state. One consequence of the increased integration of Lashkar members with these other, sometimes more extreme, outfits was to put pressure on the leadership to expand the group's involvement in the global jihad against America and its allies. The 2008 Mumbai attacks were launched amidst this environment. They had multiple objectives, one of which was to harm the group's historic enemy. Another was to to boost Lashkar's reputation and integrate its war against India with the global jihad.

Anger at perceived American meddling in Pakistan and the occupation of Afghanistan, as well as alleged US favoritism toward India, were recurrent themes in every interview the author conducted with Lashkar members. These parochial concerns were viewed through the prism of a wider American-led 'war against Islam,' in which many Western countries were seen to take part. However, Lashkar's leaders did not intend the group's growing involvement in the global jihad against America and its allies to come at the expense of war against India. This policy of attempting to have it both ways opens the group up to splintering and factionalism, which are more common in larger organizations that embrace multiple causes than in smaller ones united behind a single objective. Indeed, Lashkar's leaders still face challenges to their legitimacy because they continue to prioritize the jihad against India when forced to choose. This has alienated some members, as have their leaders' close ties to the army and ISI and continued policy of abjuring attacks against the Pakistani state. The longer the insurgencies last in Afghanistan and Pakistan, the more difficult it may become to control the next generation of Lashkar militants. Yet it would be a mistake to presume the growing threat comes only from potentially rogue operatives; since the Mumbai attacks Lashkar, as an organization, has expanded the scope of its jihad even further.

What does this mean for the future of the group? Specifically, is it poised to become the new al-Qaeda, as some analysts suggest? In Lashkar's present incarnation the short answer is no. The propensity to analogize it to al-Qaeda is understandable to the degree that both have transnational attack capabilities and grand ambitions. It also may result from the tendency to view the next potential 'big threat' through the prism of the present one. However, as this book has attempted to illustrate, Lashkar is its own unique organization and, to paraphrase one of Clausewitz's many famous dictums about war, we must not mistake it for nor try to turn it into something that it is not.[7]

CONCLUSION

Unlike al-Qaeda Central (the core organization hiding in Pakistan's Tribal Areas), which confronts a challenging security environment and relies heavily on other outfits for assistance with launching attacks, Lashkar controls a robust infrastructure that operates in plain sight. Its leadership operates out of Lahore and Pakistan-administered Kashmir, not from a hidden redoubt somewhere along the Afghanistan-Pakistan border, though the group has increased it presence there. This freedom of movement carries with it a number of benefits the core al-Qaeda organization does not enjoy, but also serves as a leverage point that can be used to constrain Lashkar's activity. The leadership's ongoing relationship with the ISI and susceptibility to state pressure robs it of legitimacy in the eyes of some jihadis, who respect the sacrifices al-Qaeda leaders have made and the forthright manner in which they challenge the US as well as its many allies. At present, Lashkar or at least significant elements within it, are still 'tamed by the ISI' as one former member observed.[8] The group no longer needs financial or much operational support; rather it requires protection and the freedom to continue its military as well as social welfare activities. In the 1990s the group needed the state to build up its infrastructure, whereas now it is reliant on the army and ISI not to tear it down. It is worth highlighting Lashkar's devotion to dawa through the delivering of social services—a capacity al-Qaeda lacks—and the fact that protecting its domestic infrastructure has at times limited its military adventurism.

Regional dynamics also continue to exert considerable and direct influence on Lashkar's behavior. The leadership retains an element of nationalism that is distinctly at odds with al-Qaeda and still finds common ground, as it has since the 1990s, with elements in the army and ISI. The two remain co-dependent: each afraid of the repercussions that might stem from splitting with the other, and bound together by their belief that India is a mortal enemy. Nor is Lashkar's prioritization of India as the main enemy solely a function of its relationship with the army or ISI. The group did not launch a jihad against India in order to solicit state support, though receiving it influenced its decision to prioritize that fight. Two decades spent waging war against India has hallowed that cause, to paraphrase another German philosopher, for many of the group's members.[9] This remains the case even as Lashkar's leaders admit that some of their cadres now are driven more by the fight against America.

If one reframes the question 'Is Lashkar the next al-Qaeda,' however, to read 'Does Lashkar threaten the US and its Western allies at home and abroad' then the answer is yes. First, its role in Afghanistan is expanding, though it remains a secondary player. Lashkar boasts a stable of explosives experts and its fighters are adept at small unit tactics, meaning it can make a qualitative contribution to the cause even without substantially increasing its quantitative input. Second, the inclusion of foreign targets for attacks in India is part of a trend that could continue. Third, Lashkar appears prepared to consider acting as the lead agent in terrorist attacks against Western countries, having done so in Australia during the early years of the decade and in Denmark more recently. Yet, Lashkar need not take the lead role in order for its training apparatus and transnational networks to be used against the US or its Western allies. Indeed, the current threat to Western interests comes from a conglomeration of actors working in concert. Notably, working as part of a consortium provides cover for the group, since shared responsibility makes it easier for Lashkar to conceal its fingerprints. One could imagine a scenario in which would-be Western jihadis looking to fight in Afghanistan linked up with a facilitator connected with Lashkar to access a training camp in territory controlled by the Haqqani Network where al-Qaeda convinced them to launch a terrorist attack in a Western country and Lashkar trainers provided some of the instruction. In addition to the contributions it can make in Pakistan, nodes in the group's transnational networks are able to provide reconnaissance, financial support or other logistical assistance for such an attack. Elements from such a scenario have occurred already, as this book has illustrated with regard to Lashkar trainees and members operating in the US, UK and Europe, Persian Gulf and Australia.

The threat comes not only from Lashkar as a stand-alone group or from its collaboration with other actors. Rather, individuals or factions within the organization can utilize its domestic infrastructure as well as transnational capabilities to pursue their own operations. Because members who leave do not necessarily cut ties with the group, or may bring elements within it with them, the threat also comes from Lashkar's alumni network. Thus, when assessing the dangers of Lashkar's expansion, one must consider the capability of current and former members both to steer the organization in an increasingly internationalist direction as well as to leverage its infrastructure for these purposes whether or not the leadership approves. Further, enhanced organizational integration with other outfits also heightens the opportunities for freelancing, thus increasing the chances that some of the group's capabilities might be used for attacks without the leadership's consent.

Lashkar's threat to India remains greater as well as more straightforward. After a period of calm following the Mumbai attacks, evidence suggests Lashkar's leash was loosened once again. The potential costs to the group for attacks against India remain lower than for its global jihadi activities because they are less likely to result in ISI sanction and so Lashkar is able to plan, prepare for and operationalize attacks against India with greater ease. Thus, the threat to Pakistan's neighbor is not simply about the likelihood or frequency of attacks, but also their scale since Lashkar can more fully capitalize on its extensive organizational capabilities for these operations. Moreover, although degraded, it appeared at the time of writing that the indigenous terrorist network in India that Lashkar helped to build was being regenerated with the help of external support. The Indian Mujahideen network is part of a wider jihadi project in India, and many indigenous militants have connections to multiple actors in Pakistan. On the whole, however, Indian jihadis are closest to Lashkar, which continues to train and support them. Although it appears the ISI remains able to influence Lashkar to modulate its terrorist activities vis-à-vis India, the group's regional presence in the Gulf as well as other South Asian countries means that its ability to inflict damage is not limited to what it can accomplish from Pakistan. While Lashkar's transnational networks can be used for multiple purposes and Western security officials are therefore correct to worry about the threats they pose to their own countries, the group still employs them primarily for attacks in India. Furthermore, their existence means that Lashkar would remain able to support or execute attacks against India were Pakistan to crack down on its domestic infrastructure. Should this occur, these networks also could be unleashed on the many countries they currently permeate, or on Pakistan.

Lashkar is unlikely to launch attacks inside Pakistan short of a sudden volte-face by the state and an attempt to smash the group. Yet that does not mean Pakistan is immune to the consequences of Lashkar's violence. Its involvement in a terrorist attack against America or one of its allies would imperil US-Pakistan relations, and could lead to retaliatory action. Another terrorist spectacular in India is of potentially greater concern. War between two nuclear powers was avoided after the Mumbai attacks, but it is questionable whether any government in New Delhi would show similar restraint were India to suffer another mass casualty attack at Lashkar's hands. For these reasons, some of those with whom the author spoke in the Pakistani security establishment evinced unease about the group's activities. Nor should one forget the impact that its non-violent activities have on Pakistan. Members of the security establishment have implied to the author that one day, provided Kashmir is settled appropriately, JuD could be used as a mechanism to move Lashkar fighters toward non-violence. However, many local interlocutors fear the long-term threat to moderate values in the country even more than they do Lashkar's martial capabilities. Although the group had only limited success at converting people to its interpretation of Ahl-e-Hadith Islam, 'JuD is steadily eating into Pakistan's social fabric' to quote one prominent journalist.[10] Yet its above-ground operations continue relatively unchecked. Meanwhile, the army and ISI continue attempting merely to modulate the group's militant activities. Among the many problems with this approach is the fact that managing jihadis is more of an art than a science and ambiguous policies by nature create situations in which real control is impossible.

Dismantling Lashkar must be a gradual process in order to avoid provoking a major backlash that could destabilize the country. But there is no indication that such a process has been initiated. Pakistan's practice of abstaining from action against Lashkar is predicated partly on the desire to avoid driving it further into the insurgency. However, this presumes a level of organizational discipline that appears at odds with the ground reality. The group's policy remains to abjure attacks against the state, but the leadership's influence over some mid-level commanders and members of the rank-and-file has attenuated as a result. Meanwhile, Lashkar remains able to expand its already potent capabilities, penetrating society through social outreach while simultaneously increasing its integration with the militant nexus that now threatens Pakistan. 'Jihad is like the flow of water,' to quote one member of the security services.[11] Unless something changes, arresting this tide will only grow more difficult with time.

# NOTES

## INTRODUCTION

1. Various figures have been reported for the death toll. This figure does not include the nine terrorists killed and is from the final report submitted by the Chief Investigating Officer to the court in Mumbai. See: 'Final Report: in Mumbai Terror Attack Cases,' The Court of Addl. Ch. M.M., 37th Court, Esplanade, Mumbai 25 Feb. 2009.
2. It also can be translated to mean Army of the Righteous and Army of the Good. Additionally, Taiba is a name for the city of Medina in Saudi Arabia, one of the holiest sites in the Muslim world, and so the group's name can be translated to mean Army of Medina.
3. MDI website, 'Introduction: Dawa and Jihad Movement,' undated. The MDI web site is now defunct, as is its successor run under the JuD banner. Author's collection gathered from these web sites during operation as well as via the Internet Archive.
4. Roel Meijer, 'Introduction,' in Roel Meijer (ed.), *Global Salafism: Islam's New Religious Movement* (London: Hurst, 2009), pp. 3–4.
5. Author interview with Mohammad Amir Rana, Director of the Pak Institute for Peace Studies, 16 & 18 Dec. 2008, in Pakistan. Author interview with Arif Jamal, former journalist in Pakistan, 20 Aug. 2009 via phone. See also: Mohammad Amir Rana, *A to Z of Jehadi Organizations in Pakistan*, trans. Saba Ansari (Lahore: Mashal Books, 2006), p. 317.
6. Information about the year it was formed from: Author interview with Abdullah Muntazir, International Spokesperson for Jamaat-ul-Dawa, 30 Dec. 2008 in Pakistan. Information about its purpose from: MDI website, 'A Brief Introduction to the Markaz and the Lashkar,' undated. Author's collection.
7. Author interview with Arif Jamal, 20 Aug. 2009 via phone.
8. MDI website, 'Education: Al-Dawa System of Schools,' undated. Author's collection.

9. The year of its formation is given as both 1990 and 1993 by Lashkar's literature. One of the original MDI founders, who was a member of the Jamaat-ul-Dawa senior leadership at the time the author interviewed him, confirmed the date was 1990. A former Lashkar member, who belonged to the group in 1990, also confirmed that date. Author interview with member of Jamaat-ul-Dawa senior leadership, name withheld, May 2009 in Pakistan. Author interview with former Lashkar-e-Taiba member, name withheld, Jan. 2009 in Pakistan.

10. Author interview with former Lashkar-e-Taiba member, name withheld, Jan. 2009 in Pakistan.

## 1. THE PAKISTANI JIHADI MILIEU

1. Christine Fair suggests a similar form of categorization, which distinguishes Pakistani militant groups in two ways: first, by school of thought; second, by their historical and current goals. See: Christine Fair, 'Antecedents and Implications of the Nov. 2008 Lashkar-e-Taiba (LeT) Attack Upon Several Targets in the Indian Mega-City of Mumbai,' testimony prepared for the Subcommittee on Transportation Security and Infrastructure Protection of the Committee on Homeland Security to the United States House of Representatives, 11 Mar. 2009.

2. Numerous scholarly works explore Pakistan's history in detail, and at the time of writing more were on the way. See for example: Stephen Cohen, *The Idea of Pakistan* (Washington, DC: The Brookings Institute, 2004). Husain Haqqani, *Pakistan: Between Mosque and Military* (Washington, DC: Carnegie Endowment for International Peace, 2005). Christophe Jaffrelot (ed.), *Pakistan: Nationalism without a Nation?* (London: Zed Books, 2004). Owen Bennett-Jones, *Pakistan: Eye of the Storm* (London: Penguin, 2002). Shuja Nawaz, *Crossed Swords: Pakistan, Its Army and the War Within* (New York: Oxford University Press, 2008). Farzana Shaikh, *Making Sense of Pakistan* (London, Hurst & Co., 2009). Anatol Lieven, *Pakistan: A Hard Country* (London: Penguin, 2011).

3. Shaikh, *Making Sense of Pakistan*, p. 8, 180.

4. Ibid., pp. 5, 39–44. See also: Haqqani, *Pakistan: Between Mosque and Military*, p. 7.

5. Shaikh, *Making Sense of Pakistan*, p. 2.

6. Ibid., p. 67.

7. Bennett-Jones, *Pakistan: Eye of the Storm*, p. 6.

8. Joshua White, *Pakistan's Islamist Frontier* (Arlington, VA: Center on Faith & International Affairs, 2008), p. 38.

9. Haqqani, *Pakistan: Between Mosque and Military*, p. 13.

10. The North-West Frontier Province was officially renamed as Khyber Pakhtunkhwa in 2010.

11. Saeed Shafqat, 'From Official Islam to Islamism: The Rise of Daawa-ul-Irshad and Lashkar-e-Taiba,' in *Pakistan: Nationalism Without a Nation?*, p. 141.
12. J.L. Racine, 'Pakistan and the "India Syndrome",' in Ibid., p. 196.
13. The catalyst for secession came in 1970 when the Awami League, representing the overwhelming majority of Bangladeshis, won the elections held that year and were denied the right to govern. The central government postponed seating the National Assembly, and the military responded to Bangladeshi protests by launching Operation Searchlight to crackdown on the Awami League and those supporting it.
14. See, for example: K.K. Aziz, *Murder of History: A Critique of History Textbooks Used in Pakistan* (Lahore: Vanguard Books, 1998). Rebecca Winthrop and Corinne Graff, *Beyond Madrassas: Assessing the Links Between Education and Militancy in Pakistan*, (Washington, DC: The Brookings Institute, June 2010).
15. Christine Fair, Neil Malhotra and Jacob N. Shapiro, 'The Roots of Militancy: Explaining Support for Political Violence in Pakistan,' 28 Dec. 2009, http://www.humansecuritygateway.com/showRecord.php?RecordId=33506 (last accessed 15 Aug. 2010).
16. Shaikh, *Making Sense of Pakistan*, p. 147. See also: Hasan Askari-Rizvi, *The Military and Politics in Pakistan* (Lahore: Sang-i-Meel, 2000). Ayesha Jalal, *The State of Martial Law: The Origins of Pakistan's Political Economy of Defence* (Cambridge University Press, 1990). Ayesha Siddiqa, *Military Inc.: Inside Pakistan's Military Economy* (London: Pluto Press, 2007).
17. Siddiqa, *Military Inc.*
18. Nawaz, *Crossed Swords*, pp. 14–15.
19. Siddiqa, *Military Inc.*, p. 59.
20. Bennett-Jones, *Pakistan: Eye of the Storm*, p. 120.
21. Shaikh, *Making Sense of Pakistan*, p. 184.
22. Cohen, *The Idea of Pakistan*, pp. 99–110.
23. Nawaz, *Crossed Swords*, p. 385.
24. For a discussion of the communal versus universal discourses of Islam in Pakistan, see: Shaikh, *Making Sense of Pakistan*.
25. Bennett-Jones, *Pakistan: Eye of the Storm*, p. 266.
26. Cohen, *The Idea of Pakistan*, p. 110.
27. Haqqani, *Pakistan: Between Mosque and Military*, p. 159.
28. Barnett R. Rubin, *The Fragmentation of Afghanistan* (New Haven, CT: Yale University Press, 2002), pp. 83–84.
29. Mohammad Yousaf and Mark Adkin, *The Bear Trap: The Defeat of a Superpower* (Havertown, PA: Casemate, 1992), p. 25.
30. Steve Coll, *Ghost Wars: The Secret History of the CIA, Afghanistan, and bin Laden, from the Soviet Invasion to September 10, 2001* (New York: Penguin, 2005), p. 102. Rubin, *The Fragmentation of Afghanistan*, p. 182.

31. Pakistan had almost, but not complete, control according to Steve Coll whose book *Ghost Wars* recounts the CIA's funding of the Afghan jihad. He asserts that the Agency used Jalaluddin Haqqani, who later became an al-Qaeda and Taliban ally, to test new tactics and weapons systems. Haqqani was so favored with supplies that he was in a position to equip the Arab fighters who came to join the jihad. See: Coll, *Ghost Wars*, p. 202.

32. For an in-depth, insider account of the ISI's role, see: Yousaf and Adkin, *The Bear Trap*.

33. Coll, *Ghost Wars*, pp. 67–68.

34. For more on Saudi funding, see: Thomas Hegghammer, *Jihad in Saudi Arabia* (Cambridge: Cambridge University Press, 2010), pp. 25–30.

35. Ibid, p. 29. Jamil al-Rahman is also known as Maulvi Hussain. He changed his name because Hussain was associated with Shia Islam and thus not popular among the Arab Salafis. David Edwards, *Before Taliban: Genealogies of the Afghan Jihad* (Berkeley, CA: University of California Press, 2002), p. 270, fn. 61.

36. Gilles Dorronsoro, *Revolution Unending: Afghanistan, 1979 to the Present* (London: Hurst, 2005), pp. 230–231. Coll, *Ghost Wars*, pp. 82–83. Rubin, *The Fragmentation of Afghanistan*, pp. 242, 261.

37. Author interview with Noman Benotman, former head of the Political and Media committees for the Libyan Islamic Fighting Group, 3 Mar. 2010 in the United Kingdom. See also: Coll, *Ghost Wars*, pp. 82–83. Dorronsoro, *Revolution Unending*, pp. 230–231.

38. Author interview with Noman Benotman, 3 Mar. 2010 in the United Kingdom. Author interview with Michael Semple, fellow at the Carr Center for Human Rights Policy at Harvard's Kennedy School and former deputy to the European Union special representative for Afghanistan, 23 Dec. 2008 in Pakistan. Regarding Saudis joining Jamiat al-Dawa al-Quran wal-Sunna, see also: Hegghammer, *Jihad in Saudi Arabia*, p. 46. Regarding Egyptians joining, see also: Dorronsoro, *Revolution Unending*, pp. 230–231.

39. Rana, *A to Z of Jehadi Organizations in Pakistan*, p. 317.

40. MDI web site, 'A Brief Introduction to the Markaz and the Lashkar.'

41. Hegghammer, *Jihad in Saudi Arabia*, p. 43.

42. For more on al-Qaeda's founding, see: Peter Bergen, *The Osama bin Laden I Know* (London: Free Press, 2006), pp. 78–81. Kim Cragin, 'Early History of Al-Qa'ida,' *The Historical Journal* 51, no. 4 (2008).

43. Author interview with Rahimullah Yusufzai, Executive Editor of *The News International*, 3 Jan. 2009 via phone. See also: Ahmed Rashid, *Taliban* (Oxford: Pan Books, 2000), p. 132.

44. Amir Mir, 'LeT Commander Furious at JuD Chief,' *The News* 15 Jan. 2009. Syed Saleem Shahzad, 'Pakistan Groups Banned But Not Bowed,' *Asia Times*, 17 Dec. 2008.

45. Hegghammer, *Jihad in Saudi Arabia*, pp. 44–45.
46. Quintan Wiktorowicz, 'The New Global Threat: Transnational Salafis and Jihad,' *Middle East Policy Council* 8, no. 4 (2001). Olivier Roy, 'The Radicalization of Sunni Conservative Fundamentalism,' *ISIM Newsletter*, no. 2 (Mar. 1999).
47. The Sunni-Shia divide in Islam began following the death of the Prophet Mohammad in 632 CE when his followers split over his successor. Shia Muslims believe that the caliphate should have been passed down only to the Prophet's direct descendants and therefore the Prophet's son-in-law (and cousin) Ali ibn Abi Talib should have succeeded him. Instead, three other men preceded Ali. Sunnis supported the ascension of his predecessors and consider Ali to be the fourth and last of the 'rightly guided caliphs.'
48. Ayesha Jalal, *Partisans of Allah: Jihad in South Asia* (London: Harvard University Press, 2008), p. 25.
49. Barbara Metcalf, *Islamic Revival in British India: Deoband, 1860–1900* (Princeton, NJ: Princeton University Press, 1982), pp. 100–101.
50. Ibid., p. 86.
51. Rashid, *Taliban*, p. 88.
52. Jalal, *Partisans of Allah*, p. 276.
53. Luv Puri, 'The Past and Future of Deobandi Islam,' *CTC Sentinel*, 21, no. 11 (Nov. 2009).
54. White, *Pakistan's Islamist Frontier*, p. 81.
55. S.V.R Nasr, 'Islam, The State and the Rise of Sectarian Militancy,' in *Pakistan: Nationalism without a Nation?*, p. 87, 102.
56. Ibid., p. 89.
57. Ibid., p. 85.
58. Ibid., p. 91. S. Jamal Malik, 'Islamization in Pakistan 1977–1985: The Ulema and their Places of Learning,' *Islamic Studies* 28, no. 1 (Spring 1989).
59. Mariam Abou Zahab, 'The Regional Dimension of Sectarian Conflicts in Pakistan,' in *Pakistan: Nationalism without a Nation?*, p. 117.
60. Nasr, 'Islam, The State and the Rise of Sectarian Militancy,' pp. 92–95.
61. Puri, 'The Past and Future of Deobandi Islam.'
62. White, *Pakistan's Islamist Frontier*, p. 35.
63. Rashid, *Taliban*, p. 89.
64. Ibid., pp. 90–91.
65. Ahmed Rashid, 'Pakistan: Trouble Ahead, Trouble Behind,' *Current History* 95, no. 600 (Apr. 1996). Jalal, *Partisans of Allah*, p. 278.
66. LeJ ostensibly split from the SSP in 1995–1996 when the SSP appeared to be moderating, but in reality the two remained closely associated. For more on the SSP and LeJ split, see: Abou Zahab, 'The Regional Dimension of Sectarian Conflicts in Pakistan,' pp. 119–120.

67. Mariam Abou Zahab, 'Salafism in Pakistan: The Ahl-e Hadith Movement,' in *Global Salafism*, p. 127. See also: Metcalf, *Islamic Revival in British India*, pp. 268–296.

68. Dietrich Reetz, *Islam in the Public Sphere: Religious Groups in India 1900–1947* (Delhi: Oxford University Press, 2006), p. 92. Jalal, *Partisans of Allah*, p. 65. Abou Zahab, 'Salafism in Pakistan,' p. 127. Regarding the corruption or pure Sunni Islalm, see also: Quintan Wiktorowicz, 'A Genealogy of Radical Islam,' *Studies in Conflict and Terrorism* 28, no. 2 (Mar.–Apr. 2005).

69. Roel Meijer, 'Introduction,' in *Global Salafism*, p. 3.

70. Wiktorowicz, 'The New Global Threat.'

71. Abou Zahab, 'Salafism in Pakistan,' p. 127. See also: Reetz, *Islam in the Public Sphere*, p. 92, 100.

72. Wahhabis themselves often reject the term because it suggests they follow Muhammad Ibn Abd-al-Wahhab, a person, rather than God. They instead use the term 'Salafi.'

73. Abou Zahab, 'Salafism in Pakistan,' p. 129.

74. Regarding the Ahl-e-Hadith profession of loyalty to the Raj, see: Jalal, *Partisans of Allah*, p. 145. Regarding the maintenance of ties, see: Reetz, *Islam in the Public Sphere*, p. 73.

75. Jalal, *Partisans of Allah*, p. 147.

76. Sayyid Ahmad Khan, 'Review on Dr. Hunter's Indian Musalmans: Are They Bound in Conscience to Rebel Against the Queen,' in Hafeez Malik (ed.), *Political Profile of Sir Sayyid Ahmad Khan: A Dictionary Record* (Islamabad: Institute of Islamic History, Culture and Civilization, 1982), p. 272.

77. Jalal, *Partisans of Allah*, p. 146.

78. Ibid., p. 147.

79. Abou Zahab, 'Salafism in Pakistan,' p. 128.

80. Metcalf, *Islamic Revival in British India*, p. 283.

81. Yoginder Sikand, 'Islamist Militancy in Kashmir: The Case of the Lashkar-i Tayyeba,' *South Asia Citizens Web* (20 Nov. 2003).

82. Reetz, *Islam in the Public Sphere*, p. 74.

83. Abou Zahab, 'Salafism in Pakistan,' p. 130.

84. Husain Haqqani, 'The Ideologies of South Asian Jihadi Groups,' in *Current Trends in Islamist Ideology* Volume 1 (Hudson Institute, 2005).

85. Abou Zahab, 'Salafism in Pakistan,' p. 130.

86. The total number of madaris in Pakistan continued to increase following Zia's death in 1988. Deobandi madaris constituted approximately 65 per cent of the total by the year 2000, while Ahl-e Hadith seminaries accounted for only about 6 per cent. Ibid, p. 132.

87. In 2006, the number of students in Deobandi madaris was estimated at 200,000 and those in Barelvi madaris at 190,000. Ibid.

88. Ibid., p. 132, 141.

89. Jalal, *Partisans of Allah*, p. 276. Zahid Hussain, *Frontline Pakistan: The Struggle With Militant Islam* (New York: I.B. Tauris, 2007), pp. 78–79.

90. Abou Zahab, 'Salafism in Pakistan,' p. 130.

91. For a comprehensive assessment of these divisions, see: Meijer (ed.), *Global Salafism*. Quintan Wiktorowicz. 'Anatomy of the Salafi Movement,' *Studies in Conflict and Terrorism* 29, no. 3 (Apr.–May 2006).

92. Abou Zahab, 'Salafism in Pakistan,' p. 131.

93. For more about the Tehrik-e-Mujahideen's activities in Indian-administered Kashmir, see: Rana, *A to Z of Jehadi Organizations in Pakistan*, pp. 306–317.

94. Abou Zahab, 'Salafism in Pakistan,' p. 131.

95. Ibid., p. 137, fn. 38.

96. Mohammad Amir Rana, *Gateway to Terrorism* (London: New Millennium, 2003), p. 330.

97. Author interview with Michael Semple, 23 Dec. 2008 in Pakistan.

98. Author interview with Noman Benotman, 3 Mar. 2010 in the United Kingdom.

99. Roel Meijer, *Global Salafism*, pp. xii, xiv.

2. LASHKAR'S IDEOLOGY: DAWA AND JIHAD

1. Thomas Hegghammer, 'Jihadi-Salafis or Revolutionaries? On Religion and Politics in the Study of Militant Islamism,' in *Global Salafism*, pp. 257–260, 259.

2. Thomas Hegghammer, 'The Ideological Hybridization of Jihadi Groups,' in *Current Trends in Islamist Ideology* Volume 9 (Hudson Institute, 2009).

3. This section is drawn from: Hegghammer, 'Jihadi-Salafis or Revolutionaries? On Religion and Politics in the Study of Militant Islamism,' pp. 257–260. See also: Hegghammer, *Jihad in Saudi Arabia*, pp. 5–8.

4. Wiktorowicz, 'A Genealogy of Radical Islam.'

5. Sheikh Abdullah Azzam, *Defense of Muslim Lands, The Most Important Personal Duty* (Amman: Modern Mission Library, 1984).

6. For an in-depth account of the history of jihadism in South Asia, see: Jalal, *Partisans of Allah*.

7. Fair, Malhotra and Shapiro, 'The Roots of Militancy.'

8. In 1999 Lashkar published a tract outlining its rationale for jihad: Hafiz Abdul Salam bin Muhammad, *Why We Do Jihad* (Muridke: Markaz al-Dawa wal-Irshad, May 1999).

9. 'Interview with Hafiz Saeed,' *Takbeer* 12 Aug. 1999. Found in Shafqat, 'From Official Islam to Islamism,' p. 143.

10. Bin Muhammad, *Why We Do Jihad.*
11. Tajikistan witnessed only a limited intervention by jihadi groups during the first several years of its civil war.
12. Noman Benotman, who spent several months working with MDI during the early 1990s and knew Mahmoud Mohammad Ahmed Bahaziq personally, confirmed he is the man often known as Sheikh Abu Abdul Aziz or Barbaros. Benotman also confirmed his role as a founder and financier of MDI. Author interview with Noman Benotman, 3 Mar. 2010 in the United Kingdom. Two local journalists following Lashkar during the 1990s reaffirmed Bahaziq's role in the organization. Author interview with Arif Jamal, 21 Nov. 2009 via phone. Author interview with Mohammad Amir Rana, 16 & 18 Dec. 2008 in Pakistan. See also: US Department of Treasury, 'HP-996: Treasury Targets LET Leadership,' 27 May 2008. Sheikh Abu Abdul Aziz has also been identified as Abdul-Rahman al-Dosari. See, for example: Evan Kohlmann, *Al-Qaida's Jihad in Europe: The Afghan-Bosnian Network* (Oxford: Berg, 2004), p. 16.
13. Instrumental to this was the agreement by Osama bin Laden's envoy from Sudan, Jamal al-Fadl, to recommend that a small cadre of trainers be deployed from Afghanistan to Bosnia-Herzegovina. This signaled bin Laden's backing for the Bosnian jihad and contributed to enthusiasm for that cause among Arab Afghans. Hegghammer, *Jihad in Saudi Arabia*, p. 50. Regarding Jamal al-Fadl's role, see: 'USA vs. Usama bin Laden *et al.*,' District Court of Southern New York, 2001, pp. 315–316.
14. For more on the role of foreign fighters in Bosnia-Herzegovina, see: Kohlmann, *Al-Qaida's Jihad in Europe.* James Bruce, 'Arab Veterans of the Afghan War,' *Jane's Intelligence Review,* 7, no. 4 (1995).
15. Found in Rana, *A to Z of Jehadi Organizations,* p. 334.
16. 'An Interview with Mujaahid Abu 'Abd ul-Azeez "Barbaros",' *Al-Sirat Al-Mustaqeem [The Straight Path],* no. 33 (Aug. 1994).
17. 'The Jihad in Bosnia,' *Majallah Al-Dawa [Al-Dawa Magazine],* Jan. 1993.
18. 'United States of America *vs.* Enaam M. Arnaout,' United States District Court Northern District of Illinois Eastern Division, 3 Feb. 2003. Bahaziq is identified as Abdul-Rahman al-Dosari.
19. Author interview with General Javed Ashraf Qazi (Retd), Director-General of the ISI from 1993–1995, 15 Dec. 2008 in Pakistan.
20. Lashkar is believed to have sent a small number of fighters to Chechnya and the Philippines during the mid-to-late 1990s, most likely to bolster the group's transnational ties and reputation, as well as to have trained foreign militants who fought in these and other locations.
21. Author interview with first Lashkar-e-Taiba member, name withheld, May 2009 in Pakistan. Author interview with second Lashkar-e-Taiba member, name withheld, May 2009 in Pakistan. Author interview with former Lashkar-e-Taiba member, name withheld, Jan. 2009 in Pakistan.

22. Found in Yoginder Sikand, 'Islamist Militancy in Kashmir.'
23. Author interview with Jamaat-ul-Dawa official, name withheld, May 2009 in Pakistan. Hafiz Abdul Salam bin Muhammad, 'Jihad in the Present Time,' JuD website, undated. Author's collection. See also: Abou Zahab, 'Salafism in Pakistan,' p. 134.
24. Author interview with Noman Benotman, 3 Mar. 2010 in the United Kingdom. Author interview with Arif Jamal, 21 Nov. 2009 via phone.
25. Author interview with Noman Benotman, 3 Mar. 2010 in the United Kingdom.
26. Author interview with Arif Jamal, 21 Nov. 2009 via phone. Author interview with former Kashmiri journalist, name withheld, Jan. 2009 in India. See also: Rana, *A to Z of Jehadi Organizations in Pakistan*, p. 336.
27. There are reports that some Lashkar trainers occasionally beat up Barelvi Muslims who refused to convert. See, for example: Rana, *A to Z of Jehadi of Organizations in Pakistan*, p. 336.
28. Mariam Abou Zahab and Olivier Roy, *Islamist Networks: The Afghan–Pakistan Connection*, trans. John King (London: Hurst, 2004), p. 42 fn. 6.
29. Author interview with Abdullah Muntazir, 30 Dec. 2008 in Pakistan.
30. Found in Prakash Pillai, 'Lashkar Chief Says Freedom of Kashmir To Pave Way for Islamization of Pakistan,' *Hindustan Times* 2 Feb. 2001.
31. Bin Muhammad, 'Jihad in the Present Time.'
32. Bin Muhammad, *Why We Do Jihad*.
33. Bin Muhammad, 'Jihad in the Present Time.'
34. Abou Zahab and Roy, *Islamist Networks*, pp. 42–43.
35. Author interview with first Lashkar-e-Taiba member, name withheld, May 2009 in Pakistan. Author interview with second Lashkar-e-Taiba member, name withheld, May 2009 in Pakistan. Author interview with former Lashkar-e-Taiba member, name withheld, Jan. 2009 in Pakistan.
36. Author interview with Jamaat-ul-Dawa official, name withheld, May 2009 in Pakistan.

3. THE ISI'S BOYS

1. Alastair Lamb, *Kashmir: A Disputed Legacy 1846–1990* (Hertfordshire: Roxford Books, 1991), p. 83.
2. For a firsthand account of Pakistan's military efforts during the conflict from 1947–1948, see: Major General Akbar Khan (Retd), *Raiders in Kashmir* (Islamabad: National Book Foundation, 1975). See also: Nawaz, *Crossed Swords*, ch. 3.
3. Haqqani, *Pakistan: Between Mosque and Military*, p. 29.
4. Nawaz, *Crossed Swords*, p. 57, 70.

5. Ibid., p. 49.
6. China and Pakistan delimited a boundary in 1963 giving China sovereignty over Aksai Chin, a small piece of territory in Kashmir. A Sino-Pakistani protocol formalized this demarcation in 1987.
7. Regarding elections in Pakistan-administered Kashmir, see: Sumantra Bose, *Kashmir: Roots of Conflict, Paths to Peace* (Cambridge, MA: Harvard University Press, 2003), pp. 99–100. Until 2009 when the Northern Areas became known as Gilgit-Baltistan, it was administered directly by the Pakistani government. It was only in 2009 that the people living there were granted very limited political autonomy. For more, see: Rasul Bakhsh Rais, 'A Step in the Right Direction,' *Daily Times* 1 Sept. 2009.
8. The Azad Jammu and Kashmir Interim Constitution Act, 1974, full text at: http://ajkassembly.gok.pk/AJK_Interim_Constitution_Act_1974. pdf (last accessed 10 Sept. 2009).
9. Bose, *Kashmir: Roots of Conflict, Paths to Peace*, p. 97.
10. International Crisis Group, *Steps Towards Peace: Putting Kashmiris First* (3 June 2010).
11. For a detailed account of Pakistan's covert activities in Indian-administered Kashmir prior to the war in 1965 and the war itself, see: Praveen Swami, *India, Pakistan and the Secret Jihad: The Covert War in Kashmir, 1947–2005* (London: Routledge, 2007), ch. 2–3. Gul Hassan Khan, *The Memoirs of Lt. Gen. Hassan Khan* (Karachi: Oxford University Press, 1994).
12. For more on militancy in Indian-administered Kashmir in the aftermath of the civil war, see: Swami, *India, Pakistan and the Secret Jihad*, ch. 5.
13. Bose, *Kashmir: Roots of Conflict, Paths to Peace*, p. 117.
14. Ibid., p. 95.
15. Ibid., p. 112.
16. Arif Jamal, *Shadow War: The Untold Story of Jihad in Kashmir* (Brooklyn, NY: Melville House, 2009), p. 146.
17. Ibid., p. 149. Bose, *Kashmir: Roots of Conflict, Paths to Peace*, pp. 126–127.
18. Bose, *Kashmir: Roots of Conflict, Paths to Peace*, p. 129.
19. Yoginder Sikand, 'The Changing Course of the Kashmiri Struggle: From National Liberation to Islamist Jihad?,' *The Muslim World*, 91, no. 1–2 (Mar. 2001).
20. Haqqani, *Pakistan: Between Mosque and Military*, p. 226.
21. Jamal, *Shadow War*, p. 155. Manoj Joshi, *The Lost Rebellion* (New Delhi: Penguin, 1999), pp. 77–79, 86.
22. Regarding Malik's release and calls for demilitarization, see: Joshi, *The Lost Rebellion*, p. 289. Jonah Blank, 'Kashmir: Fundamentalism Takes Root,' *Foreign Affairs* 78, no. 6 (1999).

23. A splinter faction of the JKLF that still embraced violence attempted to fight on until it was crushed by Indian forces in 1996.
24. Bose, *Kashmir: Roots of Conflict, Paths to Peace*, p. 116.
25. Author interview with former Kashmiri journalist, name withheld, Jan. 2009 in India. The term 'Kashmiri group' is often used for outfits like Harkat-ul-Mujahideen and Lashkar-e-Taiba because they fought in Kashmir, but this is a misnomer. Kashmiris used the term 'guest mujahideen' or 'foreign fighters' to refer to their members because these groups were not indigenous to Kashmir.
26. These were Pakistani outfits, but in the years immediately following the fall of the Democratic Republic of Afghanistan they often included foreign jihadis from outside of South Asia who initially traveled to the region to fight against the Soviets in Afghanistan.
27. Haqqani, *Pakistan: Between Mosque and Military*, p. 287. Joshi, *The Lost Rebellion*, p. 129.
28. Sumit Ganguly, *The Crisis in Kashmir* (London: Cambridge University Press, 1997), p. 139. Victoria Schofield, *Kashmir in Conflict* (New York: I.B. Taurus, 2003), p. 173. For a summary of reforms, see: International Crisis Group, *Kashmir: Learning from the Past* (4 Dec. 2003). Alexander Evans, 'Kashmir: The Past Ten Years,' *Asian Affairs*, 30, no. 1 (1999).
29. Regarding the impact of meager funding and support as a cause, see: Jamal, *Shadow War*, p. 159. Regarding the impact of anger at the pro-accession and pro-Islamist sentiment of other groups, see: Bose, *Kashmir: Roots of Conflict, Paths to Peace*, pp. 133–134. Information regarding bribery and the threat of reprisals is from Suba Chandran, who has conducted extensive field research in Indian-administered Kashmir. Author interview with Suba Chandran, Deputy Director at the Institute of Peace and Conflict Studies, 5 Jan. 2009 in India. See also: Evans, 'Kashmir: The Past Ten Years.'
30. Bose, *Kashmir: Roots of Conflict, Paths to Peace*, pp. 133–134. Jamal, *Shadow War*, p. 159.
31. Amelie Blom, 'Kashmiri Suicide Bombers,' in Laetitia Bucaille, Amelie Blom and Luis Martinez (eds.), *The Enigma of Islamist Violence* (London: Hurst, 2007), p. 73.
32. Haqqani, *Pakistan: Between Mosque and Military*, pp. 287–289.
33. Ibid.
34. Author interview with former Kashmiri journalist, name withheld, Jan. 2009 in India. See also: Rana, *A to Z of Jehadi Organizations in Pakistan*, pp. 245–246.
35. Bose, *Kashmir: Roots of Conflict, Paths to Peace*, p. 107. Sumit Ganguly, 'Explaining the Kashmir Insurgency: Political Mobilization and Institutional Decay,' *International Security* 21, no. 2 (Autumn 1996).
36. Alexander Evans, *Kashmiri Separatists—The Harkat ul Ansar* (Monterey Institute, 2000).

37. For more about the kidnappings and HuM activities, see: Claire Barshied, *Harakat ul-Mujahedin Dossier* (Center for Policing Terrorism, 11 Mar. 2005). Ilyas Kashmiri, a HuJI commander who began working closely with al-Qaeda during the 2000s and attracted a number of renegade Lashkar operatives, also took part in the kidnapping operation. See: Arif Jamal, 'South Asia's Architect of Jihad: A Profile of Commander Mohammad Ilyas Kashmiri,' *Militant Leadership Monitor* 1, no. 1 (30 Jan. 2010).

38. Joshi, *The Lost Rebellion*, p. 382.

39. US Department of State 'Background Information on Foreign Terrorist Organizations,' 8 Oct. 1999, http://www.state.gov/s/ct/rls/rpt/fto/2801.htm (last accessed 30 July 2010).

40. Bose, *Kashmir: Roots of Conflict, Paths to Peace*, pp. 148–149.

41. Luv Puri, *Militancy in Jammu and Kashmir: The Uncovered Face* (New Delhi: Promilla & Co., 2008), ch. 2. Blank, 'Kashmir: Fundamentalism Takes Root.'

42. Bose, *Kashmir: Roots of Conflict, Paths to Peace*, p. 118, 151.

43. Luv Puri, an Indian journalist who has conducted research on both sides of the LoC and traced the ethnic, linguistic and cultural facets of the conflict, suggests that militants moving across the LoC from Pakistan were almost ethno-linguistically indistinguishable from the local population in Rajouri and Poonch. Puri, *Militancy in Jammu and Kashmir*.

44. This report was shared with Mohammad Amir Rana for his book detailing the histories of a number of militant groups in Pakistan. Rana, *A to Z of Jehadi Organizations in Pakistan*, p. 329.

45. Found in Sikand, 'The Changing Course of the Kashmiri Struggle.'

46. Author interview with former Kashmiri journalist, name withheld, Jan. 2009, in India. See also: Sikand, 'Islamist Militancy in Kashmir.'

47. Bose, *Kashmir: Roots of Conflict, Paths to Peace*, pp. 136–137.

48. Author interview with Lt. General Vinayak Patankar (Retd), Distinguished Fellow at the Observer Research Foundation, 13 Jan. 2009 in India.

49. Author interview with first Lashkar-e-Taiba member, name withheld, May 2009 in Pakistan. Author interview with former Kashmiri journalist, name withheld, Jan. 2009 in India. Author interview with Suba Chandran, 5 Jan. 2009 in India.

50. For more on rape as a tactic and crime in the Kashmir conflict, see: Asia Watch and Physicians for Human Rights, *Rape in Kashmir: A Crime of War* (New York, NY: 1993).

51. Author interview with Indian researcher, name withheld, Jan. 2009 in India.

52. Author interview with former Kashmiri journalist, name withheld, Jan. 2009 in India.

53. Ibid. Author interview with Lt. General Vinayak Patankar (Retd), 13 Jan. 2009 in India.
54. Author interview with former Kashmiri journalist, name withheld, Jan. 2009 in India. Author interview with Arif Jamal, 21 Nov. 2009 via phone. See also: Rana, *A to Z of Jehadi Organizations in Pakistan*, pp. 335–336.
55. For example, see: 'Kashmir Militant Group Warns of Further Attacks on Indian Army Camps,' Press Trust of India 22 Jan. 2001.
56. For more on Lashkar's targeting of civilians and use of mutilation, see: Mariam Abou Zahab, 'I Shall be Waiting for You at the Door of Paradise: The Pakistani Martyrs of the Lashkar-e Taiba,' in Aparna Rao *et al.* (eds.), *The Practice of War* (Berghahn Books, 2008), p. 135. Peter Chalk and Christine Fair, 'Lashkar-e-Tayyiba Leads the Kashmiri Insurgency,' *Jane's Intelligence Review*, 1 Dec. 2002.
57. Praveen Swami, 'Kashmir, Post-Agra,' *Frontline*, 4–17 Aug. 2001.
58. Fayaz Wani, 'Lashkar Not to Target Foreign, Indian Tourists in Kashmir,' *NewsBlaze.com* 9 July 2008.
59. Author interview with former Kashmiri journalist, name withheld, Jan. 2009 in India. Author interview with Lt. General Vinayak Patankar (Retd), 13 Jan. 2009 in India.
60. This was the unanimous opinion of the author's interlocutors in India.
61. This list compiled based on: Author interview with former Lashkar-e-Taiba member, name withheld, Jan. 2009 in Pakistan. Author interview with first Lashkar-e-Taiba member, name withheld, May 2009 in Pakistan. Author interview with second Lashkar-e-Taiba member, name withheld, May 2009 in Pakistan. Author interview with first Pakistan-based Western diplomat, name withheld, Dec. 2008 in Pakistan. See also: Chalk and Fair, 'Lashkar-e-Tayyiba Leads the Kashmiri Insurgency.' Ashley J. Tellis, 'Bad Company—Lashkar-e-Tayyiba and the Growing Ambition of Islamist Militancy in Pakistan,' testimony prepared for the Subcommittee on the Middle East and South Asia of the Committee on Foreign Affairs in the United States House of Representatives, 11 Mar. 2010.
62. Excerpts from Lashkar's training primer found in Chalk and Fair, 'Lashkar-e-Tayyiba Leads the Kashmiri Insurgency.'
63. Author interview with former senior ISI official, name withheld, Dec. 2008 in Pakistan. Author interview with former Lashkar-e-Taiba member, name withheld, Jan. 2009 in Pakistan.
64. Author interview with former Lashkar-e-Taiba member, name withheld, Jan. 2009 in Pakistan.
65. Indian Security Services, 'Interrogation Report of Abdul Razzak Masood,' undated. Author in possession of copy.
66. Author interview with former Lashkar-e-Taiba member, name withheld, Jan. 2009 in Pakistan. See also: Hassan Abbas, *Pakistan's Drift into*

*Extremism: Allah, the Army, and America's War on Terror* (New Delhi, India: Pentagon Press, 2005), p. 214.

67. See, for example: Kamran Khan, 'Jihadi Outfits Going Underground,' *The News*, 13 Jan. 2002.
68. Haqqani, *Pakistan: Between Mosque and Military*, pp. 245–246.
69. Full text at http://www.usip.org/files/file/resources/collections/peace_agreements/ip_lahore19990221.pdf (last accessed 13 Sept. 2009).
70. Jamal, *Shadow War*, p. 188.
71. Pervez Musharraf, *In the Line of Fire: A Memoir* (New York: Free Press, 2006), ch. 11. See also: Jamal, *Shadow War*, pp. 191–201. Haqqani, *Pakistan: Between Mosque and Military*, pp. 249–250.
72. Bennett-Jones, *Pakistan: Eye of the Storm*, p. 94. For more on the Kargil invasion, the Pakistan army's calculus and the repercussions, see: Ashley J. Tellis, Christine Fair and Jamison Jo Medby, *Limited Conflicts Under the Nuclear Umbrella: Indian and Pakistani Lessons from the Kargil Crisis* (Arlington, VA: RAND Corporation, 2001).
73. Abbas, *Pakistan's Drift into Extremism*, p. 214. Other militant groups involved included: HuM, Tehrik-e-Jihad and Al-Badr. See: Raja Asghar, 'Interview: Militants Say Afghans Fight in Kashmir,' Reuters, 28 June 1999.
74. Jamal, *Shadow War*, p. 196.
75. Ibid.
76. 'Kashmir: Militant Leader Rejects US-Pakistan Accord,' Press Trust of India, 7 July 1999.
77. The machinations leading up to Musharraf's coup are detailed in Bennett-Jones, *Pakistan: Eye of the Storm*, ch. 2.
78. Author interview with first Pakistan-based Western diplomat, name withheld, Dec. 2008 in Pakistan.
79. Alexander Evans, 'The Kashmir Insurgency: As Bad As It Gets,' *Small Wars and Insurgencies* 11, no. 1 (Spring 2000).
80. Rana, *Gateway to Terrorism*, pp. 331–333, 347–348. Bose, *Kashmir: Roots of Conflict, Paths to Peace*, p. 141.
81. Abdul Rehman Makki, 'Fidayee Activities in Sharia: Part III,' *Voice of Islam* Aug. 2001.
82. Suba Chandran, 'Intra-State Armed Conflicts in South Asia: Impact on Regional Security,' in Dev Raj Dahal and Nishchal Nath Pandey (eds.), *Comprehensive Security in South Asia* (New Delhi: Manohar, 2006), p. 170.
83. *Fidayee* can mean both 'one who sacrifices himself' and 'one who risks his life voluntarily or recklessly.'
84. Abdul Rehman Makki, 'Fidayee Activities in Sharia,' *Voice of Islam* June 2001. Abdul Rehman Makki, 'Fidayee Activities in Sharia: Part II,' *Voice of Islam* July 2001. Makki, 'Fidayee Activities in Sharia: Part III.'

85. Makki, 'Fidayee Activities in Sharia: Part II.'

86. Ibid. Makki, 'Fidayee Activities in Sharia: Part III.'

87. Abou Zahab and Roy, *Islamist Networks*, p. 40.

88. Author interview with Arif Jamal, 21 Nov. 2009 via phone. A Pakistan-based Western diplomat with extensive time spent in the region made the same allegation. Author interview with second Pakistan-based Western diplomat, name withheld, Dec. 2008 in Pakistan. See also: Abbas, *Pakistan's Drift into Extremism*, p. 214. The Indian government accused the ISI of complicity in the hijacking that freed Azhar, Sajjid Afghani and Omar Saeed Sheikh and led to JeM's founding. According to some reports al-Qaeda is believed to have helped to plan the operation as well. See, for example: Ahmed Rashid, *Descent into Chaos* (London: Penguin, 2008), p. 113.

89. Author interview with Lt. General Vinayak Patankar (Retd), 13 Jan. 2009 in India. Interview with General Gurmeet Kanwal (Retd), Director of the Centre for Land Warfare Studies, 12 Jan. 2009 in India. Regarding the number of attacks, see: Bose, *Kashmir: Roots of Conflict, Paths to Peace*, pp. 141–142.

90. Jamal, *Shadow War*, pp. 209–210.

91. Ibid., p. 210.

92. Ibid., p. 221.

93. Bose, *Kashmir: Roots of Conflict, Paths to Peace*, p. 136.

94. Ibid., p. 161.

95. Lashkar later staged a reenactment of the Red Fort attack at a stadium in Lahore, Pakistan. Despite a ban on all political assemblies at the time, Pakistani authorities raised no objection. See: Abou Zahab and Roy, *Islamist Networks*, p. 35, fn. 4.

96. Abou Zahab, 'I Shall be Waiting for You at the Door of Paradise,' p. 139.

97. Hussain, *Frontline Pakistan*, p. 58.

4. THE LONG ARM OF THE LASHKAR

1. Author interview with former Lashkar-e-Taiba member, name withheld, Jan. 2009 in Pakistan. Author interview with Mohammad Amir Rana, 16 & 18 Dec. 2008 in Pakistan. See also: US Department of Treasury, 'HP-996: Treasury Targets LET Leadership,' 27 May 2008.

2. JUD website, 'Departments,' undated. Author's collection. See also: Rana, *A to Z of Jehadi Organizations in Pakistan*, p. 320.

3. Author interview with former Lashkar-e-Taiba member, name withheld, Jan. 2009 in Pakistan. MDI website, 'Education: Al-Dawa System of Schools.' See also: Rana, *A to Z of Jehadi Organizations in Pakistan*, pp. 321–325.

4. Author interview with Arif Jamal, 21 Nov. 2009 via phone.

5. Abdul Rehman Makki is the son of Hafiz Saeed's maternal uncle and married to the younger sister of one of Saeed's wives.

6. Author interview with Arif Jamal, 21 Nov. 2009 via phone. See also: Mohammad Amir Rana, 'Jamaatud Dawa Splits,' *Daily Times* 18 July 2004. Mohammad Amir Rana, *Jihad and Jihadis: Introduction to Important Jihadi Leaders of Kashmir and Pakistan* (Lahore: Mashal, 2003).

7. Josh Meyer, 'Extremist Group Works in the Open in Pakistan,' *Los Angeles Times*, 18 Dec. 2007.

8. Rana, *A to Z of Jehadi Organizations in Pakistan*, p. 327.

9. MDI website, 'Education: Al-Dawa System of Schools.'

10. 'Hafiz Mohammad Saeed: Pakistan's Heart of Terror,' *Kashmir Herald* 2, no. 2 (July 2002).

11. Author interview with Noman Benotman, 3 Mar. 2010 in the United Kingdom.

12. Mohammad Amir Rana, 'Al-Qaeda Planned to Open Varsity,' *The Friday Times*, 11 Apr. 2003.

13. Zahab and Roy, *Islamist Networks*, p. 32.

14. Amir Mir, 'LeT Commander Furious at JuD Chief,' *The News*, 15 Jan. 2009.

15. Author interview with Abu Ehsan, Jamaat-ul-Dawa Administrator of Muridke, 8 May 2009 in Pakistan. MDI website, 'Education: Al-Dawa System of Schools.' MDI website, 'Hospital: Al-Dawa Medical Mission,' undated. Author's collection.

16. Author interview with Abu Ehsan, 8 May 2009 in Pakistan. Briefing and tour of the compound by a Jamaat-ul-Dawa staff member, name withheld, 8 May 2009 in Pakistan.

17. Author interview with Jamaat-ul-Dawa official, name withheld, May 2009 in Pakistan.

18. Briefing and tour of the Al-Aziz hospital by the hospital administrator, name withheld, 8 May 2009 in Pakistan.

19. MDI website, 'Hospital: Al-Dawa Medical Mission.'

20. MDI website, 'Education: Al-Dawa System of Schools.'

21. Winthrop and Graff, *Beyond Madrassas*.

22. MDI website, 'Education: Al-Dawa System of Schools.'

23. Haroon Rashid, 'Fertile Ground,' *Herald* May 2000.

24. MDI website, 'Education: Al-Dawa System of Schools.'

25. Ibid. Author interview with Abu Ehsan, 8 May 2009 in Pakistan.

26. Habib al-Qamar, 'Training Camps Organized by the Markaz al-Dawa wal-Irshad to Revitalize Faith,' *Majallah Al-Dawa*, April 2000.

27. Abou Zahab and Roy, *Islamist Networks*, p. 33.

28. Rana, *A to Z of Jehadi Organizations in Pakistan*, p. 324.

29. Author interview with former Lashkar-e-Taiba member, name withheld, Jan. 2009 in Pakistan. See also: Sushant Sareen, *The Jihad Factory* (New Delhi: Har-Anand Publications, 2005), pp. 60–62.

30. 'Interview with Hafiz Saeed.'
31. Abou Zahab, 'Salafism in Pakistan,' p. 137.
32. Author interview with former Lashkar-e-Taiba member, name withheld, Jan. 2009 in Pakistan. MDI website, 'A Brief Introduction to the Markaz and the Lashkar.' For more on Lashkar's camps, see: Rana, *A to Z of Jehadi Organizations in Pakistan*, pp. 332–333.
33. Author interview with former Lashkar-e-Taiba member, name withheld, Jan. 2009 in Pakistan.
34. Ibid. Indian Security Services, 'Interrogation Report of Abdul Razzak Masood.' Mohammed Ajmal Amir Kasab confession before Additional Chief Metropolitan Magistrate Rama Vijay Sawant Vagule,' verbatim translation by police for internal use and not an official document, 20–21 Feb. 2009. Author in possession of copy.
35. 'Daura-e-Suffa, Training Course for Preachers of Jihad,' *Majallah Al-Dawa*, May 2000.
36. Ibid.
37. Ibid.
38. The syllabus included 'Complete learning of prayers with translation, traditional Friday Sermon and its translation, funeral prayers and their translation, and the final ten surahs [chapters of Quran] with translation. Also, learn[ing] Koranic verses on topics related to jihad and their translation.'
39. 'Daura-e-Suffa, Training Course for Preachers of Jihad.'
40. 'Mohammed Ajmal Amir Kasab confession before Additional Chief Metropolitan Magistrate Rama Vijay Sawant Vagule.' 'Testimony of David Coleman Headley to the Indian National Investigative Agency,' 3–9 June 2010. Author in possession of copy.
41. Author interview with former Lashkar-e-Taiba member, name withheld, Jan. 2009 in Pakistan. Author interview with Amelie Blom, professor at the Lahore University of Management Studies, 31 Dec. 2008 in Pakistan.
42. Author interview with former Lashkar-e-Taiba member, name withheld, Jan. 2009 in Pakistan. Author interview with Mohammad Amir Rana, 16 & 18 Dec. 2008 in Pakistan. See also: Sumita Kumar, 'Pakistan's Jehadi Apparatus: Goals and Methods,' *Strategic Analysis* 24, no. 12 (Mar. 2001). Zaigham Khan, 'Allah's Army,' *Herald* Jan. 1998.
43. Author interview with former Lashkar-e-Taiba member, name withheld, Jan. 2009 in Pakistan. Author interview with Mariam Abou Zahab, researcher at the Centre d'Etudes et de Recherches Internationales, 7 Dec. 2008 via phone. See also: Abou Zahab, 'I Shall be Waiting for You at the Door of Paradise,' p. 142.
44. 'Daura-e-Suffa, Training Course for Preachers of Jihad.'
45. Regarding the primer, see: Chalk and Fair, 'Lashkar-e-Tayyiba Leads the Kashmiri Insurgency.'

287

46. See, for example: Abou Zahab, 'I Shall be Waiting for You at the Door of Paradise,' p. 143.
47. Author interview with former Lashkar-e-Taiba member, name withheld, Jan. 2009 in Pakistan. Author interview with Arif Jamal, 21 Nov. 2009 via phone.
48. Abou Zahab, 'I Shall be Waiting for You at the Door of Paradise,' pp. 146–149.
49. Indian Security Services, 'Interrogation Report of Fahim Ansari,' undated. Author in possession of copy. 'Testimony of David Coleman Headley to the Indian National Investigative Agency.'
50. Lashkar-e-Taiba pamphlet, undated. Author's collection.
51. MDI website, 'A Brief Introduction to the Markaz and the Lashkar.'
52. Author interview with first Pakistan-based Western diplomat, name withheld, Dec. 2008 in Pakistan.
53. Author interview with Amelie Blom, 31 Dec. 2008 in Pakistan.
54. Author interview with former Lashkar-e-Taiba member, name withheld, Jan. 2009 in Pakistan.
55. Author interview with Mohammad Amir Rana, 16 & 18 Dec. 2008 in Pakistan.
56. Mohammad Amir Rana, The Seeds of Terrorism (London: New Millennium, 2005), p. 159. Hussain, Frontline Pakistan, p. 52.
57. Lashkar-e-Taiba pamphlet.
58. Rana, The Seeds of Terrorism, pp. 160–162.
59. 'Daura-e-Suffa, Training Course for Preachers of Jihad.'
60. JuD website, 'FAQs: What Does Jamaat-ul-Dawa's Media and Publications Section Do?,' undated. Author's collection. See also: Rana, A to Z of Jehadi Organizations in Pakistan, p. 327.
61. Rana, The Seeds of Terrorism, pp. 160–162.
62. Author's collection of Lashkar literature and propaganda material. Gathered from the now-defunct MDI website and the archives at the Pak Institute for Peace Studies [PIPS] archives. The author is grateful to the staff at PIPS for their gracious hospitality and assistance with this research.
63. Author's collection of Lashkar material from MDI website and PIPS archives.
64. Abou Zahab, 'I Shall be Waiting for You at the Door of Paradise,' p. 139, 146.
65. Author interview with former Lashkar-e-Taiba member, name withheld, Jan. 2009 in Pakistan. These civil defense programs were advertised in Majallah Al-Dawa, for example: Al-Qamar, 'Training Camps Organized by the Markaz al-Dawa wal-Irshad to Revitalize Faith.'
66. Al-Qamar, 'Training Camps Organized by the Markaz al-Dawa wal-Irshad to Revitalize Faith.'

67. In Pakistan this was second only in size to the annual Tablighi Jamaat congregations, which drew up to two million people.
68. Shafqat, 'From Official Islam to Islamism,' p. 132.
69. Asfar Imran, 'Lashkar-e-Taiba... Strong Support for Muslims Fighting Against Indian Forces in Occupied Kashmir,' *Jang Sunday Magazine* 20 Dec. 1998. See also: Shafqat, 'From Official Islam to Islamism,' pp. 131–132.
70. Imran, 'Lashkar-e-Taiba... Strong Support for Muslims Fighting Against Indian Forces in Occupied Kashmir.'
71. Author interview with Ahmed Rashid, journalist and author, 29 Dec. 2008 in Pakistan. See also: Ibid.
72. Found in Rana, *A to Z of Jehadi Organizations in Pakistan*, p. 334.
73. Amir Mir, 'Lashkar-i-Tayyaba Activities Reported,' *The Friday Times* 12 Nov. 1999.
74. Author interview with Ahmed Rashid, 29 Dec. 2008 in Pakistan.
75. Haqqani, *Pakistan: Between Mosque and Military*, p. 296.
76. 'The Visit to Markaz-e-Taiba by the Governor of Punjab,' *Nawa-i-Waqt* 19 Apr. 1998.
77. Kumar, 'Pakistan's Jehadi Apparatus.' Khan, 'Allah's Army.' Rana, *A to Z of Jehadi Organizations in Pakistan*, pp. 333–334.
78. Khan, 'Jihadi Outfits Going Underground.'
79. According to Zahab and Roy, traditional madaris only provided approximately 10 per cent of recruits. Abou Zahab and Roy, *Islamist Networks*, p. 36.
80. Christine Fair, *The Madrassah Challenge: Militancy and Religious Education in Pakistan* (Washington, DC: USIP, 2008).
81. Author interview with Mohammad Amir Rana, 16 & 18 Dec. 2008, in Pakistan. See also: Kumar, 'Pakistan's Jehadi Apparatus.' Khan, 'Allah's Army.'
82. Abou Zahab, 'I Shall be Waiting for You at the Door of Paradise' pp. 139–140. See also: Kumar, 'Pakistan's Jehadi Apparatus: Goals and Methods.' Fair, 'Antecedents and Implications of the Nov. 2008 Lashkar-e-Taiba (LeT) Attack Upon Several Targets in the Indian Mega-City of Mumbai.'
83. Rana, *A to Z of Jehadi Organizations in Pakistan*, pp. 333–334.
84. Author interview with Mariam Abou Zahab, 7 Dec. 2008 via phone. See also: Hussain, *Frontline Pakistan*, p. 57.
85. Author interview with Mohammad Amir Rana, 16 & 18 Dec. 2008 in Pakistan.
86. Christine Fair, 'Militant Recruitment in Pakistan: Implications for Al Qaeda and Other Organizations,' *Studies in Conflict and Terrorism* 27, no. 6 (Nov.–Dec. 2004).
87. Rana, *Gateway to Terrorism*, p. 351.

88.  Author interview with first Lashkar-e-Taiba member, name withheld, May 2009 in Pakistan.
89.  Author interview with Lt. General Vinayak Patankar (Retd), 13 Jan. 2009 in India. See also: Puri, *Militancy in Jammu and Kashmir*, p. 97.
90.  Author interview with former Lashkar-e-Taiba member, name withheld, Jan. 2009 in Pakistan. See also: Abou Zahab, 'I Shall be Waiting for You at the Door of Paradise,' 145.' Abou Zahab and Roy, *Islamist Networks*, p. 41.
91.  Hussain, *Frontline Pakistan*, p. 58. Abou Zahab, 'I Shall be Waiting for You at the Door of Paradise,' p. 145.
92.  Ayesha Siddiqa, an independent Pakistani security analyst, has collected a photo library of various Lashkar graffiti. The author is grateful to Dr Siddiqa for providing a presentation of her work. See also: Blom, 'Kashmiri Suicide Bombers,' p. 79.
93.  International Crisis Group, *The State of Sectarianism in Pakistan* (18 Apr. 2005).
94.  Chalk and Fair, 'Lashkar-e-Tayyiba Leads the Kashmiri Insurgency.'
95.  Lashkar-e-Taiba pamphlet.
96.  Rana, *A to Z of Jehadi Organizations in Pakistan*, pp. 326–327.
97.  Author interview with former Lashkar-e-Taiba member, name withheld, Jan. 2009 in Pakistan.
98.  Author interview with Pakistani citizen, name withheld, Dec. 2009 in Pakistan.
99.  Author's collection of Lashkar material from the MDI website.
100.  Rana, *A to Z of Jehadi Organizations in Pakistan*, p. 327.
101.  Bin Muhammad, 'Jihad in the Present Time.'
102.  Author interview with former Lashkar-e-Taiba member, name withheld, Jan. 2009 in Pakistan.
103.  Author interview with Abu Ehsan, 8 May 2009 in Pakistan.
104.  Rana, *A to Z of Jehadi Organizations in Pakistan*, p. 325.
105.  Author interview with second Pakistan-based Western diplomat, name withheld, Dec. 2008 in Pakistan. Author interview with Mohammad Amir Rana, 16 & 18 Dec. 2008 in Pakistan. See also: Evans, *Kashmiri Separatists—The Harkat ul Ansar*.
106.  Amit Baruah, 'Militant Chiefs Warn Musharraf,' *The Hindu*, Feb. 6, 2000.
107.  Hussain, *Frontline Pakistan*, p. 58.
108.  Author interview with Rahul Bedi, security analyst and journalist with *Jane's Intelligence Review*, 7 Jan. 2009 in India.
109.  SIMI was first banned in India in 2001, and that ban has been extended multiple times since.
110.  Author interview with Suba Chandran, 5 Jan. 2009 in India. Author interview with Animesh Roul, Executive Director of Research at the Society for the Study of Peace and Conflict, 4 Jan. 2009 in India.

111. Author interview with Rahul Bedi, 7 Jan. 2009 in India.

112. Praveen Swami, 'The Well-Tempered Jihad: The Politics and Practice of Post-2002 Islamist Terrorism in India,' *Contemporary South Asia* 16, no. 3 (Sept. 2008); Praveen Swami, 'A Road to Perdition: India and its Invisible Jihad,' (unpublished draft). See also: Praveen Swami, 'The Spreading Tentacles of Terror,' *The Hindu*, 31 Aug. 2003.

113. Praveen Swami, 'The "Liberation" of Hyderabad,' *Frontline*, 13–26 May 2000.

114. Praveen Swami, 'Pakistan and the Lashkar's Jihad in India,' *The Hindu*, 9 Dec. 2008.

115. Ibid. 'Life Sentences for 15 for 1993 Serial Train Blasts,' *Rediff*, 28 Feb. 2004.

116. For more on these attacks, see: Hasan Zaidi, *Black Friday: The True Story of the Bombay Bomb Blasts* (New Delhi: Penguin, 2002).

117. John Rollins, Liana Sun Wyler and Seth Rosen *International Terrorism and Transnational Crime: Security Threats, U.S. Policy, and Considerations for Congress*, Congressional Research Service, 5 Jan. 2010. In addition to accusing Ibrahim of providing assistance to Lashkar, the US Government also contends he shared his smuggling routes with al-Qaeda. US Department of Treasury, 'Fact Sheet: Dawood Ibrahim,' 16 Oct. 2003.

118. Rollins, Wyler and Rosen, *International Terrorism and Transnational Crime*.

119. 'Testimony of David Coleman Headley to the Indian National Investigative Agency.'

120. Swami, 'The Well-Tempered Jihad.' Swami, 'A Road to Perdition.'

121. International Crisis Group, *The Threat from Jamaat-ul Mujahideen Bangladesh* (1 Mar. 2010).

122. Author interview with member of the Indian security services, name, date and location withheld (henceforth NDLW). Author interview with former senior US intelligence analyst, NDLW. 'Testimony of David Coleman Headley to the Indian National Investigative Agency.' Regarding the group's operations in Nepal, see also: Praveen Swami, 'Arrested Cleric Ran Lashkar's Nepal Hub,' *The Hindu*, 6 June 2009.

123. Author interview with Praveen Swami, journalist with *The Hindu*, 8 Jan. 2009 in India.

124. Ibid.

125. Swami, 'Pakistan and the Lashkar's Jihad in India.'

126. Swami, 'The Spreading Tentacles of Terror.' Joshi, *The Lost Rebellion*, pp. 176–177.

127. Author interview with Praveen Swami, 8 Jan. 2009 in India. See also: 'Lashkar Using Gulf NRIs in Network,' *The Times of India*, 29 Nov. 2002.

128. Indian Security Services, 'Interrogation Report of Abdul Razzak Masood.'
129. Praveen Swami, 'Road to Unimaginable Horror,' *The Hindu*, 13 July 2006.
130. US Department of Treasury, 'HP-996: Treasury Targets LET Leadership.'
131. Author interview with Noman Benotman, 3 Mar. 2010 in the United Kingdom. Author interview with Arif Jamal, 21 Nov. 2009 via phone.
132. Interview with member of the Indian security services, NDLW. Rollins, Wyler and Rosen, *International Terrorism and Transnational Crime.*
133. 'Indian Agency Says British Muslims Support Kashmiri Militants Financially,' Press Trust of India 13 Jan. 2002.
134. US Department of Treasury, 'HP-996: Treasury Targets LET Leadership.'
135. Author interview with first Pakistan-based Western diplomat, name withheld, Dec. 2008 in Pakistan.
136. US Department of Treasury, 'HP-1023: Kuwaiti Charity Designated for Bankrolling al Qaida Network,' 13 June 2008.
137. US Department of Treasury, 'HP-996: Treasury Targets LET Leadership.'
138. Indian Security Services, 'Interrogation Report of Abdul Razzak Masood.'
139. For more information about hawala, see: http://www.interpol.int/Public/FinancialCrime/MoneyLaundering/Hawala/default.asp.
140. Michael Jacobson, *Saudi Efforts to Combat Terrorist Financing*, The Washington Institute for Near East Policy 21 July 2009.
141. Indian Security Services, 'Interrogation Report of Abdul Razzak Masood.'
142. Ansari was arrested with hand-drawn sketches and blueprints of several of the Mumbai 2008 targets in his possession at the time. He was exonerated in court, though the Maharashtra Government was challenging the acquittal at the time of writing. He is also being tried in connection with a Lashkar attack on a Central Reserve Police Force [CRPF] base in Rampur, in the state of Uttar Pradesh, on 31 December 2007–1 January 2008. See: 'Court Issues Warrants Against 2 Acquitted in 26/11 Terror Case,' Press Trust of India, 29 Aug. 2010.
143. Indian Security Services, 'Interrogation Report of Fahim Ansari.'
144. Author interview with Jamaat-ul-Dawa member, name and date withheld, in Pakistan.
145. Author interview with British security official, NDLW. Author interview with former member of the British intelligence and security establishment, NDLW. Author interview with first Western intelligence official, NDLW. Mariam Abou Zahab, who tracked Lashkar

recruitment patterns during the 1990s, offered a similar assessment. Author interview with Mariam Abou Zahab, 7 Dec. 2008 via phone.

146. This owes partly to the Pakistani government's decision to build the Mangla Dam in Mirpur District in 1960. At that time, the government issued a passport to one member of each family displaced by dam. Many of those who received a passport and were able to travel migrated to the UK. Safdar Sial, 'Exploring the Mindset of the British Pakistani Community: The Socio-cultural and Religious Context,' *Conflict & Peace Studies*, no. 1 (Oct.–Dec. 2008).

147. For more on jihadi activity in Mirpur and attempts to influence diaspora youth, see: Ibid.

148. Author interview with member of the Metropolitan Police Service, NDLW.

149. 'Briton Sends Email to Launch Jihad in Kashmir,' *The Asian Age*, 1 Nov. 1999.

150. Author's collection of Lashkar material from MDI website.

151. Indictment in 'United States *vs*. Randall Todd Royer,' The United States District Court for the Eastern-District of Virginia, Alexandria Division June 2003.

152. Memorandum Opinion in 'United States *vs*. Masoud Khan *et al.*,' The United States District Court for the Eastern-District of Virginia, Alexandria Division, 4 Mar. 2004.

153. Regarding the Al Haramain Foundation, see: 'The Consolidated List established and maintained by the 1267 Committee with respect to Al-Qaida, Usama bin Laden, and the Taliban and other individuals, groups, undertakings and entities associated with them,' http://www.un.org/sc/committees/1267/consolidatedlist.htm (last accessed, 17 Nov. 2009).

154. Judgment in 'Republic of France vs. Rama *et al.*,' Magistrates' Court of Paris, 16 June 2005. See also: Jean-Louis Bruguière, *Ce que je n'ai pas pu dire* (Paris: Robert Laffont, 2009), p. 466. The author is grateful to Dina Esfandiary for providing a translation of Bruguière's work from the original French.

155. Bruguière, *Ce que je n'ai pas pu dire*, p. 466.

156. Judgment in 'Republic of France *vs*. Rama *et al.*'

157. Mark Franchetti and Nick Fielding, 'Britons Give Pounds 2M to Terror Group,' *The Sunday Times*, 13 Jan. 2002.

158. International Crisis Group, *Pakistan: Madrasas, Extremism and the Military* (29 July 2002).

159. Opinions of the Lords of Appeal for Judgment in 'Secretary of State for the Home Department v. Rehman,' United Kingdom House of Lords, 11 Oct. 2001.

160. 'The Secretary of State for the Home Department v. Rehman,' The Supreme Court of Judicature Court of Appeal (Civil Division), 23 May 2000.

161. Opinions of the Lords of Appeal for Judgment in 'Secretary of State for the Home Department v. Rehman.'

162. Nicola Dowling, '"Terror Threat" Cleric to Stay,' *Manchester Evening News* 21 Oct. 2002.

163. 'The Terrorism Act 2000: Proscribed Organisations.' For more about the ban, see: The Office for Security and Counter Terrorism in the British Home Office, *Terrorism Act 2000*, http://security.homeoffice. gov.uk/legislation/current-legislation/terrorism-act-2000/.' House of Commons Library, http://www.parliament.uk/briefingpapers/ commons/lib/research/briefings/snha-00815.pdf (last accessed 12 June 2010.

164. Author interview with British security official, NDLW.

165. The book was entitled *The Army of Medina*, which is one of Lashkar's aliases. In addition to meaning 'pure' Taiba is also a name for the holy city of Medina in Saudi Arabia, thus Lashkar-e-Taiba can be translated both as 'Army of the Pure' and 'Army of Medina.'

166. Michael Sheehan, *Crush the Cell* (New York: Three Rivers Press, 2009), p. 216–218.

167. US Department of Justice, 'Three British Nationals Indicted on Charges of Conspiring to Use Weapons of Mass Destruction, Providing Material Support to Terrorists,' 12 Apr. 2005. For more on Dhiren Barot's activities, see for example: Susan Schmidt and Siobhan Gorman, 'Lashkar-e-Taiba Served as Gateway for Western Converts Turning to Jihad,' *Wall Street Journal*, 4 Dec. 2008. James Sturcke, 'Man Gets Life Sentence for Terror Plot,' *The Guardian*, 7 Nov. 2006. 'Muslim Convert Who Plotted Terror,' *BBC News*, 7 Nov. 2006.

168. Martin Chulov, *Australian Jihad: The Battle Against Terrorism from Within and Without* (Sydney: Pan Macmillan 2006), pp. 102–103.

169. Peter Bergen, *An Endless War: The War on Terror and Al Qaeda's Jihad Since 9/11* (forthcoming), p. 43 in draft manuscript.

170. Michael Melia, 'Australian Gitmo Detainee Gets Nine Months,' *The Washington Post*, 31 Mar. 2007.

171. Peter Bergen, 'Al Qaeda-on-Thames: UK Plotters Connected,' *Washingtonpost.com*, 30 Apr. 2007.

172. Richard Watson, 'The One True God, Allah,' *Granta*, no. 103 (Autumn 2008).

173. The police operation that thwarted the plot was codenamed 'Crevice,' hence the name the 'Crevice Network.'

174. United Kingdom Parliament Intelligence and Security Committee, *Could 7/7 Have Been Prevented?: Review of the Intelligence on the London*

*Terrorist Attacks on 7 July 2005,* May 2009. Bruce Hoffman, 'The Global Terrorist Threat: Is Al-Qaeda on the Run or on the March?,' *Middle East Policy* XIV, no. 2 (Summer 2007).

5. AL-QAEDA QUEERS THE PITCH

1. 'Lashkar Militant Killed in Kashmir,' Press Trust of India, 12 Sept. 2001.
2. Rashid, *Descent into Chaos,* p. 27.
3. National Commission on Terrorist Attacks upon the United States, *The 9/11 Commission Report: Final Report of the National Commission on Terrorist Attacks Upon the United States* (New York: W.W. Norton, 2004), p. 331.
4. Rashid, *Descent into Chaos,* p. 30.
5. Ibid., p. 29.
6. Musharraf, *In the Line of Fire,* pp. 201–202. See also: 'Wrong Step Can Spell Disaster: Musharraf,' *Dawn,* 19 Sept. 2001.
7. Rashid, *Descent into Chaos,* p. 219.
8. National Commission on Terrorist Attacks upon the United States, *The 9/11 Commission Report,* p. 331.
9. Rashid, *Descent into Chaos,* p. 32.
10. The Musharraf regime later provided safe haven and support to the Taliban, attempting to distinguish that movement from al-Qaeda as well.
11. Rashid, *Descent into Chaos,* pp. 92–93.
12. Trial Transcript of Jamal Ahmed al-Fadl Testimony in 'United States *vs.* Osama bin Laden *et al.,*' 7 Feb. 2001. Cragin, 'Early History of Al-Qa'ida.'
13. National Commission on Terrorist Attacks upon the United States, *The 9/11 Commission Report,* p. 65. Rashid, *Taliban,* p. 133. The *9/11 Commission Report* also alleged that the ISI arranged the first meeting between the Taliban and bin Laden in an effort to promote cooperation, especially regarding the training of militants for Kashmir. See: Ibid, p. 65.
14. For more on the dynamics of and rivalries within the Salafi-jihadi movement in Afghanistan at this time, see: Brynjar Lia, *Architect of Global Jihad: The Life of Al-Qaida Strategist Abu Mus'ab al-Suri* (London: Hurst, 2008), ch. 8.
15. Abu Walid al-Masri, 'The History of the Arab Afghans From the Time of Their Arrival in Afghanistan Until Their Departure with the Taliban,' serialized in *Al-Sharq Al-Awsat* 8–14 Dec. 2004. See also: Vahid Brown, 'The Facade of Allegiance: Bin Laden's Dubious Pledge to Mullah Omar,' *CTC Sentinel* 3, no. 1 (Jan. 2010).
16. 'Foreign Pro-Taliban Fighters Inside Afghanistan Pre-hostilities,' *Jane's World Armies,* 8 Aug. 2001.

17. Rashid, *Taliban*, pp. 90–92.
18. Julie Sirrs, 'The Taliban's International Ambitions,' *Middle East Quarterly* VIII, no. 3 (Summer 2001).
19. National Commission on Terrorist Attacks upon the United States, *The 9/11 Commission Report*, p. 157.
20. Regarding HuM control of these camps and LeJ training there, see: Rashid, *Taliban*, p. 92. Abou Zahab, 'The Regional Dimension of Sectarian Conflicts in Pakistan,' pp. 120–121. Regarding the Taliban giving control to bin Laden, see: Lawrence Wright, *The Looming Tower: Al-Qaeda and the Road to 9/11* (New York: Knopf, 2006), p. 250. Rashid, *Descent into Chaos*, p. 15.
21. Contrary to some reports, no Lashkar militants were killed in these attacks. Bruce Reidel has asserted that, in addition to HuM militants, ISI trainers were also among those killed. See: Bruce Reidel, *The Search for Al Qaeda: Its Leadership, Ideology and Future* (Brookings Institution Press: Washington, DC, 2008), p. 68. For more on the HuM militants killed, see: Jason Burke, *Al Qaeda: The True Story of Radical Islam* (London: Penguin, 2003), p. 188.
22. Mohammad Amir Rana, and Rohan Gunaratna, *Al-Qaeda Fights Back Inside Pakistani Tribal Areas* (Islamabad: PIPS, 2008), pp. 24–25.
23. This was the uniform opinion of the author's Pakistani interlocutors when questioned on the subject of-al-Qaeda's closest allies among the Pakistani groups prior to the 9/11 attacks. See also: Ibid. Tim McGirk and Hanna Bloch, 'Has Pakistan Tamed its Spies?,' *Time*, 6 May 2003. Fair, 'Militant Recruitment in Pakistan.'
24. Lashkar was not a signatory as is sometimes reported. Other signatories included Ayman al-Zawahiri, amir of Egyptian Islamic Jihad, Abu-Yasir Rifa'i Ahmad Taha, of the Egyptian Islamic Group, and Shaykh Mir Hamzah, secretary of the Jamiat-ul-Ulema-e-Pakistan. See: http://www.fas.org/irp/world/para/docs/980223-fatwa.htm (last accessed 25 Jan. 2011).
25. When Maulana Azhar left HuM to form JeM he took some of the top leadership, most of the cadres and a substantial amount of the infrastructure (mainly in the form of offices and equipment) with him. A dispute erupted, and led to a series of altercations. Bin Laden finally stepped in and is said to have compensated HuM with 500,000 rupees and twelve new double cabin pick-up trucks. See: Rana, *A to Z of Jehadi Organizations in Pakistan*, pp. 220–222.
26. Rana, *Gateway to Terrorism*, p. 337.
27. Author interview with former Lashkar-e-Taiba member, name withheld, Jan. 2009 in Pakistan. Author interview with Syed Shoaib Hasan, journalist with the BBC Islamabad Bureau, 15 Dec. 2008 in Pakistan. There are reports suggesting some Lashkar members continued to train

in the al-Badr camps. See, for example: Burke, *Al Qaeda: The True Story of Radical Islam*, p. 167.

28. Edwards, *Before Taliban*, p. 301.
29. Author interview with Michael Semple, 23 Dec. 2008 in Pakistan. Regarding the Taliban's capture of Kunar, see: Rashid, *Taliban*, p. 48.
30. Author interview with Rahimullah Yusufzai, 3 Jan. 2009 via phone. See also: Rashid, *Taliban*, p. 132.
31. US Department of Defense, Verbatim Transcript of Combatant Status Review Tribunal Hearing for ISN 10016, http://www.defense–link.mil/news/transcript_ISN10016.pdf (last accessed Nov. 2010). According to Ahmed Rashid, this was done in coordination with the ISI for recruits who were then sent to fight in Kashmir. Author interview with Ahmed Rashid, 29 Dec. 2008 in Pakistan. See also: Rashid, *Descent into Chaos*, p. 48.
32. National Commission on Terrorist Attacks upon the United States, *The 9/11 Commission Report*, p. 500 fn. 5.
33. Author interview with Kathy Gannon, Associated Press correspondent for Afghanistan and Pakistan from 1986–2005, 19 Dec. 2008 in Pakistan. Author interview with Ahmed Rashid, 29 Dec. 2008 in Pakistan. See also: Angel Rabasa *et al.*, *Beyond al-Qaeda Part 1: The Global Jihadist Movement* (Arlington, VA: RAND Corporation, 2006), p. 86.
34. Nasr, 'Islam, The State and the Rise of Sectarian Militancy,' p. 99. Abou Zahab, 'The Regional Dimension of Sectarian Conflicts in Pakistan,' p. 121.
35. Rana and Gunaratna, *Al-Qaeda Fights Back Inside Pakistani Tribal Areas*, p. 85.
36. Author interview with Haroon Rashid, BBC Islamabad Bureau Chief, 19 Dec. 2008 in Pakistan. See also: 'India's Secret War Against the Taliban,' *Jane's Intelligence Review*, 1 June 2002. Rahul Bedi, 'Infiltration Continues on Line of Control,' *Jane's Intelligence Review*, 1 July 2002.
37. Author interview with Jamaat-ul-Dawa official, name withheld, May 2009 in Pakistan. Author interview with Arif Jamal, 21 Nov. 2009 via phone. Author interview with second Pakistan-based Western diplomat, name withheld, Dec. 2008 in Pakistan.
38. Author interview with Jamaat-ul-Dawa official, name withheld, May 2009 in Pakistan.
39. Rita Katz and Josh Devon, 'A Global Network,' *National Review Online* 30 June 2003.
40. 'Kashmir: Lashkar-i-Toiba Denies Hand in US Attacks; Hurriyat Against Violence,' *Radio Pakistan*, 12 Sept. 2001 via BBC Monitoring.
41. 'Kashmir: Lashkar-i-Toiba Denies Role in USA attacks,' *Ausaf*, 13 Sept. 2001 via BBC Monitoring.

42. John Burns, 'Kashmir's Islamic Guerrillas See Little to Fear From US,' *New York Times*, 23 Dec. 2001.

43. MDI website, 'Hafiz Saeed: Ummah Should Support the Oppressed Afghans,' 12 Oct. 2001. MDI website, 'Hafiz Mohammad Saeed: Terrorist Strike of Non-Muslims on Islam and Muslim World and Way of Survival for Muslims,' 9 Oct. 2001. Author in possession of hard copies.

44. MDI website, 'Decree in Support of Osama, Afghanistan,' 27 Sept. 2001. Author's collection.

45. MDI website. 'Hafiz Saeed: US Attacks Were the Doing of the Zionists. No Jihadic Organization Could be Involved in Such un-Islamic Activity,' 14 Sept. 2001. Author's collection.

46. MDI website, 'US Attack on Afghanistan Would Lead to World War— Warns Hafiz Mohammad Saeed,' 22 Sept. 2001. Author's collection.

47. Steve Coll, 'The Stand-Off,' *The New Yorker*, 13 Feb. 2006.

48. Regarding the statement by General Javed Ashraf Qazi (Retd), see: B. Muralidhar Reddy, 'Jaish Behind Parliament Attack: ex-ISI chief,' *The Hindu*, 7 Mar. 2004. Regarding the convictions in India, see: Anjali Mody, '4 Accused in Parliament Attack Case Convicted,' *The Hindu*, 17 Dec. 2002.

49. Polly Nayak and Michael Krepon, *US Crisis Management in South Asia's Twin Peaks Crisis* (Washington, DC: The Henry L. Stimson Center, Sept. 2006).

50. Rahul Bedi, 'India and Pakistan Square Up Over Kashmir,' *Jane's Islamic Affairs Analyst*, 1 Jan. 2002.

51. Author interview with Arif Jamal, 21 Nov. 2009 via phone.

52. 'Who Will Strike First?,' *The Economist*, 22 Dec. 2001.

53. 'Govt blames LeT for Parliament Attack, Asks Pak to Restrain Terrorist Outfits,' *Rediff* 14 Dec. 201.

54. Gary Bernsten, *Jawbreaker* (Three Rivers Press, 2005), p. 305.

55. Musharraf, *In the Line of Fire*, p. 265.

56. For more on bin Laden's escape from Tora Bora, see: United States Senate Committee on Foreign Relations, *Tora Bora Revisited: How We Failed to Get bin Laden and Why it Matters Today* (One Hundred and Eleventh Congress, 30 Nov. 2009).

57. Nayak and Krepon, *US Crisis Management in South Asia's Twin Peaks Crisis*.

58. Ibid.

59. Office of Foreign Assets Control, US Department of the Treasury, 'Executive Order 13224—Blocking Property and Prohibiting Transactions with Persons who Commit, Threaten to Commit, or Support— Terrorism,' http://www.ustreas.gov/offices/enforcement/ofac/pro–grams/ascii/terror.txt (last accessed 20 Sept. 2010).

60. Barshied, *Harakat ul-Mujahedin Dossier*.
61. Office of Foreign Assets Control, US Department of the Treasury, 'Executive Order 13224—Blocking Property and Prohibiting Transactions with Persons who Commit, Threaten to Commit, or Support Terrorism.'
62. 'Pakistan Freezes Accounts of Militant Group,' Reuters, 24 Dec. 2001.
63. 'Pakistan Bans Collection of Funds by "extremist Islamic organizations",' *The Frontier Post* 22 Dec. 2001.
64. Khan, 'Jihadi Outfits Going Underground.'
65. Author interview with Mohammad Amir Rana, 16 & 18 Dec. 2008 in Pakistan. Author interview with second Pakistan-based Western diplomat, name withheld, Dec. 2008 in Pakistan.
66. Nayak and Krepon, *US Crisis Management in South Asia's Twin Peaks Crisis*.
67. For date of designation, see: US Department of State, 'Chapter 6: Terrorist Organizations,' *Country Reports on Terrorism 2008*, 20 Apr. 2009.
68. 'Jamaat-ul-Dawa Pakistan Press Release,' 24 Dec. 2001. Author in possession of copy.
69. 'Lashkar-i-Toiba Changes Status, Parent Body Dissolved,' *Ausaf*, 25 Dec. 2001 via BBC Monitoring.
70. The JuD press release suggests that it had just been established. However, Abdullah Muntazir, the JuD spokesperson for international media, and Javed Ashraf Qazi, a former Director General of the ISI, confirmed this was the same organization that Saeed founded in the 1980s. Author interview with Abdullah Muntazir, 30 Dec. 2008 in Pakistan. Author interview with General Javed Ashraf Qazi (Retd), 15 Dec. 2008 in Pakistan.
71. 'Jamaat-ul-Dawa Pakistan Press Release.'
72. Mohammad Amir Rana, 'Jammat-ud-Dawa Has No Global Network or Ambitions: Mujahid,' *The Daily Times*, 25 May 2004.
73. Author interview with Abdullah Muntazir, 30 Dec. 2008 in Pakistan.
74. Author interview with Mohammad Amir Rana, 16 & 18 Dec. 2008 in Pakistan. Author interview with Arif Jamal, 21 Nov. 2009 via phone. See also: US Department of Treasury, 'Background on Jamaat ud Dawa (JUD),' http://www.treas.gov/offices/enforcement/key-issues/protecting/fto_aliases.shtml (last accessed 31 Jan. 2010).
75. Author interview with Jamaat-ul-Dawa official, name withheld, May 2009 in Pakistan.
76. Musharraf also re-banned Sipah-e-Sahaba and Tehrik-e-Jafria, a Shia organization, as well as outlawing the Tehrik-e-Nifaz-e-Shariat-e-Mohammadi [TNSM] for leading thousands of Pakistanis into Afghanistan to battle American forces there.

77. 'Pakistani Television Airs Musharraf's Taped Address,' *CNN*, 12 Jan. 2002. 'Pakistani President Bans Islamic Militant Groups,' *CNN*, 12 Jan. 2002.
78. Rashid, *Descent into Chaos*, p. 147.
79. Regarding Azhar's detention, see: 'Pakistan Arrests Head of Muslim Militant Group,' Agence France-Presse 25 Dec. 2001. Regarding Saeed's detention, see: 'Pakistan Calls for Peace, Arrests Key Militant Boss,' Agence France-Presse 30 Dec. 2001.
80. 'Lahore High Court's Review Board Orders Release of Professor,' *Business Recorder* 31 Mar. 2002.
81. Over the next two weeks the security services arrested over 2,000 militants and closed more than 600 offices, according to figures from the Punjab Home Department. Over 100 Jaish militants and more than 200 Lashkar militants were arrested, and each had almost 200 of their offices closed. Rana Mubashir, '16 Jihadis Freed for Lack of Evidence,' *The News*, 25 Jan. 2002.
82. See also: Jamal, *Shadow War*, pp. 230–231. Rashid, *Descent into Chaos*, pp. 146–147.
83. Regarding the failure to bring charges, see: Rashid, *Descent into Chaos*, p. 155. Regarding the appeal to release those who renounced militancy, see: Jamal, *Shadow War*, p. 230.
84. Regarding Pakistan's actions against militant groups, see: John Burns, 'Pakistan Is Said to Order an End to Support for Militant Groups,' *New York Times*, 2 Jan. 2002. For direction by the army and ISI to militant groups to move their offices, see: Ahmed Rashid, 'Musharraf Speech is Crucial for Stability,' *The Daily Telegraph*, 9 Jan. 2002. Khan, 'Jihadi Outfits Going Underground.'

## 6. GOOD JIHADI/BAD JIHADI

1. Author interview with member of the Punjab police, name and date withheld, in Pakistan. See also: Ashley J. Tellis, *Pakistan and the War on Terror: Conflicted Goals, Compromised Performance* (Washington, DC: Carnegie Endowment for International Peace, 2008).
2. Anwar Iqbal, 'Militants See Christians as Easy Target,' United Press International, 31 Oct. 2001.
3. Amir Mir, 'The Maulana's Scattered Beads,' *Outlook India*, 1 Sept. 2003.
4. Author interview with Syed Shoaib Hasan, 15 Dec. 2008 in Pakistan. Author interview with Ahmed Rashid, 7 May 2009 in Pakistan.
5. Author interview with former senior officer in the Pakistan Intelligence Bureau, name withheld, May 2009 in Pakistan.
6. Author interview with second Pakistan-based Western diplomat, name withheld, Dec. 2008 in Pakistan.

7. Author interview with former senior ISI official, name withheld, Dec. 2008 in Pakistan.

8. Lt. Gen. V.K. Sood (Retd) and Pravin Sawhney, *Operation Parakram— The War Unfinished* (New Delhi: Sage Publications, 2003), p. 80.

9. Ibid.

10. Nayak and Krepon, *US Crisis Management in South Asia's Twin Peaks Crisis*.

11. Celia Dugger, 'Minister Says India Won't Attack Pakistan,' *New York Times* 14 May 2002.

12. Nayak and Krepon, *US Crisis Management in South Asia's Twin Peaks Crisis*.

13. Rashid, *Descent into Chaos*, p. 147.

14. Dugger, 'Minister Says India Won't Attack Pakistan.'

15. There is general agreement that this was a Lashkar-led attack, but two groups initially took credit. One was Jamiat-ul-Mujahedin, believed to be a splinter of the Hizb-ul-Mujahideen. The other was Al-Masooran, an alias Lashkar often used for attacks in which civilians were killed. Regarding details of the attack, see: 'Family Members Killed in Kashmir Militant attack on Bus, Army Camp,' Press Trust of India, 14 May 2002.

16. Nayak and Krepon, *US Crisis Management in South Asia's Twin Peaks Crisis*.

17. Lally Weymouth, 'Voices From a Hot Zone,' *Newsweek*, 1 July 2002.

18. This information was provided independently by two Pakistani journalists with sources inside the ISI, Lashkar and JeM. Both requested anonymity for security purposes. See also: Syed Saleem Shahzad, 'Ceasefire Will Not Hold, With Same Game, New Rules,' *South Asia Tribune*, 30 Nov.–6 Dec 2003.

19. Rana Jawad, 'Musharraf Orders Crackdown on Resurfacing Militant Groups,' Agence France-Presse, 15 Nov. 2003.

20. 'Pakistan Steps up Militant Crackdown,' Agence France-Presse, 20 Nov. 2003.

21. Author interview with member of Pakistan Anti-Terrorism Force, name withheld, May 2009 in Pakistan.

22. Author interview with Jamaat-ul-Dawa official, name withheld, May 2009 in Pakistan.

23. See, for example: Amir Mir, 'Forward' in *A to Z of Jehadi Organizations in Pakistan*, p. 57, 60. Sareen, *The Jihad Factory*, p. 77.

24. Similar payments were made to the leaders of Jaish and HuM. Haqqani, *Pakistan: Between Mosque and Military*, p. 306.

25. 'Pakistan, India Joint Statement,' *Dawn*, 7 Jan. 2004.

26. Rana, *The Seeds of Terrorism*, p. 283.

27. Author interview with first Pakistan-based Western diplomat, name withheld, Dec. 2008 in Pakistan. Author interview with Pakistani journalist who covered Pakistan-administered Kashmir at the time, name and date withheld, in Pakistan. See also: Amir Mir, 'Forward' in *A to Z of Jehadi Organizations in Pakistan*, p. 57.

28. There were rumors in the organization at the time that Saeed deliberately dispatched the widow's husband on a suicide mission so that he could take her as his wife. Author interview with former Lashkar-e-Taiba member, name withheld, Jan. 2009 in Pakistan.

29. Rana, 'Jamaatud Dawa Splits.' Mir, 'LeT Commander Furious at JuD Chief.'

30. Rana, 'Jamaatud Dawa Splits.'

31. Ibid.

32. Author interview with Mohammad Amir Rana, 16 & 18 Dec. 2008 in Pakistan. See also: Ibid. Amir Mir, *The True Face of Jehadists* (Lahore: Mashal Press, 2004), pp. 68–71.

33. Author interview with first Lashkar-e-Taiba member, name withheld, May 2009 in Pakistan. Author interview with second Lashkar-e-Taiba member, name withheld, May 2009 in Pakistan.

34. Author interview with second senior officer in the Pakistan security services, name withheld, May 2009 in Pakistan.

35. Information about Abdur Rehman, Haroon and Khurram drawn from 'Testimony of David Coleman Headley to the Indian National Investigative Agency.' For open source information regarding Abdur Rehman, see: Indictment in 'United States of America vs. Abdur Rehman Hashim Syed,' United States District Court Northern District of Illinois Eastern Division 20 Oct. 2009. For open source information regarding Haroon and Khurram, see: 'Pakistani Kashmiri Militants Now Fighting NATO Forces,' *Middle East Transparent*, 28 Sept. 2009.

36. 'Pakistani Kashmiri Militants Now Fighting NATO Forces.' Syed Saleem Shahzad, 'Al-Qaeda's Guerrilla Chief Lays Out Strategy,' *Asia Times*, 15 Oct. 2009.

37. The group is named for the 313 companions of the Prophet Mohammad who fought at the Battle of Badr.

38. As of 2008, these departments were: Construction of Masajid and Madaris; Dawa-o-Islah [Calling people to self-improvement]; Education; Finance; Idarah Khidmat-e-Khalq [Humanitarian Relief]; Media and Propagation; Political (and external) Affairs; Public Relations; Doctors' Wing; Farmers' Wing; Students' Wing; Teachers' Wing; Women's Wing; and Workers' Wing.

39. Author interview with Khaled Ahmed, Editor at *The Friday Times*, 29 Dec. 2008 in Pakistan.

40. Author interview with former Lashkar-e-Taiba member, name withheld, Jan. 2009 in Pakistan.
41. JuD website, 'Welfare Projects,' undated. Author's collection.
42. Author interview with Jamaat-ul-Dawa Amir for Rawalpindi, name withheld, May 2009 in Pakistan.
43. JuD website, 'Welfare Projects.'
44. Ibid.
45. Ibid.
46. Author interview with former senior officer in the Pakistan Intelligence Bureau, name withheld, May 2009 in Pakistan.
47. Author interview with Jamaat-ul-Dawa official, name withheld, May 2009 in Pakistan. Abdullah Muntazir, 'US Concern Over Jamaat-ul-Dawa's Relief Work: The Other Side of the Picture,' Dec. 2005. Posted to the JuD website. Author's collection.
48. JuD website, 'Welfare Projects.'
49. Praveen Swami, 'The Indian Mujahidin and Lashkar-i-Tayyiba's Transnational Networks,' *CTC Sentinel* 2, no. 6 (June 2009).
50. JuD website, 'Education Wing,' undated. Author's collection.
51. Rana, *The Seeds of Terrorism*, p. 105.
52. Regarding continued funding at this time, see: Zulfiqar Ali, 'Back to Camp,' *Herald* July 2005. Regarding occasional ISI funding freezes, see: Imtiaz Gul, *The Al Qaeda Connection: The Taliban and Terror in Pakistan's Tribal Areas* (New Delhi: Penguin, 2009), p. 216.
53. Author interview with Kathy Gannon, 19 Dec. 2008 in Pakistan. Author interview with first Pakistan-based Western diplomat, name withheld, Dec. 2008 in Pakistan See also: Fair, 'Militant Recruitment in Pakistan.' Ali, 'Back to Camp.'
54. Author interview with Mohammad Amir Rana, 16 & 18 Dec. 2008 in Pakistan.
55. Author interview with former Lashkar-e-Taiba member, name withheld, Jan. 2009 in Pakistan.
56. Markaz al-Dawa flyer, 'Don't Forget Mujahideen and Refugees of Kashmir & Afghanistan During Your Eid Delights,' undated. Author in possession of copy.
57. Author interview with first Pakistan-based Western diplomat, name withheld, Dec. 2008 in Pakistan. Author interview with Syed Shoaib Hasan, 15 Dec. 2008 in Pakistan. See also: Rana, *A to Z of Jehadi Organizations in Pakistan*, p. 328.
58. Author interview with first Lashkar-e-Taiba member, name withheld, May 2009 in Pakistan. Author interview with former senior officer in the Pakistan Intelligence Bureau, name withheld, May 2009 in Pakistan.

59. Information regarding the purchase of real estate from: Author interview with second Pakistan-based Western diplomat, name withheld, Dec. 2008 in Pakistan. Author interview with Arif Jamal, 20 Aug. 2009 via phone. Author interview with Mohammad Amir Rana, 16 & 18 Dec. 2008 in Pakistan. Information regarding the number of JuD offices from: Muntazir, 'US Concern Over Jamaat-ul-Dawa's Relief Work.'
60. The group did stop making *Voice of Islam* available on its English language website.
61. Mohammad Amir Rana, 'Jihadi Print Media in Pakistan: An Overview,' *Conflict & Peace Studies*, no. 1 (Oct-Dec 2008).
62. Author's collection of Lashkar material from JuD website and PIPS archive.
63. Four Pakistani journalists made this claim to the author independent of one another, but for security reasons all requested anonymity.
64. Casualty numbers are approximate. Gathered from US Agency for International Development Relief Web, 'South Asia Earthquake: Fact Sheet #25,' http://www.reliefweb.int/rw/RWB.NSF/db900SID/KHII-6J93HT?OpenDocument (last accessed 14 Apr. 2009).
65. Hussain, *Frontline Pakistan*, pp. 186–187. Steve Coll, 'Fault Lines: After the Earthquake, Some Strange New Alliances,' *The New Yorker*, 21 Nov. 2005. 'Militant Philanthropy,' *Newsline*, Nov. 2005.
66. Rahul Bedi, 'Militants' Training Camps Wiped Out,' *The Telegraph*, 10 Oct. 2005.
67. Jawad Qureshi, 'Earthquake Jihad: The Role of Jihadis and Islamist Groups After the October 2005 Earthquake,' Humanitarian Practice Network, June 2006.
68. Ibid. See also: Catherine Philp, 'Terror Groups Move into Quake Vacuum,' *The Times of London*, 17 Oct. 2005.
69. Muntazir, 'US Concern Over Jamaat-ul-Dawa's Relief Work.' See also: Qureshi, 'Earthquake Jihad.'
70. Qureshi, 'Earthquake Jihad.'
71. 'The Future Looks Bearded,' *The Economist*, 8 July 2006.
72. Hussain, *Frontline Pakistan*, p. 188. 'We Must Outdo Jihadis in Relief Efforts,' *The Daily Times* 27, Oct. 2005.
73. Philp, 'Terror Groups Move into Quake Vacuum.'
74. 'Militant Philanthropy.'
75. JuD website, 'Speech by Pakistani Kashmir Prime Minister Sikandar Hayat Khan at Jamaat-ul-Dawa Conference in Muzaffarabad,' 2 July 2006. Author's collection.
76. International Crisis Group, *Steps Towards Peace*.
77. Author interview with former senior officer in the Pakistan Intelligence Bureau, name and date withheld, in Pakistan.
78. US Department of Treasury, 'Background on Jamaat ud Dawa (JUD).'

79. US Department of State, 'Addition of Aliases Jamaat-Ud-Dawa and Idara Khidmat-E-Khalq to the Specially Designated Global Terrorist Designation of Lashkhar-E-Tayyiba,' 28 Apr. 2006.

80. JuD website, 'Jamaat-ul-Dawa Issues Statement Refuting Allegations of Terrorism Funding, Sends Letter to US Treasury Secretary,' 1 Oct. 2006. Author's collection.

81. See, for example: Danny Kemp, 'Pakistan's "Jihadi Option" Threatens Regional Peace: Analysts,' Agence France-Presse, 16 July 2006.

82. Indian Ministry of Home Affairs, 'Level of Terrorist Violence and Security Situation in J&K—An Assessment,' http://mha.gov.in/unique–page.asp?ID_PK=306 (last accessed 18 Aug. 2009).

83. Jamal, *Shadow War*, p. 232.

84. Mir, *The True Face of Jehadis*, 96.

85. Chalk and Fair, 'Lashkar-e-Tayyiba Leads the Kashmiri Insurgency.'

86. Author interview with Suba Chandran, 5 Jan. 2009 in India. Author interview with second Kashmiri journalist, name withheld, Jan. 2009 in India.

87. The two other groups were JeM and Al-Badr. See Mohammad Amir Rana, 'Lashkar, Jaish and Al-Badr Join UJC,' *Daily Times* 22 Oct. 2003.

88. Jamal, *Shadow War*, p. 232.

89. Author interview with member of the Indian security services, NDLW.

90. 'Gujarat Riot Death Toll Revealed,' *BBC News*, 11 May 2005.

91. US Department of State, *International Religious Freedom Report 2003*, 18 Dec. 2003. For more, see: Human Rights Watch, *We Have No Orders To Save You: State Participation and Complicity in Communal Violence in Gujarat* (April 2002).

92. For more on the impact of the riots on terrorist recruiting, see: Swami, 'The Well-Tempered Jihad.' Swami, 'A Road to Perdition.' Rahul Bedi, 'Bombay Bombings Fuel Tension,' *Jane's Terrorism & Security Monitor*, 12 Sept. 2003.

93. Praveen Swami, 'Riyaz Bhatkal and the Origins of the Indian Mujahidin,' *CTC Sentinel* 3, no. 5 (May 2010).

94. Devesh K. Pandey, 'Bangladesh Blasts Confirm a Suspicion,' *The Hindu*, 24 Aug. 2005.

95. Swami, 'The Indian Mujahidin and Lashkar-i-Tayyiba's Transnational Networks.'

96. Swami, 'Riyaz Bhatkal and the Origins of the Indian Mujahidin.'

97. 'American Center Attack: SC Stays Death Sentence of Aftab Ansari,' *The Times of India*, 25 May 2010.

98. Author interview with member of the Indian security services, NDLW. See also: Pandey, 'Bangladesh Blasts Confirm a Suspicion.'

99. Swami, 'The Indian Mujahidin and Lashkar-i-Tayyiba's Transnational Networks.'

100. Author interview with member of the Indian security services, NDLW. See also: Swami, 'Riyaz Bhatkal and the Origins of the Indian Mujahidin.'

101. Swami, 'Riyaz Bhatkal and the Origins of the Indian Mujahidin.'

102. Swami, 'The Indian Mujahidin and Lashkar-i-Tayyiba's Transnational Networks.'

103. Author interview with Praveen Swami, 8 Jan. 2009 in India.

104. Ibid. Author interview with Kanchan Lakshman, Research Associate at the Institute for Conflict Management, 6 Jan. 2009 in India. See also: Animesh Roul, 'After Pune, Details Emerge on the Karachi Project and its Threat to India,' *CTC Sentinel* 3, no. 4 (Apr. 2010).

105. Author interview with member of the Indian security services, NDLW. See also: Tellis, 'Bad Company—Lashkar-e-Tayyiba and the Growing Ambition of Islamist Militancy in Pakistan.'

106. Author interview with Praveen Swami, 8 Jan. 2009 in India. Author interview with Kanchan Lakshman, 6 Jan. 2009 in India. See, for example: Namrata Biji Ahuja, 'LeT, HuJI Supply High-end Explosives,' *The Asian Age*, 30 July 2008.

107. 'Testimony of David Coleman Headley to the Indian National Investigative Agency.'

108. US Department of Treasury, 'US Designates Dawood Ibrahim as Terrorist Supporter,' 16 Oct. 2003.

109. Author interview with member of the Indian security services, NDLW. See also: Roul, 'After Pune, Details Emerge on the Karachi Project and its Threat to India.'

110. 'Testimony of David Coleman Headley to the Indian National Investigative Agency.'

111. Ibid. For an open source account, see: Roul, 'After Pune, Details Emerge on the Karachi Project and its Threat to India.'

112. The head of Lashkar's Indian operations planned the attack and one of the fidayeen killed was the nephew of the group's finance chief Haji Ashraf. 'Testimony of David Coleman Headley to the Indian National Investigative Agency.'

113. Sabauddin Ahmed is presently in judicial custody for leading a fidayeen attack against the Central Reserve Police Force [CRPF] camp in Rampur, in the state of Uttar Pradesh, on 31 Dec. 2007–1 January 2008. See: Atiq Khan, 'Acquitted Indians to Face Trial in Rampur CRPF Terror Attack Case,' *The Hindu*, 3 May 2010.He was also tried, along with Fahim Ansari, in connection with providing sketches of several of the Mumbai 2008 to Lashkar. Ahmed and Ansari were exonerated in court, though the Maharashtra Government was challenging the acquittal at the time of writing. See: 'Court Issues Warrants Against 2 Acquitted in 26/11 Terror Case.'

114. 'Lakhvi Also Behind Mumbai Train Blasts,' *Hindustan Times* 4 Jan. 2009.

115. Ibid. See also: T.A. Johnson, 'Muzammil, Lakhvi: Same Names, ISI Links in IISc Attack Probe,' *The Indian Express*, 8 Dec. 2008. Robert Worth and Hari Kumar, 'Police Foiled Earlier Plot Against Mumbai,' *New York Times*, 6 Dec. 2008. 'IISc Attack: Sabauddin Confesses to Crime,' Press Trust of India, 5 Apr. 2008.

116. 'IISc attack.' See also: Khan, 'Acquitted Indians to Face Trial in Rampur CRPF Terror Attack Case.' Presley Thomas, 'Lashkar's "Only Indian Commander",' *Hindustan Times*, 4 May 2010.

117. Author interview with Rahimullah Yusufzai, 3 Jan. 2009 via phone. Author interview with Jamaat-ul-Dawa member, name and date withheld, in Pakistan. Author interview with former Lashkar-e-Taiba member, name withheld, Jan. 2009 in Pakistan. Author interview with Western intelligence analyst, NDLW.

118. Author interview with first Pakistan-based Western diplomat, name withheld, Dec. 2008 in Pakistan. Author interview with third Pakistan-based Western diplomat, name withheld, May 2009 in Pakistan. Author interview with first senior officer in the Pakistan security services, name withheld, May 2009 in Pakistan.

119. Rashid, *Descent into Chaos*, p. 98.

120. Author interview with first Pakistan-based Western diplomat, Dec. 2008 in Pakistan. Author interview with Mohammad Amir Rana, 16 & 18 Dec. 2008 in Pakistan. See also: Asif Shahzad, 'Outlawed Groups Help Al Qaeda Suspects,' *Dawn*, 20 Apr. 2002. Michael Scheuer, *Imperial Hubris: Why The West Is Losing The War On Terror* (Washington, D.C.: Potomac Books, Inc., 2005), pp. 55–56.

121. Author interview with Tariq Pervez, former Director General of the Federal Investigation Agency and the National Coordinator of Pakistan's Counter Terrorism Authority at the time interview was conducted, 14 May 2009 in Pakistan. Author interview with Khaled Ahmed, 29 Dec. 2008 in Pakistan. Author interview with Ahmed Rashid, 29 Dec. 2008 in Pakistan.

122. Indian Security Services, 'Interrogation Report of Abdul Razzak Masood.'

123. Shahzad, 'Outlawed Groups Help Al Qaeda Suspects.'

124. Author interview with Tariq Pervez, 14 May 2009 in Pakistan.

125. Abou Zahab and Roy, *Islamist Networks*, p. 42. 'Inside the Centre that Created an Australian Traitor—David Hicks: A Terrorist in Training,' *The Daily Telegraph*, 13 Mar. 2002.

126. Gary Schroen, *First In: An Insider's Account of How the CIA Spearheaded the War on Terror in Afghanistan* (New York: Ballantine, 2005), p. 361.

127. Author interview with Ahmed Rashid, 29 Dec. 2008 in Pakistan.

128. Scott Shane, 'Inside a 9/11 Mastermind's Interrogation,' *New York Times*, 22 June 2008.
129. Hussain, *Frontline Pakistan*, p. 127.
130. 'Capture of Bin Laden's Aide Boosts US Anti-Terror Fight,' *Financial Times*, 3 Apr. 2002. Selig S. Harrison, 'Why Musharraf Clings to Power; Corruption and Extremism in Pakistan,' *International Herald Tribune*, 10 May 2002.
131. Author interview with Michael Semple, 23 Dec. 2008 in Pakistan. Antonio Giustozzi, *Koran, Kalishnikov and Laptop: The Neo-Taliban Insurgency in Afghanistan* (London: Hurst, 2007), pp. 71–72. Regarding Rohullah's arrest, see: Ian Fisher and John F. Burns, 'U.S. Troops Focus on Border's Caves to Seek bin Laden,' *New York Times*, 28 Aug. 2002.
132. For more on local dynamics in Kunar at the time, see: Brian Glyn Williams, 'Afghanistan's Heart of Darkness: Fighting the Taliban in Kunar Province' *CTC Sentinel* 1, no. 12 (Nov. 2008).
133. Author interview with Michael Semple, 23 Dec. 2008 in Pakistan.
134. Williams, 'Afghanistan's Heart of Darkness.'
135. Author interview with Arif Jamal, 20 Aug. 2009 via phone. Author interview with Mohammad Amir Rana, 16 & 18 Dec. 2008 in Pakistan. Regarding the shipment of weapons and material to Afghanistan, see also: 'Militant Group Denies Links to Ammunition Found in Afghanistan,' Agence France-Presse 27 Jan. 2002.
136. 'Testimony of David Coleman Headley to the Indian National Investigative Agency.'
137. Indian Security Services, 'Interrogation Report of Abdul Razzak Masood.'
138. US Department of Treasury, 'TG-192: Treasury Targets Al Qaida and Lashkar-E Tayyiba Networks in Pakistan,' 1 July 2009. On 29 June 2009, Arif Qasmani was added to 'The Consolidated List established and maintained by the 1267 Committee with respect to Al-Qaida, Usama bin Laden, and the Taliban and other individuals, groups, undertakings and entities associated with them.'
139. Indian Security Services, 'Interrogation Report of Abdul Razzak Masood.'
140. Mohammad Shehzad, 'Suicide Bombing Is the Best Form of Jihad,' *The Friday Times* 17 Apr. 2003. Rashid, *Descent into Chaos*, p. 228.
141. Rabasa *et al.*, *Beyond al-Qaeda Part 1: The Global Jihadist Movement*.
142. Regarding Lashkar's posting, see: Daniel Benjamin and Gabriel Weimann, 'What the Terrorists Have in Mind,' *New York Times*, 27 Oct. 2004. Regarding the figure given by Indian media, see: Praveen Swami and Mohammad Shehzad, 'Lashkar Raising Islamist Brigades for Iraq,' *The Hindu*, 13 June 2004.

143. Information regarding the use of JuD offices for recruitment from: Author interview with third Pakistan-based Western diplomat, name withheld, May 2009 in Pakistan.

144. Author interview with Mohammad Amir Rana, 16 & 18 Dec. 2008 in Pakistan.

145. Ibid. Author interview with second Lashkar-e-Taiba member, name withheld, May 2009 in Pakistan.

146. For a sample of the breakdown of foreign fighters in Iraq by country, see: Joseph Felter and Brian Fishman, *Al-Qa'ida's Foreign Fighters in Iraq: A First Look at the Sinjar Records* (West Point: Combating Terrorism Center, 2007).

147. Author interview with first Western intelligence official, NDLW. See also: US Department of Treasury, 'HP-996: Treasury Targets LET Leadership.' According to Ahmed Rashid, at least seven Lashkar members were known to have been killed fighting in Iraq in 2003–2004. See: Rashid, *Descent into Chaos*, p. 228.

148. Richard Norton-Taylor, 'Britain Aided Iraq Terror Renditions, Government Admits,' *The Guardian*, 26 Feb. 2009.

149. E. Blanche, 'Lashkar-e-Taiba Spreads its Tentacles,' *Jane's Terrorism & Security Monitor*, 1 Sept. 2004. Praveen Swami, 'The Long Arm of Lashkar,' *Frontline*, 24 Apr.–7 May 2004.

150. This information was gathered by Declan Walsh, *The Guardian* correspondent in Pakistan at the time, during his interview of the senior British Foreign Office official in question. Author interview with Declan Walsh, 13 Dec. in Pakistan.

151. Gul, *The Al Qaeda Connection*, p. 27.

152. Chulov, *Australian Jihad*, p. 151.

153. Abou Zahab, 'Salafism in Pakistan,' p. 140.

154. Mir, *The True Face of Jehadists*, p. 70.

155. Author interview with first Pakistan-based Western diplomat, name withheld, Dec. 2008 in Pakistan. Author interview with first former US intelligence officer, NDLW. Author interview with Haroon Rashid, 19 Dec. 2008 in Pakistan. See also: Meyer, 'Extremist Group Works in the Open in Pakistan.'

156. Judgment in 'Republic of France *vs.* Rama, *et al.*'

157. Bruguière, *Ce que je n'ai pas pu dire*, pp. 468–471.

158. Ibid, p. 471 fn. 8.

159. Ibid, 471. See also: Myra MacDonald, 'Pakistan and Afghanistan: "The Bad Guys Don't Stay in Their Lanes",' Reuters, 4 Dec. 2009.

160. Superseding Indictment in 'United States *vs.* Ali Al-Timimi,' The United States District Court for the Eastern-District of Virginia, Alexandria Division, Feb. 2005 Term. Indictment in the 'United States *vs.* Randall Todd Royer; Ibrahim Ahmed al-Hamdi; Masoud Ahmad

Khan; Yong Ki Kwon; Mohammed Aatique; Seifullah Chapman; Hammad Abdur-Raheem; Donald Thomas Surratt; Caliph Basha Ibn Abdur-Raheem; Khwaja Mahmood Hasan; Sabri Benkhala,' The United States District Court for the Eastern-District of Virginia, Alexandria Division, June 2003 Term. See also: Indictment in 'United States *vs.* Ali Al-Timimi,' The United States District Court for the Eastern-District of Virginia, Alexandria Division, Sept. 2004 Term. Memorandum Opinion in 'United States *vs.* Masoud Khan, *et al.*,' The United States District Court for the Eastern-District of Virginia, Alexandria Division, 4 Mar. 2004.

161. Indictment in 'United States *vs.* Ali Asad Chandia and Mohammed Ajmal Khan,' The United States District Court for the Eastern-District of Virginia, Alexandria Division, Sept. 2005 Term.

162. Plea Agreement in 'United States *vs.* Mohammed Aatique,' The United States District Court for the Eastern-District of Virginia, Alexandria Division. Plea Agreement in 'United States *vs.* Khwaja Mahmood Hasan,' The United States District Court for the Eastern-District of Virginia, Alexandria Division. Superseding Indictment in 'United States *vs.* Ali Al-Timimi.' Indictment in 'United States *vs.* Randall Todd Royer; Ibrahim Ahmed al-Hamdi; Masoud Ahmad Khan; Yong Ki Kwon; Mohammed Aatique; Seifullah Chapman; Hammad Abdur-Raheem; Donald Thomas Surratt; Caliph Basha Ibn Abdur-Raheem; Khwaja Mahmood Hasan; Sabri Benkhala.' See also: Memorandum Opinion in 'United States *vs.* Masoud Khan, *et al.*'

163. A British court sentenced Mohammed Ajmal Khan to nine years, and he will be deported to stand trial in the US once his prison term in the UK is complete. Metropolitan Police Service, 'British Man Jailed for Nine Years for Terrorism,' 17 Mar. 2006.

164. Indictment in 'United States *vs.* Ali Asad Chandia and Mohammed Ajmal Khan.' Memorandum Opinion in 'United States *vs.* Masoud Khan, *et al.*'

165. Muhammed Aatique was sentenced to ten years and two months in prison; Ibrahim al-Hamdi to seventeen years; Ali al-Timimi to life in prison; Asad Ali Chandia to fifteen years in prison; Seifullah Chapman to eighty-five years; Khwaja Mahmood Hasan to eleven years and three months; Masoud Ahmad Khan to sixty-five years; Yong Ki Kwon to eleven years and six months and Randall Todd Royer to twenty years. Several other men who did not train with Lashkar, but were involved in the Virginia Jihad Network, were sentenced to short prison terms as well. For a detailed list of indictments, plea agreements and trial outcomes, see: The Investigative Project, 'The Rise of Lashkar-e-Tayyiba,' 2010, Appendix B.

166. Sajid Mir was known to the men as Abu Baraa, one of his many aliases. Memorandum Opinion in 'United States *vs.* Masoud Khan, *et al.*'

167. United States Attorney's Office Eastern District of Virginia, '"Virginia Jihad" Member Convicted of Perjury, Obstruction,' 5 Feb. 2007.

168. Indictment in 'United States *vs.* Ali Asad Chandia and Mohammed Ajmal Khan.'

169. United States Attorney Southern District of New York, 'Bronx Martial Arts Instructor Pleads Guilty to Conspiring to Support al Qaida,' 4 Apr. 2007.

170. Ibid.

171. Brent pled guilty to conspiring to provide material support to Lashkar and was sentenced to fifteen years in prison. Shah pled guilty to conspiring to provide material support to al-Qaeda and agreeing to train would-be jihadis in martial arts. He also received fifteen years in prison. Sabir was convicted of providing material support to al-Qaeda and sentenced to thirty years in prison. See respectively: United States Attorney Southern District of New York, 'Maryland Man Sentenced to 15 Years For Providing Material Support to Terrorist Organization,' 25 July 2007. United States Attorney Southern District of New York, 'Bronx Martial Arts Instructor Pleads Guilty to Conspiring to Support al Qaida.' United States Attorney Southern District of New York, 'Florida Doctor Convicted of Conspiring and Attempting to Support Al Qaida,' 21 May 2007.

172. United States Attorney's Office Northern District of Georgia, 'Terrorism Defendants Sentenced: Ehsanul Islam Sadequee Receives 17 Years in Prison; Co-defendant Syed Haris Ahmed Receives 13 Years,' 14 Dec. 2009.

173. United Kingdom Crown Prosecution Service, 'Terrorist "Mr Fix-It" Convicted With Two Others of Terrorism Offences,' 19 Aug. 2008.

174. Regarding the US government charge, see: Ibid. Regarding Khan's testimony, see: 'Testimony of Aabid Khan,' Blackfriars Crown Court, 17 July 2008. Found in Evan Kohlmann, *Anatomy of a Modern Homegrown Terror Cell: Aabid Khan et al.* (The NEFA Foundation, Sept. 2008).

175. Raffaello Pantucci, 'Operation Praline: The Realization of Al-Suri's Nizam, la Tanzim?,' *Perspectives on Terrorism* II, no. 12 (2008).

176. United Kingdom Crown Prosecution Service, 'Terrorist "Mr Fix-It" Convicted With Two Others of Terrorism Offences.'

177. United States Attorney's Office Northern District of Georgia, 'Terrorism Defendants Sentenced: Ehsanul Islam Sadequee Receives 17 Years in Prison; Co-defendant Syed Haris Ahmed Receives 13 Years.'

178. Ibid.

179. Kohlmann, *Anatomy of a Modern Homegrown Terror Cell.*

180. Ibid.

181. 'Testimony of Aabid Khan.'
182. Regarding Ahmed and Sadequee meeting with a member of the Toronto 18, see: Stewart Bell, 'Alleged "Toronto 18" Ringleader Named in US Terror Case,' *National Post* 5 Feb. 2009. For a comprehensive account of the Toronto 18, including the outcomes of legal action taken, see: Isabel Teotonio, 'Toronto 18,' *The Star*, http://www3.thestar.com/static/toronto18/index.html (last accessed 17 Nov. 2009).
183. United States Attorney's Office Northern District of Georgia, 'Terrorism Defendants Sentenced: Ehsanul Islam Sadequee Receives 17 Years in Prison; Co-defendant Syed Haris Ahmed Receives 13 Years.'
184. Indictment in 'United States of America *vs.* Syed Haris Ahmed and Ehsanul Islam Sadequee,' United States District Court for the Northern District of Georgia, 19 July 2006.
185. United States Attorney's Office Northern District of Georgia, 'Terrorism Defendants Sentenced: Ehsanul Islam Sadequee Receives 17 Years in Prison; Co-defendant Syed Haris Ahmed Receives 13 Years.' For more on Tsouli, who plead guilty to incitement to commit acts of terrorism on the internet, see: Gordon Corera, 'The World's Most Wanted Cyber-jihadist,' *BBC News*, 16 Jan. 2008.
186. Indictment in 'United States of America *vs.* Syed Haris Ahmed and Ehsanul Islam Sadequee.'
187. United States Attorney's Office Northern District of Georgia, 'Terrorism Defendants Sentenced: Ehsanul Islam Sadequee Receives 17 Years in Prison; Co-defendant Syed Haris Ahmed Receives 13 Years.'
188. Khan and Tanweer are known to have met with Khyam at least four times in Britain and been in telephone contact with him as well. See: United Kingdom Parliament Intelligence and Security Committee, *Could 7/7 Have Been Prevented?*.
189. Ibid. See also: Simon Israel, '7/7 an Intelligence Failure?,' *Channel 4 News*, 1 May 2006. Nicola Woolcock, Daniel McGrory, Michael Evans, Sean O'Neill and Zahid Hussain, 'Meeting of Murderous Minds on the Backstreets of Lahore,' *The Times of London*, 1 May 2007.
190. United Kingdom Parliament Intelligence and Security Committee, *Could 7/7 Have Been Prevented?*.
191. Peter Foster and Nasir Malick, 'Suicide Bombers Flew to Pakistan Together,' *The Telegraph* 19 July 2005.
192. Author interview with first Western intelligence official, NDLW. Author interview with second Western intelligence official, NDLW.
193. Ewen MacAskill and Luke Harding, 'Ambassador Denies Pakistan Linked to Bombs,' *The Guardian*, 18 July 2005. Andrew Gilligan, 'On the Conveyor Belt of Terror,' *The Evening Standard*, 24 Aug. 2006.

194. Tanweer also visited a JeM madrasa in Lahore during his final trip. See: Foster and Malick, 'Suicide Bombers Flew to Pakistan Together.'

195. Author interview with former member of the British intelligence and security establishment, NDLW. Author interview with first former US intelligence officer, NDLW.

196. Author interview with British security official, NDLW. Author interview with former member of the British intelligence and security establishment, NDLW. Author interview with second Pakistan-based Western diplomat, name withheld, Dec. 2008 in Pakistan. See also: Anthony Loyd, 'The "Charity" That Plotted the Mumbai Attacks,' *The Times of London*, 8 Dec. 2008.

197. Praveen Swami, 'Evidence Mounts of Pakistan Links,' *The Hindu*, 12 Aug. 2006.

198. Henry Chu and Sebastian Rotella, 'Three Britons Convicted of Plot to Blow up Planes,' *Los Angeles Times*, 8 Sept. 2009. John Burns, '3 Sentenced in London for Airline Plot,' *New York Times*, 12 July 2010.

199. Dexter Filkins and Souad Mekhennet, 'Pakistani Charity Under Scrutiny In Financing of Airline Bomb Plot,' *New York Times*, 13 Aug. 2006. Joshua Partlow and Kamran Khan, 'Charity Funds Said to Provide Clues to Alleged Terrorist Plot,' *Washington Post*, 15 Aug. 2006. 'UK Police Probe Terror Money Trail: Investigators Believe Alleged Plot Tied to Asian Quake Relief,' *CNN.com*, 16 Aug. 2006.

200. Reid took multiple trips in advance of his attempted attack on AA Flight #63, including to Israel, Egypt, Turkey, Pakistan, the Netherlands and Switzerland.

201. US Department of Defense, Verbatim Transcript of Combatant Status Review Tribunal Hearing for ISN 10024, Revised as of 15 Mar. 2007, http://www.defenselink.mil/news/transcript_ISN10024.pdf (last accessed 17 Nov. 2010).

202. Judgment in 'Republic of France *vs.* Rama, *et al.*'

203. 'Shoebomb Plotter Given 13 Years,' *BBC News*, 22 Apr. 2005.

204. Author interview with Jean-Louis Bruguière, former leading French Magistrate for counter-terrorism investigations, 28 Aug. 2010 via phone.

205. John Tagliabue, 'France: Prison for Man Linked to "Shoe Bomber",' *New York Times*, 17 June 2005

206. Judgment in 'Republic of France *vs.* Rama, *et al.*'

207. Ibid.

208. Author interview with Jean-Louis Bruguière, 28 Aug. 2010 via phone.

209. Sarah Ferguson, 'The French Connection,' *Sunday, Nine Network*, 8 Feb. 2004.

210. Chulov, *Australian Jihad*, p. 138.

211. Author interview with Jean-Louis Bruguière, 28 Aug. 2010 via phone.

212. Appeal Judgment in 'Fahim Khalid Lodhi *vs.* Regina,' New South Wales Court of Criminal Appeal, 20 Dec. 2007.
213. Chulov, *Australian Jihad*, p. 151.
214. 'Committal Hearing of Faheem Khalid Lodhi,' Downing Centre Local Court, Sydney 17 Dec. 2004. Found in Ibid. See also: Natasha Wallace, 'Court Battle Over Secret Evidence,' *The Sydney Morning Herald*, 18 Dec. 2004.
215. Chulov, *Australian Jihad*, p. 153
216. Bruguière, *Ce que je n'ai pas pu dire*, p. 469.
217. Ibid., p. 472.
218. Ibid, p. 473.
219. Judgment in 'Republic of France *vs.* Rama, *et al.*'
220. Appeal Judgment in 'Fahim Khalid Lodhi *vs.* Regina.' Bruguière, *Ce que je n'ai pas pu dire*, p. 472 endnote 170. 'Frenchman Played "Major" Role in Australia Terror Plot, Court Hears,' Agence France-Presse, 8 Feb. 2007.
221. Appeal Judgment in 'Fahim Khalid Lodhi *vs.* Regina.' Bruguière, *Ce que je n'ai pas pu dire*, p. 473.
222. Appeal Judgment in 'Fahim Khalid Lodhi *vs.* Regina.'
223. Bruguière, *Ce que je n'ai pas pu dire*, p. 473.
224. Chulov, *Australian Jihad*, pp. 116–124.
225. Ibid., p. 129.
226. Appeal Judgment in 'Fahim Khalid Lodhi *vs.* Regina.'
227. Australian Federal Police Fact Sheets, April 2004. Found in Chulov, *Australian Jihad*, p. 144.
228. Appeal Judgment in 'Fahim Khalid Lodhi *vs.* Regina.'
229. Chulov, *Australian Jihad*, p. 166.
230 Author interview with former Australian security official, NDLW. See also: Chulov, *Australian Jihad*, p. 143. Liz Jackson, 'Program Transcript: Willie Brigitte,' *ABC*, 9 Feb. 2004.
231. Author interview with former Australian security official, NDLW. See also: Bruguière, *Ce que je n'ai pas pu dire*, p. 473.
232. Musharraf, *In the Line of Fire*, pp. 244–257. Rashid, *Descent into Chaos*, pp. 230–231.
233. Author interview with first Pakistan-based Western diplomat, name withheld, Dec. 2008 in Pakistan. Author interview with second former US Intelligence officer, NDLW.
234. Author interview with Arif Jamal, 21 Nov. 2009 via phone.
235. 'Pakistani Kashmiri Militants Now Fighting NATO Forces.' Shahzad, 'Al-Qaeda's Guerrilla Chief Lays Out Strategy.'
236. 'Testimony of David Coleman Headley to the Indian National Investigative Agency.'
237. Rashid, *Descent into Chaos*, p. 231.

## 7. EXPANSION AND INTEGRATION

1. Nayak and Krepon, *US Crisis Management in South Asia's Twin Peaks Crisis.*
2. Author interview with Rahul Roy-Chaudhury, former member of the Indian Prime Minister's National Security Council Secretariat and currently Senior Fellow for South Asia at the International Institute for Strategic Studies, 31 Aug. 2010 via phone.
3. Author interview with Pakistani Ministry of Foreign Affairs official, name and date withheld, in Pakistan.
4. Ibid.
5. Author interview with Rahul Roy-Chaudhury, 31 Aug. 2010 via phone.
6. Steve Coll, 'The Back Channel: India and Pakistan's Secret Kashmir Talks,' *The New Yorker*, 2 Mar. 2009.
7. Ibid.
8. Ibid.
9. Author interview with Rahul Roy-Chaudhury, 31 Aug. 2010 via phone.
10. Armitage also added that indigenous violence and the violation of human rights in Indian-administered Kashmir continued as well. See: US Department of State, 'Armitage Finds Pakistan-India Relations Improving,' http://www.america.gov/st/washfile-english/2004/Jul y/20040716182403ndyblehs0.939068.html (last accessed 15 Jan. 2010).
11. Ali, 'Back to Camp.'
12. Author interview with second Pakistan-based Western diplomat, name withheld, Dec. 2008 in Pakistan. Author interview with first Western security official, NDLW.
13. Author interview with first Pakistan-based Western diplomat, name withheld, May 2009 in Pakistan.
14. Ibid. Author interview with third Pakistan-based Western diplomat, name withheld, May 2009 in Pakistan. See also: Praveen Swami, 'Signs of Another Kind of Line of Control,' *The Hindu*, 14 May 2007.
15. Author interview with first Pakistan-based Western diplomat, name withheld, Dec. 2008 in Pakistan. Author interview with second Pakistan-based Western diplomat, name withheld, Dec. 2008 in Pakistan. Author interview with second Lashkar-e-Taiba member, name withheld, May 2009 in Pakistan.
16. Author interview with Kathy Gannon, 19 Dec. 2008 in Pakistan. Author interview with Ahmed Rashid, 7 May 2009 in Pakistan. Author interview with Haroon Rashid, 19 Dec. 2008 in Pakistan.
17. US Department of State, 'Ch. 2: South and Central Asia Overview,' *Country Reports on Terrorism 2007* 30 Apr. 2008.
18. David Wood, 'Commanders Seek More Forces in Afghanistan: Taliban Prepare Offensive Against US, NATO Troops,' *The Baltimore Sun*, 8 Jan. 2007.

19. Giustozzi, *Koran, Kalashnikov and Laptop*, p. 1.
20. Ibid., pp. 34–35.
21. Author interview with Ahmed Rashid, 29 Dec. 2008 in Pakistan. Author interview with second senior officer in Pakistan security services, name withheld, May 2009 in Pakistan. Author interview with first Western intelligence official, NDLW. See, also: Kathy Gannon, 'Foreigners Boost Insurgency in Eastern Afghanistan,' Associated Press, 12 Aug. 2010.
22. Author interview with Jamaat-ul-Dawa official, name withheld, May 2009 in Pakistan. 'Testimony of David Coleman Headley to the Indian National Investigative Agency.'
23. Author interview with third Pakistan-based Western diplomat, name withheld, May 2009 in Pakistan.
24. Author interview with Pakistani journalist based in Pakistan-administered Kashmir at the time, name and date withheld, in Pakistan.
25. Author interview with member of Pakistan Anti-Terrorism Force, name withheld, May 2009 in Pakistan.
26. Intikhab Amir, 'The Waiting Game,' *Herald*, Aug. 2006.
27. Author interview with first Lashkar-e-Taiba member, name withheld, May 2009 in Pakistan.
28. Indian Ministry of Home Affairs, 'Level of Terrorist Violence and Security Situation in J&K—An Assessment.'
29. Author interview with Wilson John, Senior Fellow at the Observer Research Foundation, 11 Dec. 2008 in India.
30. Author interview with Rahul Roy-Chaudhury, 31 Aug. 2010 via phone. See also: 'Musharraf Urges India to Consider his Proposals,' Press Trust of India, 5 Feb. 2006.
31. Author interview with Pakistani journalist based in Pakistan-administered Kashmir at the time, name and date withheld, in Pakistan. See also: Jamal, *Shadow War*, p. 270.
32. Author interview with second Lashkar-e-Taiba member, name withheld, May 2009 in Pakistan. Author interview with former Lashkar-e-Taiba member, name withheld, Jan. 2009 in Pakistan.
33. Coll, 'The Back Channel.'
34. Author interview with Kanchan Lakshman, 6 Jan. 2009 in India. See also: Swami, 'Signs of Another Kind of Line of Control.' Jamal, *Shadow War*, p. 270.
35. Author interview with former Kashmiri journalist, name withheld, Jan. 2009 in India.
36. Author interview with Suba Chandran, 5 Jan. 2009 in India.
37. Swami, 'Signs of Another Kind of Line of Control.'
38. Author interview with member of the Indian security services, NDLW. Author interview with Kanchan Lakshman, 6 Jan. 2009 in India. Author interview with Praveen Swami, 8 Jan. 2009 in India. See also:

Praveen Swami, 'New Proof on Mumbai Blasts,' *The Hindu*, 1 Aug. 2006. Swami, 'The Well-Tempered Jihad.'

39. 'Testimony of David Coleman Headley to the Indian National Investigative Agency.'

40. Author interview with Rahul Roy-Chadhury, 31 Aug. 2010 via phone.

41. Tellis, *Pakistan and the War on Terror*.

42. 'Pakistan Arrests Lashkar-e-Tayyiba Founder,' *Jane's Terrorism Watch Report* 10 Aug. 2006.

43. 'The Kashmir Connection,' *Jane's Terrorism & Security Monitor*, 13 Sept. 2006. He was released on 17 Oct. when the court again ruled against his continued detention. See: 'Pakistani Court Orders Release of Militant Group Founder,' Press Trust of India, 17 Oct. 2006.

44. Author interview with Praveen Swami, 8 Jan. 2009 in India.

45. Swami, 'Riyaz Bhatkal and the Origins of the Indian Mujahidin.'

46. Praveen Swami, 'The Jihad in Paradise,' *South Asia Intelligence Review*, 19 Nov. 2007.

47. Swami, 'The Indian Mujahidin and Lashkar-i-Tayyiba's Transnational Networks.'

48. K. Srinivas Reddy, 'Islamist Terrorists Planned Blasts in Goa,' *The Hindu* 2 Feb. 2008. Johnson, 'Muzammil, Lakhvi: Same Names, ISI Links in IISc Attack Probe.'

49. Praveen Swami, 'Nasir Can Help Unravel HuJI Network: Sleuths,' *The Hindu*, 29 Jan. 2008.

50. Author interview with member of the Indian security services, NDLW. See also: Josy Joseph, 'Mumbai, Goa's Beaches, Gujarat were Terror Targets,' *Daily News & Analysis of India*, 4 Feb. 2008.

51. B. Raman, 'Mumbai Terror; The Anti-Israeli Angle,' *Outlook India*, 4 Dec. 2008.

52. Author interview with Indian journalist, name withheld, Jan. 2009 in India. Author interview with member of Indian security services, NDLW. See also: Joseph, 'Mumbai, Goa's Beaches, Gujarat were Terror Targets.'

53. 'FACTBOX-Indian Mujahideen Islamic Militant Group,' Reuters, 13 Sept. 2008.

54. For details of the targets and attacks, see: Animesh Roul, 'India's Home-Grown Jihadi Threat: A Profile of the Indian Mujahideen,' *Jamestown Terrorism Monitor* 7, no. 4 (3 Mar. 2009).

55. '"Indian Mujahideen" Claims Responsibility,' *The Hindu*, 27 July 2008.

56. Author interview with member of the Indian security services, NDLW. See also: Roul, 'India's Home-Grown Jihadi Threat.' Swami, 'Riyaz Bhatkal and the Origins of the Indian Mujahidin.'

57. Giustozzi, *Koran, Kalishnikov and Laptop*, p. 1.

58. Tellis, *Pakistan and the War on Terror*.
59. Alissa Rubin, 'Militant Group Expands Attacks in Afghanistan,' *New York Times*, 15 June 2010.
60. Author interview with former member of the British intelligence and security establishment, NDLW. Author interview with Anatol Lieven, Professor of War Studies at King's College London, 25 Aug. 2010 via phone.
61. Lt. General David Barno (Retd), 'Afghanistan on the Brink: Where Do We Go from Here?,' testimony to the Committee on Foreign Affairs in the United States House of Representatives, 15 Feb. 2007.
62. 'An Interview with Richard L. Armitage,' *Prism: A Journal of the Center for Complex Operations* 1, no. 1 (Dec. 2009).
63. Mark Mazzetti, Jane Perlez, Eric Schmitt and Andrew Lehren, 'Pakistan Aids Insurgency in Afghanistan, Reports Assert,' *New York Times*, 25 July 2010.
64. Rohan Gunaratna and Anders Nielsen, 'Al Qaeda in the Tribal Areas of Pakistan and Beyond,' *Studies in Conflict and Terrorism* 31, no. 9 (Sept. 2008).
65. Brian Glyn Williams, 'The CIA's Covert Drone War in Pakistan, 2004–2010: The History of an Assassination Campaign' *Studies in Conflict and Terrorism* 33, no. 10 (Oct. 2010).
66. Gul, *The Al Qaeda Connection*, p. 12.
67. Nicholas Schmidle, *To Live or To Perish Forever: Two Tumultuous Years in Pakistan* (New York: Henry Holt and Company, 2009), p. 143.
68. Abou Zahab, 'Salafism in Pakistan,' p. 140.
69. Schmidle, *To Live or To Perish Forever*, p. 154.
70. 'Testimony of David Coleman Headley to the Indian National Investigative Agency.'
71. Jamal, *Shadow War*, p. 270.
72. Author interview with Arif Jamal, 21 Nov. 2009 via phone.
73. Author interview with member of Jamaat-ul-Dawa senior leadership, name withheld, May 2009 in Pakistan. Author interview with Jamaat-ul-Dawa official, name withheld, May 2009 in Pakistan.
74. Author interview with first Lashkar-e-Taiba member, name withheld, May 2009 in Pakistan. Author interview with second Lashkar-e-Taiba member, name withheld, May 2009 in Pakistan.
75. 'Testimony of David Coleman Headley to the Indian National Investigative Agency.'
76. Author interview with first Western intelligence official, NDLW. Author interview with third Pakistan-based Western diplomat, name withheld, May 2009 in Pakistan.
77. Author interview with Jamaat-ul-Dawa official, name withheld, May 2009 in Pakistan.

78. 'Testimony of David Coleman Headley to the Indian National Investigative Agency.'
79. Author interview with first Western intelligence official, NDLW. Author interview with third Pakistan-based Western diplomat, name withheld, May 2009 in Pakistan. Author interview with Haroon Rashid, 19 Dec. 2008 in Pakistan. See, also: 'Cross-border Hardcore,' *Jane's Terrorism and Security Monitor*, 5 Sept. 2008. Rubin, 'Militant Group Expands Attacks in Afghanistan.'
80. Author interview with first senior officer in the Pakistan security services, name withheld, May 2009 in Pakistan. Author interview with third Pakistan-based Western diplomat, name withheld, May 2009 in Pakistan. Author interview with Mohammad Amir Rana, 11 May 2009 in Pakistan.
81. 'Testimony of David Coleman Headley to the Indian National Investigative Agency.'
82. Author interview with first senior officer in Pakistan security services, name withheld, May 2009 in Pakistan. Author interview with Mohammad Amir Rana, 11 May 2009 in Pakistan.
83. Author interview with Mohammad Amir Rana, 11 May 2009 in Pakistan. See also: Williams, 'Afghanistan's Heart of Darkness.'
84. Author interview with Mohammad Amir Rana, 11 May 2009 in Pakistan. Author interview with Rahimullah Yusufzai, 3 Jan. 2009 via phone. Author interview with Michael Semple, 23 Dec. 2008 in Pakistan.
85. Author interview with Mohammad Amir Rana, 11 May 2009 in Pakistan.
86. Author interview with member of Jamaat-ul-Dawa senior leadership, name withheld, May 2009 in Pakistan. Author interview with Jamaat-ul-Dawa official, name withheld, May 2009 in Pakistan. Author interview with second Lashkar-e-Taiba member, name withheld, May 2009 in Pakistan.
87. Author interview with Rahimullah Yusufzai, 3 Jan. 2009 via phone. Author interview with Jamaat-ul-Dawa member, name withheld, May 2009 in Pakistan. Author interview with former Lashkar-e-Taiba member, name withheld, Jan. 2009 in Pakistan. Author interview with first senior officer in the Pakistan security services, name withheld, May 2009 in Pakistan. Author interview with Western intelligence analyst, NDLW.
88. Author interview with first senior officer in the Pakistan security services, name withheld, May 2009 in Pakistan. Author interview with third Pakistan-based Western diplomat, name withheld, May 2009 in Pakistan. See also: Michael Petrou, 'The Extremists who Hit Mumbai

are Poised to Strike Again,' *Macleans*, 2 Dec. 2009. Rubin, 'Militant Group Expands Attacks in Afghanistan.'

89. Author interview with first Pakistan-based Western diplomat, name withheld, Dec. 2008 in Pakistan. Author interview with third Pakistan-based Western diplomat, name withheld, May 2009 in Pakistan. Author interview with former US security official, NDLW.

90. Michael McConnell 'Annual Threat Assessment of the Director of National Intelligence,' testimony to the United States Senate Select Committee on Intelligence, 5 Feb. 2008.

91. Author interview with first Pakistan-based Western diplomat, name withheld, Dec. 2008 in Pakistan. Author interview with former US security official, NDLW.

92. For more about the other groups operating in Bajaur, see: Gul, *The Al Qaeda Connection*, p. 88.

93. Author interview with Jamaat-ul-Dawa official, name withheld, May 2009 in Pakistan.

94. Author interview with Zahid Khan, the spokesperson for the Awami National Party in the NWFP, 31 Dec. 2008 in Pakistan. Author interview with Haroon Rashid, 19 Dec. 2008 in Pakistan. See also: Intikhab Amir, 'Flashpoint Frontier,' *Herald*, June 2006.

95. Author interview with Michael Semple, 23 Dec. 2008 in Pakistan.

96. Author interview with first Pakistan-based Western diplomat, name withheld, May 2009 in Pakistan. Author interview with third Pakistan-based Western diplomat, name withheld, May 2009 in Pakistan. Author interview with Pakistani journalist based in southern Punjab, name withheld, May 2009 in Pakistan.

97. Kathy Gannon gathered this information during interviews with the families of recruits. Author interview with Kathy Gannon, 19 Dec. 2008 in Pakistan. Several Afghan news organs reported on Lashkar's burgeoning recruitment activities in Peshawar in 2006. For example, see: 'Pakistani Party Incites Afghan Refugees Against Government,' *Afghan State TV*, 5 Oct. 2006 via BBC Monitoring. 'Pakistan Needs To Do More To Prevent Terrorism,' *Afghan State-Run Hewad*, 17 Oct. 2006 via BBC Monitoring.

98. Mushtaq Yusufzai and Carol Grisanti, 'How Two Teens Were Recruited For Jihad,' http://worldblog.msnbc.msn.com/archive/2007/03/28/103138.aspx (last accessed 8 Sept. 2008).

99. Regarding the leaked US military reports, see: Mazzetti, Perlez, Schmitt and Lehren, 'Pakistan Aids Insurgency in Afghanistan, Reports Assert.' Regarding the rise in suicide bombings, see: Christine Fair, 'Suicide Attacks in Afghanistan, 2001–2007,' United Nations Assistance Mission in Afghanistan, 9 Sept. 2007.

100. Regarding the different actors present in the Korengal, see: Williams, 'Afghanistan's Heart of Darkness.' Kathy Gannon, 'AP Impact: Pakistan Militants Focus on Afghanistan,' Associated Press, 13 July 2008.

101. David Morgan, 'RPT Analysis: US Sees Rise in Pakistani Fighters in Afghanistan,' Reuters, 31 July 2008.

102. 'Cross-border Hardcore.'

103. 'Surge of the Insurgents,' Jane's Terrorism and Security Monitor, 5 Sept. 2008. Carlotta Gall and Eric Schmitt, 'Taliban Breached NATO Base in Deadly Clash,' New York Times, 15 July 2008.

104. 'Surge of the Insurgents.'

105. 'Kabul Bomber Identified as Pakistani,' Daily News & Analysis, 4 Aug. 2008.

106. Praveen Swami, 'Kabul Attack: US Warning was Accurate,' The Hindu, 3 Aug. 2008. Regarding the Haqqani Network planning the operation, see: Mark Mazzetti and Eric Schmitt, 'C.I.A. Outlines Pakistan Links with Militants,' New York Times, 30 July 2008.

107. Mazzetti and Schmitt, 'C.I.A. Outlines Pakistan Links with Militants.'

108. Jane Perlez, Eric Schmitt and Carlotta Gall, 'Pakistan is Said to Pursue Foothold in Afghanistan,' New York Times, 24 June 2010. Mazzetti, Perlez, Schmitt and Lehren, 'Pakistan Aids Insurgency in Afghanistan, Reports Assert.'

109. Author interview with first former US intelligence officer, NDLW. See also: Rubin, 'Militant Group Expands Attacks in Afghanistan.'

110. Author interview with Jamaat-ul-Dawa official, name withheld, May 2009 in Pakistan. Author interview with former senior officer in the Pakistan Intelligence Bureau, name withheld, May 2009 in Pakistan.

111. Gul, The Al Qaeda Connection, p. 193.

112. Ibid., p. 101.

113. Ibid., p. 102. 'Taliban Kill Rival Group Leaders,' The Daily Times, 20 July 2008.

114. Author interview with Rahimullah Yusufzai, 3 Jan. 2009 via phone.

115. Gul, The Al Qaeda Connection, p. 102. 'Taliban Kill Rival Group Leaders.'

116. Mukkaram Khan, 'TTP "Arrests" 2 Intelligence Operatives in Mohmand,' The Daily Times, 22 July 2008. Iqbal Khattak, 'Mohmand Agency Now Under Taleban's Control,' The Daily Times, 24 July 2008.

117. Gul, The Al Qaeda Connection, pp. 102–103.

118. Author interview with first senior officer in the Pakistan security services, name withheld, May 2009 in Pakistan. Author interview with member of Pakistan Anti-Terrorism Force, name withheld, May 2009 in Pakistan.

119. Author interview with first senior officer in the Pakistan security services, name withheld, May 2009 in Pakistan. Author interview with

second senior officer in the Pakistan security services, name withheld, May 2009 in Pakistan.

120. Author interview with Kathy Gannon, 19 Dec. 2008 in Pakistan.

121. Author interview with Tariq Pervez, 14 May 2009 in Pakistan. Author interview with member of Pakistan Anti-Terrorism Force, name withheld, May 2009 in Pakistan. Author interview with first senior officer in the Pakistan security services, name withheld, May 2009 in Pakistan. Author interview with third Pakistan-based Western diplomat, name withheld, May 2009 in Pakistan.

122. Author interview with Tariq Pervez, 14 May 2009 in Pakistan. Author interview with member of Pakistan Anti-Terrorism Force, name withheld, May 2009 in Pakistan. Author interview with third Pakistan-based Western diplomat, name withheld, May 2009 in Pakistan.

123. 'Testimony of David Coleman Headley to the Indian National Investigative Agency.'

124. Ibid.

## 8. STORMING THE WORLD STAGE

1. 'Mohammed Ajmal Amir Kasab confession before Additional Chief Metropolitan Magistrate Rama Vijay Sawant Vagule.' '"Sir, mujhe mera gunaah kabool hai [Sir, I admit my crime]",' *The Times of India*, 21 July 2009.

2. At some point during those three weeks, Muzaffar's older brother came to the camp and took him home.

3. 'Mohammed Ajmal Amir Kasab confession before Additional Chief Metropolitan Magistrate Rama Vijay Sawant Vagule.' See also: '"Sir, mujhe mera gunaah kabool hai [Sir, I admit my crime]".'

4. Ibid.

5. Praveen Swami, 'Gaps in Pakistan's 26/11 Investigations Worry India,' *The Hindu*, 30 July 2009.

6. Lydia Polgreen and Souad Mekhennet, 'Militant Group Is Intact After Mumbai Siege,' *New York Times*, 29 Sept. 2009.

7. According to Kasab, all of them were killed by Indian security forces.

8. 'Mohammed Ajmal Amir Kasab confession before Additional Chief Metropolitan Magistrate Rama Vijay Sawant Vagule.' See also: '"Sir, mujhe mera gunaah kabool hai [Sir, I admit my crime]".'

9. 'Kasab Used Fake I-card, Says Principal of Hyderabad College,' *The Times of India* 19 May 2009.

10. 'Mohammed Ajmal Amir Kasab confession before Additional Chief Metropolitan Magistrate Rama Vijay Sawant Vagule.'

11. 'Final Report: Mumbai Terror Attack Cases.'

12. 'Kasab Gives More Details on 26/11 Attacks,' *The Times of India*, 21 July 2009.

13. 'Testimony of David Coleman Headley to the Indian National Investigative Agency.'

14. 'Mohammed Ajmal Amir Kasab confession before Additional Chief Metropolitan Magistrate Rama Vijay Sawant Vagule.' 'Dossier of Evidence Relating to Mumbai Terrorist Attacks,' Prepared by the Indian Ministry of External Affairs, 9 Jan. 2009. Author in possession of copy.

15. 'Dossier of Evidence Relating to Mumbai Terrorist Attacks.'

16. 'Final Report: Mumbai Terror Attack Cases.'

17. 'Dossier of Evidence Relating to Mumbai Terrorist Attacks.'

18. Dan Reed, 'Terror in Mumbai,' *Home Box Office*, 23 Nov. 2009.

19. 'Dossier of Evidence Relating to Mumbai Terrorist Attacks.' See also: Reed, 'Terror in Mumbai.'

20. 'Dossier of Evidence Relating to Mumbai Terrorist Attacks.'

21. 'Testimony of David Coleman Headley to the Indian National Investigative Agency.'

22. Reed, 'Terror in Mumbai.'

23. Ibid.

24. Ibid.

25. 'Final Report: Mumbai Terror Attack Cases.'

26. Reed, 'Terror in Mumbai.'

27. Ibid.

28. 'Final Report: Mumbai Terror Attack Cases.'

29. Ibid.

30. Reed, 'Terror in Mumbai.'

31. Ibid.

32. 'Final Report: Mumbai Terror Attack Cases.'

33. Kenny Kemp, 'An Indian Nightmare Revisited,' *The Times of London*, 9 Aug. 2009.

34. 'Final Report: Mumbai Terror Attack Cases.'

35. Reed, 'Terror in Mumbai.'

36. Angel Rabasa *et al.*, *The Lessons of Mumbai* (Arlington, VA: RAND Corporation, 2009).

37. 'Final Report: Mumbai Terror Attack Cases.'

38. Reed, 'Terror in Mumbai.'

39. Ibid.

40. 'Terrorists Ring Up India TV Twice During Siege Using Hostages' Cellphones,' *India TV*, 27 Nov. 2008. See also: 'Pak Owns Up to Two More Mumbai Attackers,' *The Times of India*, 20 July 2009.

41. 'Translation of Message From "Deccan Mujahideen",' *Wall Street Journal*, 28 Nov. 2008.

42. David Headley identified Sajid Mir as the handler speaking to the fidayeen at the Chabad House. 'Testimony of David Coleman Headley to the Indian National Investigative Agency.'

43. Reed, 'Terror in Mumbai. US court documents in which Mir is identified as 'Lashkar Member A' discuss his attempt to facilitate Kasab's release. See: 'Superceding Indictment in 'United States of America vs. Ilyas Kashmiri, Abdur Rehman Hashim Syed [a/k/a 'Major Abdur Rehman,' a/k/a 'Pasha'], David Coleman Headley [a/k/a 'Daood Gilani'], Tahawwur Hussain Rana,' United States District Court Northern District of Illinois Eastern Division, 14 Jan. 2010.

44. 'Final Report: Mumbai Terror Attack Cases.'

45. Sebastian Rotella, 'FBI Was Warned Years in Advance of Mumbai Attacker's Terror Ties,' ProPublica, 15 Oct. 2010.

46. Saikat Datta, 'The Gateway of India,' Outlook India, 29 Nov. 2009.

47. S Balakrishnan, '26/11 Panel Severely Indicts Maharashtra Govt,' The Times of India, 29 July 2009.

48. Rabasa et al., The Lessons of Mumbai.

49. Ajai Sahni, 'Mumbai: The Uneducable Indian,' South Asia Intelligence Review 7, no. 21 (Dec. 2008).

50. Rabasa et al., The Lessons of Mumbai.

51. 'Dossier of Evidence Relating to Mumbai Terrorist Attacks.'

52. Since the 2008 Mumbai attacks, several additional bases around the country have been opened.

53. Rabasa et al., The Lessons of Mumbai.

54. Sahni, 'Mumbai: The Uneducable Indian.'

55. Pranab Dhal Samanta, 'Only One Taj Master Key, No Hotel Maps, NSG Walked in Hands Tied,' India Express, 7 June 2009.

56. Rabasa et al., The Lessons of Mumbai.

57. Samanta, 'Only One Taj Master Key, No Hotel Maps, NSG Walked in Hands Tied.'

58. Ibid.

59. Reed, 'Terror in Mumbai.' Marie Brenner, 'Anatomy of a Siege,' Vanity Fair Nov. 2009.

60. 41 calls totaling 147 minutes were made from Taj Mahal Hotel, 62 calls totaling 261 minutes were made from the Trident Oberoi Hotel and 181 calls totaling 586 minutes were made from the Chabad House. 'Final Report: Mumbai Terror Attack Cases.'

61. Author interview with member of the Indian security services, NDLW. See also: Reed, 'Terror in Mumbai.'

62. Accounting of the material found on board the ship, from: 'Dossier of Evidence Relating to Mumbai Terrorist Attacks.'

63. Reed, 'Terror in Mumbai.'

64. 'Mohammed Ajmal Amir Kasab confession before Additional Chief Metropolitan Magistrate Rama Vijay Sawant Vagule.'
65. '26/11 Accused Kasab Confessed Voluntarily: Magistrate,' *The Times of India*, 30 Sept. 2009.
66. For the published account, see: '"Sir, mujhe mera gunaah kabool hai [Sir, I admit my crime]".'
67. Regarding guilty verdict, see: '26/11: Kasab Guilty; Ansari, Sabauddin Shaikh Acquitted,' *The Times of India* 3 May 2010. Regarding sentencing, see: Rahi Gaikwad, 'Kasab Sentenced to Death on Five Counts,' *The Hindu* 7 May 2010.
68. Saeed Shah, 'Revealed: Home of Mumbai's Gunman in Pakistan Village,' *The Observer*, 7 Dec. 2008.
69. 'Zardari Distances Pakistan from Mumbai Attack,' *BBC News*, 17 Dec. 2008.
70. 'Dossier of Evidence Relating to Mumbai Terrorist Attacks.'
71. 'Pak Concedes India Has Got Proof Against Pak Nationals,' *The Times of India*, 17 Jan. 2009. Rama Lakshmi and Shaiq Hussain, 'Assault on Mumbai Planned in Pakistan,' *Washington Post*, 13 Feb. 2009.
72. Ketaki Gokhale, 'Singh Defends Move to Mend Pakistan Ties,' *The Wall Street Journal* 30 July 2009.
73. 'Testimony of David Coleman Headley to the Indian National Investigative Agency.'
74. Plea Agreement in 'United States *vs.* David Coleman Headley [a/k/a 'Daood Gilani'],' The United States District Court for the Northern District of Illinois, Eastern Division, 18 Mar. 2010.
75. 'Mohammed Ajmal Amir Kasab confession before Additional Chief Metropolitan Magistrate Rama Vijay Sawant Vagule.'
76. The three are described in US court documents as Lashkar-e-Taiba Members A, B and C. See: Plea Agreement in 'United States of America vs. David Coleman Headley [a/k/a 'Daood Gilani'].' Superceding Indictment in 'United States of America vs. Ilyas Kashmiri, Abdur Rehman Hashim Syed [a/k/a 'Major Abdur Rehman,' a/k/a 'Pasha'], David Coleman Headley [a/k/a 'Daood Gilani'], Tahawwur Hussain Rana.' See also: Baqir Sajjad Syed 'India Comes Up With Six New Names In Mumbai Case,' *Dawn*, 4 July 2010. '6 "Guilty" of 26/11 Still Free, Pak Told,' *The Times of India*, 29 June 2010.
77. Major Iqbal is described in US court documents as Person A. See: Superceding Indictment in 'United States of America vs. Ilyas Kashmiri, Abdur Rehman Hashim Syed [a/k/a 'Major Abdur Rehman,' a/k/a 'Pasha'], David Coleman Headley [a/k/a 'Daood Gilani'], Tahawwur Hussain Rana.' See also: Jane Perlez, Eric Schmitt and Ginger Thompson, 'U.S. Had Warnings on Plotter of Mumbai Attack,' *New York Times*, 16 Oct. 2010.

78. Author interview with first former US intelligence officer, NDLW. Author interview with second Western security official, NDLW. See also: Bob Woodward, *Obama's Wars* (New York: Simon & Schuster, 2010), p. 46. Polgreen and Mekhennet, 'Militant Group Is Intact After Mumbai Siege.' Sebastian Rotella, 'Mumbai Case Offers Rare Picture of Ties Between Pakistan's Intelligence Service, Militants,' *ProPublica*, 29 Dec. 2010.

79. 'Testimony of David Coleman Headley to the Indian National Investigative Agency.'

80. Ginger Thompson, 'A Terror Suspect With Feet in East and West,' *New York Times*, 21 Nov. 2009.

81. Plea Agreement in 'United States *vs.* David Coleman Headley [a/k/a 'Daood Gilani'].'

82. Rotella, 'FBI Was Warned Years in Advance of Mumbai Attacker's Terror Ties.'

83. Joseph Tanfani, John Shiffman and Kathleen Brady Shea, 'American Suspect in Mumbai Attack was DEA Informant,' *McClatchy*, 14 Dec. 2009.

84. 'Testimony of David Coleman Headley to the Indian National Investigative Agency.' Regarding Headley's training, see also: US Department of Justice 'Chicago Resident David Coleman Headley Pleads Guilty to Role in India and Denmark Terrorism Conspiracies,' 18 Mar. 2010.

85. 'Testimony of David Coleman Headley to the Indian National Investigative Agency.'

86. Plea Agreement in 'United States *vs.* David Coleman Headley [a/k/a 'Daood Gilani'].'

87. Sebastian Rotella, 'Feds Confirm Mumbai Plotter Trained with Terrorists while Working for DEA,' *ProPublica*, 16 Oct. 2010.

88. Ibid. Rotella, 'FBI Was Warned Years in Advance of Mumbai Attacker's Terror Ties.'

89. Perlez, Schmitt and Thompson, 'U.S. Had Warnings on Plotter of Mumbai Attack.'

90. Rotella, 'FBI Was Warned Years in Advance of Mumbai Attacker's Terror Ties.'

91. Perlez, Schmitt and Thompson, 'U.S. Had Warnings on Plotter of Mumbai Attack.'

92. Rotella, 'FBI Was Warned Years in Advance of Mumbai Attacker's Terror Ties.'

93. Author interview with member of the Indian security services, NDLW. Author interview with Western security official, NDLW. 'Testimony of David Coleman Headley to the Indian National Investigative Agency.' Regarding Samir Ali, see also: 'India Asks Pakistan to Hand Over 2 Army Officers,' *The Times of India* 26 Feb. 2010. '26/11 Linked to the ISI:

US Research Group,' *The Express Tribune* 13 July 2010. Tom Wright, 'Pakistan Investigates Ex-Army Officers in Mumbai Attacks,' *The Wall Street Journal* 20 July 2010.

94. 'Testimony of David Coleman Headley to the Indian National Investigative Agency.' See also: Plea Agreement in 'United States *vs.* David Coleman Headley [a/k/a 'Daood Gilani'].'

95. 'Testimony of David Coleman Headley to the Indian National Investigative Agency.' See also: Plea Agreement in 'United States of America vs. David Coleman Headley [a/k/a 'Daood Gilani'].' Superceding Indictment in 'United States of America vs. Ilyas Kashmiri, Abdur Rehman Hashim Syed [a/k/a 'Major Abdur Rehman,' a/k/a 'Pasha'], David Coleman Headley [a/k/a 'Daood Gilani'], Tahawwur Hussain Rana.'

96. 'Testimony of David Coleman Headley to the Indian National Investigative Agency.'

97. Ibid.

98. Ibid. Regarding Headley's reconnaissance of the National Defence College, see also: Plea Agreement in 'United States of America vs. David Coleman Headley [a/k/a 'Daood Gilani'].'

99. 'Testimony of David Coleman Headley to the Indian National Investigative Agency.'

100. Ibid.

101. Ibid. Regarding Headley's surveillance of potential landing sites, see also: Plea Agreement in 'United States of America vs. David Coleman Headley [a/k/a 'Daood Gilani'].' Superceding Indictment in 'United States of America vs. Ilyas Kashmiri, Abdur Rehman Hashim Syed [a/k/a 'Major Abdur Rehman,' a/k/a 'Pasha'], David Coleman Headley [a/k/a 'Daood Gilani'], Tahawwur Hussain Rana.'

102. 'Testimony of David Coleman Headley to the Indian National Investigative Agency.'

103. Regarding Headley's surveillance of all the targets struck during his final reconnaissance trip, see: Plea Agreement in 'United States of America vs. David Coleman Headley [a/k/a 'Daood Gilani'].'

104. 'Testimony of David Coleman Headley to the Indian National Investigative Agency.'

105. The Israeli government made a request through diplomatic channels to try to save the hostages. When Sajid directed the fidayeen at the Chabad House to kill them he evinced the hope that doing so would 'spoil relations between India and Israel.' See: Reed, 'Terror in Mumbai.'

106. The training schedule aligns with the one Kasab described in his confession. 'Mohammed Ajmal Amir Kasab confession before Additional Chief Metropolitan Magistrate Rama Vijay Sawant Vagule.' See also:

Plea Agreement in 'United States of America vs. David Coleman Headley [a/k/a 'Daood Gilani'].' Superceding Indictment in 'United States of America vs. Ilyas Kashmiri, Abdur Rehman Hashim Syed [a/k/a 'Major Abdur Rehman,' a/k/a 'Pasha'], David Coleman Headley [a/k/a 'Daood Gilani'], Tahawwur Hussain Rana.'

107. 'Testimony of David Coleman Headley to the Indian National Investigative Agency.'

108. According to Kasab's confession, the fidayeen also went through the Daura-e-Ribat during this time. 'Mohammed Ajmal Amir Kasab confession before Additional Chief Metropolitan Magistrate Rama Vijay Sawant Vagule.'

109. 'Testimony of David Coleman Headley to the Indian National Investigative Agency.'

110. 'Mohammed Ajmal Amir Kasab confession before Additional Chief Metropolitan Magistrate Rama Vijay Sawant Vagule.'

111. 'Testimony of David Coleman Headley to the Indian National Investigative Agency.'

112. Author interview with second Pakistan-based Western diplomat, name withheld, May 2009 in Pakistan. See also: Polgreen and Mekhennet, 'Militant Group Is Intact After Mumbai Siege.'

113. Al-Yaqeen Media Center, 'Bombay Operations: A Study of the Local, Regional and International Dimensions,' posted to As-Sahab Foundation for Media Production, 6 Jan. 2009, http://as-sahab.blog.com/20009/01/06/al-yaqeen-media-presentsbombay-operation/ (last accessed 8 Jan. 2009). See also: 'Popularity of LeT Zooms on Jihadi Websites, Chatrooms,' The Times of India, 13 Dec. 2008.

114. Siobhan Gorman and Susan Schmidt, 'Officials Worry Attacks in Mumbai Could Spur Copycats in the West,' The Wall Street Journal, 11 Dec. 2008.

## 9. DAYS OF RECKONING

1. Tariq Naqash and Syed Irfan Raza, 'Operation Against LeT-Dawa Launched in AJK,' Dawn, 9 Dec. 2008.

2. Jane Perlez and Salman Masood, 'Pakistan Raids Group Suspected in Attacks,' New York Times, 8 Dec. 2008.

3. 'Zardari Distances Pakistan from Mumbai Attack.'

4. 'UN Bans Jamaat-ud-Dawa; Declares it a Terror Outfit,' The Times of India, 11 Dec. 2008. The other two men were Mahmoud Mohammad Ahmed Bahaziq and Haji Mohammad Ashraf. Several more Lashkar leaders were added later. The complete list can be found at: United Nations, 'The Consolidated List established and maintained by the 1267 Committee with respect to Al-Qaida, Usama bin Laden, and the Taliban

and other individuals, groups, undertakings and entities associated with them.'

5. 'UN Bans Jamaat-ud-Dawa; Declares it a Terror Outfit.'

6. Jane Perlez and Salman Masood, 'Pakistan Detains Founder of Group Suspected in Mumbai Attacks,' *New York Times*, 11 Dec. 2008.

7. 'Government Takes Control of Dawa Headquarters,' *The Daily Times*, 26 Jan. 2009. 'JuD Camps, Websites Shut, Chief Arrested: Pak,' *The Times of India*, 15 Jan. 2009.

8. 'Mumbai Terror Attacks: Details of 5 Accused Arrested and 13 Accused Declared Proclaimed Offenders,' Police Station SIU FIA Islamabad Case No. 01/2009, 12 Feb. 2009. Author in possession of copy.

9. 'Document Details Mumbai Charges,' *BBC News*, 4 Dec. 2009.

10. 'Pakistan Charges Seven over Mumbai Attacks,' *The Guardian*, 25 Nov. 2009.

11. Zahid Hussain, '"Mastermind" of Mumbai Attack Preaches at Mosque in Lahore,' *The Times of London*, 21 Nov. 2009.

12. Author interview with member of the Indian security services, NDLW. See also: 'Pakistan "Not Obliged" to Arrest Hafiz Saeed: Malik,' *Dawn* 2 Sept. 2009. Abhishek Sharan, 'Saeed Monitored 26/11: Headley,' *Hindustan Times*, 8 July 2010.

13. 'India Asks Pakistan To Hand Over 2 Army Officers.'

14. Wright, 'Pakistan Investigates Ex-Army Officers in Mumbai Attacks.'

15. Nirupama Subramanian, 'The Flaw That Let JuD Chief Hafiz Saeed Off the Hook,' *The Hindu*, 3 June 2009. 'LHC Orders Release of Hafiz Saeed,' *Geo News Television*, 2 June 2009.

16. Author interview with Matthew Rosenberg, journalist with the *Wall Street Journal*, 11 June 2009 via phone. Matthew Rosenberg and Glenn Simpson, 'Money Eludes Pakistan's Crackdown on Accused Terror Group,' *Wall Street Journal*, 13 Dec. 2008.

17. Markaz al-Dawa flyer, 'Don't Forget Mujahideen and Refugees of Kashmir & Afghanistan During Your Eid Delights.'

18. Author interview with first Pakistan-based diplomat, name withheld, May 2009 in Pakistan. Author interview with third Pakistan-based diplomat, name withheld, May 2009 in Pakistan.

19. Author interview with former Punjab provincial government official, name withheld, May 2009 in Pakistan.

20. Rosenberg and Simpson, 'Money Eludes Pakistan's Crackdown on Accused Terror Group.'

21. Sachin Parashar, 'Zardari's Move on Terror Aliases an Eyewash?,' *The Times of India*, 7 Oct. 2009.

22. Author interview with third Pakistan-based diplomat, name withheld, May 2009 in Pakistan. Declan Walsh, *The Guardian*'s Pakistan correspondent observed this fundraising first hand while covering FIF relief

efforts. Author interview with Declan Walsh, 14 May 2009 in Pakistan. See also: Matthew Rosenberg, 'A Year After Mumbai Attack, Militants Thrive,' *The Wall Street Journal*, 24 Nov. 2009.

23. Praveen Swami, 'Saeed's Release Raises Fears of Fresh Terror Wave,' *The Hindu*, 3 June 2009. Declan Walsh, 'Banned Group Helping Swat Refugees,' *The Guardian*, 13 May 2009.

24. FIF web site, http://www.fif.org.pk/ (last accessed 20 Nov. 2010).

25. Two Pakistani journalists observed this practice; both requested anonymity. This claim was also reported in the Indian media. See: Praveen Swami, 'The Red Hot Line,' *Outlook India*, 4 Sept. 2009.

26. Author interview with Jamaat-ul-Dawa official, name withheld, May 2009 in Pakistan. Author interview with Jamaat-ul-Dawa Amir for Rawalpindi, name withheld, May 2009 in Pakistan.

27. Walsh, 'Banned Group Helping Swat Refugees.'

28. Ibid.

29. Saeed Shah, 'Pakistan Floods: Islamic Fundamentalists Fill State Aid Void,' *The Guardian*, 3 Aug. 2010.

30. Myra MacDonald and Kamran Haider, 'Islamist Charity Aims to be Pakistanis' Salvation,' Reuters, 3 Sept. 2010.

31. Author interview with former Punjab provincial government official, name withheld, May 2009 in Pakistan.

32. Intikhab Hanif, 'Govt Takes Over Dawa Offices in Muridke,' *Dawn*, 26 Jan. 2009.

33. Author interview with Abu Ehsan, 8 May 2009 in Pakistan.

34. 'Pakistan "Gave Funds" to Group on UN Terror Blacklist,' *BBC News*, 16 June 2010.

35. 'Jamaat-ud-Dawa Easily Evades Ban,' *Dawn*, 24 Feb. 2010.

36. 'Pakistan "Gave Funds" to Group on UN Terror Blacklist.'

37. 'Punjab Bans 23 Outfits Acting Under New Names,' *Dawn*, 6 July 2010.

38. The men responsible for arranging meetings with Lashkar militants requested anonymity.

39. Petrou, 'The Extremists who Hit Mumbai are Poised to Strike Again.'

40. Syed Shoaib Hasan, 'Banned Pakistani Groups "Expand",' *BBC News*, 30 June 2009.

41. Praveen Swami, 'Lashkar-e-Taiba Flourishes on Facebook,' *The Hindu*, 13 Apr. 2010.

42. JuD Youtube page, http://www.youtube.com/user/JamaatudDawah (last accessed 11 Nov. 2010).

43. Author interview with member of Jamaat-ul-Dawa senior leadership, name withheld, May 2009 in Pakistan.

44. Abdullah Ghaznavi claims to operate from Indian-administered Kashmir, but it has been alleged the name is an alias for a Pakistan-based member of JuD. See, for example: Amir Mir, 'Jamaatul Daawa Spokes-

man Impersonates As Lashkar-e-Toiba Spokesman,' *Middle East Transparent*, 4 Jan. 2009. Regarding the claim of credit following the March 2009 offensive, see: M. Saleem Pandit, 'Lashkar Hand in J&K Encounter, Group Warns of More Attacks on Army,' *The Times of India*, 26 Mar. 2009. For details of the operation, see: Animesh Roul, 'Lashkar-e-Taiba Resumes Operations Against Indian Forces in Jammu and Kashmir,' *Jamestown Terrorism Monitor 7*, no. 8 (3 Apr. 2009).

45. Hari Kumar, '4 Dead After 20-Hour Gun Battle in Kashmir,' *New York Times*, 7 Jan. 2010.
46. International Crisis Group, *Steps Towards Peace*.
47. 'Vale of Tears,' *The Economist*, 28 Aug.–3 Sept. 2010.
48. Swami, 'The Red Hot Line.'
49. 'Only 500 Militants Active in Kashmir: J&K Police Chief,' *The Times of India*, 15 June 2010.
50. Swami, 'The Red Hot Line.'
51. International Crisis Group, *Steps Towards Peace*.
52. 'Strike Triggered by Teen's Death Shuts Indian Kashmir,' *Voice of America*, 14 June 2010.
53. Hafsa Kanjwal, 'A Dispatch from Srinagar, Kashmir,' *The AfPak Channel*, 12 July 2010.
54. Ben Arnoldy, 'Kashmir Intifada? New View of India, Pakistan Territory Dispute,' *Christian Science Monitor*, 13 July 2010.
55. 'Vale of Tears.'
56. Rubin, 'Militant Group Expands Attacks in Afghanistan.'
57. Author interview with first former US intelligence officer, NDLW. Author interview with second Western security official, NDLW. See also: Rubin, 'Militant Group Expands Attacks in Afghanistan.'
58. Kevin P. Bell, 'July 3: Afghan-ISAF Operations in Eastern Afghanistan,' ISAF Joint Command—Afghanistan, 3 July 2010.
59. Karin Brulliard, 'Afghan Intelligence Ties Pakistani Group Lashkar-i-Taiba to Recent Kabul Attack,' *Washington Post*, 3 Mar. 2010.
60. Ibid.
61. Lynne O'Donnell, 'Eight Killed in Suicide Attack Near Kabul Hotel,' Agence France-Presse, 14 Dec. 2009. Rubin, 'Militant Group Expands Attacks in Afghanistan.'
62. Jason Motlagh, 'Pakistani Insurgent Group Expands in Afghanistan,' *Time*, 10 Sept. 2010.
63. Brulliard, 'Afghan Intelligence Ties Pakistani Group Lashkar-i-Taiba to Recent Kabul Attack.' Rubin, 'Militant Group Expands Attacks in Afghanistan.'
64. 'German Bakery Blast: 2 LeT Men with Pak Links Arrested,' Press Trust of India, 8 Sept. 2010. 'Indian Police Arrest Two over Pune Bakery Bombing,' *Dawn*, 8 Sept. 2010.

65. Mateen Hafeez & Asseem Shaikh, 'German Bakery Blast Mastermind Arrested,' *The Times of India*, 9 Sept. 2010.
66. Praveen Swami, 'Pune Bombing Could Herald Renewed Lashkar Offensive,' *The Hindu*, 15 Feb. 2010.
67. Roul, 'After Pune, Details Emerge on the Karachi Project and its Threat to India.' Diwakar and Pervez Iqbal Siddiqui, 'Arrested IM Terrorist Says Fresh Attacks on Course,' *The Times of India*, 7 Mar. 2010. 'Pune Blast Part of Lashkar's "Karachi Project"?,' *The Times of India*, 15 Feb. 2010.
68. 'Testimony of David Coleman Headley to the Indian National Investigative Agency.'
69. Plea Agreement in 'United States of America *vs.* David Coleman Headley [a/k/a 'Daood Gilani'].'
70. 'Testimony of David Coleman Headley to the Indian National Investigative Agency.'
71. Ibid. For open source accounts, see: Plea Agreement in 'United States of America *vs.* David Coleman Headley [a/k/a 'Daood Gilani'].' Superceding Indictment in 'United States of America *vs.* Ilyas Kashmiri, Abdur Rehman Hashim Syed [a/k/a 'Major Abdur Rehman,' a/k/a 'Pasha'], David Coleman Headley [a/k/a 'Daood Gilani'], Tahawwur Hussain Rana.'
72. Criminal Complaint in 'United States of America *vs.* David Headley [a/k/a 'Daood Gilani'],' United States District Court Northern District of Illinois Eastern Division, 11 Oct. 2009.
73. Plea Agreement in 'United States of America *vs.* David Coleman Headley [a/k/a 'Daood Gilani'].'
74. 'Testimony of David Coleman Headley to the Indian National Investigative Agency.'
75. Ibid. Regarding Headley's surveillance of Chabad Houses and the National Defence College in India, see also: Plea Agreement in 'United States of America *vs.* David Coleman Headley [a/k/a 'Daood Gilani'].'
76. Ibid.
77. Author interview with member of JuD senior leadership, name withheld, May 2009 in Pakistan. See also: Plea Agreement in 'United States of America vs. David Coleman Headley [a/k/a 'Daood Gilani'].'
78. Plea Agreement in 'United States of America *vs.* David Coleman Headley [a/k/a 'Daood Gilani'].'
79. 'Testimony of David Coleman Headley to the Indian National Investigative Agency.'
80. Plea Agreement in 'United States of America *vs.* David Coleman Headley [a/k/a 'Daood Gilani'].' Information regarding the funding for Headley's travel from: 'Testimony of David Coleman Headley to the Indian National Investigative Agency.'

81. 'Testimony of David Coleman Headley to the Indian National Investigative Agency.'

82. Plea Agreement in 'United States of America *vs.* David Coleman Headley [a/k/a 'Daood Gilani'].' Information about the visits to the UK and Sweden from: 'Testimony of David Coleman Headley to the Indian National Investigative Agency.'

83. Rotella, 'Feds Confirm Mumbai Plotter Trained With Terrorists While Working for DEA.'

84. Criminal Complaint in 'United States of America *vs.* Abdur Rehman Hashim Syed [a/k/a 'Pasha,' 'Major,' 'Abdur Rahman'].'

85. 'Testimony of David Coleman Headley to the Indian National Investigative Agency.'

86. Superceding Indictment in 'United States of America *vs.* Ilyas Kashmiri, Abdur Rehman Hashim Syed [a/k/a 'Major Abdur Rehman,' a/k/a 'Pasha'], David Coleman Headley [a/k/a 'Daood Gilani'], Tahawwur Hussain Rana.'

87. Criminal Complaint in 'United States of America *vs.* Abdur Rehman Hashim Syed [a/k/a 'Pasha,' 'Major,' 'Abdur Rahman'].'

88. Plea Agreement in 'United States of America *vs.* David Coleman Headley [a/k/a 'Daood Gilani'].'

89. Superceding Indictment in 'United States of America vs. Ilyas Kashmiri, Abdur Rehman Hashim Syed [a/k/a 'Major Abdur Rehman,' a/k/a 'Pasha'], David Coleman Headley [a/k/a 'Daood Gilani'], Tahawwur Hussain Rana.'

90. 'Bangladesh Police Arrest Three Pakistani Suspects,' *Dawn* 13 Nov. 2009.

91. David Montero, 'Pakistani Militants Expand Abroad, Starting in Bangladesh,' *Christian Science Monitor*, 5 Aug. 2010. Kailash Sarkar, 'Lashkar Plotters Identified,' *The Daily Star—Bangladesh*, 8 Nov. 2009.

92. Montero, 'Pakistani Militants Expand Abroad, Starting in Bangladesh.' Shariful Islam, '2 Lashkar Men Held inside Indian Border,' *The Daily Star—Bangladesh*, 24 Nov. 2009.

93. Montero, 'Pakistani Militants Expand Abroad, Starting in Bangladesh.'

94. Author interview with third Western security official, NDLW. Author interview with Bangladeshi security official, NDLW.

95. Interview with Western intelligence analyst, NDLW.

96. Regarding information provided by Headley, see: 'Bangladesh Police Arrest Three Pakistani Suspects.' Regarding the interception of conversations with Syed, see: Praveen Swami, 'David Headley's Arrest Preempted Strikes in India,' *The Hindu*, 13 Nov. 2009. Regarding the provision of funding and instructions, see: Sarkar, 'Lashkar Plotters Identified.'

97. 'Testimony of David Coleman Headley to the Indian National Investigative Agency.'

CONCLUSION

1. Ashish Sen, 'Double Take: The US Now Acknowledges Lashkar-e-Toiba's Global Ambit,' *Outlook India* 12 Apr. 2010.
2. Author interview with former senior ISI official, name withheld, Dec. 2008 in Pakistan.
3. Author interview with second senior officer in Pakistan security services, name withheld, May 2009 in Pakistan.
4. Author interview with ISI officer, name and date withheld, in Pakistan.
5. Author interview with Jamaat-ul-Dawa member, name and date withheld, in Pakistan.
6. Haqqani, *Pakistan: Between Mosque and Military*, p. 3.
7. Carl von Clausewitz, *On War*, eds. Michael Howard and Peter Paret (Princeton, N.J.: Princeton University Press, 1976), pp. 88–89.
8. Author interview with former Lashkar-e-Taiba member, name withheld, Jan. 2009 in Pakistan.
9. Friedrich Nietzsche *Thus Spoke Zarathustra*, trans. R.J. Hollingdale (London: Penguin, 1969), p. 74.
10. Author interview with Zaffar Abbas, Editor of *Dawn*, 24 Dec. 2008 in Pakistan.
11. Briefing by the Pakistan security services, 15 May 2009 in Pakistan.

# INDEX

Aatique, Mohammed: member of
Virginia Jihad Network, 157
Afghani, Sajjad: arrest of (1994), 55
Afghanistan: 11, 24, 82, 100–1, 118,
148, 154, 162, 194, 196, 204, 227,
233, 249, 264, 266; and India, 18;
Coalition forces in, 177, 188–9,
232; Combat Outpost Wanat
attack (2008), 199; Deobandi
militant groups in, 29; Durand
line, 18, 114, 201, 265; fall of
Democratic Republic of (1992),
53; government of, 18, 104;
insurgency in, 245, 263; Invasion
of (2001), 102, 110, 112, 123, 130,
149, 151, 158; Islamists in, 18, 70;
Kabul, 18, 106, 110, 248; Kunar,
19–20, 41, 109, 151, 194, 197, 247;
Nangarhar, 247; NATO presence
in, 188; Paktia, 2, 20; presence of
Lashkar-e-Taiba in, 6, 106, 178;
Salafism in, 41, 109, 150–1, 198;
Soviet Invasion of (1979–89),
2–3, 11, 17–19, 27, 38–9, 41–2,
54, 92, 108, 186, 189, 198; suicide
bombings in, 198; Taliban presence in, 25, 29–30, 56, 82, 110,
186–7; Tora Bora, 113;

Ahl-e-Hadith, 2–3, 11, 20, 129, 181,
200; criticism of, 26; followers of, 84, 88, 109, 207; funding
received from Saudi government, 27; ideology of, 25–6, 60,
75; influence of, 27, 178, 261;
interpretations of, 74, 96, 268;
madaris of, 27–8, 83; organisations, 28–9, 79, 195, 260; presence in Pakistan, 29; presence in
South Asia, 26
Ahmad, Nazir (Abu Umer):
participation in Mumbai attacks
(2008), 212
Ahmed, Lt. Gen. Mahmud: and
Richard Armitage, 104; Director-General of ISI, 103
Ahmed, Maqbul: head of MDI
Farmers and Workers' Wing, 87
Ahmed, Sabauddin: role in CRPF
Rampur attack (2007), 147; role
in IISc attack, 146–7; alleged role
in 2008 Mumbai attacks, ch. 6
fn. 113.
Ahmed, Syed Haris: 162; background of, 160
Akhtar, Qari Saifullah: amir of
Harkat-ul-Jihad-al-Islami, 110;
relations with Taliban, 110

335